TAKING THE LAND
TO MAKE THE CITY

Mary P. Ryan

—

TAKING
the
LAND
to
MAKE
the
CITY

—

A Bicoastal History
of North America

UNIVERSITY OF TEXAS PRESS 〜 AUSTIN

Copyright © 2019 by the University of Texas Press
All rights reserved
Printed in the United States of America
First edition, 2019

Requests for permission to reproduce material from this work should be sent to:
  Permissions
  University of Texas Press
  P.O. Box 7819
  Austin, TX 78713-7819
  utpress.utexas.edu/rp-form

♾ The paper used in this book meets the minimum requirements of ANSI/NISO
Z39.48-1992 (R1997) (Permanence of Paper).

LIBRARY OF CONGRESS CATALOGING-IN-PUBLICATION DATA

Names: Ryan, Mary P., author.
Title: Taking the land to make the city : a bicoastal history of North America /
  Mary P. Ryan.
Description: First edition. | Austin : University of Texas Press, 2019. | Includes
  bibliographical references and index.
Identifiers: LCCN 2018019184
  ISBN 978-1-4773-1783-9 (cloth : alk. paper)
  ISBN 978-1-4773-1784-6 (library e-book)
  ISBN 978-1-4773-1785-3 (non-library e-book)
Subjects: LCSH: San Francisco (Calif.)—History—19th century. | Baltimore (Md.)—
  History—19th century. | City planning—California—San Francisco—History. |
  City planning—Maryland—Baltimore—History. | Social change—Environmental
  aspects.
Classification: LCC F869.S357 R93 2019 | DDC 979.4/6104—dc23
LC record available at https://lccn.loc.gov/2018019184

doi:10.7560/317839

For Robert Roper, truly a mountaineer

CONTENTS

TAKING THE LAND
TO MAKE THE CITY

INTRODUCTION

*An hour ago I shut up my book & started on my afternoon
stroll home. Today I took a new route. Crowds of workmen in red
& blue shirts were drilling & blasting rock to extend and widen a
street—Leaving them and emerging into "Broadway," on my left
were the "Franklin House", the "St Louis Hotel" and other ambitious
"Houses" with high sounding names and gaudy signs, each having
a full complement of loafers and redolent of Gin and Tobacco.
Mexican Girls and women were laughing and chatting with each
other in the door way of some houses, and then a Mexican boy would
appear driving before him his little jackass with a backload of wood.*

BENJAMIN WINGATE, SAN FRANCISCO, MAY 1, 1853

Benjamin Wingate's route home from work on May 1, 1853, proceeded down Broadway and turned onto Montgomery Street, the central commercial thoroughfare, where "whiskered dandies" and "simple maidens with little jaunty bonnets" joined him. Changing his course, he came upon a "row of Irish Cabins," where he spied "more happiness than among the rich on other streets." On July 4, Wingate joined "Germans and Frenchmen," "native Californians," and "Americans who had come over the plains" to celebrate the "national jubilee" in the city's central plaza. "All hands entered into the spirit of the occasion with great zest" and were "as much delighted as children," he wrote. Such were the impressions that the city of San Francisco left on an ambitious young man and devout Christian from a small town in New Hampshire.[1]

To stroll along the streets of San Francisco with Benjamin Wingate is to be bombarded by the cacophony of sensations to be found in nineteenth-century American cities. Sights, sounds, colors, and smells stream in from

1

all sides. To scan the skyline is to be awed by the facades of lavish buildings. To cross a street is to navigate through the noise and disarray of the many construction projects continually in progress. To make one's way through the commotion requires cognitive skill, the ability to scan the sidewalk and discriminate between "laborers and loafers," rich and poor, natives and immigrants of multiple national origins. To walk a city street is to risk moral danger as well as mental challenge: the temptations of liquor, tobacco, gambling, and worse. (Benjamin Wingate assured his wife that he did not go abroad at night.) In the best of times—like July 4—the stimulation of the city could render the wide-eyed pedestrian "as delighted as a child." The sensory plentitude of movement through a city street cannot be captured in a still photograph or in lines upon a page. Nonetheless, the delirium of the city street and a "zest" for the urban spectacle are what inspired this book.[2]

The public space of the city is also an especially fitting place for serious historical study. Evidence about every aspect of human experience is strewn along the street without any particular order, chiding the historian who thinks she can reduce the past to a simple story or single logic. To stumble into a marketplace or onto a major thoroughfare is to brush up against a wide spectrum of human differences and to disturb any comfortable sense of unity and certainty. No place is as capacious as a city. It displays the full pallet of human differences: Wingate likened the population of San Francisco to "as many shades of color as in a box of worsted." The public street is also awash with conflict, the site of brusque encounters, raucous political rallies, protest marches, riots, even revolutions. Wingate's letters home recorded the results of vigilante justice: bodies "hung on the plaza or the public square."[3] Renamed Portsmouth Square by the conquering Americans, San Francisco's plaza was inherited from Mexican predecessors and plotted on land that had been worked by human hands for thousands of years, as long as four millennia, in fact, along the shores of San Francisco Bay. The city is a momentous historical construction project, its foundation dug deep in the past. The rugged durability of the city prompted the audaciously simple questions that propelled the research for this book: Just how do you create something as complex as a city, from the depths of the pavements to the heights of the skyline? How is it that cities are constructed and relentlessly renovated over such long stretches of time?

Over a long academic career, I was slow to comprehend the fundamental significance of the historical process of city-making. My re-education began in the classroom over a decade ago when I determined to ground my

—

undergraduate courses on the turf where my students lived and where they exercised citizenship. I stumbled into urban history along with troops of students, walking the row-house-lined streets from Johns Hopkins University down to Baltimore's Inner Harbor, and boarding a BART train connecting the Berkeley campus to the metropolis that spanned the territory around San Francisco Bay. In Baltimore, we encountered the seedlings of democracy at the base of a monument to the War of 1812; in San Francisco, we found relics of both a Mexican pueblo and a vigilante hanging in a ragged square where immigrants from China were playing mahjong. At the outset I intended to start my research for this book with a familiar time and place, the period of American history that was my field of specialization, the late eighteenth and early nineteenth centuries. That starting point was also a pivot of American political history, the auspicious moment when two fledgling republics, one the United States of America and the other the Estados Unidos Mexicanos, were founded. From this location an extended research trip commenced, going far back in time and connecting up with a sequence of pivotal events in the history of North America.

Taking the Land to Make the City reports on this experiment in tracing the origins of one nation from the history of two cities. From the start and at its heart, this volume is an urban history written by a city lover, and one for whom Baltimore and San Francisco are cherished home places. But as it happened, these two cities were built on land especially rich in evidence about larger historical issues and events. They were situated, first of all, in unusually fertile ecological zones, great estuaries where a mix of fresh and sea water bred the abundant plant and animal nutrients that would sustain the earliest human occupants of the Americas for upward of one hundred centuries. To do justice to the urban landscape required recognition of its prehistory, the prolonged period before cities were built upon the surface of the earth. In much more recent times, those two estuaries were also magnets for the first Europeans to colonize the New World. Captain John Smith toured up the Chesapeake early in the seventeenth century, past what would be Baltimore Harbor, at the same time that the Spanish began searching for the fabled Bahía de San Francisco.

After the *entrada* of Europeans, the land along the estuaries would never be the same. The British promptly carved the shores of the Chesapeake into parcels of private property in the Colony of Maryland, while the settlers of Alta California claimed their region for the Roman Catholic Church, the Spanish Crown, and some humble Mexican families. Those who trolled the great

—

bays quickly spied the commercial prospects of the waterways: the wide bend in the Patapsco River, where it entered the Chesapeake, and the commodious cove named Yerba Buena on the western shore of San Francisco Bay. These two ports became busy hubs of political and economic activity. Citizens of Baltimore fought off the British in 1776 and again in 1814; soon thereafter, the liberal leaders of Alta California would rebel against the governors imposed by the Spanish. Most presciently, the citizens of Baltimore and San Francisco would each practice self-government at the local level, becoming precocious republicans. In the 1850s and 1860s, Baltimore and San Francisco were both caught up in the fractious politics that led to civil war, as the concluding chapters of *Taking the Land to Make the City* will explore.

In sum, the land upon which the cities of Baltimore and San Francisco were sited, the first in 1796 and the second in 1834, proved to be an intersection of major historical events. I set out to mine the rich deposits of evidence to be found there in order to see what they might tell us about the history of cities and the nation of which they are a part. My strategy was somewhat like that of an archaeologist: I started digging in a small but carefully chosen place and traced history up through one layer of material evidence after another. I plumbed these sites for answers to a set of questions particular to each place. My first goal was to understand how you make a city. Because Baltimore and San Francisco were erected so suddenly, both of them on sparsely settled land, and at the same time that colonists were winning independence from European empires, they offer opportunities to watch the creation of a city from the ground up and at an auspicious moment. At this intimate local level, furthermore, I hoped to detect the handiwork of ordinary citizens in the construction of the city. These research sites also foreground a dimension of urban history that is too often neglected. The city of Baltimore and the pueblo of San Francisco were established in advance of the juggernaut of industrial capitalism when so much of the history of American cities is said to commence. Furthermore, Baltimore, born of the late eighteenth century, and San Francisco, shaped early in the nineteenth, grew up on their own, through local practices largely independent of the states of Maryland or California, and at a time when federal institutions were relatively weak. This was the second major goal of my investigation—to show, using municipal records, how cities are more than the results of larger economic forces. Indeed, they are active agents of historical changes writ large.

—

A third advantage of the peculiar geography of this urban history is that it demonstrates that there is no single formula for how to build an American city. These two sites, one on the Atlantic, the other on the Pacific, show that there is more than one cultural lineage to American urban history. Rather than simply extending the Anglo American narrative along a linear, westward-leaning frontier, this pairing of San Francisco and Baltimore focuses in on two of the multiple channels of urban history, one of them traced through New Spain and up from Mesoamerica, with its ancient moorings in the Aztec capital of Tenochtitlan.

These two locations also complicate national history in another way: by showing us two different ways of construing race. Baltimore, a port on the Atlantic, in a slave state but not far south of the Mason-Dixon Line, saw its slave population decline well before the American Civil War, when it became home to a large population of free people of color. The first citizens of Alta California, in contrast, were largely mestizo in origin, and the Republic of Mexico abolished slavery at an earlier date, without recourse to war. By looking east from the Pacific and north from Mexico, this book therefore provides an alternative vantage point on our nation's racialized history, contradicting the geography of race that so often partitions US history along a stark divide between North and South, the free and the slave.

I would never have attempted to answer these preposterously large questions—how do you make a city, what role do cities play in the development of the nation, and where, beyond the Atlantic anchorage, are the moorings of American urban culture—without the guidance of geographers and political scientists as well as historians. Over the past few decades, scholars in a number of related fields have come to regard space as well as time as a critical dimension of social life, giving new relevance to the discipline of geography. Political geographers, in particular, have provided an indispensable tool for historians by reminding them that history is made at multiple scales—at the level of the municipality as well as state and federal government. At the forefront of this body of scholarship, which came to be known as the "spatial turn" in historical studies, was one volume written over forty years ago. The very title of Henri Lefebvre's *The Social Production of Space* is a prolegomenon for historians of the city. His formulation of a uniform theory of space challenged urbanists to regard the shape of the world around them as relentlessly in the process of creation. It was manifest in three inextricable dimensions: as it is conceived, as it is perceived, and as it

—

is lived. Lefebvre set a high standard for urban historians, challenging us to do justice to the city as an idea, as a material place, and as a living organism created by the quotidian practices of those who inhabit it.[4]

Appreciation of the material and everyday lived experience of the city is the stock-in-trade of the field of vernacular architecture. The guidance of scholars in this field focused my attention on the inconspicuous physical places in the city and taught me to ask how they came into being, and in turn, how they came to shape experience and effect historical change. Scholars of vernacular architecture, such as my mentors Paul Groth, Marta Gutman, and Dell Upton, interpret the physical environment as the creation not just of engineers and designers but also of anonymous Americans who shape the city in their own way and according to their own sense of beauty. The artistry of their homes, their stoops, and their neighborhood gathering places merit J. B. Jackson's paean to the ordinary American landscape, which he understood as a place of "hard work, stubborn hope and mutual forbearance striving to be love." Everything from the whimsy of amateur builders to the rivalry between neighbors becomes a creative part of the urban vernacular, its patterns, its disarray, its surprises, its discomforts, and its sensory delights. The plazas of the American Southwest as much as the Paris of Henry IV, and the New York of Jane Jacobs as well as that of Robert Moses, exemplify how multitudes of everyday artists shape the city.[5]

The final body of literature that guided this project consists of those histories, too countless to catalog, that depict the city as a material and physical space, as a human construction upon the land. The city of New York has been especially favored by historians attentive to the deep texture of the urban landscape: Hendrik Hartog, who excavated the street plan; Elisabeth Blackmar, who exposed the matrix of urban real estate; Russell Shorto, who recognized its Dutch foundation; Ted Steinberg, who watched it grow on water as well as on land; Catherine McNeur, who traced it through a sequence of nineteenth-century environmental transformations. America's Second City, Chicago, was the subject of perhaps the most masterful and influential volume in the genre to date, a work that became the model for a spatially grounded but expansive urban history: William Cronon's *Nature's Metropolis*, linking Chicago to its natural habitat, to its commercial hinterland, and to the vast sweep of nineteenth-century capitalism. As Cronon's book widened the scale of urban history, other historians of Chicago, notably Robin Einhorn, penetrated to the granular level of urban space, right down to the city's sidewalks, lined up block by block. And thanks to the opus of Carl

—

Smith, we can see that cities like Chicago were built on ideas as well as with bricks. The people of Chicago mortared a city together with hard thinking and fervid deliberation about such material concerns as protection from fire and provision of water. Meanwhile, countless scholars are still filling in the spatial patchwork of urban history, with studies north to Detroit, east to Boston, south to New Orleans, along the border with Mexico, and everywhere in between.[6] But the bicoastal history in this book is particularly indebted to the work of all the political scientists, archaeologists, and other historians who have assiduously studied the cities of Baltimore and San Francisco. The depth of knowledge and civic commitment among local historians never ceases to amaze, humble, and guide me.[7]

One team of social scientists and historians has placed cities in their global and oceanic context, linking them to one another and to the rest of the world through networks of trade, transportation, and commodity exchange.[8] I have not taken on the task of drawing Baltimore and San Francisco into this web of transnational commerce. In *Taking the Land to Make the City*, I hope to complement this work by turning inward from the harbors on the Atlantic and the Pacific and tracing the development of the local, landed, urban political economy. In a way, this volume returns to what Frederick Jackson Turner called "the Great West," but approaches it from another angle. The urban history of the continental United States did not proceed simply as a slow-moving frontier or shifting borderland. It actually leapt across a vast landscape to San Francisco Bay beginning in the late eighteenth century, where it intersected with migrations up the Pacific from Spanish America. Seen from the perspective of cities on both sides of the North American continent, land takes on a complex of different meanings: as habitat, as property, as real estate, as the different patterns that Ohlone and Powhatans, Spaniards and Englishmen, San Franciscans and Baltimoreans inscribed upon the shores of two great estuaries.

Looking inland and deep into the history that evolved along the shores of the Chesapeake and the San Francisco Bay has brought three historical subjects to the forefront of this urban history. These themes, matters of land, sovereignty, and capitalism, are the central foci of the three chronological parts of *Taking the Land to Make the City*. The book begins by exploring the deep roots of urban history, focusing on the exceptional habitat of two great bays that framed the North American continent. These intricate and elegant carvings of water onto stone, earth, and sand abutted the vast oceans whose waters flow over two-thirds of the globe's surface. When the Europeans

–

arrived on the shores of the great bays, the land had long been tended by human settlers who had made their passage across the Pacific over twelve thousand years before. Thus the introduction acknowledges the distinctive ways in which Algonquian nations along the Chesapeake, and the small communities around San Francisco Bay now given the common name Ohlone, made the land into sustainable habitats, each in their own distinctive ways. Each city still embraces its magnificent bay and still shares in the natural beauty and bounty enjoyed by its original inhabitants.

Part I, "Taking the Land," goes on to show how the decisions of the first European settlers etched the different cultures of Spain and Britain onto these shorelines, culminating in a brutal act of taking Indian land on both sides of the continent and converting it into individual private property, parcels large and small carved out in different ways by Spaniards and Englishmen. The construction of cities, and with it capitalism and nation-building, could not commence in North America until the land had been taken to clear the space for building, resulting in a presidio and a mission on the San Francisco Peninsula and a town on the Chesapeake. Yet neither the Spanish nor the British managed to retain hegemony for very long. Although the Spanish missionaries of California and the English colonists of Maryland—with critical help from the deadly microbes they carried across the Atlantic—swiftly displaced Indians from their land, they did not shape it into cities. Neither did they reproduce the landscape from whence they had come. The English carved the Atlantic tidewater into huge parcels of land that became plantations, devoted to tobacco production, while the coast of California was made into a vast pasturage, at first the property of the missions, but soon converted into private ranches. Neither planters nor ranchers invested much effort in city-building—San Francisco and Baltimore would grow up on their own. The tenacious colonists of Baltimore broke free of the British in 1776, and the first humble settlers of Alta California, called *los pobladores*, ousted the Spanish from their imperial outpost in 1821. The town of Baltimore and the pueblo of San Francisco became vital centers around which two North American republics would grow.

Once the colonists had secured independence from Great Britain, the process of land-taking sped across the continent. The United States Land Act of 1785 superimposed a rigid checkerboard of townships on the map of North America extending as far as the Mississippi River, heedless of any topographical obstacles. In 1848, this matrix for disposing of American land was extended all the way to the Pacific, on territory conquered from the

—

Republic of Mexico. By 1867, the US Land Office had surveyed and distributed two billion acres of once public land.

Part II, "Making the Municipality: The City and the Pueblo," recounts how the settlers of the port along the Chesapeake and the scattered inhabitants around San Francisco Bay reshaped European precedents and created their own independent and distinctive urban polities. By practicing self-government at the local level, in the fundamental political institutions of the city council and what Mexicans termed the *ayuntamiento*, North Americans produced urban space without much guidance from higher authorities. The municipality of Baltimore was a particularly energetic city-builder. The citizens acted to construct the docks and wharves from which to launch international trade and taxed one another in order to open the roads to inland markets. The booming city, which grew to become the third largest in the United States, was not a free-wheeling marketplace, however, but a carefully regulated local economy whose merchants and artisans, buyers and sellers, were constrained by hundreds of ordinances enacted in the name of the public good. The conversion of the shores of San Francisco into political space came later, but it also vested sovereignty, including the initiative in distributing land, in the local polity. Municipal governance, Hispanic style, was particularly careful about retaining large parcels of land, including common pastures and a public shoreline, for the good of the public.

The urban landscape of Baltimore served as an ideal laboratory in which to examine how cities take their polyglot shape. Blocks of brick row houses, interspersed with domed public buildings and dotted with monuments, still stand as testimony to an extraordinarily prolific and creative season of city-building at the turn of the nineteenth century. The records of the mayors and city councils of Baltimore prove that making the city was not just the work of individual actors and untrammeled imagination but a complex social construct requiring collective action and associated effort, both public and private. Individual entrepreneurs might take the initiative in laying out the land for commercial profit, but to be successful they had to act in collaboration with their fellow citizens and within the purview of government. City-building in Baltimore was an essentially political project conducted within the chambers of local government and according to the rules of local, state, and national sovereignty. The expansion of representative government in the early nineteenth century brought a wide range of citizens into the ranks of city-builders. It was no accident that Alexis de Tocqueville collected vital testimony about *Democracy in America* on a visit to Baltimore in 1831.

—

Baltimoreans, some of them émigrés directly from the British Isles, or from the agricultural hinterland or the nearby city of Philadelphia, were schooled in the political arts of city-building that are deeply rooted in the history of Anglo-America, including the institution of the city charter, with its compendium of rights and duties dating back as far as the twelfth century. The municipality was also a key element in Spain's colonizing project. Spanish conquistadores, like those making English expeditions into the New World, immediately planted cities on the shoreline, making the formation of urban jurisdictions, *ciudades* and pueblos, the essential building blocks of colonization. The municipalities of Mexico even sent delegates to Spain's first national assembly, the *Cortes*, meeting in Cadiz in 1812. When Mexicans seized independence from Spain in 1821, the settlers of San Francisco Bay quickly proceeded to plot out the surrounding land into private property, with rights protected by the power of the federated state. The two new republics built cities that were different enough to add the spice of variety to the urban landscape of North America. Furthermore, the cities were vital stakeholders in the struggle for territory between the two republics. While the border between Mexico and the United States was in dispute until at least 1848, and national sovereignty was unstable in both republics into the 1860s, the cities of Baltimore and San Francisco continued to practice a robust popular politics and energetic city-building.[9]

Part III, "Making the Modern Capitalist City," shows how the citizens of both Baltimore and San Francisco molded the urban land into the shape of the modern city with its gridded downtown, outlying parks, and rudimentary streetcar suburbs. By the 1850s, the two cities had come to resemble one another, in part a consequence of the Yankee conquest of Mexican territory in 1848, followed immediately by the Gold Rush and the movement of eastern capital across the continent. But the cities astride the estuaries were not joined together by fiat of the nation-state; they also played a role in its creation. The Port of Yerba Buena along San Francisco Bay beckoned politicians and merchants westward even before the Gold Rush, when they created an anchor for commerce along the Pacific Rim and stimulated an appetite for western expansion among Washington politicians. The municipality of Baltimore was a major funder of the first long-haul railroad, which was built to open markets in the West, and the city fathers of San Francisco fought aggressively to profit from taking up the land of the *Californios*. At the same time, enterprising businessmen bristled under the yoke of municipal regulation, setting the private sector apart from the public by

—

10

chartering corporations and devising increasingly sophisticated financial instruments. Unleashed from municipal controls, the process of taking land became the business of real estate developers in Baltimore and the cause of frenzied cycles of boom and bust in San Francisco.

Part IV, "These United Cities," finds Baltimore and San Francisco linked together under one federal government, but each still exercising a significant measure of city sovereignty and retaining a distinctive urban character. When slavery threatened to rend the United States apart, neither Baltimore nor San Francisco rushed to take sides in the sectional conflict. The vast majority of Baltimore's African Americans were emancipated and laboring in the free market for paltry wages. Meanwhile, the Constitutional Convention of California, summoned in the San Francisco Plaza in 1849, had promptly abolished slavery. Even as the United States suffered the horrific carnage of civil war, the men and women of Baltimore and San Francisco continued along their separate paths, taking up more and more land to accommodate the populations streaming into their regions from across the Pacific and the Atlantic. The numbers of these immigrants were larger than those of the pioneers venturing slowly westward by the wagonload. The sale of city lots in both cities was a booming capitalist market and, unlike the road to capitalism through slave labor in the cotton fields of the South, it was not obstructed by sectional rivalry and war.[10]

Individual cities followed their own courses through time, making small ripples in the multifarious stream of events from which scholars and writers compose the history of one nation. Nonetheless, refracted back and forth through the prism of the two estuaries, the process of taking land to make the cities of Baltimore and San Francisco does raise some larger historical issues. For now, these intimations of the impact of urban history beyond the city limits of Baltimore and San Francisco had best be raised as a few open-ended questions.

First, I am tempted to ask whether the city should not be acknowledged as an essential space out of which new nations formed in the eighteenth and early nineteenth centuries. This hypothesis seems particularly warranted in the case of New Spain and Mexico. Cities grew up quickly in places where the conquistadores planted the Spanish flag, and national boundaries often took shape around them. The richest city in New Spain grew up around the Aztec plaza of Tenochtitlan. South of Mexico, Spanish America splintered into separate nation-states, which were often anchored by a single city. The separate nation of Guatemala, for example, cohered around the port

—

11

of its namesake city, and the nucleus of Argentina was the Port of Buenos Aires. Before that, the nation-state of Spain took shape when the Hapsburgs located the court of Philip II in Madrid. The national polity that would become the United States began to take shape in a coterie of colonial urban centers. The development of urban space for a national capital along the Potomac came later; it was something of a ruse, designed to remove federal institutions from the social and political tumult of cities such as New York, Philadelphia, and Baltimore. California had no sooner been admitted to that national union than it became the most urbanized state in the country, with San Francisco as its natal place. At least this much is true: be it in Europe or in North, South, or Central America, the federal capital, often called the "general" or the "superior" government, was not the sole location of sovereignty but part of a multi-scaled system of political authority that entrusted sizable responsibilities to cities. Before the 1860s, with the assertion of more centralized federal authority in both North American republics, towns and cities, pueblos, and *ciudades* exerted a major political force in the course toward nationhood.[11]

A second question would follow from this premise. Did the municipalities of North and Central America nurture a distinctive political culture in the New World? Did cities like Baltimore and San Francisco, in other words, exemplify the process whereby republican ideas and democratic practices germinated in postcolonial urban spaces? This line of reasoning commences with the observation that when the freedoms first formulated in the city charters granted by English monarchs were transferred to North America, they quickly habituated American colonists to local self-government and the exercise of those rights that would be written into state and federal constitutions. Similarly, the *pueblos* of New Spain and the *ayuntamientos* of Alta California elected *alcaldes* and *regidores* (roughly mayors and councilmen) as prescribed by Iberian plans of colonization. Exported to the Americas, the representative municipal institutions of Britain and Spain transferred power far from nobles and monarchs to plebian settlers. It is worth asking, therefore, whether the city, including the urban spaces where the public congregated, the streets and *calles*, the squares and the plazas, the American city halls and the *cabildos* (Spanish government buildings), deserve special credit for cradling democracy in North America.[12] If the city as much as the agricultural frontier is the anvil on which American political culture was molded, one has to ask if it forged rugged individualism or a different set of virtues and vices, among them boosterism, civic association, social

—

12

activism, political ingenuity, city bosses, and the financial wizardry of those who trafficked in urban real estate. As we shall see, those who prospered in San Francisco and Baltimore were not backwoodsmen but more often inveterate joiners, adept political strategists, and zealous entrepreneurs.[13]

Which raises another cause for speculation: How did towns and cities give shape to American capitalism? The entry of émigrés from across the Atlantic into lands where human history had developed independently for over ten thousand years opened a vital bridge toward modernity and economic expansion. Baltimore and San Francisco are two nodes in the dense network of cities and towns that constituted one of the most prolific growth sectors in the nineteenth-century economy. The city sector was a powerful component in the expansion of all sorts of commodities across the global marketplace, the trading center for the grain of the Mid-Atlantic region and the cattle of Alta California no less than for the cotton and tobacco of the South. Moreover, the shores of the great estuaries were transformed into a major staple of economic growth: land packaged as real estate. Those who settled port cities along the great bays came to regard the land not as a source of subsistence or modest production for the market but as a component of economic growth and a means of upward mobility. Investors large and small used such devices as stock shares, mortgages, corporate charters, and government subsidies to carve the land into lots and blocks to be sold at inflated prices. Cities, therefore, harbor important evidence about the nature of American capitalism. They may tell an idyll of middle-class equality or portend a widening gulf between landlords and the landless, between rich and poor. They invite speculation about how the rise and development of American capitalism might have been propelled and altered by its circuit through the cities.[14]

A final question arises as well from these two sites on the map of North American history: Does the focal event of nineteenth-century US history, the Civil War, look different from an urban vantage point? It has long been recognized that slavery did not fare well in the urban economy. The peculiar institution of the South had almost died out in Baltimore by 1860, when it accounted for only 2 percent of the population. Mexico had outlawed slavery by 1829, effectively excluding the institution from Alta California. Advanced urban economies increasingly dependent on industrial production, finance capital, and global markets did not welcome the disruption of civil war. Neither secessionists nor radical republicans rolled up large urban majorities in the 1860 election—prompting one to dare to ask whether slavery might

—

have ended with less bloodshed, and been followed by a less prolonged racial inequality, if the debate had been conducted by pragmatic politicians working out their differences in the chambers of municipal government. While such counterfactual reasoning is poor ground for reaching sound historical conclusions, the process of land-taking and city-building at these two urban locations does reframe the political geography of the Civil War era in instructive ways. While the nation was breaking apart on the North/South axis, East and West were coming together, linked by a system of free wage labor, the technology of rail and telegraph, and a network of cities. And so this urban history will end with this query lurking in the margins: How was the path to Civil War paved or diverted by another powerful historical force, the taking of land and the making of cities?

The making of cities was not scripted by a single author or plotted out once and for all according to a tidy plan. It was the work of multitudes of thinking men and women, all scrambling for a comfortable place and perhaps a modicum of wealth and power within the material limits and social structures they helped to shape. The men and women who took the land and then made the cities of San Francisco and Baltimore are not the towering figures venerated in popular histories of the United States; the vast majority of them will remain nameless in the chapters to follow. The spatial imagination of ordinary people was seldom committed to writing. It was stored in their diurnal practices and lodged in their mental maps. A very rough facsimile of this deep visual knowledge of the urban landscape can be gleaned from the scores of maps scattered throughout this volume. They register something of the tenacious effort and expert skill required to make and navigate a city.

A varied cast of characters had a hand in creating these iconic cities, some as august as a signer of the Declaration of Independence by the name of Charles Carroll, others as humble as an illiterate mestizo dairy farmer named Juana Briones. Minor political figures—such as Jesse Hunt, a mayor of Baltimore, and Francisco de Haro, an *alcalde* of Yerba Buena—made some critical decisions that still determine the lines along which Baltimoreans and San Franciscans walk today. A few more renowned historical personages also appear in the chapters that follow. Take Stephen J. Field, who served as *alcalde* in a tiny Sierra settlement and then as the jurist who cleared the way for a key land grab in San Francisco, all before he wrote some of the most important and controversial decisions of the Supreme Court of the United States. Or consider Roger Taney, well known in Baltimore and excoriated for his decision in the Dred Scott case. He went on to sign

—

many other controversial Supreme Court documents, some that conferred, or denied, land titles to the Californios. Men and women like these, no less than kings and presidents or massive, impersonal historical abstractions, such as feudalism, imperialism, capitalism, or nationalism, created these two unique works of urban art, Baltimore and San Francisco. This book is a walk through these two urban construction sites where history lurks on every corner, issuing reminders, warnings, challenges, and inspiration to those who live together upon the land.

Making a city is a complicated and often unsavory project. The noise of the churning population, the disorder of the crowd, and the clash of interests defy any proclamation of a singular and harmonious national identity. Yet anyone who looks down on Baltimore from Federal Hill, or takes in the view from Twin Peaks in San Francisco, cannot help but see the majesty of these creations and marvel at the human effort needed to build them. The meaner streets of the two cities—Pennsylvania Avenue in Baltimore, or Mission Street in San Francisco—put the resilience of city people, including those who are dealt an uneven hand in the pursuit of the so-called American Dream, on display. If you look down on the pavement in either city, you might also see a notice to refrain from sending polluted water into the gutters and thereby help to "Save the Bay." In countless, routine ways, our cities serve as an admonition not to take but to tend the waters and the land. I hope that readers will find in this history of Baltimore and San Francisco a sense of the place, the time, and the commonweal that is the city.

—

Abraham Ortelius, Americae Sive Novi Orbis Nova Descriptio *(Americas, or the new world, new description) (Antwerp: Gielis Coppens van Diest, 1570). Courtesy of the David Rumsey Map Collection, Stanford University.*

PART I

TAKING THE LAND

Taking the Land to Make the City focuses on two small patches of land on the surface of the earth, but it is intended as a point of entry into a wider history, a space as large as the earth itself as imagined by the earliest maps of the Western Hemisphere. Soon after Columbus crossed the Atlantic, European mapmakers attempted to tame the wilderness by containing it within lines drawn upon parchment. In 1527 the mapmaker Diogo Ribério plotted the North American continent all the way from the Atlantic to the Pacific. Within a few decades a number of cartographers had scripted the names of European empires upon that land. The Dutch mapmaker Abraham Ortelius placed the labels "Nova Francia" on the northeastern corner of the continent and "La Hispania" to the west and south. Another of Ortelius's maps, *Americae Sive Novi Orbis* (Americas, or the new world), published

—

in 1570, left the interior of North America almost empty, except for an imaginary river that sliced across the land from the craggy coast of the Atlantic to the largest body of water in the world—the Pacific, then called the South Sea. The eastern shore of the continent was indented as far as a northern river called San Lorenzo. While Ortelius creased the southern portion of the Pacific coast with inlets and place names, he drew the northern shoreline as a relatively smooth surface, marked with only a few labels, none of them familiar today.[1]

In the next century mapmakers refined the lines along the coasts of North America and inscribed the northern tier of the continent with the sign of another empire, New Albion. Maps drafted in the seventeenth century gave further definition to the eastern coastline colonized by Britain, including the fine lines of an estuary called the Chesapeake. The Pacific coastline of North America was still poorly charted. A mythical place, said to be the domain of Amazons and called California, was often depicted as an offshore island. A few Latin names, ostensibly designating anchorages or potential ports, dotted the charts of the western shore of North America, including the landing of Sir Francis Drake near Point Reyes in 1577. As late as 1769, however, the portal to the rumored Bay of San Francisco still eluded the European explorers and merchant vessels trolling the Pacific.

The firm black lines Ortelius drew around the landmass of North America represented the continent as a silhouette bounded by two great oceans in which European monarchies waged wars of conquest. *Taking the Land* moves inland from the imperial map for a closer view of the newly "discovered" continent of North America. It homes in on two estuaries that had long sustained human life, and would eventually become urban places. It is a story of North American land, rather than the waterways patrolled by Europeans. While early maps of North America testified to the

—

artistry of cartographers and printers, and to the daring explorations of the seafarers who ventured into the strange new world, they failed to acknowledge the prior history enacted within those borders and were slow to recognize how the first settlers moved quickly to the interior and reshaped the landscape. Part I will zoom in on two great estuaries overlooked by European mapmakers in order to capture a more intimate view of how the land was prepared for the making of cities.

The material life around the estuaries is the topic of Chapter 1. The rocky shores and sandy beaches of the two estuaries were relics of galactic events that occurred some four billion years before Europeans first trod upon them. It had taken hundreds of millions of years to shape the great estuaries of North America, another score of millennia before *Homo sapiens* would stand erect upon the earth. Humans did not migrate into the Western Hemisphere until many centuries later, when, around fifteen thousand years ago, small bands of men and women came from Asia, traveled down the Pacific, and quickly, by some yet unknown route or routes, inhabited much of the North American landmass, including the two especially fertile estuaries on each side. The native population of the continent numbered in the millions by the time of the European *entrada*.

Although the first peoples of the Americas had made a living off the land for hundreds of generations, they never "took it" in the terms practiced by European invaders. Englishmen, in particular, devised an elaborate language for taking possession of the earth, first "kingdoms" and "fiefdoms," then "enclosures," and finally "private property," which could be "owned" in "fee simple" by individuals and families. European notions of property set the larger global context for Chapters 2 and 3, but the intrepid men and women who followed after the explorers quickly devised their own ways of taking land and making space. Those who stayed on

—

and settled in the coastal areas, or moved farther into the interior of the continent, converted the land into the diversified farms, wheat fields, and tracts of tobacco of the British colonies and the pastures, gardens, and silver mines of New Spain. The English settlers (Chapter 2) and the *pobladores* of New Spain (Chapter 3) would draw a tight web of private properties upon the land, not just the plantations of Virginia and Maryland, or the haciendas of New Spain, but also the finer outlines of what would someday become urban places: boundaries between town lots near the Chesapeake harbor and the *solares* (small plots) scattered near the presidios and missions named for Saint Francis.

The colonists were also drawing political borders around their property and improvising rules for governing their new habitat. Soon after the settlers along the Patapsco River formed themselves into the town of Baltimore, they declared independence from Britain, dispelled monarchy, and constructed a government on republican principles. Within three decades the native sons of Alta California were also contesting imperial rule, winning independence from Spain in 1821. The Americans and the Californios were not just reshaping the land around the great bays; they were also building the spaces in which to practice self-government in ways that would make waves back in the Old World.

CHAPTER 1

BEFORE THE LAND WAS TAKEN

.

A t the shallow southern tip of San Francisco Bay, dense fields of tall green reeds—the Spanish named them *tule*—wind through shimmering marshes. In the autumn, sunshine bathes this gently sloping landscape, a place where men and women have walked, worked, and celebrated for thousands of years. The elixir of sea air is apt to lift the spirits and the imaginations of those who gather here. One recent communicant with the landscape conjured the vision of a spirit called Hawk, who "caught cross currents of air to soar above the hills and survey the activities below." From her bird's-eye view, Hawk looked down on "the People, caretakers of this place who had been here before, but had been hidden for a while. Hawk felt she knew them": "Now," she added, "once again, the people of this central coast locale were gathering to celebrate and share a wealth of knowledge preserved, passed on, reacquired, and cherished among them."

This particular reverie was recorded in October in the year 2010. The people who gathered near the bay called themselves Ohlone and had been assembling for seventeen years, "still honoring ancestral spirits" in song, story,

—

and dance. One celebrant told her "grandmother's story"; others reenacted the "1,000 Hummingbird Ceremony for healing the earth." An Ohlone leader named Beverley Ortiz rose to claim a heritage of generosity and fair play that had been passed down among her people for generations. Following reports about ongoing efforts to preserve this land and other material relics of the Ohlone past, the ceremony concluded with a "sacred shell mound walk" along the eastern shore of the bay.

The Ohlone are hardly alone in attempting to capture their history by communing with a sacred spot on the surface of the earth. Many tribes claim a stake in landmarks like the site of the annual Ohlone festival. It takes place on public property, at Coyote Hills in the East Bay Regional Park District (the employer of Beverley Ortiz). Since as far back as the 1930s, conservationists have worked to protect this small slice of the earth from urban development. Caring for the land, and protecting what remains of America's open space, requires arduous and tenacious efforts by many hands, working in many different ways.[1]

Men and women from diverse backgrounds and sundry institutions share in the task. Much of this work is done by scientists and highly specialized academics. By meticulously scrutinizing local dialects, linguists have identified scores of different cultural groups that inhabited the shores of the San Francisco Bay five hundred years ago. Archaeologists have devoted their careers to excavating the shell mounds that are sacred to the Ohlone. For over a century, they have been sifting through the soil and refuse looking for evidence of human life around the bay as long ago as 5000 BC. They have made a direct material connection with the first caretakers of the San Francisco Estuary and have concluded that the mound dwellers "stretch[ed] across generations in their accumulation, signifying the successes of people's ancestors in amassing food and other resources." Ethno-historians have scoured the archives on both sides of the Atlantic seeking documentation of these complex human cultures that predated the arrival of Europeans. They have summoned the voices of the Ohlone ancestors from historical witnesses, such as the Spanish priest who, over two hundred years ago, reported that the captives of Misión San Francisco de Asís yearned to travel out to sea after death, hoping to find freedom from the Mission's captivity in the waters off the Pacific shore.[2]

The descendants of Native American groups often dispute the interpretations of archaeologists and ethno-historians and sometimes compete for access to precious artifacts, claimed as scientific evidence by the one and as sacred totem by the other. Yet both tribal groups, with their heartfelt claims upon ancestral land, and academics, in zealous pursuit of scientific knowledge, look to the land in order to recover the past. The shores of the great estuaries of San Francisco and the Chesapeake have inspired a fecund spatial imagination and sense of place. It can be expressed and handed down for generations by the Ohlone legend of the Hawk, or dated by radiocarbon measurements: put another way, contemporary investigators of the ancient history of the great American estuaries are part of a continuous intellectual project of "Taking the Land," capturing it in a mental map if not by physical conquest. The persistent quest to find meaning written on the prehistoric landscape cannot, however, reduce the past to a single unchanging heritage or irrefutable scientific profile. Accordingly, this chapter should not be read as a definitive factual account of life in pre-Columbian San Francisco Bay and in the Chesapeake region. It strives merely to piece together enough physical evidence to serve as a prologue to the city-building that commenced in North America after 1600.

The humans who began to occupy the great estuaries over ten thousand years ago demand at least this recognition, for they performed the longest, hardest work of making the land a habitat for humanity. They did so in varied and distinctive ways. The ancestors of peoples now called Ohlone, as well as the Algonquian-speaking tribes along the Chesapeake, such as the Powhatan and Piscataway, reaped the maximum sustenance from the great bays, but they never quite *took* the land, or controlled the waters, that have been sustaining a human population for millennia.

If we are to believe the legends passed down from the Ohlone and the Algonquian, neither did they set man fully apart from other creatures in the position of absolute hegemony over the earth. The Ohlone did not create a god in their own image, but rather venerated "Hawk" and a whole assembly of animal creatures, including an extended avian menagerie of Eagle, Falcon, and Hummingbird, plus terrestrial spirits such as Coyote, Woodchuck, Bear, and Lizard. Founding deities, including Coyote and Woodchuck, tended to be a rather capricious and devious crew; though not entirely trustworthy, they were still good-humored godheads. While Coyote rescued his people when the bay was first flooded, he also bickered with competing animal-gods and selfishly hid a catch of salmon from his hungry children.

The mythic creators of the Chesapeake Bay peoples appear to have been more reliable and benevolent, but, like the founding spirits of the Ohlone, they assumed the shape not of man, but of a cast of animals. In the settlement

—

23

of Patawomeck in 1610, long before either Indians or colonists could imagine building a city near the Chesapeake Bay, an Algonquian leader named Iopassus recounted how the earth and humankind came into being. It was the work of a kindly creature named Ahone, or "The Great Hare." This local deity gave shape first to the earth and next to men and women. After the second act of genesis, Ahone reconsidered the order of creation. Fearful that the earth was a hostile environment for the infant human species, he wrapped woman and man together in a bag and stowed them away under his protection until the world had been rid of menacing cannibalistic creatures and populated with sufficient flora and fauna to sustain humankind. It would seem that the first settlers around the great estuaries sought spiritual allies among creatures of nature like themselves, who used their instincts and their wits to survive on the grudging earth.[3]

Stories like these are an invaluable but corrupted form of historical evidence. They come to us either through European informants or passed down through remote Indian descendants whose recollections have been filtered through many generations and a tumultuous history. In some ways the physical remains left on and in the earth by the earliest inhabitants offer more reliable testimony about the distant past. With the assistance of geologists, archaeologists, and botanists, we can place ourselves in the material spaces where humans scratched out a living as long ago as 12,000 BC. This map to the past, although subject to revision because of a new scientific breakthrough or the latest archaeological discovery, actually takes us through the same territory where our species walked a score millennia ago.

This abridged survey of the lands around the bays will establish four propositions that are essential background to the history written by Europeans. The first is a reminder of the prior force of nature that still sets the limits of human agency. Second, the prehistory of the bay lands was not static but a high drama in which geology, climate, flora, fauna, and then humankind acted out their common fate. At a critical moment at about the end of the most recent ice age, *Homo sapiens* migrated out of Asia and down the Pacific coast. Soon the clear and indelible footprints of humans appeared upon both the eastern and the western shores of the North American continent. Finally, by the time the Europeans arrived, the settlements on the two great estuaries had been shaped into native lands bearing the distinctive marks of two different cultures, one the Spanish called Costanoan, and the other whose name the English translated as Algonquian.

—

24

THE LAND TAKES SHAPE

The people whom the Spanish called Costanoan claimed the name Ohlone for themselves a century ago. They anchored their creation story in landmarks above San Francisco Bay, Mount Tamalpais on the northwest and Mount Diablo to the south and east. From those peaks on a clear day in times past, one might see out over the Pacific to the Farallon Islands and eastward to the Sierra Nevada. These rocky shapes were relics of the cataclysmic events that had transpired on the planet billions of years ago and have been evolving ever since. Two hundred million years ago, the earth's crust was relatively unbroken all the way from the Pacific to the eastern edge of Eurasia and Africa. Thereafter the ancient platform of rock began to split apart, giving shape to separate tectonic plates whose lumbering movement eventually split North America off from the western edge of Europe and opened the Atlantic Ocean. The rock would push westward until, about 145 million years ago, the North Atlantic tectonic plate collided with another bordering the Pacific, giving rise to the great mountain ranges of the West. The Sierra Nevada was a younger landmark, rising on the California skyline only five million years ago. Geologists tell the early history of the land as the spectacular "buckling, faulting and folding," the "shoving" and "driving," of rock, earth, and water.[4]

The earth would keep moving, and with particular ferocity along the Pacific tectonic plate. The forces beneath the surface of the earth were powerful enough to deposit Sierra granite near the San Francisco Estuary. Having given shape to the dramatic topography of the Bay Area, the earth quieted down for the next one hundred thousand years. The small tremors of earthquakes did not disturb the basic geological structure that would serve as the platform for the human history that commenced many millennia later. The bands of mountains running nearly the length of present-day California opened to the sea at only one narrow passage; one day it would be called the Golden Gate to San Francisco Bay.[5]

Across the continent, the rocky outlines of what would become the Chesapeake formed a gentler terrain, testimony to less cataclysmic creative forces at work within the earth. The eastern estuary was longer and more level than that of San Francisco; the major elevation rose gradually from the shoreline upward three thousand feet toward the Appalachian Mountains. In the long-distant future, the bands of coastal rock would be called the fall line, along which a string of cities—Fredericksburg, Richmond, Washington, and Baltimore—would be sited. But this quieter landscape also bore the marks

—

of the violent force of nature. Not just movements within the earth, but also cataclysmic incursions from the galaxy, set the spatial parameters for human life to come. One of these reminders of the power of the cosmos occurred thirty-five million years ago, when some colossal object crashed through the earth's atmosphere and landed on the continental shelf near present-day Virginia Beach. It created a deep crater fifty miles in diameter, now buried under sea level and laden with more than a thousand feet of sediment.[6]

Another natural force, our capricious climate, allied with geology to create the foundation for the next stage in the earth's history. Over the past two hundred million years, the climate waxed from frigid to cold, from freezing to thawing, timed to small alterations in the earth's axis and consequent changes in radiation and air currents. During the ice age, North America was covered with glaciers up to three kilometers deep. About fifty million years ago, an interglacial warming cycle, called the Pleistocene, sent water pouring down from the Sierra in the west and the Appalachians in the east, carving out valleys, craters, and caverns along each side of the continent. Fluctuations in climate, within a prolonged period of frigid weather, made

Satellite image, Chesapeake Bay. United States Geological Survey.

—

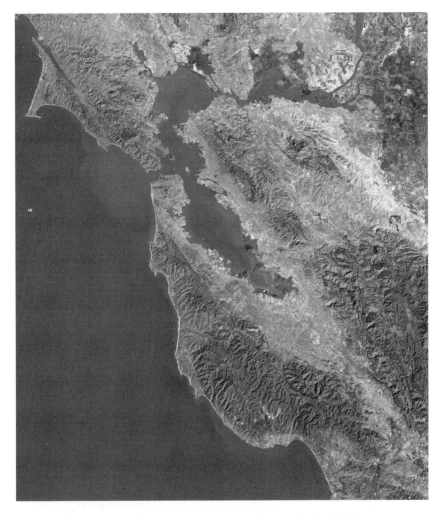

Satellite image, San Francisco Bay. United States Geological Survey.

the glaciers ebb and shift over the millennia, in cycles usually lasting around ten thousand years. One such interglacial warming period began approximately fourteen thousand years ago. This was the cue for another force of nature to chisel out the American landscape. The cycle of warmth, marking the transition to the Holocene era, filled up the ancient rock formations with melted waters and created two prominent estuaries, one on each side of the continent.[7]

—

As the glaciers melted, water rushed down the Susquehanna to fill the Chesapeake while the San Joaquin and Sacramento Rivers flowed toward the Golden Gate, creating the San Francisco Bay on their way. The Atlantic would rise more than three hundred feet in fifteen thousand years, moving the coastline sixty miles inland. Meanwhile, the shores of the Pacific moved inward forty to fifty kilometers, from the Farallon Islands to the entry point of San Francisco Bay. When the flood subsided, two estuaries stood like bookends on the eastern and western shores of North America. The Chesapeake was the largest on the continent, over three hundred miles long; the western estuary was smaller but deeper, with northern and southern branches. The northern arms were named Suisun and San Pablo Bays; the outlet to the Pacific, along with the southern branch, would be named San Francisco Bay.[8]

Earth, water, climate, all moving with unbridled force but over languorous stretches of time, had created two unique and dramatic shapes on the surface of the globe. More than that, they brought with them the materials that would sustain life. Only during the interglacial period that ended the ice age did the earth become more hospitable to plant and animal life. The cascading waters had carried a bounty of rich alluvial soil to the bays' shores and left behind a filigree of rivers and streams. Five rivers indented the western shore of Chesapeake Bay. The largest was the Potomac, whose tributaries drained approximately fifteen thousand square miles of land, extending all the way from Pennsylvania down to southern Virginia. A multitude of species—estimates range from five hundred to two thousand—populated the estuary biomass. The rich and varied soil deposited there sprouted with a dense forest of pines, beeches, and towering oaks on the northern and western shores. The oaks were an especially tenacious species; one of their offspring survived over five hundred years, only to die in 2002. The oaks native to San Francisco Bay were also prolific, but sparser and crouched lower to the ground than the Chesapeake Bay area's oaks, residing in soil that was most hospitable to grass, bulrush, and sedge. The plant life in the marshes around the bay played a critical ecological role, fortifying the shorelines against the battering of wind and water. Higher up from the shores rose the groves of giant redwoods nestled above the carpet of tiny plants gripping the creek-sides. The life of the estuary was fecund and sustainable. Geologists who sampled the estuary floor south of San Francisco in 2011 found that most of the species that inhabited the shallow shore of the bay today were present 125,000 years ago.[9]

—

The lush spectacle of flora around the estuaries was the stage-set for a drama performed by prolific fauna. Myriad species of shellfish—abalone, oysters, clams, and mussels—spawned in the bays and the surrounding wetlands. Shellfish found a particularly congenial habitat at the places where freshwater and seawater mingled, at the mouths of creeks, or up the river drainage. Abundant marshlands along both coasts supported yet more species of fish and fowl. Some species, such as the salmon and steelhead of San Francisco, adapted to both habitats. Amphibians and reptiles, snakes and turtles, found a happy habitat in Chesapeake swamps. The land surrounding the estuaries to the east and west was alive with mammals both small and large. An array of four-legged creatures thrived in the intricate network of streams around both bays. White-tailed deer in the East and black-tailed ones in the West cohabited with other prolific species, including the packs of grizzly bears that once lorded over the San Francisco terrain. During the period that the estuaries were settling into their modern shapes, even more menacing species had prowled the land. Twenty thousand years ago, mammoths, saber-toothed cats, bison, and camels ranged around the bays. Ten millennia later, they disappeared, harbingers of another momentous turn in natural history.[10]

THE ARRIVAL OF HUMANS

The last days of the mega-mammals overlapped with the debut of *Homo sapiens*. Some archaeologists have even speculated that humans helped to expedite the exodus of the humongous species. All we know for sure is that mammoths reigned between twenty thousand and ten thousand years ago, their demise occurring within the window of time when humans arrived in North America. The exact date and itinerary of that epic human migration is now a matter of dispute among archaeologists. Some have pushed the timing back as far as thirty-five thousand years ago, while the number of possible routes out of Africa and through Asia has expanded from one to as many as four, some by land, some by water. Tentatively, the scholarly consensus, pieced together through the conflicting evidence of skeletal and archaeological remains, linguistic analysis, and various samplings of DNA, is that humans made their way into North America fifteen thousand years ago, crossing into the continent over the Bering Land Bridge and proceeding either by land or by water, probably leapfrogging along the warm and fertile shores of the Pacific before finding routes across the North American continent.[11]

The consensus is highly volatile, however, subject to frequent revisions

—

with each new skeletal find or advance in the technology of genetic analysis. Spearheads recently found in Oregon, for example, suggest that two distinctive lineages of the human family may have made their way to America a score of millennia ago. One thing remains clear, however: the original people of this continent did not pass through Europe, but came out of Asia. Once they were here, it took less than one thousand years for them to make their way along the Pacific and then across the continent. The first North Americans took advantage of the warming temperatures at the end of the ice age to spread across North America along rivers and lakes stocked with sustaining animal life.[12]

Wherever they hailed from, however they got there, and whatever the number of their caravans, these pioneers quickly found their way to the bountiful habitats of the San Francisco and Chesapeake Bays. Small bands of men and women settled in the near vicinity of present-day San Francisco and Baltimore, arriving in plenty of time to see the deep valleys filled up to create the two largest estuaries on the continent. As one scholar put it, "the sea advanced and the estuaries formed literally at the people's hearth sides." In fact, the waters released by the melting glaciers sometimes buried the early Americans and their campsites. For roughly the next five thousand years, the bay peoples left little archaeological evidence of their undoubtedly heroic encounters with the last mammoths, retreating glaciers, and rising waters of the bays.[13]

By making their way to this fecund environment, the first bay peoples had taken a critical step forward in American history. Our yet unnamed forefathers and mothers planted the species on two of the sweetest spots on earth, where freshwater and seawater mingled along a fine web of rivers and creeks and fed the marshes and wetlands with a cornucopia of fish and crustaceans. The shores and nearby forests harbored deer, bear, and waterfowl. All could be captured with the help of simple tools fashioned from bone and stone. Hunters and foragers followed flocks and herds, gathering the most easily accessible and bounteous berries, grasses, fruit, seeds, and nuts. To say that the people of the bays reaped the bounty of the land would account for only a fraction of their livelihood. They had happened upon littoral economies, gaining sustenance from marine life for an estimated 50 percent of their diet, not including the oysters and mussels that flourished at the shoreline. For critical years, when human survival hung in the balance, men and women gathered nutrients on the move, not only over the land, upon foot, but also over water, in vessels shaped of bark, made of skins, or woven of reeds.[14]

———

Life along the bays was not easy or uneventful. Examination of skeletal remains suggests that the supply of nutrients was subject to periodic depletion
on both coasts. Archaeologists have determined that about five thousand
years ago Paleo-Indians suffered from a decline in the consumption of protein from big game, including deer, elk, and sea otter. Even on the bountiful
shores of San Francisco Bay, men and women had to use their wits and
wrestle with the capricious forces of nature to reap their survival. Regular
seasons of drought, fire, an occasional earthquake, and perhaps their own
success in "overkilling" large mammals forced these peoples to make difficult
adaptations to environmental change.

Approximately three thousand to four thousand years ago, climatic
forces lent a hand to these enterprising early Americans. The glacial melt
had stopped, the borders of the bay stabilized, and the land was readied
for a more sedentary human existence. Small groups, centered in a few
families, seized this auspicious moment to make marks upon the landscape
that would endure even until the arrival of the Europeans. They built
structures upon the land whose outlines are still visible in the environs of
San Francisco and in remote regions of the Chesapeake. One shell mound
can be found north of the Patuxent River in an Indian settlement called
Opanient. This site, while of relatively recent construction, is a facsimile
of an ancient mound found to the south in the Chesapeake watershed. The
older shell midden, located near Pope's Creek, Virginia, once rose up to 26
feet high and was constructed 3,000 years ago.[15] Even before this date, an
elaborate network of shell mounds lined the shores of San Francisco Bay.
Some 425 such constructions have been identified circling the bay, some
of them dated over 5,000 years ago; one of them was 30 feet high, 100 feet
wide, and 330 feet long. The shell mounds mark the land with another major
human accomplishment, quasi-permanent settlement. The composition of
the middens suggests that the settlers often occupied the site through four
seasons of the year. Plumbing down through the layers of shell, sand, and
ash, archaeologists have found evidence that some of these ancient ancestors
inhabited the same place for as many as 1,900 years. By collecting plants and
animal resources around established campsites, the peoples of the estuaries
secured a commanding place in the environment.

The huge piles of oyster shells and animal bones demonstrated that these
enterprising people had found a way to feed themselves for generations,
and with few interruptions, despite a still capricious climate. Found within
the mounds are artifacts made in America thousands of years ago. The

—

baskets and large containers testify that the mound builders were no longer at the mercy of nature's arbitrary seasonal largess. They managed both to save resources for future use and acquire desirable objects from a distance. Objects crafted of material unavailable within easy traveling distance from the mound site, such as olivella (snail oil) or obsidian, indicate that the bay people had become long-distance traders. Indeed, the mound itself might have served as a marketplace. Building higher and higher over the waters of the bay, the mound people could easily launch their rafts or canoes and visit the other settlements that hugged the shore; from present-day Oakland to San Francisco was an easy trip in their swift, sleek barks.[16]

The shell mounds tell us, through their archaeological translators, that the bay peoples did not live on oysters alone. The mounds also bore the outlines of hearths and ovens, evidence of innovative food-ways and of the sustained social bonds that form around the preparation and sharing of meals. Some hearths were encircled by a floor plan, the earliest evidence of domestic architecture. Others served as the site of carefully arranged burials. The arrangement of these human remains has led some archaeologists to speculate about the symbolic and cultural life of these very early Americans. The proximity between discarded oyster shells and human burials has even been interpreted as evidence that these ancient peoples were so deeply attached to their own ancestors that they practiced the quotidian ritual of dining above the family skeletons.

Recent evidence suggests an alternative interpretation. Many of the shell mounds were not burial sites, and, more intriguingly, some mounds were devoted exclusively to depositing human skeletons. These burial mounds were stocked with symbolic objects, such as the skeletons of California's elegant condors, clusters of charm-stones, or ornamented mortars and grinding stones. The contents of these burial sites seem to hold a complex cultural meaning and serve a wider social function—as a place to honor ancestors, for example, or to perform ceremonies and display sacred objects. Yet more elaborate architectural evidence lies buried in another mound, which was constructed not of the usual grass or bark fabric, but of a hard-packed yellow and brown clay. This decorative facade, found in a San Francisco shell mound that was devoted exclusively to nondomestic uses, constitutes physical evidence that the San Francisco Bay people were no longer locked in the drudgery of eking out their survival. They had begun to build for some larger, spiritual, aesthetic, or social purpose. As late as the 1920s, this architectural

—

pile still stood outlined against the landscape of the bay, testifying to heroic and creative human efforts to reshape the land.[17]

The shell mounds around San Francisco Bay, like those still entombed beneath the dense urban development of the Eastern Seaboard, were part of a wider network of human habitations. The pattern of occupying space around the bay featured small settlements placed at a regular distance from one another, varying over time between two and three kilometers. Smaller shell middens clustered around larger mounds suggested a hierarchical relationship between the sites. The favorite places to settle and build mounds were along freshwater streams tumbling into San Francisco Bay or astride the rivers, swamps, and marshes lining the Chesapeake. For several thousand years, the mound culture flourished around the San Francisco Estuary. When the bay peoples ranged far afield of their settlements to trade with distant peoples, they sometimes marked their borders with petroglyphs in the coastal mountains.[18]

The shell mounds reigned over the San Francisco Bay landscape fifteen hundred years ago, a golden age when they were the center of trade, feasting, ceremony, and some accumulation of wealth for a small elite. Then this impressive built environment was slowly abandoned, including three sites at Coyote Hills, where Ohlone descendants now celebrate their history. We do not know the cause of the retreat from the shell mounds: a period of global warming and drought (called the medieval warming period) may have played a role, or the shift may have resulted from the very successes of the Paleo-Indians in exploiting their natural habitat (leading to the extinction of several species of coastal shellfish and abalone). Whatever its cause, however, the retreat shows that the prehistory of the San Francisco Bay peoples was not a smooth arc of triumph, man over nature. A few centuries in advance of the European *entrada*, the peoples of the San Francisco Bay scattered and moved into smaller, more homogeneous communities, where they resumed the struggle for survival, intensifying their exploitation of the land and looking up the creeks and hillsides for more plants and animals with which to sustain themselves.[19]

The bay peoples were not reverting to some simpler accommodation with nature. Quite to the contrary, about a millennium ago they undertook a major new production of space, redoubling their labor and renovating their technology. The people of San Francisco Bay devised an exhausting labor system of processing the bitter fruit of the oak trees, not just gathering but

—

also bleaching, grinding, cooking, and storing the harvest of acorns. Environmental pressures also sparked technological innovation, such as carving mortars in the bedrock in the hills above the bay, and weaving baskets for storage and cooking. Such adaptations to environmental changes were commensurate with major social changes. Women took on the task of grinding acorns, giving sharper definition to a gendered division of space and labor. Some millennia later, similar processes, including times of drought and overexploitation of big game, would provoke an even more dramatic change along the Chesapeake: the domestication of plant life. With such ingenious strategies, bay people made a home on the land and established that they were the keystone species of North America. They took the helm of history and began to reshape the land even more decisively.[20]

In sum, by about one millennium ago, the bay peoples, while still subject to the vagaries of climate, the limits of natural resources, and the available technology, had settled into a modest but resourceful existence just inland from the shores of both the Atlantic and the Pacific. They successfully managed their riverine habitats and established a stable relationship with the land as well as a sustainable subsistence. Once again, galactic changes in the atmospheres and oceans had played a role in a shift in the course of human civilization. Increasing temperature in the medieval warming period, combined with the hard human labor of processing acorns and planting corn, brought bountiful harvests and hunts that could support a larger human population. By 1600, the Chesapeake was sustaining thirty thousand people, seven thousand along the Potomac alone. The densest region north of Mexico, present-day California, supported an estimated pre-Columbian population of three hundred thousand inhabitants, approximately ten thousand of whom clustered around San Francisco Bay. The warmer waters and richer alluvial soil on the east side of San Francisco Bay, like the southern and eastern shores of the Chesapeake, were particularly strategic places from which to exploit, manage, and replenish local resources. Relatively secure in their habitat, the aboriginal tribes of the Chesapeake and San Francisco Bays had taken a more forceful hand in managing their environment. As a consequence, the landscape began to take on more distinctive manmade shapes on each coast. Accordingly, we can now give them names, such as the Powhatans of the East and the Ohlone of the West. The diverging stories of the San Francisco and Chesapeake regions will now be told separately, beginning on the Pacific coast, where humans first arrived on this continent. Because both groups remained in place until that time when Europeans docked along

—

34

their shores, we can cautiously piece together their cultural geography with help from the written accounts of Spaniards and Englishmen.

THE COMPLEX HUNTER-GATHERERS OF SAN FRANCISCO

During a cycle of drought beginning about fifteen hundred years ago, the natives of San Francisco Bay sited villages and set up seasonal camps so as to exploit the wide variety of plant and animal life of the estuarial ecology. Following the course of the creeks, the Ohlone designed a distinctive agrarian economy and the associated social space. That economy has been labeled "complex" or "intensive" hunting and gathering, and the social space was called a "tribelet" (by the anthropologist Alfred Kroeber). Both terms denote successful ways of shaping the land and making it productive, but without resorting to the complete domestication of plants. By virtue of occupying these same lands into the nineteenth century, the people of San Francisco Bay achieved a common cultural identity. It has been estimated that seven different languages and fifty or sixty different dialects were spoken around the San Francisco Bay before the Europeans arrived. The population spread out into hundreds of small encampments, in groups usually ranging in size between one hundred and two hundred people. They understood each other's dialects, interacted, traded, intermarried, and sometimes battled one another, but never melded into one large tribe. Now linked together under the name Ohlone (a name reputedly in use for a century, and taken from one Indian settlement in the South Bay), the local tribelets bore myriad linguistic monikers, from the Napa in the north to the Aptos in the south and the Josmite in the far east. The tribelets spread out roughly equidistantly along the creeks and maintained clear, but unfortified, boundaries with one another.[21]

Plotting the settlements of these different groups on a two-dimensional map is not a simple matter. The people who bore distinctive names, and who spoke these different variations of the seven languages heard around the bay, took winding paths, eight to ten miles apart, up and down the web of streams that meandered down to the bay. They formed their own principal villages, with populations as large as five hundred, as well as smaller encampments spaced so as to exploit seasonal variations in plant and animal resources. Some tribelets built a specialized complex of structures in the larger villages, including small round domiciles fashioned out of saplings, roofed with grass, and with a fire pit at the center. Higher up the hillside, they might

—

Reproduction of an Ohlone hut, East Bay Regional Park. Author's photo.

make use of redwood bark to construct conical shelters. The major villages also featured larger round houses, in which to gather for ceremonies and dances, as well as such segregated spaces as menstrual huts for women and sweathouses for male hunters.[22]

The Ohlone had worked out a unique way of living off the land and waters of the bay. Their mastery of a salubrious environment did not require that they adopt the hardscrabble regimen of farmers, but neither were they desperate foragers like their ancestors, those bands of roving hunter-gatherers who had been the custodians of the global landscape for much of human history.[23] Each tribelet effectively harnessed marine life with expertly designed nets, weirs, and fish poisons. They would master the technology of bow and arrow to fell deer, elk, and other large game and devised ways to trap smaller mammals, fowl, and insects. The exploitation of plant life was an especially arduous and creative adaptation to the microclimates and various elevations of the Bay Area. Skillful foragers traveled their hinterland, finding patches of plant life that could be manufactured into edible protein—by blanching

———

36

and grinding the nuts of oak and pine trees, for instance. Not stopping there, they carefully improved on nature by pruning and weeding, and, some say, even by transplanting vegetation or planting wild seeds. The Ohlone's most forceful way of sculpting the land was to employ the technology of fire to redistribute plant life, refurbish the soil, and clear destructive underbrush. Ohlone women handed down to their descendants a catalog of native plants that would rival that of Linnaeus, along with instructions on how to make use of every iota of vegetation, from root to seed to flower. The resulting harvest was stored in the Ohlone's gallery of containers: tightly woven, waterproof baskets in a variety of shapes and sizes. The surplus would sustain the small bands through the winter and enable them to withstand the caprices of nature—the droughts, floods, fires, and occasional earthquakes that still plague this corner of the earth.[24]

The San Francisco Bay was not a paradise; nor were its residents practitioners of the most sophisticated agrarian technology. But they had met their basic needs and created a subsistence economy on a small scale. Busied upon their own fecund creeks, they had made the land and the waterways their own and created a quite distinctive living space: a landscape of small, autonomous, relatively self-sufficient tribelets. Side by side, they traipsed up and down the creeks that fed into the San Francisco Bay along serpentine, closely spaced, but separate paths. The tribelets seem not to have erected physical barriers between one another, neither fences nor palisades, yet they marked off their common land and the provenance of different families according to the contours of the bay, the shifting currents of the creek, and the nutritious patches of grass and forest. Much of their diet came from the marine life that thrived in the streams, the marshes, and the great bay. A water habitat is difficult to partition. Neither could the bounty of fowls in the sky overhead be held as private property. Like micronations, these longest-living inhabitants of the San Francisco Bay region established social cohesion among themselves as well as a loose kind of sovereignty over the land and water from which they reaped their subsistence.

The Ohlone survived for generations without fully domesticating plants or developing a steep political or social hierarchy. The villagers constructed gathering places around the bay in which some women as well as men could assume leadership and perform such roles as shaman and chieftain. A round structure in the center of the principal settlements was the meeting place for the council, where both sexes may have presided. The landscape does not reveal much further detail about social arrangements, such as information

—

about relations between the sexes, political organization, or social stratification. Although the first Europeans to penetrate the Golden Gate reported being welcomed by "chiefs" and "captains," they provided little evidence that the bay people had erected a steep and durable social hierarchy. Uniformly humble domiciles formed the village skyline; individual families maintained the similarly small stashes of acorns or smoked fish. The built environment is equally mute about how those sixty tribelets of the Bay Area maintained the borders between them. The archaeological record is ambiguous, containing some battered skeletons but neither major arsenals nor signs of the bellicose reputation of tribes like the Chumash, who created a more highly stratified society to the south. We can only assume that the Ohlone worked out ways to coexist in such close quarters. They also communicated with more distant tribes, conducting exchange through the medium of beads and cylinders of shell, clam, and abalone.[25]

By some standards, the peoples of San Francisco Bay were a simple culture, placed low on that scale of human civilizations ranking agriculture above hunting and gathering. Yet the Ohlone were not entirely ignorant of

Louis Choris, Bateau du port de San Francisco *(Boat of the Port of San Francisco),*
ca. 1815, fG420.K84C6 1822, Part 3, Plate X. Courtesy of the Bancroft Library,
University of California, Berkeley.

—

alternate ways of managing the land. They were aware of tribes to the south and east that cultivated corn and had developed more organized political structures, approximating a state, but the Ohlone did not adopt these innovations. The peoples of San Francisco Bay are a case in point for those anthropologists who now question the practice of ranking agriculturalists a strata above simple hunters and gatherers. The Ohlone did not plow or plant or pay tribute to tribal leaders. Yet they endured and even prospered around the San Francisco Bay, one of the most densely populated regions in the Americas north of Mexico. In fact, their way of life was enviable to some. There is mounting evidence that some horticulturalist tribes east of the Sierra Nevada were won over by the lifestyle of the Ohlone, and turned away from the arduous regimen of domesticating native plants. Be that as it may, the Ohlone had mastered their own distinctive and durable way of living on the land and the waters of the bay. They had produced a very special American place many centuries before the arrival of Europeans.[26]

THE CHIEFDOMS OF THE CHESAPEAKE

The warming climate also nurtured increasingly varied life along the great estuary of the Atlantic and the dense network of waterways that fed into it. The *longue durée* of clement weather, sometimes interrupted by either drought or torrential rainfall, fostered a renaissance among the nomadic bands who found their way to the Chesapeake over ten thousand years ago. Between 8000 and 1000 BC, small groups of kin migrated toward the warmer southern waterways of the Potomac basin, where they might feast on turkey as well as venison, soft-shell crabs, and oysters as well as cherries and strawberries. Once the bay and the rivers had settled into their contemporary shapes, around three thousand years ago, the peoples of the Chesapeake, much like the Ohlone, became more sedentary, for at least a season. They began to regularize their movements through the landscape and found the niches of the pine forest best suited for hunting, and the points along the rivers that were stocked with the most varied and abundant marine life.[27]

By the dawn of the first millennium, the Algonquian-speaking people had installed themselves as the keystone species of the Chesapeake. Under pressure from the same climatic conditions as the Ohlone, they adapted their settlement patterns and devised new methods of subsistence. Taking advantage of the warming climate, they improved their hunting and gathering technology. They hunted with spears and bows, fished from log canoes,

—

processed groundnuts and seeds with stone tools, cooked at large hearths, and ate off clay pots. They also worked out a seasonal accommodation with their riverine environment and built principal villages near the mouths of rivers, or upstream along rich marshland, and established small seasonal campsites where they hunted in the winter. Unlike the Ohlone, the peoples of the Chesapeake did not rest comfortably in the hunter-gatherer economy, however complex. Around one thousand years ago, the Chesapeake peoples enacted that much-heralded transformation in the relationship between man and land, the Neolithic revolution, said to first occur ten thousand years ago at other sites around the world. The domestication of plants pioneered by the corn farmers of Mesoamerica migrated north and entered the Chesapeake region from west of the fall line. It soon spread to the equally congenial soils of the coastal plain, particularly on the eastern shore and on the banks of the great rivers that drained into the west side of the bay: the James, York, Rappahannock, Potomac, Patuxent, and Patapsco. Soon the Algonquian tribes, including the Powhatans along the Potomac and the Piscataway farther north, were planting the tidewater with squash and beans as well as corn. Chesapeake peoples took control of the land with a new sense of purpose and intensity. They harnessed fire to clear and replenish the land. When the dense shorelines of forest did not yield compliantly, they took to killing the trees by slashing their barks or felling their trunks with axes. This was man's work, preparatory to women's labor of disturbing the soil with hoes, penetrating it with alien seeds, and uprooting vegetation at harvest time. The peoples of the Chesapeake were more than complex hunters and gatherers; they had become horticulturalists.[28]

The Neolithic revolution, a period marked off in Chesapeake archaeology as the Woodland period, was accompanied by a spate of spatial innovations. Because cultivated crops required constant tending, and protection from the invading species of weeds and animal predators, the Powhatan and Piscataway peoples built permanent structures around the cornfields. They fashioned small thatch and bark domiciles and interspersed them with houses that would comfortably accommodate larger families. They crafted elongated oval buildings, capacious enough to shelter nearly a whole village, and furnished them with raised platforms on which they might enact a ceremony or worship a tribal god. These elevated structures also provided the sacred spaces where the Powhatans elaborately prepared their kinsmen for burial. Baskets sufficient to contain a small surplus of recently foraged food gave way to self-standing warehouses that could contain a plentiful

—

annual corn crop and store it for another season. In the late Woodland period, a few settlements exhibited a yet higher order of spatial change. The village of Pomeiooc on Albemarle Sound, for example, grouped dwellings, a storehouse, and a temple-like structure in a circle and surrounded them with the defensive structure of a palisade. These new constructions upon the land signaled that the Algonquians had accomplished major economic, social, and cultural changes.

In the four hundred years before the arrival of the English, various tribes of Algonquian speakers settled around the Chesapeake Bay, shaping the land into farmsteads, nucleated (small but dense) villages, and larger, more specialized locations, for which they devised a name that approximated the term "town." This complex built environment was emblematic of a specialized division of labor and a relatively steep social hierarchy. The English would call the heads of the larger households the "Big Men." The Chesapeake people had other names for them, *werowance* or *tayac*. A second order of village notables, called *wiso*, *cockaroos*, *cronoco*, or *weroansqua*, presided at a rung below this. The first three titles of this group denoted counselors; the last designated a lower rank of authority, open to women. The linguistic recognition of both a single dominant figure, usually male, and those who held council at a rung below him announced that the peoples of the Chesapeake had created a formal government, complete with a dominant authority figure and some semblance of a deliberating public body. This political stratification had economic consequences; commoners were required to give the ruling *werowance* a portion of their corn crop in tribute.

One large settlement near the James River was called Werowocomoco, and its archaeological footprint is as complicated as its name. In the four hundred years before the arrival of Europeans, the inhabitants of Werowocomoco had sculpted a relatively baroque habitat, complete with domiciles large and small, elaborate earthworks suitable for public ceremonies, and a deep trench that seemed to set off a separate residential district. The chief resident of this auspicious place at the time of the Jamestown landing in 1607 was Wahunsenacawh, better known as Powhatan, the chief of the most powerful of the Algonquian tribes of Chesapeake. Powhatan's political stature rested in part on a spatial hierarchy—he reigned in the grandest of dwellings and presided at the central place of an extended tribe. His kingdom spun out from the principal settlement to small hamlets scattered in a patchwork of fields and along a chain of rivers, all linked together under a common name.[29]

—

The lattice of hamlets and villages on the south side of the Potomac River was called Powhatan, and the territory to the north went by the name of Piscataway, with its own presiding *tayac*. The English were quite right to call these political spaces kingdoms, for like the emerging nations across the Atlantic, the Algonquian tribes brought the land under the tutelage of a single ruler who exacted tribute from his subjects. Ethno-historians estimate that as many as fifty such political jurisdictions occupied the Chesapeake at the end of the Woodland period. Most of them spoke a variant of the Algonquian language, abided in adjacent territories, and traded with one another for luxury goods—copper, beads, and pearls—and sometimes they warred with one another. King Powhatan and the Piscataway *tayac* maintained difficult relations with one another and with the other kingdoms that had formed in the natural pockets of the Potomac watershed. While more distant tribes came from across the fall line to raid the Piscataway, the Powhatans made aggressive moves toward the south and east.[30]

The warfare on the Chesapeake became more frequent and brutal when the climatic good fortune of the medieval warming period began to abate after 1400. The austerity of this "little ice age," which would last into the nineteenth century, drove tribes from the colder regions, such as the Iroquois-speaking Susquehannocks in the north and the Sioux to the west, into the more fertile Algonquian lands, tempted by their more ample stocks of corn. Ethno-historians speculate that this increasingly aggressive stance toward their neighbors was a consequence of the taste for political power and excessive material goods fostered by the social hierarchy of the Powhatans. The *tayac* of the Piscataway, like King Powhatan, sought to aggrandize more Indian territory. Chief Uttapoingaskennum led a confederacy of several tribes and claimed the title of emperor. Centered in the village of Moyoane, he presided in earshot of present-day Mount Vernon, soon to be the home of another celebrated American chief.[31]

INDIAN LANDS ON THE EVE OF THE ENCOUNTER WITH EUROPEANS

The longtime residents along the shores of San Francisco and Chesapeake Bays had survived brutal conditions on the natural landscape, settled the most advantageous regions, made the land productive, and passed it on from generation to generation. Yet, when John Smith ventured up the Chesapeake in 1608, or when Gaspar de Portolá sighted San Francisco Bay in 1769, the land had not yet been fully taken. Aside from the small stock of surplus corn in the coffers of Algonquian *werowances*, Indians seldom took much more than their subsistence from the land. Ninety-five percent of the Chesapeake watershed was still forest, broken by a few small cornfields. What Powhatan took in tribute was traded largely for luxury goods, not staples. The basic needs of their quite autonomous communities were met by carefully tending the fields and gardens, relying on the bounty of the estuaries, streams, marshes, meadows, and forests, and holding the land and waterways as the common resource of the tribe or tribelet. Although the diverse peoples of the bay regions recognized, and sometimes violated, the complex borders between the Algonquian kingdoms or Ohlone tribelets, they seldom erected barricades between them, not even a flimsy fence around a cornfield or a dam along a salmon run.

In the late Midland period, around one thousand years ago, when climate worsened once again, the custodians of the Chesapeake Bay might have been on the cusp of making more drastic changes in the management of the land, but they had not yet marked off slices of earth as separated parcels and labeled them with the names of individual owners. Meanwhile, in the more beneficent climate around San Francisco Bay, the natural abundance of the wetlands showed few signs of being exhausted. Life along the estuaries was not idyllic, and nature was only prolific enough to sustain a limited population. Life expectancy among the Ohlone and the Algonquian hovered around the age of thirty-five, on average. Nonetheless, the bay peoples had maintained a presence in North America for millennia and accomplished some laborious and momentous transformations of space, including the creation of sedentary communities, complex economies, and organized villages and towns. Some would argue that they had presided over one of the most momentous transitions in the history of the earth. Geologists, aware of the perilous condition of the planet in the twenty-first century, are debating about when to mark the date at which humankind began to effect climatic events and transform the environment with a force that rivaled nature in its power. Was it only after World War II, when the atomic bomb introduced its noxious waste into the atmosphere, or did it begin with industrialization in Britain in 1800? Or was it earlier, in the seventeenth century, when European empires laid claim to the Western Hemisphere, bringing virtually all the lands around the globe under their oversight? Which of these watershed moments might mark a new geologic era called the Anthropocene, in recognition of the agency of humans in shaping basic environmental conditions? A number of archaeologists argue that this historical accomplishment

—

could be dated to that time when the distant ancestors of the Ohlone and the Algonquians landed in North America some fifteen thousand years ago. The bay peoples had indeed left marks of their own artistry around the great estuaries on both sides of the continent, but they never quite took the land in the decisive ways marked by imperial edicts, national boundaries, or deeds of property.

The arrival of Europeans, beginning in 1492, portended a harsher use of the bay habitat. But the displacement of the bay people would not be sudden or simple. As the meeting at Coyote Hills testified, the claims of the earliest Americans upon the land around the great estuaries did not terminate once and for all around 1500, with the arrival of either Juan Rodríguez Cabrillo on the Pacific or John Cabot on the Atlantic. Some Miwoks from the north shore of San Francisco Bay, for example, escaped from Spanish missions and could be found several generations later resettled near an ancient shell mound. Some of their descendants might have been among the celebrants at the Ohlone festival in 2010, held not far from an ancient shell mound and the hunting grounds of a tribelet called Chochenyo. Back East, the Piscataway traced a line of *tayacs* going back twenty-eight generations. In 1987, approximately one hundred members of the tribe buried their leader at Moyoane, their sacred ancestral space. One of the celebrants claimed his people's right of return to their "land and their spiritual roots." Chief Billy Tayac elegized that "we are so intermingled with this earth that when you pick up one fistful of dirt you pick up life."[32]

Neither the Ohlone nor the Algonquians had constructed anything resembling the great cities to be found across the Atlantic or in Mexico and South America. They left the immediate sites of Baltimore and San Francisco largely unsettled. Baltimore was located below the fall line along the Patapsco River on rocky soil that was cut off from the bay by rugged cliffs, and subject to raiding by the fearsome tribes of Iroquois in the north and Sioux in the west. As for the future site of San Francisco, on the west side of its bay, its dry landscape, wind, and fog attracted only two of the region's sixty tribelets, each with only one or two small villages. These largely vacant and unmarked patches of land present a stark backdrop to the changes that European colonizers would soon bring to the great estuaries. Although the Ohlone and the Algonquians had not created cities, they had shaped their own unique and intricate spaces along the shores of the Atlantic and the Pacific. These two native cultures, separated by thousands of miles, each managed the Herculean task of sustaining human life in one place for many

—

Their rype corne

Their greene corne

Corne newly sprong

SECOTON

John White, An Algonquian Village on the Pamlico River, *1585.*
Courtesy of the Library of Congress.

generations, and they did it in their own unique and inventive ways. The Ohlone fashioned a complex hunting and gathering economy framing San Francisco Bay, while the Algonquian tribes arranged a hierarchy of towns along the rivers of the Chesapeake. Their accomplishments are lasting testimony to the ingenuity, tenacity, adaptability, and originality with which humankind wrests a living along the water and off the land. The Native Americans, furthermore, retained custody over the great estuaries for an expanse of time at which the newcomers could only marvel.

CHAPTER 2

THE BRITISH AND THE AMERICANS TAKE THE CHESAPEAKE

V arious tribes of Europeans were hovering around the Chesapeake at the turn of the sixteenth century. John Cabot had passed along the Atlantic coast in 1498 and claimed the territory of North America for Henry VII of England. Soon thereafter, Spaniards and Portuguese ventured north from their imperial outposts in Florida and gave the name Bahía de Santa María to the estuary that Algonquians reputedly gave such names as "Great Shellfish Bay" or "Big River." The Susquehannocks, who reigned over the northern tip of the Chesapeake, had become regular trading partners with the French, who offered beads and guns in exchange for the beaver skins coveted by continental men of fashion. The Powhatan and Piscataway tribes were not particularly alarmed when pale-skinned men speaking a strange tongue sailed all the way up the Chesapeake in 1607 and passed by a river they named Bolis, near where the city of Baltimore would rise almost two centuries later. Long after the arrival of Captain John Smith, the Chesapeake peoples and seafaring agents of competing European empires would skirmish around the great bay and along the Atlantic shores without any one nation evicting the others or definitively taking the land.

The tide of empire had turned by the middle of the eighteenth century. In 1763, at the conclusion of seven years of war, the European powers agreed to split their claim to the land between the Atlantic and the Pacific roughly in half, between the English and Spanish monarchs. This pretense of a boundary would endure until the end of another war in 1848, this one between two independent federated states, the United States of America and the Republic of Mexico. The time in between was an extraordinary historical epoch, marked not just by European conquest, followed swiftly by the revolt of their colonies, but also by a fundamental transformation in the way humans occupied the North American continent. As seen from the Chesapeake Bay region, this revolution unfolded as a convulsive succession of overlapping changes: the destruction of the Algonquian ecological system, the implantation of a kind of agricultural economy unknown in either hemisphere, and the founding of a commercial settlement at the mouth of the Patapsco River that would link the Atlantic port to a hinterland that was moving rapidly and aggressively westward.

By the middle of the eighteenth century, a set of contiguous towns clustered at the mouth of the Patapsco announcing a new regime of land and labor. Nested together on the jagged coast of the bay, the ports of Fells Point, Jonestown, and Baltimore formed a commercial hub, exchanging local agricultural produce for European goods and conducting frantic sales of small pieces of land they called "lotts." On these wharves and lots, a booming market economy and nascent popular democracy would one day rise. As we shall see, the men and women who founded these Chesapeake towns were inveterate land-takers, and although their towns were not granted city charters or the political status that would accompany such charters, they demonstrated their capacity to produce dense urban spaces.

The revolution upon the land started quietly enough, with largely harmonious encounters between the first European interlopers and the natives of the Chesapeake. It took roughly a century and a half to complete the first stage of remaking the land: displacing most of the native inhabitants. Surveying the colony called Maryland in 1759, the English governor, Horatio Sharpe, counted only 120 Indians in what he termed "the populous part of the Province," and these had been reduced to a "scattered Remnant of a confused Nation."[1] The governor's account of the displacement of the native population was simplified, exaggerated, and foreshortened. For well over a century, neither the Indian nor the European "Nation" held absolute dominion over the land and waterways of the Chesapeake. The landscape was a piebald mix of clashing kingdoms, not just Indians and Europeans, but different combinations of Susquehannock, Piscataway, and Powhatan Indians as well as the rival nations of Spain, France, Holland, and England. The Colony of Maryland was also cleaved by religion, between Catholics and various sects of Protestants. Within a few years of Governor Sharpe's pronouncement of the extinction of the Indians, the British tribe would also be banished from the Chesapeake, ousted by American settlers claiming their independence. This unruly country would not be easily tamed into one nation. Neither would the notion of a methodically advancing frontier or a transitional middle ground capture the untidy and earth-shaping process of taking land along the northern shores of the Chesapeake.[2]

COHABITING THE LAND: INDIANS AND ENGLISHMEN

The Europeans arrived in the "New World" confident that they could make the strange land conform to their sense of order, and they carried a critical set of tools with which to do so. The Dutch and the Spanish had learned to transcribe the shapes of the land and water onto parchment in the form of maps and atlases, and the French had become master cartographers. One amateur English mapmaker—Captain John Smith—put these skills to work along the Chesapeake. His map of Virginia, published in England in 1612, reduced a plentitude of knowledge about the New World to some lines on a two-dimensional surface. Smith charted the paths along which Indians and colonizers would walk and live fleetingly together. But his map relied on local Indian knowledge and was very much a collaborative production.

A map, as Smith knew well, was a massive abstraction designed to convert the inscrutable variety of the land to a synopsis of useful information. Smith inscribed his chart of the Chesapeake with a wealth of political knowledge, much of it written in the symbols of royalty. He took care to perch the English crown atop a coat of arms at the center of his map. The keen-eyed explorer-politician also placed the insignia of a second kingdom on his map. An image of Powhatan dominated the upper left side; the *werowance* was seated on a platform above his subjects, who congregated in a tall, finely woven, temple-like building. Smith gave the native king priority of space and some artistic embellishment. He also found an economical way to represent the social order of the kingdom of Powhatan. In a cartouche, Smith explained the "signification of the marks" upon his map. He labeled larger dwellings the "King's Houses," and the smaller, undifferentiated shelters "Ordinary."

John Smith's map of the Chesapeake Bay, 1608. Virginia, Discovered
and Described by Captayn John Smith *(London: William Hole, 1624).*
Courtesy of the Library of Congress.

Smith discerned the social hierarchy that had recently grown up around the
Chesapeake. From the vantage point of John Smith—on the ground around
the Chesapeake in the first decade of the seventeenth century—the kingdoms
of the Tudors and the Powhatans were analogous.[3]

John Smith's map was a fine-grained portrait of the land and the waters
he had traveled. At a "Scale of Leagues and half Leagues," he traced a filigree
of rivers and creeks running from the fall line down to the Chesapeake and as
far north as the domain of the "giant like people," the Susquehannocks. What
caught Smith's eye more than anything else were the settled communities:
the map sited no less than 166 Indian villages hugging the shores of the
Chesapeake and lining its tributaries from the James to the Susquehanna.
The English expedition is known to have actually visited only 58 of those 166
villages depicted on Smith's map. In order to identify the rest, he depended
on the local knowledge of his Indian guides.

—

Although neither the Piscataway nor the Powhatans had paper maps of their own, they were clearly capable of translating their intimate knowledge of the land into words and images. They knew the rough tribal boundaries of different hunting grounds and where the soil was fertile, the game abundant, and the waters prolific. They could communicate their knowledge in symbols, sometimes marking their trails with blazes on trees, and readily plotting locations by lines in sand or ash, upon bark or deerskin, or with an arrangement of pine cones. While the 1612 map of Virginia bore the caption "discovered and described by Captayn John Smith," it transcribed "the information of the Savages . . . according to their instructions." Native American informants furnished Europeans with their first atlases of the yet untaken land around the Chesapeake.[4]

The collaborative mapmaking of John Smith and the Algonquians was typical of the first encounters between the people of the Chesapeake and the visitors from Europe. Although later accounts of the meeting between King Powhatan and Captain Smith highlighted conflict, inspiring the mythic story of Pocahontas, their relationship actually proceeded in a less dramatic and more amicable manner. Powhatan held the upper hand and beneficently offered Smith not his daughter but a territory, an area called Capahowasick, and conferred upon him the title of *werowance*. Proceeding on with his explorations in 1608, Smith came upon one hundred Piscataway Indians at the village of Moyoane and reported another friendly reception, writing, "The people did their best to content us." Smith's diary sometimes reads more like a report from summer camp than a frontier war story. In one entry, he wrote of a day spent in "fetes, dancing and singing, and much like mirth." The procession of Englishmen into the region of the Chesapeake followed along this path of relative equanimity. When Leonard Calvert arrived in the Chesapeake to claim Maryland for his brother George Calvert, the 1st Baron Baltimore, or Lord Baltimore, in 1634, a *tayac* named Archihu made a proposal: "We will eat at the same table, my followers too shall go to hunt for you: and we will have all things in common."[5]

First encounters were seldom as idyllic as these reports imply; nor were relations between the natives and the immigrants to remain pacific for very long. Indians and Englishmen jockeyed for position along the Chesapeake, keenly searching for advantageous political alliances and access to material resources. To the Indians, the English were late-coming players on an already complex and contentious chessboard of tribal rivalries. The Piscataway were particularly eager for allies against tribes pressing in on them

—

from three sides, from the Powhatans to the south, the especially aggressive Masswomeks in the east, and the Susquehannocks in the north. Although the Europeans' need for Indian allies would not become acute until the next century, during the Seven Years' War with France, different tribes were occasionally enlisted in the internecine European rivalries. In 1655, the border between Virginia and Maryland was bloodied by religious enmity between Protestants and the Catholic lord proprietor, Lord Baltimore. What was called the Sabbath Battle of that year left fifty Englishmen dead. In this context, Maryland colonists made haste to reach a diplomatic accord with the Susquehannocks on their northern border. Embattled Indian tribes also resorted to protective alliances with the English. Some Piscataway, eager for any allies they could muster, made peace with the settlers of Maryland by briefly converting to Catholicism. Indians also used alliances with the English to settle their own internal quarrels. The *tayac* Kittamaguund, for example, used his ties with the English as a shield against his own tribe after he reputedly murdered their chief, his own brother.[6]

More than fealty to king, God, and country was at stake in the fragile détente along the Chesapeake. Indians and Europeans forged their tenuous peace through the exchange of material objects. Explorers like John Smith and the first settlers at places like Roanoke, Jamestown, or St. Mary's desperately needed the agricultural surplus that the Algonquian peoples had cultivated so assiduously. Jamestown became a marketplace where corn was exchanged for copper and the white beads the Indians called *reoanoke* or *peake*. Accordingly, the English arrived with a boatload of trading goods. The galley of *The Ark and the Dove*, the vessel that brought the first settlers to Maryland, contained a stock of cloth, brass, kettles, knives, and beads, along with the guns and metal hatchets coveted by Chesapeake warriors. Englishmen readily accommodated such desires. William Claiborne, a Virginian poaching in the Maryland waters around Kent Island, went into business with the Susquehannocks by exchanging guns for hides. One historian has called the commerce around the Chesapeake "a transatlantic network stretching from the beaver dams of America to the docks of London." By trading in arms, this embryonic global marketplace was also a harbinger of ethnic conflicts to come.[7]

In the short term, however, these reciprocal material desires gave both Indians and Europeans reason to maintain peaceful relations. The first tense encounters often ended in stalemate. By and large, both sides saw an advantage in maintaining workable relationships. Neither was compelled to

—

banish the other from the land they cohabited. Indians, for their part, were not about to leave the land they had occupied for centuries. The Piscataway *tayac* Uttapoingassenem boasted to the English that his royal lineage went back thirteen generations. The first appearance of a few traders and adventurers from across the Atlantic was not likely to provoke either migration or surrender. Neither were the English initially eager to remove the Indians from the land. The fierce imperialist battle for dominion over the New World was based on claims of first discovery, patrol of the high seas, mineral bounty, and occasionally conversions to Christianity. The English quest for Indian souls, however, was brief and lethargic. The mission mounted by the Jesuits in Maryland was even briefer, minuscule in scale compared to the Franciscan campaign to Christianize California. In matters spiritual and material, minimizing conflict was in the interest of both natives and immigrants to the Chesapeake.

At times, colonial leaders assumed a protective relationship with the Indians. In 1652, the Virginia Assembly took the unusual action of granting titles to the peoples who had inhabited the land so long before them. Concerned about the "wrong done to the Indians in taking away their lands," and fearful that they might take some "desperate course of themselves," Virginia officials ordered that "all the Indians of this colony shall and may hold and keep those seats of land that they now have. And that no person or persons whatsoever be suffered to intrench or plant upon such place." With this paternalistic gesture, however, the English governor presumed sovereign power and made the allocation of American land contingent on his permission.[8]

When George Calvert, the first Lord Baltimore, secured a royal charter declaring him the "True and Absolute Proprietor" of the land to the north of Virginia, his "to Have, hold, Possess and Enjoy," he was not unaware of the prior claims of Chesapeake natives. He acknowledged the Indian patrimony with the annual diplomatic gesture of having two Indian arrows delivered to Windsor Castle. On the ground, in the Colony of Maryland, the proprietor offered the "particular tribes" their "guaranty and protection." Well into the eighteenth century, George Calvert and his heirs patrolled a tenuous boundary between Indian and European land. The governor of Maryland advised the settlers to go gently into the lands of the Indians, writing, "It is most for the safety of the province to continue them neer us." Accordingly, the colonial policy, as designed by three generations of Calverts and implemented by their colonial agents, acknowledged Indian land rights by the act of purchase or by granting them "reserves." In 1668, the Council of Maryland offered the

—

Piscataway title to their own patch of land "provided it stands with their King." Large chunks of land on the Eastern Shore were granted to Nanticoke and Choptank Indians, tendered as "an act for the continuation of peace with, and protection of our neighbors and confederates."[9]

Colonial authorities maintained an official policy of reserving and respecting Indian territory. An act of 1721 established a commission to survey Indian lands and hear complaints about the violation of their borders. Two years later, the Nanticokes protested before the commission that English settlers were encroaching upon their hunting grounds, leading the commission to assert that the Indians had a right to protection against trespass. Should the Indians agree to sell or lease their ancestral land, the commission also enforced the terms of sale and the payment of rents.[10]

Were it just a matter of the colonial policy drafted in England and enforced by appointed governors, the relations with the Indians might have been reasonably harmonious. What disrupted the tenuous accommodation with native people was the arrival of Englishmen intent on enclosing land into farms and plantations. Historian James Rice recounted an ominous example of the incompatibility between English farming and Algonquian horticulture. It occurred in 1665 in Charles County and demonstrated the fundamental contradictions between English and Indian land practices. The conflict ensued when the English set their hogs free to root about in the Indian cornfields in the village of Mattawoman. The Indians retaliated by violating English property lines, hunting deer within the bounds of an English family's homestead. Tensions escalated into violence between the two offended parties, leaving two children dead by Indian tomahawks. Two irreconcilable ways of living upon the land had confronted one another. The Englishmen had not only brought domesticated animals into the Indians' unprotected cornfields, but had built fences where they had once freely hunted game. Yet despite this extreme provocation—a violation of English prerogatives of land use ending in violent death—the colonial governor made peace with the Indian *tayac*. The murderers were executed, and the Mattawoman leader volunteered to lead his people farther into the woods. The English settled in; the Indians moved on.[11]

While the conflict at Mattawoman was apparently resolved to the satisfaction of both parties, it was an omen of greater difficulty ahead. A new wave of English settlers was sweeping ashore in the Chesapeake. They came not in search of glory or beaver skins, but for profitable farmland. One Indian leader, named Queen Portobacco, clearly perceived the threat posed by land-hungry

—

54

Englishmen. She was reported to lament that her people were being pushed to the "utmost bounds of their lands." Even the Virginia Assembly recognized that the rising tide of European immigration was "taking away their lands, and forcing the Indians" into narrow straits and places where "they cannot subsist, either by planting or hunting." Leaders of Virginia and Maryland responded to this dilemma with the same strategy. They escorted the Indians to a separate, remote tract of land, something that would later be called a reservation. One Maryland treaty required Indians to fence their lands and stay within arbitrary boundaries in Charles County.[12]

The Indians of the Chesapeake adapted to the new circumstances of the seventeenth century, including English codes of property. Some even complied with the edict that Indian "land be with all convenient speed layd out for them by certain meets and bounds, with which no English man shall *take up* land" (emphasis mine). In 1705, one group of Chesapeake Indians petitioned to trade in the remnants of their kingdom for one thousand acres of their ancestral land. Another Indian chief, Betty Caco, adopted European ways of taking the land. She offered six pounds to lease some land from an Englishman named Edward Norton. Terms like "metes and bounds," "acres," "leases," "pounds sterling," "fences," and the regular use of that word "taking" introduced the Indians to a complicated new language of space, and one that some of them mastered.[13]

Unaccustomed to being fenced in, Indians most often rejected European offers of confinement on a single tract of land. Instead they moved on in search of open hunting and planting grounds. The Powhatans had moved quietly westward by the 1690s. The Susquehannocks exited with a military flourish; joining the Covenant Chain of the Iroquois, they would live to fight the English another day. The Piscataway receded far enough away by 1759 for Governor Sharpe to explain that "time and circumstances eventually prevailed over love of place."[14] Governor Sharpe was not very discerning. He was oblivious to how the Indians had occupied the Chesapeake and used its land and waterways for so many generations. With growing numbers of English settlers trespassing on their native habitat, most tribesmen and women chose to move on to places where they could use the land and waters more freely. The last decree of the colonial Assembly of Maryland regarding Indian land, dated 1768, captures the slow somber way land was taken from the Indians. The displacement of Maryland's native population was transcribed in the colonial record with the perfunctory notice that "the greatest part of the tribe of Nanticoke Indians had left the province, and

—

that the few still remaining were, as appeared by their petition, desirous to depart, and join themselves with the Indians of the six nations, but prayed that some compensation should be made to them for quitting claim to the land formerly granted to their tribe." The Nanticoke petition was granted. The tribe surrendered three thousand acres of land; their compensation was "six hundred and sixty-six dollars and two thirds of a dollar." By the close of the eighteenth century, then, the devolution of the Indian ecology was measured in acres and money, down to two-thirds of a dollar. Indians had been parties to this wholesale reshaping of the land, choosing, when pressed, to move on to new territory farther to the west, or, at other times, bargaining as best they could for the sale of the coastal lands that they had long held in common. They did not make an advantageous or even a fair bargain, but neither did they abjectly surrender to the English colonizers. Due in part to decimating disease and voluntary migration, the tribes of the Chesapeake lost their habitat to European newcomers—clearing the ground for further experiments in reshaping the land.[15]

TAKING MARYLAND

The swift determination with which the Maryland colonists fenced off farms and plantations around the Chesapeake was something of a novelty in the seventeenth century. The language of absolute, individualistic landholding was not that widely spoken on either the European or the American side of the Atlantic until relatively recent times. Although English monarchs and noblemen held nominal title to vast territories before the sixteenth century, they were not much more precise about drawing boundaries than was Powhatan. While all land customarily belonged to the king, his loyal noblemen had the use of it, and took their tribute from the fields cultivated by the peasantry, often along separate, parallel strips. Pasturage was held in common, and if fields were partitioned, it was only by a low hedge. It took centuries, commencing around 1300, for lords, and then yeomen farmers, to mark off their estates into clearly bounded portions of land along those lines called "metes and bounds." This simple technology of land-taking drew chains (divided into one hundred links and totaling twenty-two yards) tautly across the terrain to measure off the land into irregular parcels. The "bounds" were commonly set between such natural landmarks as trees, stones, creeks, and larger bodies of water. The "metes" were the points where these lines drawn on the landscape intersected. Taking these measurements became the

—

work of a specialized occupation, that of the surveyor. By the late sixteenth century, surveyors were at work in the English countryside marking off more and more of the land into these roughly geometrical plots. This fundamental social transformation acquired a fitting name, "enclosure."[16]

In the seventeenth century, the English settlers carried this technology for partitioning land across the Atlantic, where it provided the incentive, the method, and the language for moving inland from the coast. John Winthrop, patriarch of the "City on the Hill" in the Massachusetts Bay Colony, was one of many practitioners of the new method of land-taking. Winthrop's family had purchased enclosed fields in England, and he justified claiming title to land in the New World on the principle that the Indians "inclose no land, neither have they settled habitations." A similar logic excused the taking up of the land in the Colony of Maryland. According to the royal charter issued in 1632, the land granted to Lord Baltimore was "hitherto uncultivated and occupied in part by savages, having no knowledge of the Divine Being." The legal principle cited here, termed *vacuum domicilium*, justified claiming any land "not now actually possessed by any Christian Prince, nor inhabited by Christian People." By 1718, the Maryland proprietor had appointed nine surveyors to carve up land in each of the colony's counties. From the vantage point of the enclosing colonists, the eastern and western shores of the Atlantic seemed to fit together like two pieces of a giant jigsaw puzzle: from the east came the land-takers, and to the west lay a boundless expanse of open space free for the taking. The first Europeans to map the Chesapeake anticipated brilliant prospects, declaring, "No place is more convenient for pleasure, profit, and man's sustenance."[17]

Rudimentary schemes of English land-taking had portentous consequences when transported across the Atlantic: they can be gleaned from the writings of one of the most forward-looking thinkers of the day, John Locke. Before he wrote the prolegomena to the rights of private property and the labor theory of value, *The Second Treatise on Government* (1682), Locke had served as secretary to the lords proprietor of the colony of Carolina, chartered in 1663. For six years, Locke put his pen to work recording such legerdemain matters as the measurement of the new colony into parcels, both large and small. When he sat down at the drawing board to write the *Fundamental Constitutions of Carolina*, he had practical land matters on his mind. "Every county is to consist of forty square Plots, each containing twelve thousand Acres," he declared. He proceeded to construct a social and economic hierarchy atop this cadastral map. To each of the twelve proprietors he assigned huge tracts; eight more large parcels would go to the "nobility," and twenty-four others were divided among "the people." Locke's political philosophy is a transcript of the property transactions of the proprietors, surveyors, and settlers of the American colonies. He would have been aware of applicants for land grants such as William Hilton of Carolina, who argued, first, that the natives did not make proper use of the land, and, second, that he, an Englishman, would adhere to other principles, of "freedom of Trade, Immunity of Customs, and Liberty of conscience." Those powerful words, soon to be the trademark of liberal individualism, rested on a material foundation that included the abundant possibilities promised by the North American continent, which, when cleared of a native population, would be there for the taking by those who ventured across the Atlantic.[18]

The momentous consequences of these changes on the land are well known, beginning in Virginia, a colony that was primarily a commercial venture, the work of a joint stock company. The Virginia Company banked on profiting from agricultural production. Over the course of a century, surveyors carried their chains over the soil, rocks, mountains, marshes, and water, grafting metes and bounds and perches (about 5.5 linear yards) upon the land of the Chesapeake colony. The pioneers seem to have had a selective memory of the English countryside. They placed little stock in nucleated villages, common lands, or strip farming. They quickly dispersed instead to their separate "plantations." Enclosed fields, gardens, fences, corrals, and domesticated animals soon followed, closing off and trampling over the Indian landscape. The most productive parcels of private property would be planted with tobacco for export to Europe. The enterprise of the Virginia Company did not have an auspicious start, however. Converting vast acreage into a cash crop required human labor, a scarcity around the Chesapeake. By the close of the seventeenth century, most of the Indians had fled the Chesapeake, and the supply of English volunteers was small as a result of the scourge of disease and a high mortality rate. The Virginia colony adapted to the labor shortage by enacting a brutal immigration policy, importing slaves from Africa. Forced labor made Virginia land profitable and closed a worldwide circuit of merchant capital with a major nexus along the Chesapeake Bay. The commerce in tobacco was conducted on plantations dispersed around the Chesapeake, some on the Eastern Shore, but most in the southern tidewater. The crop was carried to market along the colony's densely spaced rivers and crossed directly to Europe, seldom stopping in any American port town and nary a city.[19]

—

58

The pattern of settlement in the northern section of the Chesapeake was a similarly sobering story—a story of commercial prosperity built on a landscape for the cultivation of tobacco and the enslavement of Africans. Yet the lords proprietor of the Colony of Maryland, George Calvert and his successors, managed lands in their own way and opened some other possibilities for the production of space. Calvert was a convert to Roman Catholicism, and as such had been denied civil liberties by Britain's reigning Protestant monarch, Charles I. To him the New World beckoned like a feudal retreat promising him a noble's prerogatives over the land. The terms of his royal land grant circumvented the recent reforms, whereby Parliament prohibited such practices as quitrents, paid to the lords of the land upon which his tenants toiled. Calvert codified his old-fashioned ideas about how to take up land in the eighteenth paragraph of the Maryland charter. It permitted the lord proprietor and his heirs to grant land "to Persons willing to take or purchase the same . . . [b]y . . . Customs and Rents of this Kind, as seem fit and agreeable." Lord Baltimore's son and heir, Cecil Calvert, the second Baron Baltimore, took further steps to re-create an English barony in Maryland. He conveyed large tracts to secondary proprietors, who would in turn take up the land, place tenants on small parcels, and exact quitrents. His father had imagined an aristocratic fiefdom, complete with rural manor houses, two designated for each county. The Calvert family would continue exacting quitrents from Maryland landowners and tenants for over a century, right up through the American Revolution.[20]

While George Calvert returned to England to enjoy his noble stature, his agents in Maryland, first his brother Leonard and then his son Cecil, went to work carving out the land around the upper Chesapeake and updating their colonizing strategies. Cecil Calvert immediately hired a surveyor and began issuing land grants in "fee simple" to "heirs forever." He recruited settlers, whom he called "adventurers," by promising warrants that entitled them to select a certain tract, survey the land, and then obtain a patent. The land was still subject in perpetuity to a quitrent originally payable in tobacco or "good wheat as usually grows in England." When few Englishmen took up the initial offers, the Calverts fine-tuned the "Conditions of the Plantation" by adjusting the rents and the acreage and offering additional parcels, or "headrights," to anyone pledging to transport servants or family members into the colony, hence increasing the supply of labor. Originally the Calverts invited only natives of Ireland or Britain to take up land in Maryland, but the scarcity of immigrants prompted them to offer land to the French, Italians, and Dutch.

—

The Calverts zealously pursued the land business throughout the seventeenth century, even amid the colonial disorder caused by the English civil wars. In 1675 the proprietorship of the family estate passed from Cecil to Charles Calvert, the 3rd Baron Baltimore, who also continued to reside in England. The management of the Calvert estate in Maryland was entrusted to a team of local agents headed by Henry Darnall, a Maryland planter. The Calverts' new agent issued a proclamation that fundamentally restructured the process of land-taking. Prospective settlers were informed

> that all persons adventurers or others of British and Irish descent, inhabiting, resideing or trading into this province, desirous to take up any quantity or quantitys of land within this our province, shall pay or secure to be paid unto us or our heirs or such officer or officers as shall be appointed by us and our heyres . . . the just quantity of one hundred and twenty pounds of tobacco . . . together with two shillings sterling yearly rent for every fifty acres of Land.

The Calverts had opened a marketplace for land on the shores of the Chesapeake, making tracts of various sizes available for purchase with English currency or the crop produced by the labor of African slaves. By 1683, virtually the entire shoreline of the great estuary had been sold. As the tidelands were already settled, the Maryland Land Office surveyed and sold land out in the "frontiers," including a county they called New Ireland, which was put up for sale at discounted prices.[21]

When Henry Darnall died, his assistant and son-in-law, Charles Carroll, took charge of the family business. The terms of Carroll's appointment reveal just how much the process of land-taking had changed by 1705. Now the Calverts employed twelve surveyors and teams of secretaries who calculated and collected rents, with the help of local sheriffs when necessary. The barony of Maryland was not the feudal manor Lord Baltimore had imagined. The land had become a commodity traded on an international market—it could be called real estate. By 1700, titles to American plots of land could be acquired in exchange for credit, local produce, or English currency. The third Lord Baltimore authorized Charles Carroll to seek payment in "Money," and redeem debts "by account, or otherwise howsoever." Carroll accumulated a fortune by carving the land into smaller parcels and offering interest-bearing mortgages to prospective buyers. The Maryland Land Office became a thriving venture in producing space and taking profits. Henry

—

Darnall helped himself to eighteen thousand acres of Maryland. Charles Carroll, differentiated from his namesakes by the suffix "settler," would reap handsome profits from selling pieces of Maryland and soon became one of the richest men in the English colonies.[22]

The Calverts and the Carrolls painted the Chesapeake landscape with a broad brush. As one local observer observed, the land was being measured

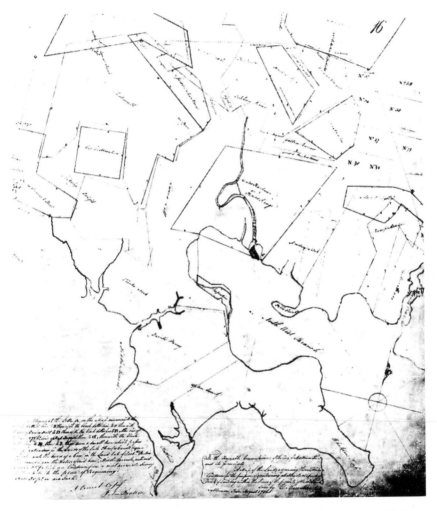

Map of the land adjoining Baltimore Town showing original parcels around the Basin, 1786. Baltimore City Courthouse, from Sherry Olson, Baltimore: Building an American City *(Baltimore: Johns Hopkins University Press, 1997).*

—

by the acre rather than in square footage. Still, the land office dealt in more than large plantations. To make the land profitable in the English market economy would require that humbler men and women—servants, peasants, yeomen farmers, and ultimately, slaves—till the soil and generate agricultural profits. The Calverts and Carrolls resorted to selling headrights for small parcels in order to lure a labor force to Maryland. These grants typically involved plots of one hundred acres. While the lord proprietor's favorites were granted large chunks of Maryland, those acquiring headrights were generally less prosperous settlers; even indentured servants could redeem their headrights, purchase other modest parcels, and slowly consolidate them into plantations of a few hundred acres. When grantees failed to settle on their patents, they were forced to surrender them by the rule of escheat, and the land was put back on the market at cheaper prices. Farmers took up these smaller parcels of land as private property in fee simple and inscribed a new pattern onto the land: they scattered onto individual plots, disdaining either common fields or village centers, and gave a distinctive shape to rural America. The countryside was blanketed with relatively humble homesteads, typically anchored by wood-framed, shed-like houses of less than five hundred square feet. Soon the colonies of Virginia and Maryland, from the tidewater region to the frontier, would be overlaid with a distinctive matrix of private properties large and small. They formed a patchwork of geometric yet irregular shapes suggesting both the rationality of the survey and the capriciousness of natural boundaries.

The rural landscape of the Chesapeake Bay region, like the northern and western parts of the Colony of Maryland, became an agricultural hinterland that differed from the tidewater to the south. George Calvert, the first lord proprietor, cognizant of the vulnerability of the Virginia Company's reliance on a single-crop economy, encouraged the settlers to plant wheat for subsistence as well as tobacco for export. Settlers up the Chesapeake in Anne Arundel County, for example, had taken this advice as early as 1700, planting wheat and corn along with tobacco. By 1776 the local farmers had replaced tobacco with wheat as the cash crop. These small farmers distinguished themselves from the planters south of the colony in other ways as well. The Calverts encouraged immigrants from Germany to take up freeholds in Maryland. Augmented over the next decades by a flood of migrants from Pennsylvania and Western Maryland, the northern Chesapeake became host to a diverse population. German, Scotch Irish, and Swedish as well as English, they worshiped as Methodists and Quakers, Catholics and Anglicans.[23]

—

The taking of agricultural land in the north and west of the Colony of Maryland had created an alternate hinterland lying in wait for a town or city to come into being. This land, upriver from tributaries of the Chesapeake, including the Patapsco, Jones Falls, and Gunpowder Falls, turned out to harbor more than good soil for producing wheat. When a Devonshire miner named John Moale discovered iron a few miles up the Patapsco River from the Chesapeake, he purchased another parcel and named it "David's Fancy." Soon, western and northern Maryland was producing not just a surplus of wheat but also significant exports of iron. As iron mining prospered it brought the northeastern shore of the Chesapeake to the attention of large land barons, the Carroll and the Dulany families among them. The Dulanys went to work aggressively selling land in Western Maryland, laying out small farm plots and a whole town, which they named Frederick. Farmers streamed in through Pennsylvania to take up available land, most of them of German and Scotch Irish descent. This land became fruitful with wheat production and sent a bountiful harvest to Philadelphia for export to Europe and the West Indies. The personnel and the materials with which to create an Atlantic port astride the Chesapeake were slowly falling into place by the 1720s.

The land agents of the Colony of Maryland did not figure the creation of cities into their plans for colonial development. The Dutch merchant Augustine Hermann drew a map in the seventeenth century charting the tobacco trader's itinerary along the rivers to dispersed plantations, oblivious to the nucleated settlements of either Indians or Europeans. The conversion of Maryland into a tobacco economy did not speed the growth of either Annapolis or St. Mary's and largely bypassed the northwestern coastline of the Chesapeake, which bordered the area then called Baltimore County. There were no villages on the river that Smith named the Bolis, but known to the Indians as the Patapsco—no portent, that is, of a site for the city of Baltimore.

At the same time, the Maryland Land Office was well aware that it needed to arrange ways for landowners to transport their agricultural surplus to offshore markets. To that end, the colonial government fostered private ventures in transportation, such as the incorporation of a turnpike, and a few services conducted by the counties, including the construction of the Baltimore jail, perched above "the Neck" in the curvature of Jones Falls. In 1683, the General Assembly of Maryland authorized the "erecting of towns" along the colony's rivers. The intent was not to encourage urban development per se, but to serve a specific economic purpose: the "procuring of money and the

—

advancement of trade." The towns, three of which were within a few miles of where the Patapsco flowed into the bay, were basically depots for the transport of tobacco. The tobacco station set up near the mouth of the Patapsco never did much business. The steep slopes and rocky shoreline were not fit for tobacco production, making land a hard sell in Baltimore County. The major purchaser of land in the area during the seventeenth century was Thomas Cole, who in his patent pledged "fealty" to the lord proprietor and to the Virgin Mary. As of the 1720s, Thomas Cole was listed as the sole occupant of the shoreline that would be Baltimore. The historical roots of the city of Baltimore will not be found within the landscape of tobacco and slavery.[24]

SHAPING A PORT ON THE PATAPSCO: FROM PARCELS TO LOTS

Like the tobacco planters, the growers of wheat and miners of iron were not working the land merely for their own sustenance, or even for local markets. The iron mines along the Patapsco sent tons of ore to Britain, while the farmers of Western Maryland became the breadbasket for the sugar plantations in the West Indies. To reach these markets, the Patapsco farmers and miners initially retraced their steps back through Pennsylvania, to the docks of Philadelphia. Some perspicacious farmers and merchants, however, surmised that the northern reaches of the Chesapeake provided a closer port with easy access to the Atlantic and the colonies of the Caribbean. The parcels of land around the mouth of the Patapsco that had once languished now became desirable properties. Quaker immigrants from Lancashire, England, William and Edward Fell, took up Thomas Cole's parcel. Because Cole had never settled on the land, the English law of escheat permitted the Fells to purchase the tract at a reduced price. Settling above a deep harbor near where the Jones Falls entered the Patapsco, the Fells made the first attempt to create a port upon the Chesapeake.[25]

Despite the natural advantage of their dock site, the Fells' land business developed very slowly and was soon surpassed by the efforts of shipping merchants who docked just to the south, astride a shallow but broad stretch of the Patapsco called simply "the Basin." A harbor began taking shape there in the 1740s, fed by more migration out of Pennsylvania. A turnpike opened to Frederick in 1744, allowing country products from western points to be brought to wharves along the Basin and onto oceangoing vessels, whose captains often hailed from Pennsylvania and Western Maryland; a number of them were in fact from the same congregations of Scottish Presbyterians.

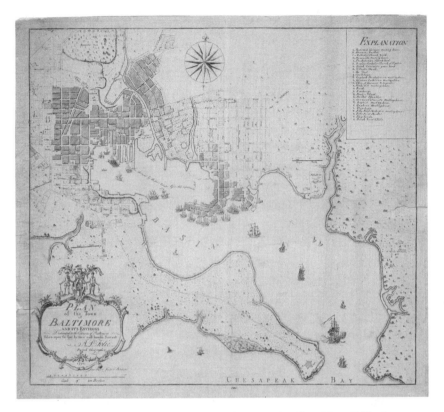

A. P. Folie's Plan of Baltimore, 1792, Baltimore City Sheet Maps Collection.
Courtesy of the Eisenhower Library, Johns Hopkins University, Baltimore,
and JScholarship, the digital repository at the Sheridan Libraries of
Johns Hopkins University, jscholarship.jhu.edu.

Among those who crafted this new feature on the Chesapeake landscape was Samuel Smith of Carlisle, Pennsylvania, who migrated south along with his brothers-in-law Archibald and James Buchanan and a flock of other Pennsylvania Presbyterians: the Gilmors, Gittings, McHenrys, Olivers, and Steuarts—the founding dynasties of mercantile Baltimore. Having the foresight to predict that the country produce of Western Maryland or Southern Pennsylvania would fetch a handsome price in Barbados, the pioneers went to work constructing a port. They imagined a bridge of commerce that extended from the northwestern regions of Maryland and southern Pennsylvania down through the Chesapeake and across the Atlantic, often taking

—

a profitable Caribbean detour. The crucial commercial hinge between sellers and buyers would be located at the Basin near the mouth of the Patapsco River. It would become the nucleus and center of Baltimore Town.[26]

Building the commercial bridge called Baltimore would require something more than the land-taking skills of farmers and planters. Merchants like the Smiths and Buchanans did not rely on nature to provide the arteries of commerce, however; they went to work improving on the Patapsco watershed. They built roads to the farms of Reisterstown, Maryland, and York, Pennsylvania. To compensate for the natural disadvantages of the shallow harbor, enterprising merchants built artificial arteries out into the water, wharves that extended the street over marshland and out toward the shipping lanes. Said to be no more than tree trunks plopped down at the shoreline, rival wharves stretched farther and farther out into the Basin. Samuel Smith built one street upon the water that extended out one thousand feet beyond the shoreline, flush with the dock of his fellow Presbyterian William Spear.

A newcomer named James Sterett, part of the chain migration out of Carlisle, Pennsylvania, devised a yet more basic technique for converting land and water into a profitable commercial space: he poured 550 loads of sand into the marsh that bordered his property. The Maryland General Assembly endorsed such practices with alacrity. In 1747, the colonial legislature in Annapolis approved the plan of Alexander Lawson and Captain Darby Lux for "laying out ground into the Water the extent of his Lott and as far out as conveniently he can." The wording of the state's authorization of a commercial project proposed by William Hammond captures the radical nature of this intervention in the natural environment. It sanctioned Hammond's intention not just to take land, but to "make land" below the banks of the Patapsco. By the last quarter of the eighteenth century, making and reshaping the natural landscape had become quite standard practice. A coordinated group of merchants changed the whole course of Jones Falls in order to provide a straighter watercourse to the agricultural hinterland that bordered it. That done, they remodeled the shoreline to better accommodate the legal institution so essential to orderly commercial relations, the courthouse. They dug a tunnel underneath the Baltimore County Courthouse so that trade could be conducted more expeditiously along the street below.[27]

The construction of a commercial port along the Chesapeake entailed reshaping both water and land. The settlers of Jones Falls (incorporated into the town of Baltimore in 1745) considered the authority to shape land and channel water a basic right of property, worthy of codification in the town

---

66

charter. The charter of Jonestown specified that improvements "made out of the water, or where it usually flows, shall, as an encouragement to such improvements, be deemed forever the right, title and inheritance of such Improvers, their heirs and assigns forever."[28] The enterprising merchants along the Patapsco were determined to convert the land they had taken into commercial profits, even at the expense of manufacturing their own land and waterways.

But commerce could not live on water and land alone. To operate a port and conduct regional and transnational trade required many human hands and shoulders, everyone from the haulers of agricultural products to the readers of law books, not to speak of the women who birthed and fed and nurtured the town's growing population. The common laborers essential to running a port far outnumbered the shipping merchants, and all of them needed land under their feet and roofs over their heads. To shelter and support the workforce of the port would require building a town around the docks. The three settlements near the junction of the Chesapeake and the

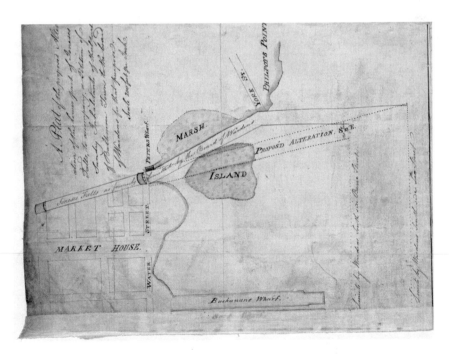

Making land around the Basin. Cartographic Records, BRG 12-4-2. Courtesy of the Baltimore City Archives.

—

Patapsco, at Fells Point, the Basin, and Jonestown, were consolidated in 1745 and given the name Baltimore. The General Assembly placed the new town under the jurisdiction of Baltimore County to be managed by commissioners, whom they appointed for life terms.[29]

The colonial government did not draw boundaries around Baltimore Town. The initial shape of the port settlement was determined by the same processes that had created the tobacco plantations and the rural landscape, the plotting and purchasing of parcels of land. Legal historian Garrett Power carefully mapped this nascent urban landform. The whole ragged coastline had already been carved into grants by the last quarter of the seventeenth century. Most parcels were two hundred to five hundred acres in size, more substantial than a house lot or city block, but far smaller than a tobacco plantation. The patents were identified by the names of the new owners, conjoined with some natural features of the landscape: Cole's Harbor, Jones' Range, and Mountney's Neck, for example. Some patents conveyed a bit of personality as well as the mark of ownership on the landscape. Ridgely's Delight, David's Fancy, Fell's Prospect, and Bold Venture were among the inscriptions filed at the patent office. Among them was a grant to the sons of the Calverts' land agent. Charles Carroll of Annapolis and his brother Daniel Carroll laid claim to a patent at the shoreline of the Patapsco, just where it turned out toward the Chesapeake at Fells Point. These parcels remained fallow until the middle decades of the eighteenth century, when the landlords undertook a more fine-tuned division of their parcels.[30]

As the commercial traffic around the confluence of Jones Falls and the Patapsco grew more congested, the surrounding spaces became the template for a new urban geography. John Fell, representing the second generation of his namesake family, earned the title "Land hunter" in recognition of his success in buying up idle patents near the dock at bargain prices, and slicing them up for sale at a profit. Farther up the Falls, David Jones was carving out space to build a town in his own name. Charles and Daniel Carroll carved their parcel of sixty acres into over one hundred small lots. Appropriately, the new towns were named for the owners of land patents—one for David, Peter, and Philip Jones, another for John and William Fell, and the third for Lord Baltimore (whose land agent went by the name of Carroll). The first towns began as little more than a cluster of small land patents near the Chesapeake shore.

The patents laid out at the intersection of the Patapsco, Jones Falls, and the Chesapeake were prime commercial sites and as such inspired more

—

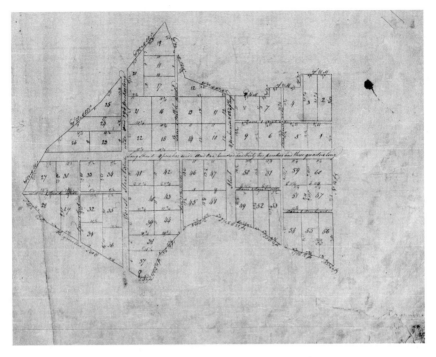

Jehu Bouldin, plat of original Baltimore Town, ca. 1729. Cartographic Records,
BRG 12-2-1. Courtesy of the Baltimore City Archives.

intricate designs for holding property. The map of the evolving town of
Baltimore was drawn at the scale not of the plantation or the rural parcel,
but of the lot. This method of marketing space got under way in a clumsy
fashion in the first quarter of the eighteenth century. Fells Point came into
existence when the founding landowners fashioned one hundred acres above
their dock into a tight grid of twenty lots and put them up for sale. Peter
Jones offered another ten small lots for sale, neatly lined up along the Falls.
Carroll's survey of Baltimore was more irregular; some described it as a
left-pointing arrowhead; those more poetically inclined likened it to a lyre.
Whatever the geometrical metaphor, the spaces within the borders of the
town were partitioned into uniform rectangular spaces. By the midpoint
of the eighteenth century, all of the patents lining the commercial arteries
of Baltimore Town were divided into lots, tidy packages for taking and selling the land.[31]

Measured by the foot rather than the acre, the lot was distinguished from previous partitions of land in Maryland by its size, its shape, and the method of distributing it. Lots were the products of a more fine-grained survey, as required by colonial policy and undertaken at the behest of the patentee. The first surveyors of the land around the Basin set their compass around natural features. The survey commissioned by Philip Jones Jr. in 1729 laid out the boundaries of his land as a dizzying circuit of the Patapsco River. He began "at the bounded red oak and running then east five perches and half" and proceeded to the next tree and measured an acre, "more or less." Other surveyors marked off space with a mathematical calculation of degrees of longitude and latitude. David Jones's entry in the early town records specified that his grant would be "surveyed, laid out, and divided as near as may be, into Twenty equal lots," which he promptly put up for sale.[32]

For all its aura of rationality, legality, and exact boundaries, a mere survey of private property was not sufficient to make a town. Although Charles Carroll owned much of the land that would be incorporated into Baltimore, he played a minor role in converting it into a political entity. His name was not among the "several inhabitants in and about the Patapsco River" who petitioned the General Assembly to create Baltimore Town in 1729. The signatures on the petition appeared above the phrase "with the further endorsement of Daniel and Charles Carroll." The General Assembly appointed seven commissioners of the new town and authorized them to meet with the Carrolls to set a price for the purchase of sixty acres. With tens of thousands of acres of more valuable agricultural land, the Carrolls did not strike a hard bargain. "Several inhabitants" of Baltimore County bought a port town at the cost of forty shillings an acre "of current money of Maryland or else tobacco at one penney lb."[33]

The General Assembly of the Colony of Maryland appointed the same seven men as commissioners and instructed any three of their number to meet with a surveyor to lay out the town. The procedure for town planning was perfunctory: "The same sixty acres to be mark'd stak'd and divided . . . marked by some Posts or Stakes the streets or Lands, with number One, Two, three, four and so on to sixty. To be divided and laid out." Like the "bold ventures" of the colonial patentees, those markings on the land were merely the imagining of a town, not a transcription from material reality. They registered the promise or hope of exchanging small plots of land for money or tobacco. Furthermore, the formal transfer of title to the land was hedged in by conditions, many of them traditional English constraints on the land

---

market. For the first four months, only inhabitants of Baltimore County were permitted to purchase a lot. Even thereafter, the selling of Baltimore Town did not operate as a completely open market: "The owner or Owners of the said land shall have his or their first Choice for one lot; and after such Choice, the remaining Lots may be taken up by others; and . . . no Person shall presume to purchase more than One Lot within the said Sixty Acres . . . during the first four Months after laying out the same." Buyers were required to occupy the land and improve it by building a house of at least four hundred square feet within a space of eighteen months. If this condition was not met, the putative owner was liable for a fine, payable in tobacco, and the property could be taken up a second time by another buyer.[34]

Such constraints on the free market in land did not temper the lust for lots in Baltimore Town. At least three of Baltimore's seven commissioners can be categorized as land speculators. Six of the seven original commissioners immediately purchased a lot on the Carroll tract, and a frenzy of land sales ensued. Take the case of Dr. George Walker, who acquired Lot 53 at the time of the town's founding and acquired a second, contiguous lot in 1731. In 1736, Walker added Lot 20 to his inventory, and then Lot 13, which he sold in 1738. In 1747, he listed two lots in Jonestown, now part of the consolidated town of Baltimore. Another commissioner, William Hammond, lost his initial lot for failing to make a payment, but took it up again a few years later. Richard Gist, his fellow commissioner, acquired a second lot, number 48, within a year of his first purchase, Lot 59. Meanwhile, the land had captured the attention of other investors. Charles Ridgley, an iron manufacturer, and John Eager Howard, whose plantation was due north of the Basin, began surveying the land to the west and north of the Carroll patent.[35]

The Fells were also aggressively expanding their domain. First the brothers William and Edward Fell took up vacated patents at as low a cost as forty shillings per hundred acres, plus four shillings of annual quitrent. When one Mary Hanson forfeited a lot by not improving it, an act of the General Assembly "entered the name of Ann Fell," widow of Edward, on the ledger of property. Ultimately, the names Ann, William, or Edward Fell appeared on lot numbers 1, 4, 6, 15, 16, 19, and 20. Such wizardry in land-taking became known as "stringing" and enabled shrewd land speculators like the Fells to maintain control of what was potentially the most valuable property along the shore of the Patapsco.[36]

For another two decades, the chief business of Baltimore's town commissioners was to monitor the piecemeal taking and retaking of the land within

—

the porous boundaries of the town. They authorized voluminous sales, extended the eighteen-month grace period for occupying and improving property, and reclaimed and resold abandoned lots. After the initially exuberant land rush, lots were left vacant as frequently as they were purchased. In 1747, the commissioners had a name for the slump in sales; they spoke of "fallen lots." By 1750, they had become downright pesky about "sundry persons taking up Lotts therein and Neglecting to pay the Purchase Money to remove." They reprimanded three delinquent landlords in particular for not building on their lots: "It impeded the increase of the Town by having these Lotts unbuilt upon." The town commissioners summarily put "the numbers 21, 22 and 26 up for sale at auction." Singled out for this scolding was William Hammond, who had been one of the first town commissioners.[37]

In the third quarter of the eighteenth century, trade picked up markedly around the mouth of the Patapsco, and newcomers to the town began to join the land grab. Darby Lux and George Buchanan proceeded to Baltimore to make their fortunes from the land they acquired along the Basin. Thomas Harrison, owner of no less than fourteen thousand acres, much of it in Western Maryland, targeted Lots 52 and 53 near the Baltimore Harbor as prime investment property. He filled in the marshland that separated the Basin from Fells Point and put it up for sale divided into some eighty lots. After thousands of years of human occupation, the land around the northern Chesapeake was now clearly marked as a salable commodity, and it was a windfall for some of the early European settlers of Baltimore. Packaged as lots, the earth could be sold once, and then sold again and again, in the space of a few years, through boom times and bust. Geographer Sherry Olson put it aptly when she concluded that the founding of Baltimore "was a great speculation." The rapid acceleration in the marketing of land was already well under way before Baltimore officially became a city. It was a precocious expression of the commercial energy that was advancing the market economy at the Patapsco port.[38]

The early inhabitants and commissioners of Baltimore Town drew lines upon the land according to the prescriptions of the Colony of Maryland and consistent with the practices of the local residents, primarily migrants from Pennsylvania, Western Maryland, England, or Northern Ireland. Transplantation in the New World, however, inevitably led to mutations in the genotype of English land policies. These changes could be gleaned from the final passage in the act dated 1745 that joined the settlements near the Patapsco together as the town of Baltimore: "And whereas there are several very valuable Improvements made in said Towns, by Virtue of the Laws already made, and whereby they were erected into a Town; Be it Enacted by the Authority aforesaid, by and with the Advice and Consent aforesaid. That all Takers-Up of Lots . . . shall have a sure and indefeasible Estate of Inheritance in Fee Simple in said Lots taken up by him or them; any Law, Usage, or Custom to the contrary not withstanding."[39]

The founders of Baltimore were explicit and definitive in their allegiance to private landownership and the "sure and indefeasible" rights of property. In addition, "as Encouragement to such improvers" of the land, they were granted the "right, Title, and inheritance to whatever owners or leaseholders built upon the land or out to the water where it usually flows." Those repeated phrases, "Takers-up" and "Improvers," became the vernacular names for the founders of Baltimore Town. Those labels were in use before such terms as "Citizen" or "American" entered the vocabulary of the first townsmen along the Chesapeake.[40]

The first maps of Baltimore, Fells Point, and Jonestown were little more than a record of taking up the land. They consisted principally of a sketch of property lines and were rarely interrupted by a street or a road, much less a public square or village commons. Clearly the writing was on the land: the men and women who were creating a dense patchwork of lots where the Patapsco River emptied into the Chesapeake had made a clean break with feudal and mercantile constraints and packaged plots of land as salable commodities and legally protected private property. In the third quarter of the eighteenth century, large landowners, including the Carrolls and other veteran land agents; patriarchs of large plantations, such as the Howards and the Ridgeleys; and enterprising newcomers, including the likes of Thomas Harrison, bought up land near the Basin and carved their parcels into small lots, sometimes only a fraction of an acre, affordable to relatively impecunious "takers-up."

A less affluent but especially enterprising group of land speculators, including the Fells and the original town commissioners, specialized in the turnover of small lots near the dock across Jones Falls from the Basin. One of them, the widow Ann Fell, has been credited with perfecting another strategy that would expand her profits and at the same time promote widespread property ownership in Baltimore Town. Fell updated the English practice of charging ground rent by issuing ninety-nine-year leases—virtual lifetime ownership of a lot—in exchange for a small annual rent, rather than selling the property outright. Baltimore's pioneer land merchants followed in her

—

Row houses of early Baltimore. Courtesy of the Library of Congress, E. H. Pickering, photographer, Historic American Buildings Survey (compiled after 1933).

footsteps, essentially amortizing debt over time and enabling them to occupy the lots on which to build their own homes. Amounting to a small sum annually, ranging from one to three pounds, the ground rent functioned much like a mortgage and was estimated to yield the creditor 6 percent in interest.

When this strategy was first implemented in the 1750s, it was advantageous not only to those who sold and those who leased the land, but also to the town itself. Those holding large grants could lease the land and secure the long-term promise of a stream of rental income; those leasing it secured a home site at a relatively affordable price; and the town grew and prospered lot by lot. Enterprising carpenters and builders soon took advantage of the new form of credit. With a small amount of capital they could lease lots, slowly stock them with housing units, sell the houses, sublet the land, and invest their profits to purchase additional building sites. By the time of the American Revolution, the town boasted over five hundred houses, which sheltered five thousand people. Most of these structures were very tiny— twelve feet wide or less, and only one or one and a half stories high—but they were what today would be called "owner occupied."[41]

The measuring, buying, selling, and leasing of land constituted the essential spatial practices that created a town called Baltimore. By the mid-eighteenth century, the shores of the Chesapeake had been securely taken, but in a complicated two-step process. The surveyors who arrived with Lord Baltimore had converted the mouth of the Patapsco into large parcels of private property as early as the 1670s. After 1730, the land was divided into a fine web of small lots. This frenetic pace of land-taking could leave the clerk who recorded the actions of the town commissioners breathless and dizzy. To locate "the bounds of Captain Philip Graybell's lot on Baltimore street," for example, required circling from "a part of the Original town lott No. 31 between Charles and Hanover on the North East corner of a Brick store built by John Ridgely Esquire and now belonging to Mrs. Hudson." This, according to the records, was only the boundary on the east side of Graybell's property; the western border, on Baltimore Street, was "the north West corner of the Brick House where John Stock now keeps tavern." And still the dimensions of the lots were incomplete: "There is a surplus of Twenty inches on the front of the said Lotts which they have divided between the said Lotts and the Same."[42]

The conversion of land into lots like Captain Graybell's, measured in inches and nestled between adjoining properties, was repeated hundreds of times until it accomplished a spatial revolution. It erased the subtle lines

—

the Algonquians had written on the land and waterways of the Chesapeake, modified English notions of property relations, and created an ad hoc American town. Those who first expropriated the Indian lands, the owners of large parcels around the Basin, such as the Carrolls and the Howards, prospered and sired the heroes of the Revolution as well as the leaders of the new republic. By selling their land in small lots and reinvesting ground rents, they made private landownership accessible to men and women of relatively modest means. The numbers of "takers-up" expanded geometrically in the new republic. First families, such as the Smiths, the Buchanans, and the McElderrys, would also convert land and water into markets and wharves, thereby opening employment and opportunity to tradesmen, mechanics, ship carpenters, caulkers, draymen, washerwomen, and servants, some of them bound out to their employers. The extensive, piecemeal process of taking land had the effect of building both opportunity and inequity into the landscape. The expanding class of property owners was divided between the large landowners and the small leaseholders, both set off from the propertyless majority. In time these divisions would express themselves as economic grievances and political disagreements.

FROM BRITISH COLONY TO AMERICAN TOWN

This landscape of lots was assembled by individual acts of buying and selling very loosely coordinated by the Maryland General Assembly and the town commissioners the assemblymen appointed. It certainly was not the design of King George or the British Parliament. Yet, without a plan or much political oversight, the denizens of Baltimore Town created a template for making history as well as for building houses. The town grew up on its own, capitalizing on the weakness of colonial authority and the interruption of international trade during the imperial wars of the eighteenth century. Busy building their port town, the landlords and merchants of Baltimore Town paid little mind to the British even though all their parcels, lots, and leases were technically a feudal fiefdom. The act of the Maryland Assembly that authorized the erection of the town of Baltimore reserved royal hegemony over American land, explicitly reminding the "takers-up" of lots along the Patapsco of the prerogatives of "his Most Sacred Majesty, his Heirs and Successors, [and] the Right Honorable the Lord Proprietary, [and] his Heirs and Successors." It would take a revolution for the General Assembly to declare that paying quitrent to an English nobleman was "highly improper

—

for, and derogatory of the citizens of this sovereign and independent state." Having converted a relatively small piece of land along the Chesapeake into a prospering port, Baltimore townsmen hastened to sever their ties to Great Britain. The last British governor of Maryland called Baltimore the vanguard of revolution, and the local contingent of the "Sons of Liberty" the "most pronounced rebellious and Mischievous" in the province.[43]

Three Marylanders would eventually sign the Declaration of Independence, among them the most prominent landlord around the Patapsco, Charles Carroll. The Carroll family had reason to maintain loyalty to Great Britain. Among other things, independence would bring an end to thousands of pounds of income in quitrents. When the Maryland revolutionary government confiscated loyalist landholdings and property, however, the Carrolls would not regret their decision to cast their fortunes with the cause of independence. Nor would the owners of nearby plantations like the Howards. The elite merchants and ship captains of Baltimore Town also profited from the rebellion. British mercantilist policies were a costly tax upon the likes of Samuel Smith and his brother-in-law George Buchanan, who prospered by selling Maryland flour to the West Indies and to Europe. Smith, Buchanan, and other Baltimore merchants led the opposition to the Stamp Act in 1766 and again led their peers in 1770 when the Intolerable Acts further restricted their trade. They would grow even richer once the colonies severed their ties to England. The revolutionary war reduced competition by diverting shipping from the rival port of war-torn Philadelphia. In addition, more than fifty ships moored in the Basin were commissioned as privateers, meaning they were authorized to plunder British vessels and keep much of the booty.[44]

It took more than the self-interested efforts of land speculators and privateers to make a revolution. As the grievances against the British mounted, the protest meetings in front of the Baltimore County Courthouse welcomed not just freemen—those property holders entitled to vote for delegates to the General Assembly—but also the propertyless inhabitants of Baltimore Town. The organization that coordinated revolutionary activities in Baltimore went by a plebian name, the Mechanical Company. Relatively impecunious artisans—such as the hatter David Shields—would become officers in the revolutionary militia. Humble sailors, victims of the most flagrant personal assault against the rights of Englishmen—being impressed into service on the high seas by the Royal Navy—waged the War of Independence on Baltimore's streets. Occasionally they joined merchants and gentlemen in tarring and feathering loyalists. Religious and ethnic grievances could also

—

contribute to the chorus of independence rising along the Patapsco. The Irish Catholic Carrolls, no less than recent immigrants from Ireland, some of whom had been purchased as indentured servants on the docks of Baltimore and Fells Point, were happy to lend their voices to the call for independence.

In sum, building a port town in the New World had prodigious political consequences. The same ships that carried wheat and iron across the Atlantic returned to Baltimore with an increasingly diverse population, conflicting economic interests, and rebellious political ideas. Frenchmen, including refugees from Canada, joined the English and the Scotch Irish. Relations between the different groups were not always harmonious—the national divisions were compounded by religious differences: the Germans came as Protestants, Catholics, and Jews; the English included Quakers and Methodists as well as Anglicans and unbelievers. But this demographic tinderbox ignited some radical revolutionary ideas. The Mechanical Company boasted: "Our meetings have been held in public. Our records are free and open for inspections. From the public we receive our authority not by personal solicitations, but a free and voluntary choice: to that tribunal we submit our actions." In the same egalitarian spirit, the Baltimore rebels solicited contributions for the war effort from all inhabitants, apologizing if the war placed too much of a burden on the town's less affluent families. The large planters who presided over the General Assembly in Annapolis complained of the rowdy politics of Baltimore Town. To Maryland's few loyalists, the Baltimore contingent of the revolutionary militia was "A Band of Ruffians, Mulattoes, or Negroes, Fifers and Drummers."[45]

The trade winds of revolution also threatened to unmoor the racial hierarchy along the Chesapeake. On the Eastern Shore, a black wheelwright named John Simons plotted an armed revolt, while others sought their freedom by joining the British Army. The spirit of liberation chafed at the conscience of whites as well. In 1783, in advance of federal policy, the state of Maryland outlawed the international slave trade. The cosmopolitan mix of migrants into the port city stirred up challenges to slavery in several quarters. The Methodist congregation meeting in a mixed-race assembly near the harbor questioned the godliness of enslaving fellow Christians. The antislavery sentiments surged in 1791, when several hundred Baltimoreans heard "an Address upon the Moral and political evil of Slavery delivered at public meeting of the Society for Promoting the abolition of Slavery, and the Relief of Free Negroes." The orator was none other than George Buchanan, a fitting spokesman for the freedoms and opportunities of the port town. He had secured a ninety-nine-year lease of waterfront property, built a wharf, and collected privateering profits in partnership with the revolutionary leader Samuel Smith. The members of the Baltimore antislavery association were mostly merchants, but humbler workingmen, such as the hatter David Shields, the tradesman George Presstman, and the tavern-keeper Nathan Griffith, also joined the cause.[46]

Other prominent revolutionary leaders were not so quick to embrace the spirit of liberation that wafted through Baltimore. Although Charles Carroll signed the document declaring that all men were created equal, he never felt compelled to free his three hundred slaves, most of whom toiled on his plantation outside the port town. Resistance to emancipation among large planters could be brutal. In Dorchester County, three slaves were hanged and quartered for the affront of allying with the British in hopes of securing their freedom. The port town, however, was not so deeply and desperately invested in slavery. The rate of manumissions rose steadily in the late eighteenth century, leaving a sizable and growing population of free persons of color in Baltimore Town. Many of them were runaways from plantations who found jobs and hiding places in and around the docks. The culture of servitude eroded in the heady atmosphere of a thriving port in the time of revolution, as can be read off the manumission papers of one Charlotte Matthews, who was granted her freedom, according to her former owner, "for the cause that she has repeatedly asked to be free of my service, and is not satisfied to remain in slavery."[47]

At least one freeborn white woman partook of the rising tide of opportunity in the port town. Her name was Mary Goddard. She came to the booming port in 1774 from Connecticut via Philadelphia, arriving in time to take up her brother's editorial duties at the *Maryland Journal*'s office on Market Street. She also served as the local postmaster through the critical years of war and nation-building, from 1775 to 1789, when she was summarily dismissed. Goddard was responsible for the first official printing of the Declaration of Independence. Later, aware of her rights, she called her firing an affront to the "love of justice" and "an extraordinary act of oppression." She and her sex would have to wait some time to redeem the promises of the Declaration. Thomas Jefferson decreed that "the appointment of a woman to office is an innovation for which the public is not prepared, nor am I."[48]

On July 29, the Declaration of Independence became the cause of public celebration in front of the Baltimore County Courthouse, followed by an illumination of the whole town and a parade through the principal streets.

—

The most impressive public assembly in Baltimore Town would come a few years later, with the ratification of the US Constitution. The procession in honor of the national union was said to enroll three thousand men, who were arrayed to represent the various contingents of humanity required to build the port city. The mechanical trades, organized into forty different marching units, were joined by separate delegations representing "the liberal professions." The mobile throng took off from Philpot Hill at 9:00 a.m. and proceeded through the town, circling down to the harbor. The jubilant marchers towed a fitting symbol of the local economy along the parade route: a full sailing rig called the *Federalist*. The ship docked near the Basin, where dinner was served to a crowd that had grown to four thousand. The site of the celebration was given the name it still bears today, Federal Hill.[49]

The fetes of revolution and nation-building were staged in fitting locations. That courthouse, those streets, and that port town had spearheaded independence; they had set the essential spatial conditions for a revolutionary movement. The protests that led to the decisive break with Great Britain began with calls to meet in public spaces, most often the unpaved and unshapely open turf outside of the Baltimore County Courthouse. In Baltimore, the path of revolution cycled through the entire social structure. The resistance was ignited among the merchant leaders and gained strength in the popular quarters. The militancy in the plebian districts, along the docks of Fells Point and the artisans of Oldtown, spread across the bridge over Jones Falls. It crested in a public meeting at the courthouse, just up from the Baltimore Harbor. It took a whole town, a dense concentration of people, to assemble the combustible mélange of ideas, interests, and vitality required to break the bonds with the British Empire. Those scattered through the Colony of Maryland, who came together irregularly at county courthouses or owed deference to large landowners and slave masters, would have had difficulty mustering the collective human resources and energy needed to propel such a radical course forward.[50]

Officially, the port along the Patapsco was merely a town, a minor and emasculated place within the colonial political structure, subordinated not just to King George and Parliament but also to the General Assembly in Annapolis and the mostly rural Baltimore County. The townsmen of Baltimore experienced the late eighteenth century as a season of governmental deprivation. Burdened with increasing urban needs and invigorated by the infusion of energy from a growing and diversifying population, the powers of local self-government were severely limited, held hostage by the state legislature that appointed the town commissioners. Among other things, the town could not tax itself to perform such prosaic functions as paving the streets or clearing them of animal and human waste. The anemic state of municipal governance was apparent in the act of the Maryland Legislature that joined Jonestown to Baltimore in 1745. After appointing commissioners, for lifetime terms, and instructing them to proceed with their major function, selling land and laying out lots, the legislature issued only one additional mandate: "And further they pray, that no Swine, Sheep, or Geese may be kept or raised within said Town, unless kept in Inclosure. All which this general Assembly think reasonable to be Enacted." In order to do so much as erect a lamppost, the town commissioners would have to petition the General Assembly of Maryland. With such little autonomy, the commissioners' position was not a very demanding one. They were instructed to meet only once a year. As the town grew, and lot sales boomed, the meetings became more frequent. Still, the town commissioners seldom convened more than once a month, and did so as if they were a private gathering, assembling in the home of one of their members or at DeWitt's Coffee House.[51]

Rather than languishing in this political purgatory, the self-governing leaders of the Patapsco port devised their own means of meeting public responsibilities. Not only that, they organized a revolution in the manner of a voluntary society. The "Ancient and Honorable Mechanical Company of Baltimore" that mobilized resistance to the British also performed many of the essential public services required in a growing port town. Founded in 1763 and incorporated by an act of the Maryland General Assembly two years later, the Mechanical Society was far more than a military company or a revolutionary militia. It had a hand in building the first wharves, bridges, and schools along with a hospital, a flour mill, and, of course, that iconic voluntary society, a fire company. The Mechanical Company was just one of the nodes in a loose web of civil society that gave functional shape to the town along the Chesapeake port.

The enterprising people who fought a revolution and founded a town did not await state authorization before conducting public business. They moved aggressively to meet their municipal goals on an ad hoc basis. In 1768, for example, a group of townspeople proposed that the county seat be moved from the upriver village of Joppa to Baltimore Town. A map attached to this petition nicely captured the hubris of the first town on the Chesapeake. It drew an outline of the course of the Patapsco and all its tributaries spreading over the county. A primitive and distorted piece of cartography compared

—

to John Smith's handiwork, this map sketched a grid of lines near the Basin at the southern border of the county and affixed to it the caption "Baltimore Town Center of the County." Despite this questionable geography, the petition was granted. Town commissioners, acting on the authority granted by the colony, proceeded to purchase five lots on the west side of Calvert Street for the purpose of building a jail and a courthouse. Without the authority to tax, the commissioners relayed the project on to private citizens. Meeting in the home of Robert Adair, Esq., they voted to "authorize and Empower Alexander Well to receive and collect the Several sums Subscribed by the different Persons whose Names are Mentioned in this list and that he pay the Same to Andrew Buchanan One of the commissioners."[52]

Like the courthouse, sundry other municipal projects were funded by private subscription. Individual citizens, acting in concert, with the support of the town commissioners and as approved by the General Assembly of Maryland, took up the responsibility of financing a variety of those construction projects necessary to create a commercial entrepôt: wharves, bridges, marketplaces, and the public watch were all private initiatives. The commissioners scrambled to secure the funds, payable in currency or tobacco, for a variety of essential public projects, sometimes relying on revenue from the sale of lots to finance them. In 1745, for example, the General Assembly acceded to a request from the commissioners of Baltimore that "the sum still unpaid for those who took up lots . . . be applied to the Use of the Town." The financial windfall from delinquent lot buyers was converted to the construction of a "good bridge serving travelers as well as the towns."

In the 1780s, the town commissioners managed to wrest a modicum of control over these key commercial projects from the General Assembly. In 1782, the legislature appointed "street commissioners" for Baltimore Town. The office of Port Warden was created in 1784. Even then, however, the local authorities were empowered only to coordinate the initiatives of private landowners. The instructions to the street commissioners still construed the town as a parcel of private land: it allowed the commissions to lay out streets, lanes, and alleys through the Carrolls' tract. That process had not proceeded very far as late as 1792, when the street commissioners heard complaints that the primitive pathway called Market Street was clogged with wagons and carts and could not be navigated without collisions with pedestrians. When, in 1793, the street commissioners created a thoroughfare named East Street, they acted "on the Consent of the Owners and proprietors of that part of the land situated on East land."[53]

—

To meet vital public needs, private citizens often volunteered portions of their land or extended loans to the town commissioners. Colonel John Eager Howard, the landlord of much of the western flank of the harbor, opened his own marketplace and used it as a bargaining chip with the state of Maryland. He offered to build a statehouse there on the condition that the Assembly agree to move the capital from Annapolis to Baltimore. The landlords of Baltimore Town made many a shrewd bargain with state and local government. Thomas McElderry, Esq., "offered to lend the Commissioners of Baltimore Town one hundred pounds free and clear of Interest for the Purpose of filling up and paving the Lower End of the Center Market House." It turned out that McElderry and his partner, Cumberland Dugan, had already developed an elaborate commercial space at that very spot, complete with a canal and a fashionable assembly room. The commissioners consented with one proviso: that the private canal be widened and lengthened.[54]

The political instrument that authorized such town projects was an act of incorporation. Petitioners to the Maryland General Assembly secured state charters that permitted them to issue and sell stock in order to fund a variety of projects, everything from churches and colleges to roads and bridges. The pervasiveness of such devices led geographer Sherry Olson to characterize the development of Baltimore in the eighteenth century as the work of a "corporate private enterprise." The public party to this corporate enterprise resided in Annapolis, where the colonial and then the state government held the authority to grant the exclusive privilege of selling stock to selected citizens. Private entrepreneurs, working collaboratively at the local level, used corporate charters to provide public services and build urban infrastructure, prospering personally along with the town. These urban pioneers had happened upon a port of opportunity where they enjoyed corporate privileges and wide-open prospects of landownership and commercial profit.[55]

Private incorporation and voluntary civic action were not enough to sustain urban growth. While the population grew exponentially, reaching thirteen thousand in 1780 and twenty-six thousand by 1800, the structure of government remained rudimentary. Their administrative powers stretched to their limits, the town commissioners began in 1782 to petition the General Assembly for the city to be chartered as a "public corporation" with authorization to act for the general good of the growing population. More than ten years later, they were still pleading with the state to grant them the power of self-government. The committee that drafted the original appeal was not a representative body of the port town; it was dominated by the town elite,

—

not the popular elements of the Mechanical Society. Nine merchants, a bank clerk, a clerk of court, and a physician—and not a single mechanic, much less a slave, a free person of color, a servant, a sailor, or a woman—signed the petition for a municipal charter. The elite design for government emulated the constitution devised by the planter-dominated state government: it featured the indirect election of a senate and a governor and severely restricted access to voting and holding office. The first draft of the city charter made the Mayor's Office an outpost of aristocracy, open only to someone owning at least $2,000 in property.

This first effort to establish municipal sovereignty in Baltimore did not meet with universal approval. This haughty blueprint for government was anathema to the artisans, to the shopkeepers, and to the "ruffians" who had fought against the Tories. To them, "corporations" connoted an elite monopoly. The tradesmen who celebrated Maryland's ratification of the US Constitution in 1788 alongside merchants and large landholders did not join the campaign to secure a conservative municipal charter. Having exercised their political muscles building a town and repelling the British, workingmen were not about to withdraw from the public sphere. Without popular support, the first appeal for a city charter stalled. The workingmen allied with the Jeffersonian opposition to the Federalists and became the mainstay of the first prototypes of partisan politics, called "republican societies." The process of building a port town at the mouth of the Patapsco had the potential both to expand the pie of property and to create political conflict between and among the landlords, the leaseholders, and the landless.

Until the last decade of the eighteenth century, the liminal politics of Baltimore Town were conducted without much official sanction. In the language of statecraft that was coming into use at the time, the people who had created a functional municipality along the Patapsco lacked formal sovereignty, official authorization to take collective actions in their own behalf. Yet, like many other citizens of the sovereign states of the federal union, they managed a robust if unofficial self-government. They created a polity by their associated actions within their shared space on common local ground, not as authorized by long-standing customs or established institutions and procedures. The townsmen of Baltimore exercised what historians and political theorists have called "collective sovereignty" or "vernacular democracy." Without much official sanction, the population that concentrated at the point where the Patapsco River spilled into the Chesapeake constructed a thriving urban space. At that junction of land and water—a place spurned

—

by Algonquians, passed over without a single notation on John Smith's map, and unfit for tobacco growing and plantation slavery—migrants from the countryside and across the Atlantic laid the groundwork for a city yet to be founded. By the end of the revolutionary war, the inhabitants of Baltimore Town had fertilized the land and waterways with their ambition and their wits. The town was politically subordinate to authorities stationed elsewhere—at the Baltimore County Courthouse, at Annapolis, or in the tenuous federal government that met first in Philadelphia, then in New York, then at a disheveled outpost on the Potomac named after the first president. In the process of producing the space of the town, the men and women of Baltimore contributed their political creativity to the age of democratic revolution: habits of self-government, civic activism, and voluntary association.[56]

Independence from Great Britain also brought a bounty of yet more land to the former colonists. In 1784, the Continental Congress made a momentous decision by voting to reserve a vast territory to the west of the thirteen original colonies for the creation of new states. The former New England colonies resisted the move, claiming their own right to the lands stretching out to the Ohio River. The states of Virginia and Maryland, however, were key supporters of the bill, introduced in Congress on October 15, 1783, that created the Northwest Territory. The chief sponsor of that act was Daniel Carroll, brother of Charles and co-owner of the parcel of land on which Baltimore was built. Much as the Carrolls had chosen to give up their quitrents and cast in their lot with the future of an independent United States, the new state of Maryland relinquished its claim on the Northwest Territory, investing instead in the uncharted future of the United States, its expansion across the continent no longer blocked by the British. One eminent American historian called this initiative "the boldest assertion of national sovereignty and of the rights of eminent domain over the Western Territory." It also connected the land-takers of Maryland and Baltimore Town to a major dynamic of US history. Opening the Northwest Territory to sale and settlement would sanction the voracious appropriation of western land by the likes of George Washington, who would claim and survey a huge chunk of the newly opened territory. The future president advertised the sale of twenty thousand acres in Ohio with the stipulation that it could be divided "into any sized tenements that may be desired."[57]

That foundational document of the new nation, the Northwest Ordinance, also created the template for Thomas Jefferson's design for surveying and selling off the continent. The Land Act of 1785 carved the West up into

—

townships measuring thirty-six square miles and put them up for sale in orthogonal parcels whose shapes defied the natural topography. Ultimately, that great grid would extend all the way to the Pacific, and even to the shores of San Francisco Bay. But that is a story for a later chapter. For now, suffice it to say that the pioneers of Baltimore had not only taken up the land around the Chesapeake, but also taken a hand in moving the border of the United States of America farther west.

The British Empire did not have much to do with building the port town of Baltimore. Neither King George nor the English Parliament could take time to mourn the loss of the lands around the Chesapeake. Consumed with their long ongoing wars between rival European empires, the British quickly conceded a vast territory to the American rebels, stretching as far as the Mississippi on the west, Florida to the south, and the Great Lakes in the north. On paper, at least, the borders of the new American republic were drawn at the outer limits of the Spanish Empire. In fact, the Spanish did not begin to colonize a region called Alta California until the 1760s. At the time that the denizens of Baltimore were boasting of making a town and winning independence, José de Gálvez, the *vistador generál* (inspector general) of New Spain, or Nueva España, was drawing up elaborate plans for taking and shaping the land of California. His designs bore little resemblance to the crude maps of Baltimore Town. But the Spanish plans for shaping land into urban space would turn out to be as chimerical as Lord Baltimore's dream of re-creating a feudal fiefdom in Maryland.

CHAPTER 3

THE LAND OF SAN FRANCISCO BAY

Cleared but Not Taken

T he rebellion of the townsmen of Baltimore in 1776 was a small tempest in the war between European navies roving the seas and vying to take control of the Americas. The storm had subsided briefly in 1763 after the English victory in the Seven Years' War, known in the North Atlantic colonies as the French and Indian War. The Treaty of Paris reduced the French presence on the imperial map of North America and left much of the continent divided along the Mississippi between the British and the Spanish, at least theoretically. In reality, the alignment of empires and boundaries of nation-states remained contested and ambiguous well into the nineteenth century. Napoleon deposed the Spanish monarch in 1808. Four years later, the United States went to war with Britain once again. Meanwhile, the lines of territorial dominion drawn in the palaces of Paris, London, and Madrid exercised little authority on the ground in the great swath of land between the Atlantic and the Pacific. Britain's former colonists moved westward, heedless of the borders established by heads of state, be they European monarchs or American presidents. Imperial control was

—

87

especially tenuous in the coastal areas of the Northern Pacific, where Russians hunting sea otters contested both British and Spanish claims. All the while, colonizers and creoles alike faced increasingly aggressive resistance from the native peoples of the Americas.[1]

Nonetheless, Spain was still the dominant European presence in the Western Hemisphere as of 1800. The British had only a toehold in the North Atlantic, while the Spanish claim extended from the tip of South America through the center of the hemisphere, and north into the provinces of Florida on the east and Texas, New Mexico, and Arizona in the west. The Spanish were far more than imperial figureheads of an obsolescent *ancien régime*. In the judgment of many historians, they were the vanguard of global capitalism. The mines they opened in Peru and Mexico in the sixteenth century produced the silver that circulated not just to Europe but also to China by way of the Philippines, setting a worldwide trade network in motion. Spain's imperial pretensions expanded in the eighteenth century. Commissioned by Bourbon reformers, José de Gálvez, the *vistador generál*, sent colonizing expeditions up the Pacific coast as far as San Francisco Bay. They were seeking to dislodge the Russians and challenge British claims to New Albion.

The Spanish grounded their imperial ambitions in urban planning. Since the sixteenth century, the Castilian monarchs had solidified their control of territory by building fortified cities, first on the land they wrested from the Moors and Jews, in the south of the Iberian Peninsula, and then when they sent Columbus on his way to America. The Leyes de Indias (Law of the Indies), first codified in 1573 during the reign of Philip II, outlined the spatial foundation of Spanish colonization. It envisioned the colonized territory of the New World as a network of urban spaces of varying sizes, from villas and pueblos to *ciudades*. At the time that the scattered British ports along the North Atlantic harbored fewer than 20,000 settlers, the population of Mexico City stood at an estimated 150,000. As one historian of Mexico put it, "urban life occupied center place in the minds of the Spaniards who first encountered Mexico." The term "pueblo" became the generic term for the small nucleated urban settlements that proliferated throughout Mexico. When the Spanish miners and ranchers spread north in the late eighteenth century, toward what would become the province of Alta California, they propagated pueblos among the Indians of Sonora, Sinaloa, and present-day Arizona.[2]

By the time Gálvez sent the first colonizing party to San Francisco Bay, the Northern Pacific provinces of Mexico were organized into pueblos and villas, some of them relatively autonomous Indian settlements, others

---

overseen by Spanish missionaries, and most of them with a mix of statuses and ethnicities. While the conquistadores plundered the continent in order to extract bullion, those Spaniards who stayed on quickly intermarried and procreated with the native Indians. They also carried the bacteria that would ultimately decimate the native population. Nevertheless, after a century of colonization, the population of New Spain not only blended Iberians with natives but also incorporated significant numbers of Africans and Moors into a complex human lineage. This mix of peoples, habituated to living together in distinctively Mexican urban spaces, would become the pioneers of Alta California, setting off from Sonora and Sinaloa under the command of Juan Bautista de Anza in 1774. These pioneers, charged with taking the land called Alta California for Spain, carried with them the potential to create a distinctive territory along the North Pacific, a rival to the fragile alliance of former colonies that would become the United States.[3]

Given the metropolitan dimension of the Hispanic spatial imagination, the king of Spain must have rejoiced in 1774 when he received the message that San Francisco Bay opened up to "a plain of enormous size . . . capable of supporting many large cities."[4] When José de Gálvez sent colonizing expeditions out from northern Mexico up the Pacific and on to San Francisco Bay, he did not think the native inhabitants would present an obstacle to Spain's urban ambitions. "It should not be difficult," he reasoned, "to take possession of some advantageous site there, granting that the natives of the place show themselves as peaceful and friendly as they have on other occasions." Gálvez's expectation of pacific relations with the natives of the area proved correct. Converting the lands of the Ohlone into an extension of the Spanish Empire, however, would be a vexed and ultimately unsuccessful project. Between 1769 and 1821, the brief period when the Spanish flag flew over the coastline of Alta California, both Indians and Europeans had only a tenuous hold on their habitat. The Ohlone, as described in Chapter 1, occupied the land and waters of the bay with a loose grip, without recourse to fixed boundaries and fenced lands. Hovering offshore, in the aspirations of the Spanish monarchy and Roman Catholic missionaries, was a baroque plan to build Spain anew in the wilderness. While the tenure of the Ohlone on the land was precarious, so, too, was the grasp of the Iberian Empire.[5]

The Spanish would brutally assault the native habitat and ultimately clear the San Francisco Peninsula of most of the Indian settlements. They would not, however, replace what they destroyed or build very substantial or enduring structures on the land of the Ohlone, nothing like the intricate designs for

—

urban space that agents of the Spanish Crown had devised over the previous two centuries and established in Mesoamerica. Such architectural ambitions would leave only a sorry shamble of decaying adobe near the shore of San Francisco Bay when, in 1821, the Mexican settlers won their independence. A chapter of Western civilization abruptly closed early in the nineteenth century when Spain's attempt to take California land ended in failure.

When imperial rivalries subsided at the turn of the nineteenth century, the Spanish did leave something more substantial behind, however: some rugged and tenacious *novohispano* settlers. These *pobladores* would become the ultimate conquistadores, the decisive pioneers of the Northern Pacific. They carried forward the project of taking and reshaping the northwest coast of the Americas. They would make a new world, trampling over the Indian landscape, defying the fiats of European monarchs, and reordering the relationship between humans and their natural environment. Along the Pacific, the most redolent portent of this new landscape was a space called California.

SIGHTING SAN FRANCISCO BAY

The complex urban organization of New Spain did not reach very far north during the Spanish era—certainly not as far as San Francisco Bay and the land of the Ohlone. Europeans had trolled the Pacific for almost two hundred years without disturbing the natives. From Valparaiso in the south up through major Mexican ports, such as Acapulco and San Blas, Spain ruled the waves and the trade routes, leading some Europeans to regard the Pacific as a "Spanish Lake." Still, European seafarers could not find the illusive San Francisco Bay until late in the eighteenth century.[6] The topography itself, that unique arrangement of land and water that was the San Francisco Estuary, thwarted Spain's imperial aspirations. The entrance to what they called a "great arm of the sea" was hidden behind the barricade of the Farallon Islands, veils of fog, and a narrow point of entry. In 1579, Sir Francis Drake came ashore at a more modest inlet of the Pacific to the north, now known as Drake's Bay. A Spanish seafarer, Sebastián Rodríguez Cermeñio, thought he sighted the estuary again in 1594. Neither explorer had set eye—or foot— anywhere near the current site of the city of San Francisco.[7]

The Spanish ventured up the Pacific coast again in 1769 in hopes of fending off the territorial claims of the British and the Russians. On instructions from Spain, Gaspar de Portolá searched for the great bay by sea in 1769

The obstacles impeding discovery of the entrance to San Francisco Bay.
Louis Choris, Voyages pittoresque autour du Monde *(Picturesque voyages*
around the world), 1822. HathiTrust Digital Library, ffG420.k84C6,
original from Bancroft Library, University of California, Berkeley.

and reported sighting it from a distance. He failed, however, to find a point
of entry from the Pacific. In frustration, Portolá called San Francisco Bay
"a chest with many locks." Land expeditions in search of the bay also ended
in frustration. Still, the landing in Monterey Bay to the south merited an auspicious ceremony in June 1770. On that date, two Spanish expeditions, one
by land and the other by sea, converged. The seaborne explorers included
Padre Junípero Serra, a Roman Catholic priest who designed a string of missions up the coast, posing a spiritual counterpoint to the secular intentions
of the Bourbons. Padre Serra presided over a lavish ceremony upon reaching
his destination. As bells chimed and hymns rang out, two processions came
together under a giant cross, planted upon the beach. After unfurling the
flags of the monarchy and the church, the congregation "shouted at the top
of our voices, 'long live the Faith! Long Live the King!'" Serra concluded his
account of this celebration of Spain and Catholicism with a hasty glance at
the landscape to the south of San Francisco Bay. After burying a sailor who
had died on the arduous trip north from Mexico, he "sprinkled with holy
water all the fields around."[8]

—

Junípero Serra's understanding of the land he claimed in the name of God and country was seriously flawed. The natives of Northern California had not carved the land into fields—*suertes* in Spanish, meaning those carefully defined tracts of domesticated plants found in the Old World. To the Costanoans, the land was open terrain, a complex patchwork of marshes, creeks, hillsides, and oak forests, which they had tended and hunted, but never plowed. The Indians were no doubt mystified, if not alarmed, by the Spanish. The sounds they first heard on that day—the Latin liturgy, the clang of metal bells, and the blast of muskets—must have confounded the villagers who had resided around the bay largely undisturbed for so many generations.

From their beachhead in Monterey, small parties of Mexican explorers went in search of the illusive bay to the north, in the process acquiring a more intimate acquaintance with the native land and people. In 1770, a small party set out from Monterey and wandered north; they sighted

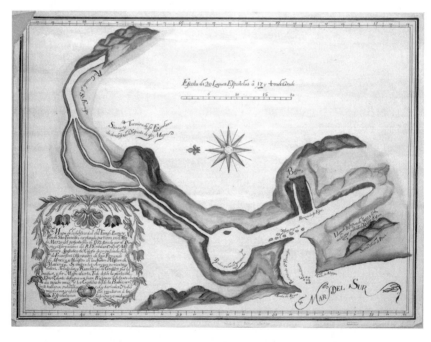

Juan Cresp's map of San Francisco Bay, Mapa de lo substancial del Famoso Puerto y Rio de San Francisco (*Essential map of the Famous port and river of San Francisco*), 1772. Case XB, GO4362 S22 1772 X. Courtesy of the Bancroft Library, University of California, Berkeley.

Drake's Bay, but turned back when another large body of water blocked their path (probably the Carquinez Strait, at the northeastern extension of the estuary now called San Pablo Bay). In 1772, yet another small party of explorers, led by Pedro Fages, became sidetracked by the delusion that the northern arms of the estuary might be the mouth of a great river. Thinking it might provide access to the interior of the continent claimed by the English, they followed it north and east. The Fages expedition arrived above what is now the town of Berkeley and looked down to see an inlet of the Pacific grander than anything they had anticipated. The first crude map of what would one day become the metropolitan region of San Francisco was drawn from that vantage point. It showed the estuary deeply indented from the Pacific, with branches splayed north and south. Still, it would not be until 1776 that a Spanish ship actually penetrated the bay from the great body of water they called the Mar del Sur, passing through the narrow, fog-enshrouded entrance they named the Boca del Puerto de San Francisco; John C. Fremont would name it the Golden Gate in 1846. Finally, in the fall of that year, the Spanish came ashore and planted their flag on the ground where the city of San Francisco now stands.[9]

This period of exploration produced firsthand reports on the lay and the look of the land around San Francisco Bay. The diaries of the priest who accompanied the Fages expedition, Fray Juan Crespí, are especially informative. He had a keen and curious eye—not just for the strategic advantage of a port, or even for souls awaiting Christian salvation, but also for the flora, fauna, water, and vegetation of the bay, providing us with an observant description of them as they first appeared to European eyes. Crespí looked down from the eastern shore of the bay upon "some beautiful plains well adorned with trees" and a "most noble estuary." His running account of the passage up the east side of the bay painted a picture of a lush and plentiful landscape gently sloping to the sea. It was striped with arroyos flowing with water even in the arid season. Every few miles, the explorers crossed a creek and gushed their appreciation: "A good stream of water . . . flowed through the middle of the large plain and estuary . . . a considerable flow of water and a bed well-wooded," Crespí wrote. "All the water is excellent, cool and clear." Those streams spawned large beds of mussels, on which the explorers feasted to the point of gluttony, perhaps accounting for an outbreak of dysentery. Other gustatory pleasures lined the streams: shellfish in "great abundance . . . large and good." Occasionally, the voracious explorers broke their march to hunt, dress, and consume wildlife. The deer came in herds, numbering

—

as many as fifty, and shared the habitat with plentiful rabbits, antelopes, and geese. Although less welcome animal life, such as bellicose grizzly bears and pesky mosquitoes, also accompanied the Spanish on their search for San Francisco Bay, they were a minor interruption of the movable feast. Dessert was also provided: "It is a pleasure to see the great number of blackberries," Crespí noted.[10]

The Ohlone diet was not milk and honey, but still tasty and nutritious fare. According to Crespí, the eastern shore of the bay was a landscape of "abundant forage and countless other kinds of herbage, and of its own accord produces as food for the numerous Indians plentiful harvests of the crops from which they make the good pinole and atole on which they live." He collected an array of positive impressions of this foreign land, and at the same time he cherished the ways in which it resembled his homeland. On tasting the fruit of the madrone trees, he pronounced them comparable to the nuts of his native Spain. Amid the California grasslands and flower-lined creeks he spotted roses that reminded him of home.[11]

Juan Crespí did not mistake this natural beauty and bounty for virgin land. The East Bay was teeming with people: "Judging by the fires that we have seen on the beach," he wrote, "it must be well populated with villages." He also detected signs that the Ohlone were carefully managing this landscape, noticing "much grass although it was burned." This first impression was correct. Every few miles along the fine web of creeks, he discovered that "all the land is populated with a large number of Indians." He was speaking as a priest, not a naturalist. "We have found so many heathen in all this area that it would be a great pity if so many thousands of souls which have lost so many centuries should be abandoned forever." Whatever his missionary intent, however, Crespí could not suppress his appreciation of the Ohlone, their bodies as well as their characters. Of the different parties he met along the way, he would report, "good hair and very long," "fair [and] well-formed," "fair and bearded," "gentle, generous, and well-formed."[12]

"Gentle" and "generous"—these words came easily and repeatedly to Crespí's mind when he met small groups of Indians along the well-trod paths of the East Bay. Although the Spanish search party came equipped for warfare, armored in "Leather Jackets," only one Indian hunting party greeted them with the least hostility—"ferocity and ill temper," in Crespí's words. More often, the small groups encountered along the labyrinth of paths through the East Bay appeared shy and timid, traits that Crespí found less common among the women. The Indians' curiosity routinely overcame

—

their fears. Above all, the Ohlone greeted the members of the Fages party with magnanimity. They came with baskets of food, fruit, and nuts. As the Spanish visitors circulated around the bay, more Indians appeared bearing more gifts. They were especially eager to have the foreigners visit their different villages. One tribelet prepared a seat of grass for their European visitors, offered refreshment and entertainment, begged them to stay, and only reluctantly bid good-bye.[13]

Crespí was an especially keen and receptive observer, and he passed through a section of the Ohlone habitat at an especially verdant time in the fall of 1772. But members of other expeditions and less tolerant observers echoed his appraisal of the place and the people. Pedro Font, the steely Spanish priest accompanying the land expedition of Juan Bautista de Anza (arriving in 1775), reported passing through green meadows covered with familiar species of violets and lilies, onions and tobacco. He was impressed by the plentitude of fish and the skills of native fishermen; in just fifteen minutes he saw five boats pass from one shore to another, and he estimated the size of one village at over 425 persons. The Ohlone greeted the Spanish expedition with "singular demonstrations of joy, singing, and dancing" as well as processions set to the music of handcrafted instruments. Font, who disparaged the Indians of the Southwest as "wretched," living in "ignorance, misfortune . . . and continual warfare," described the natives of the San Francisco Bay area as "pleasant," "docile," and "polite," adding that they were "pleasure-loving, happy and kind," and "great talkers." Font found the local Indians to be gregarious in the extreme, greeting the invaders with profuse gifts of food, shouting their welcome "until they were hoarse," and offering entertainment until late into the night. When Padre Vicente de Santa María arrived by the water route in 1775, members of the Huimen and Huchiun language groups greeted the Spanish with a dance performance and a demonstration of "their great liking for us." As news of the visitors spread, more villagers came bearing gifts of food.[14]

In sum, the first reports of Spanish and *novohispano* explorers concurred in their assessment of the San Francisco Bay area and its people. The lands around the bay, and especially those on the eastern and northern shores, were beautiful and bountiful and populated with a friendly and generous people. Although none of these informants were particularly attentive to social geography, their itineraries also indicate that the Ohlone occupied the land around the estuary in a distinctive manner. They clustered in small, autonomous villages that coexisted side by side along the streams that flowed

—

down to the great bay. The visitors from Mexico called them *rancherías*, the same term they used for the well-organized Indian villages in Sonora and Sinaloa. Pedro Font was surprised to find that groups of Indians who resided in very close proximity to one another spoke different languages.[15]

These first encounters seldom inspired fear or hostility in either the Ohlone or the Spanish. After fumbling attempts to communicate, they struck up amiable relations with one another. Crespí offered beads of white glass in exchange for native foods, politely visited different villages, and then quickly moved on. An expedition into the North Bay greeted a delegation from the Huchiun tribe with some apprehension but mollified its members with a gift of chocolate; the Indians reciprocated with the gift of a "fairly sweet" tamale. Padre Santa María went immediately and earnestly to work converting the Indians. At the same time that he attempted to learn their tongue, he resorted to Catholic chants and rituals as a nonverbal mode of communication. The padre approached the apparent headman of the tribe, and, "taking his hand, began to move it in the sign of the Cross, and he, without resisting, began repeating my words with so great clearness that I stood amazed, and so did those who were with me." Reports such as these reveal both the cultural gulf between the Spanish and the Ohlone and the mutual capacity to bridge it.[16]

Much of this intercultural reconnaissance was gathered even before the Spanish had set foot on the plot of land that would one day be the city of San Francisco. When the Spanish finally found their way through the Golden Gate in 1774, they cast an appreciative glance at their surroundings. Crespí became reverent upon arrival at the destination that bore the name of the patron saint of his order. He pronounced the Bay of San Francisco the ideal place in which to plant a cross and to begin to convert the Indians who lived around the estuary. Pedro Fages joined in with the chorus of praise, extoling "the beautiful sites that we had marked out for the mission and presidio of San Francisco." The site of San Francisco even evinced a bit of poetry from Juan Bautista de Anza, a normally hardheaded agent of the Spanish Crown. Anza pronounced that San Francisco "could be well settled like Europe[.] [T]here would not be anything more beautiful in all the world, for it has the best advantages for founding in it a most beautiful city." A seasoned Mexican settler, Anza saw San Francisco as a future port town "with all the conveniences desired, by land as well as sea, with that harbor so remarkable and so spacious, in which may be established shipyards, docks, and anything that might be wished." Such urban visions leapt quickly into the imaginations of

—

the first Europeans to drop anchor in San Francisco Bay, but they would not materialize under the aegis of the Spanish Empire.[17]

In the summer of 1776, Anza wrote to the Spanish monarch offering "the most endless congratulations upon the praiseworthy news of the new discovery of the Great Bay of San Francisco." Then he promptly went to work implementing the imperial instructions that had sent him on the arduous journey north from Mexico: to choose the appropriate sites for a presidio and a mission. The proper site for a military outpost—*uno presidio*—was obvious to Anza: a promontory just inside the entry to the estuary was "so commanding that with muskets it can defend the entrance to the mouth." Anza chose a sunnier spot for the mission, one along a creek three miles to the southeast. On September 17, 1776, the scouting party commissioned by José de Gálvez and inspired by the evangelical fervor of Junípero Serra took formal possession of the site of the mission. Four priests celebrated a solemn High Mass attended by a small audience of about twenty families, most of them headed by the soldiers who had journeyed from Mexico with Anza. The Te Deum, a hymn of praise, was accompanied by peals of bells and repeated salvos from cannons and muskets.[18]

There must have been a few Ohlone within hearing distance of this rite of conquest. Although the land near the sites chosen for the presidio and the mission was not blessed with the natural bounty that Crespí had found on the east side of the bay, it did support at least two small Indian settlements of 150 to 200 people. The Yelamu language group had a small village near the site of the presidio, and the Petlenuc had an encampment along the creek and lake where Anza had chosen to locate the mission. Although Anza was not concerned about the presence of natives, the expedition's missionary, Padre Francisco Palóu, allowed that the cacophony of Latin chants and clanging bells, gunshots, and cannon "doubtless terrified the heathen, for they did not allow themselves to be seen for many days." For the next eight months the Indians rarely ventured near the Spanish encampment. When a few boys came hunting duck on the lake the Spaniards had named Nuestra Señora de Dolores, they offered a gift of some fowl and accepted beads in return.[19]

Shortly thereafter, in August 1777, the peace was broken. As Palóu reported it, a young Indian hunter made a menacing turn of his bow toward a resident of the mission. The Spanish sergeant stationed there retaliated with an arrest and a flogging in the mission guardhouse. Hearing the screams of their comrade, the Indians came to his defense. One belligerent move led to another, and Indian arrows met Spanish gunfire. The sergeant "ordered

—

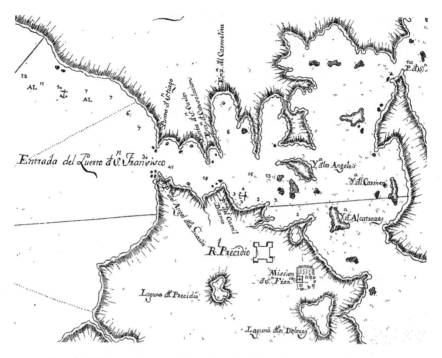

Jose de Cañizares, Plano del Puerto de San Francisco *(Map of the Port of San Francisco), 1776, from Neal Harris,* The Maps of San Francisco Bay *(San Francisco: Book Club of California, 1950), Map 9. Courtesy of the Earth Science and Map Library, University of California, Berkeley.*

the men to fire, and the wounded citizen brought down [an Indian] with a ball, and he fell dead in the water of the bay." The natives retreated from the tip of San Francisco Peninsula, never a particularly coveted spot for habitation. The Spanish had taken a beachhead. Unimpeded by the natives, who had been stewards of the land for thousands of years, the small band of colonists began to refashion the environment according to imperial Spanish instructions.[20]

Upon landing inside the Golden Gate, the emissaries of the Spanish Crown hoisted an image of "our Seraphic Father San Francisco, patron of the port, presidio, and mission," and carried it in procession. The tattered remains of two of the three structures represented on that banner, the presidio and the mission, would be the only relics the Spanish left on the northern shores of San Francisco Bay. Erecting a town or a pueblo at the Port of San Francisco

—

did not seem to be a priority for San Francisco's first European and Mexican settlers. Anza, like Junípero Serra, would return to Mexico by boat, leaving two priests and a few soldiers and their families to uphold the Spanish claim to the great estuary.[21]

RELICS OF SPANISH SAN FRANCISCO: PRESIDIO AND MISSION

The first priority of the conquering Europeans was to secure a military and diplomatic outpost near the bay. To that end, the pioneers of San Francisco promptly set about constructing a presidio as prescribed by Spanish law. It was modeled after impressive structures of the type that had been built across New Spain since Columbus's landing in Hispaniola. Anza, of Sonoran birth, and formerly the *comandante* of a modest presidio in northern Mexico, began constructing a rustic facsimile of the Spanish model within three months of arrival in San Francisco Bay. On paper, El Presidio Real de San Francisco (the Royal Fortress of St. Francis) was a simple, orthogonal design. Its four sides were joined at right angles and broken by windows only on the interior courtyard. There was just one point from which to enter and exit. Initially drafted in Mexico, the first plans projected a presidio of only 92 square *varas* (a vara equals approximately one yard). The Presidio underwent renovations in later years. The last floor plan, dated 1815, called for a quadrangle measuring 192 by 172 varas. Each wall of the fortress would consist of cell-like rooms that were flush with one another and opened onto the interior. The chapel, a sacristy, the quarters of the *comandante*, warehouses, and workshops were to occupy larger spaces on the third wall. The blueprints called for adobe walls, tile roofs, and a second defensive barricade around the inner perimeter.[22]

Constructing even a simple structure in such a remote area proved a challenge. The original building was made of local materials, including thatch for the roof and timber hauled from across the bay. Construction inched upward slowly: two walls had risen only two and a half yards by 1779—and then they all crumbled away. "During a rainfall in the month of January of 1779," one report read, "the stores, the slaughter house, the church, the houses of the commandant and of the troops and the greatest part of the four pieces of wall fell," washing away years of labor to establish a Spanish presence on San Francisco Bay. When a British observer, Admiral George Vancouver, docked within the Golden Gate in 1792, he found not an impressive bastion of empire, but a disheveled settlement that looked to him like a mud corral.

—

A remodeling plan drafted in 1794 envisioned a slightly larger structure of tile and adobe; its completion was celebrated with another Te Deum, but it had received little financial support from the Crown. There is no evidence that the Presidio Real de San Francisco was ever fully enclosed on all four sides.[23]

The flimsiness of this fortress of empire was emblematic of the vulnerability of Spain itself. Preoccupied with wars in the Atlantic, fighting off the British, French, and Dutch, the Crown had little left over to invest in its Northern Pacific domains. The Presidio was all that protected the northern border of a beleaguered empire. It was designed first of all to house the soldiers and their families, who had trekked north from Mexico with Anza. Having fended off the attacks of the fierce Apache, Seri, and Yaqui on their way north from Mexico, Anza's troops were assigned to guard duty at the mission and sent out on military expeditions far inland. The courtyard that took up most of the footprint of the Presidio was meant to enclose the mundane

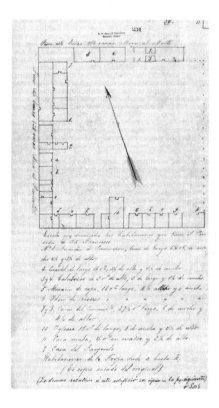

Hermenegildo Sal, Plan for the Presidio of San Francisco, 1792. From Historic Resource Study, El Presidio de San Francisco *(Washington, DC: US Department of Interior, 1992).*

work of empire-building on the northern frontier: open-air cooking, textile manufacturing, pottery making, the slaughter of cattle, and the construction of the building itself. Most of this labor was the work of local Indians.

The first Spanish and Mexican families of the San Francisco Peninsula quickly became restless within the Presidio's walls. When Vancouver passed through the bay in 1792, he spied "thatched roofs of . . . low small houses" scattered outside the Presidio. Three decades later, another visitor found more small frame houses strewn about—something that was out of alignment with the Spanish urban plan. By this time, the first soldiers had tired of their military duties and sought land of their own. They migrated to riparian valleys to the east and south of the Presidio, where water sources and arable soil could support farming and grazing for some of the cattle they had brought with them from Mexico. Unlike the Presidio, with its Spanish-style construction and materials, the houses outside the quadrangle were often rounded rather than orthogonal in shape. They were built of local materials and stocked with Indian crafts as well as European artifacts. Constructed of mud and branches, or with upright poles supporting flat straw roofs, they were not that much different from the rustic homes of rural Mexico, or even those of the Ohlone.[24]

After 1810, the Spanish were also besieged by rebellion in their Mexican colony. By 1821 when Mexico secured its independence, the Presidio was an empty shell. Russians who were anchored nearby in the 1820s described it as "a rather formless pile of half-ruined dwellings, sheds, store houses, and other structures." Well before that date, Spain's European rivals had intruded into Alta California. As early as 1803, the British had come ashore near the Presidio, first to repair their ships, then to trade with the missions, and in short shrift to defy Spanish tariffs and restrictions on international commerce. A few years later, agents of John Jacob Astor's Hudson Bay Company were trading furs there, while Russian trappers camped just a few miles away. By 1824, the Russians had settled in; they even established a bakery just outside the Presidio walls.[25]

El Presidio Real de San Francisco did not meet the architectural standards of the Spanish Crown; nor did it serve the Crown's imperial purposes. When Alta California passed from the Spanish to the independent Republic of Mexico, the Presidio fell quickly into disuse. The California-born commandant Mariano Vallejo proposed that its remains be sold to pay the back wages of the soldiers. After the United States conquered California in 1848, New York's 7th Regiment took up residence within the Presidio's crumbling adobe

—

walls. What was left of the Presidio was later buried under a US Army base. The only material sign of the Spanish imperial authority remaining near the site today is a portion of one wall of the former officer quarters. It was not just the shifting course of military and imperial history that undermined El Presidio Real—the force of nature played a supporting role. The climate of the Golden Gate mocked the imperial aspirations of the first European settlers. Arriving in the warm and gentle fall, or disembarking in the sunnier microclimates on the east side of the bay, they did not anticipate the torrents of winter rain that quickly eroded the walls of the first rustic fortress near the Golden Gate. Then, in 1808, the remodeled Presidio was shaken by one of the many earthquakes to come.

Juan Bautista de Anza chose a more temperate site on which to construct the second architectural embodiment of Spanish Empire, the mission. Situated inland from the Presidio, it was sheltered from the punishing winds off the Pacific and watered by a creek called Dolores that ran down to the eastern shore of the bay. This place was chosen for a religious rather than a diplomatic or military purpose. Initially named Misión San Francisco de Asís, it quickly became known locally as Dolores. The first Spanish chapel was in place by October 1776, and a second structure was built in 1782. A much restored and renovated relic of the original still stands in that spot, just up from Mission Street fronting on Dolores, testament to the lofty ambitions of the Order of St. Francis and Padre Serra. The red tile roof, wide adobe walls, and modest ornamentation of the chapel announced the European presence on Ohlone land. Unmistakably a Spanish church, with its belfry and columned facade, the Mission also bespoke the eighteenth century, the resurgence of classicism, and glimmers of enlightenment.

A California mission was more than a church. The chapel was surrounded by a cluster of other structures, starting with the "principal house," where the padres resided, apparently quite comfortably, for they requisitioned such luxuries from Mexico City as chocolate, saffron, and fine wines. The padres' mission became a serious business. Lined up next to their quarters was the *escolta*, the guardhouse for soldiers sent from the Presidio. The adobe walls extended to encompass a string of dormitories and a series of workplaces: a tannery, spinning rooms, two mills, a soap factory, a laundry, and a filter house for purifying water. This ensemble created an orthogonal compound with an inner courtyard, the hub of missionary endeavor. The geography of the Mission extended well beyond the adobe walls to gardens, orchards, and the irrigation ditches that watered them. Far beyond, extending along the

Pacific coast and linked in a chain of twenty missions, was a vast pasturage for thousands of head of cattle.[26]

Functionally, this compound resembled a company town, whose intended product was Indian converts to Catholicism, called neophytes. Louis Choris, a Ukrainian artist who visited Mission San Francisco in the company of Russian explorers in 1816, described the daily routine in and around the site in images that resemble a Mexican *hacienda* or a slave plantation along the Chesapeake Bay. Choris saw it as a "village" inhabited by 1,500 Indians: "There they are given protection, clothing, and an abundance of food. In return, they cultivate the land for the community. Corn, wheat, beans, peas, and potatoes—in a word, all kinds of produce—are to be found in the general warehouse." Choris also noted that the Indians worked fields of their own just outside the mission walls, cultivating onions, garlic, cantaloupes, watermelons, pumpkins, and various fruits. This bounteous inventory demonstrated that the Spanish had swiftly carried out an agricultural revolution. They brought the Ohlone land into cultivation, reenacting the Neolithic revolution that had arrived along the Chesapeake centuries earlier.[27]

Choris's description of the "fair-sized village" at Mission San Francisco also testified to the fact that the missionaries had recruited and organized a local labor force. Indian workers filed into "a large square in the middle of the village," where they took their collective meals at designated hours three times a day. Reports like these demonstrate that the Spanish had designed a distinctive social and economic space in Alta California, a means of not just taking the land but also making it productive by European standards. The mission economy was designed to provide subsistence for both the Presidio soldiers and the padres who managed the mission complex. By fiat of the Spanish government, Ohlone habitat was converted into what Carey McWilliams would later call a "factory in the fields." Under their stern Franciscan taskmasters, the Indians quickly supplied the sustenance for the Spanish soldiers and Mexican settlers and left something to spare. Soon the two padres who managed the Mission's economy were trading with passing ships, exchanging their agricultural produce (including some well-regarded wines) for European manufactures and Chinese luxuries.[28]

To devout Franciscans, however, the purpose of a mission was to produce not just a workforce but Christians. An undertaking of such hubris, daring to virtually reconstruct a whole cultural system, required a drastic reordering of social space. Columbus had hardly returned from his first encounter with the native population of the Western Hemisphere when King Ferdinand and

Queen Isabella decreed a detailed plan for the occupation and Christianiza-
tion of the New World. It was from the first a program for the urbanization
of the Indian population. Ordinance number 148 in the Law of the Indies
instructed the colonists of New Spain to "see with great care that these
Indians be settled into towns, and that, within these, churches be built so
that the Indians can be instructed into Christian doctrine and live in good
order." This project, called *congregación*, was updated in the *Recopilación de
las Leyes de los Reinos de Indias* (Compilation of the Laws of the Kingdom
of the Indies) in 1680, and reinforced by Bourbon reformers in the eighteenth century. By the time Junípero Serra arrived in San Francisco Bay, the
institution of the mission was out of favor with the Crown and the Viceroy.
The Bourbons exiled the Jesuits from the missions of northern Mexico and
sent the Franciscans into the California frontier on a secular assignment:
feeding the soldiers who would fend off the other Europeans who coveted the
land of Alta California. When the expedition of José María Padrés and José
María Híjar set out for San Francisco Bay from Mexico in the 1830s, they
also intended to consolidate the Indians into villages complete with central
plazas and dense compounds of families. While the Indians were entitled to
"build their houses" in pueblos of their own, Mexican policy stipulated that
they "shall not be permitted to do so outside the lines traced for forming
the streets."[29]

The Spanish plans to convert Indians into townsmen seemed promising
at first. The Ohlone came voluntarily into the Mission in the late eighteenth
century, attracted by such things as relief from a season of drought, protection from hostile tribes to the south, or a chance to replenish the empty
winter larder. Whole villages of Huchiuns and Saklan arrived at Mission San
Francisco in 1794 and 1795. At its height, the Mission was the residence of
one thousand Indians, making it far more populous than a typical Ohlone
tribelet of one or two hundred.[30] Once within the jurisdiction of the padres,
the Indians were subjected to a comprehensive program of assimilation. First,
the Indian population was re-sorted according to Franciscan specifications.
Women and men were segregated from one another. Young women were
housed in dormitories for their sexual protection. Indians who converted
and married were permitted to take up residence in conjugal households
outside the perimeter of the compound. During working hours the central
complex became the domain of women, children, and their clerical supervisors; adult Indian men were sent to the fields, or to construct and reconstruct
the Presidio. At rigidly scheduled mealtimes, everyone was paraded into

the center of the Mission for a repast suited to a Mexican palate. Heavy in beef and beans, it led the Indians to pine for a diet of fresh fish and ground acorns. A sequence of bells signaled the regimented movements of the day. Prayers and attendance at Mass were required. Discipline was enforced with whips and goads wielded by the padres or their Indian subordinates.

There was, of course, a bitter irony at the heart of the Franciscan experiment in social organization and coercive urbanization. Incarceration in the Mission led to demographic disaster for the natives, eviscerating the very population the padres sought to save. All the pious regimentation and spatial engineering of the Franciscans had a devastating effect on the Indians of San Francisco Bay. The number of births never exceeded deaths within Mission San Francisco. The death rate was such that it would require the arrival of an estimated two hundred additional Indians annually to maintain the mission population of about one thousand. Once again, nature seemed to rise up to mock the conquistadores and the missionaries. In 1795, a measles virus struck the vulnerable immune systems of California natives. Its deadly course accelerated in the densely packed, close quarters of the Mission, leaving three-quarters of the Indian children dead. Another measles epidemic, in 1806, took the lives of half the women of childbearing age, half the boys,

Louis Choris, Danse des habitans de Californie à la mission de San Francisco *(Dance of the inhabitants of California at the Mission San Francisco), ca. 1815, fG420.K84.C6. Courtesy of the Bancroft Library, University of California, Berkeley.*

———

and all the Indian girls. Syphilis was a second major cause of demographic crisis among the natives of California. It coursed through the Spanish Empire along a sinister and ironic path. Although the virus had existed in a benign form in the New World, it mutated into a virulent strand upon its transmission to Europe and then returned to California to fatally inflict the native as well as the colonizing population.[31]

This demographic catastrophe aborted the Christianizing project and stopped far short of the original Spanish intention of converting the land of the New World into Indian pueblos. Still, the Indians found ways to adapt the mission spaces to their own desires and cultural ends. One of Choris's sketches finds them gathered in the courtyard in front of Mission San Francisco for dances and games, much as they once did in their native villages, in a central spot that Pedro Fages called a "level spot like a plaza." Indian handiwork could also be found within the Mission chapel: its ceiling, for example, was adorned with a colorful geometric design resembling Native American decorative motifs. As an example of either Spanish or Ohlone heritage, however, the Mission on the San Francisco Peninsula paled in comparison to the architectural splendors of Mexico City.[32]

THE SPANISH AND INDIAN INTERREGNUM

The future looked bleak at the beginning of the nineteenth century for the Franciscans as well as for the Ohlone. Understandably, the Ohlone lost faith in their Christian protectors. In the aftermath of the 1795 measles epidemic, some 280 Indians went missing. Running away from the Mission became so endemic that the recapture and return of Indians became the primary task of the mission guard and the chief assignment of soldiers from the Presidio. The actions of one former Presidio resident, José María Amador, exemplified the brutal turn in the fortunes of the Indians. Amador boasted of raiding Indian villages as far east as present-day Livermore and Stockton. He marched his captives back across the bay, the women to Misión San José de Guadalupe and the men to the Presidio, where they would be put to work making bricks. Amador's tales about his life as a California soldier are as lurid as a violent scenario shot in contemporary Hollywood. He told of Indian captives oozing blood through their brains, of daggers emptying out intestines, and of one hundred prisoners being lined up for simultaneous baptism and execution.[33]

Another gruesome vignette in Amador's account, a description of Indian prisoners "tied from the thumbs to a stick that ran across the back of their necks," has visual documentation: a sketch drawn by Louis Choris of Indians harnessed in such a fashion and being marched back into captivity at the Presidio. The missionaries took to brutal methods of Christianizing the recalcitrant natives. Shackles and whips became part of the clerical costume, at the ready even in the chapel, where they were used to enforce a requirement that Indians maintain a properly supplicant posture before the Christian god. A Padre Olbes, stationed nearby at Misión de Santa Cruz, was said to regularly inflict twenty-five lashes, "on the buttocks or the belly, according to his fancy of the moment." Amador's reports may well have been exaggerated, a figment of his flamboyant imagination, flawed memory, and contempt for the missionaries, whom he called "rancid Spaniards." But the conditions in the missions had become desperate enough by 1797 to provoke an angry protest from a young priest as well. José María Fernández had a simple explanation for the epidemic of escapes from the Mission: "I know why they have fled. It is due to the terrible suffering they experienced from punishments and work." An interrogation of some of the runaway captives who were returned to the Mission in 1797 substantiated Fernández's charges. The twenty-three testimonials reported multiple reasons to flee. Nine captives cited physical abuse from priests armed with whips, cudgels, and clubs. The missionaries installed an Indian named Raymundo, who was native to Baja California, to oversee the local labor force. He used a heavy cane to cripple one Indian's hand.[34]

The missionary archives record the emotional and physical pain inflicted on the Ohlone and other tribes of the Bay Area. Chief among these tortures was watching a relative die in captivity. An Indian named Macario, questioned by a Presidio official about his attempted escape from the Mission, "testified that he fled because his wife and one child had died, no other reason than that." Another native, named Ostano, the official said, escaped the mission only after his wife, one child, and two brothers had died there. Sexual abuse from soldiers also provoked Indian flight. An escapee named Otolón left Mission San Francisco after "the *vaquero* Salvador had sinned" with his wife. More routinely, in eight cases, Indians cited hunger—their own or that of their kin—as the cause of their flight from the Mission. A man named Toribio said he "was always very hungry." Another Indian, Milán, ran away "to look for clams to feed his family," and one named Orencio tried to escape because he saw his niece die of hunger.[35]

Hunger, physical brutality, the destruction of families—and sometimes all

---

three combined—drove Indians from the Mission. The chain of compounded violations is exemplified by the personal testimony of an Indian named Homobono: "His brother had died on the other shore, and when he cried for him at the mission they whipped him," said the official's report. The *alcalde* Valeriano then "hit him with a heavy cane for having gone to look for mussels at the beach with Raymundo's permission." Christianized Indians like Raymundo and Valeriano were often deputized to discipline the Mission's labor force, driving them to work, to Mass, and toward sobriety. Their title of *alcalde* denoted the chief municipal authority in a pueblo, be it in Spain or the Americas. According to the *Recopilación de las Leyes de los Reinos de Indias*, the elected office of *alcalde* could be held by Indians presiding over an Indian community. Although Indian pueblos were commonplace elsewhere in New Spain, they were exceptionally rare and ephemeral in Alta California. The Spanish did not build an Indian pueblo near San Francisco Bay, but instead coerced the local population into living and working at the Mission. This spatial strategy would end in the betrayal of the Franciscans' Christian intentions as well as the rapid termination of the effort of the Spanish Crown to colonize San Francisco Bay.[36]

The outcome was apparent by the first decade of the nineteenth century. Throughout California, the missions were losing workers as well as souls—to death, escape, and open rebellion. José María Amador and the other soldiers of the San Francisco Presidio were kept busy fending off active resistance, which took the form of an assassination of a priest at Mission Santa Cruz; a violent revolt involving as many as one thousand Indians, led by the rebel Estanislao; and routine raids for horses and cattle. The flight of the Indian labor force undermined the productivity of the fields and pastures of the missions. By the 1810s, the Spanish government had diminished its support for missions. In 1813, it announced a policy of secularization that stripped the padres of their political authority. The Mission went the way of the Presidio, but only after inflicting a heavier human cost. The highest, most selfless goals of the missionaries had degenerated into a scourge of the Ohlone and their environment.[37]

In the last analysis, the distance between the Spanish Empire and the Ohlone way of life could not be bridged. By repeatedly escaping from Mission San Francisco, the Ohlone enacted a desperate rejection of the way Europeans lived off the land and the waterways. Louis Choris read it in Ohlone faces in 1816, reporting: "In winter, bands of Indians come from the mountains to be admitted to the mission. They find it irksome to work continually and to have everything supplied to them in abundance. In their mountains, they live a free and independent, albeit a miserable existence. After several months spent, they usually begin to grow fretful and thin, and they constantly gaze with sadness at the mountains which they can see in the distance."[38]

The Ohlone's tenacious allegiance to their ancestral way of living on the land posed a challenge to the fundamental principles of early modern European civilization. Padre Fermín Lasuén, writing in defense of the missions, acknowledged that there were advantages to the Indians' way of life. They had an unshakable attachment to their own arduous but rewarding ways of "procuring a sustenance from the open spaces." He even saw the virtues of the Ohlone economy. While the Ohlone way of making a living off the land was "free and according to their liking," he noted, the Mission's regimen was "prescribed, and not according to their liking. . . . The uncultivated soil supports their manner of life. . . . They live on herbs while they are in season, and then gather the seeds for the winter, and as a rule, they celebrate the end of it by holding a feast or a dance." After acknowledging the coherence, integrity, and pleasures of the Ohlone way, Padre Lasuén stepped back and went through a series of logical contortions to justify its destruction. As Lasuén saw it, the Indians violated "the law of self-preservation which nature implants in us." They "enjoy life as long as they can sustain it with ease, and without having recourse to what they regard as work. . . . They satiate themselves today and give little thought to tomorrow." To Padre Lasuén, the "law of self-preservation" mandated that humankind labor beyond what is necessary to sustain life. Only the inculcation of a punishing work regimen would "transform a savage race such as these into a society that is human, Christian, civil, and industrious."[39]

Aware that the Ohlone had survived on the land and off the waters of the bay for many generations without the benefit of Christian supervision, Padre Lasuén became defensive and confused. In order to justify the missionary enterprise, he mobilized an assortment of arguments: invocations of penitential Christianity, a kind of labor theory of value, and even a version of the survival of the fittest. At the same time that he upheld the "law of self-preservation which nature implants in us," he conceded that raising the Ohlone to the European standards of civilization "could only be accomplished by denaturalizing them." Lasuén acknowledged that recasting human nature would be difficult: "It is easy to see what an arduous task this is, for it requires them to act against nature." In one stroke he invoked the law of nature and called for the "denaturalization" of native Californians. Padre Lasuén's tortured logic revealed just how confusing the encounter with the Ohlone was for a thoughtful Spaniard. It also exposed the deep chasm in the history of ideas between the Old World and the New and raised some fundamental questions about how the Europeans organized land and labor.[40]

The Ohlone way of life could not be reconciled with the Spanish regime of taking land and saving souls, but the brutality would dissipate, at least for a while. The Indians who survived the trauma of the missions moved out of the orbit of the Franciscans. Some reassembled across the bay in a string of reconstituted Indian villages, or *rancherías*. Others quietly merged into the evolving world of the Californios; a few intermarried with the soldiers of the Presidio. Still others lived as Christians, and many re-created themselves by forming new communities out of the once separate tribelets of bay peoples. Archaeologists have discovered impressions of Ohlone survival and adaptation in some of the home sites scattered just outside the Presidio and the Mission. They found stone tools interspersed with iron, adobe walls enclosing Indian hearths, and diets that combined cornmeal and acorns. One group of Miwoks who were put to work on a ranch in the North Bay in the 1830s continued to eat acorns as well as beef, used the mortars their ancestors carved into the rocks, and preferred their own woven baskets to Mexican clay pots. Long after the Spanish had departed, Indians continued to range the Bay Area, salvaging the remaining natural bounty. They traveled down to the beaches to collect mussels and up the eastern slopes to harvest favorite berries and seeds. As late as 1836, the administrator of San Francisco de Asís defended the territorial rights of some of the natives of San Francisco Bay who were occupying a "tract of land lying between the first willow-grove and San Mateo." This was, he said, the "lawful possession" of Indians, according to Spanish regulations.[41]

The Ohlone, in any case, did not disappear when the Spanish Empire lost its claim on North America in 1821. They had not become extinct. Like the Algonquians, the California natives had adapted to the hostile intrusions into their habitat and reassembled in spaces of their own choosing. At the time the Spanish retreated from Alta California, the Indians still far outnumbered them. Although the Indian population of California would be reduced from an estimated three hundred thousand to thirty thousand by 1900, most of the decimation occurred after the land was ceded to the United States. The numbers of self-identified Ohlone would begin growing again early in the twentieth century. Descendants of the sixty tribelets that

---

dominated the great estuary of the Pacific two hundred years ago can still be seen on the California landscape. They are reclaiming their names and languages, holding annual harvest ceremonies, recovering the remains of their ancestors for Indian reburial, and retrieving their history.[42]

The Ohlone land, however, would never be quite the same. The damage had begun even before the Anza party set foot on the San Francisco Peninsula. Foreign microbes and invasive European species traveled north from Mexico in advance of soldiers and missionaries, playing havoc with the delicate biosphere. The herds of cattle driven north by the Anza expedition trampled on the vegetation vital to the Ohlone diet. Soon thousands of cattle, horses, oxen, and plows were dislodging the soil and destroying the tender herbs that Ohlone women once gathered. Stripped of native grasses, the hillsides became overgrown with rugged chaparral. Contemporary estimates of the damage are staggering: an estimated 17 percent of the vegetation and 40 percent of the fish species soon became extinct. The last free run of salmon in the creeks of the East Bay was in the 1850s. Immense environmental change occurred in a nanosecond of natural history. The complex and delicate mode of survival on the land that sustained the Ohlone for hundreds of years could not withstand the environmental assault of a few score Spaniards camped within the Golden Gate.[43] The California missions converted up to eight million acres of land into agricultural and pastoral production, accomplishing one of the largest single land-grabs in history, and dwarfing the scale of the patents the English had surveyed in Maryland.

The chapel of Misión San Francisco de Asís, much restored, stands on the corner of Dolores and Sixteenth Streets, a small, unprepossessing relic of the Spanish Empire amid the neighborhood's trendy restaurants and bustling *taquerías*. An imposing Catholic basilica down the street serves as the parish church for hundreds of Spanish speakers. But they are mostly immigrants from elsewhere in the Americas with no historical connections to the Ohlone. By removing the Ohlone and converting the vast acreage around the San Francisco Estuary into pasture, Misión San Francisco de Asís had prepared the land around the great estuary for the city people who would someday follow. Neither the Spanish Empire nor the Order of Saint Francis were able to complete the act of securing the land for Europeans, however. The Mission compound, like the Presidio, was in ruins within half a century of its construction. The Mexicans officially secularized the Franciscan landscape in 1833, leaving only the chapel, which was entrusted to one beleaguered priest. A visitor from the United States writing in 1837

—

Mission Dolores, 1850s. In G. R. Fardon, San Francisco in the 1850s: 33 Photographic Views by G. R. Fardon *(New York: Dover, 1977).*

described Mission San Francisco as "a miserable place as can well be imagined, consisting of nothing more than a few rows of wretched hovels for the Indians and one row of whitewashed houses . . . for the people attached to the Mission." In the 1860s, the Lincoln administration would formally grant the title to the small plot of land on which the Mission chapel rested to the Roman Catholic Archdiocese of San Francisco.[44]

POBLADORES WITHOUT A PLAZA OR A PUEBLO

If the Presidio was in ruins and the Mission reduced to a parish church, the third iconic feature of the Spanish landscape, the pueblo, was a phantom. When Mexico won its independence in 1821, the Spanish left hardly a trace of nucleated urban settlement within the boundaries of present-day San Francisco, not even a space as dense as an Ohlone village. It was also difficult to locate the anchor of Spanish colonial town planning, a central plaza, among the few remains of empire scattered around the San Francisco Peninsula. Numerous prototypes of the sixteenth-century Spanish plans can be found elsewhere in Latin America and the American Southwest, but none were laid out at the future site of the city of San Francisco during the Spanish era.[45]

The absence of these iconic Hispanic spaces around San Francisco Bay is a notable exception to the widespread human predilection to anchor society in a concentration of homes around a central public space—a practice common everywhere from ancient China to pre-Columbian America. The grand ceremonial plazas of Cahokia near present-day St. Louis long predated the humble square of William Penn's Philadelphia, just as the royal pretension of the Plaza Major in Madrid paled beside the vast spaces and elaborate architecture of the Aztecs' Tenochtitlan. Mesoamericans set a standard for urban planning that the Spanish hastened to emulate. The exacting prescription of urban spaces that the Spanish Crown laid down in 1573 specified the exact dimensions of plazas, the precise intersection of streets, the location of churches and houses of government, and generous provisions for public land as well as private lots. According to the Law of the Indies, the land stretching out from the plaza should be overlaid in a complicated spatial design "with uniformity and in proportion to the amount of land." Commonly extending out four leagues for a pueblo, and much more for the populous *ciudad*, the ideal Spanish urban complex encompassed an extensive public domain, *ejidos*, *baldios*, and *propios*—spaces designated for the village commons, shared pastures, and future use—along with a shared shoreline. Yet the first settlers near the entry to San Francisco Bay, like those who were building a town along the Chesapeake at about the same time, did not make urban planning, the creation of plazas, or reservation of public land an immediate priority.[46]

When José de Gálvez mounted his expedition to colonize Alta California, his urban plans were modest: he focused on propagating private property and a few small but cohesive pueblos. The Spanish governor of Alta California, Felipe de Neve, reiterated the credo of the pueblo in 1781 and adapted it to local conditions and priorities. In keeping with Bourbon policies, Neve's *Reglamentos* (Regulations) called for the election of the officers of the pueblo, that is, the *alcaldes* and *regidores* (roughly mayors and council members). The *Reglamentos* also prescribed an urban strategy for assimilating California Indians. They would settle the Christianized Indians of California around a plaza, set them to working land that they held in common, and authorize them to elect their own leaders. Finally, Neve's *Reglamentos*

---

anticipated that Indian pueblos would comply with the most up-to-date European principles for holding the land. In the governor's opinion, the best way to carry out the Spanish imperial project was "to bind individuals to society by the powerful bond of property." Although Neve, like every other governor of California, failed to create Indian towns, he did sanction another kind of pueblo, a colonial settlement of migrants from Mexico "who being gathered together, shall promote the planting and cultivation of crops, stock raising and in succession the other branches of industry so that in the course of a few years their produce may suffice to supply the presidio."[47]

One such pueblo, designed for settlers from Spain or Mexico rather than California Indians, was laid out near the southernmost shore of San Francisco Bay. In 1771, Neve sent sixty-eight soldiers south from the San Francisco Presidio to establish the pueblo near Misión San José de Guadalupe. The first urban pioneers of Alta California dutifully marked off a plaza and allotted *suertes* (fields) and *solares* (town lots) to the first settlers. A few years later, a second, even smaller settlement, the Villa de Branciforte, was charted yet farther away from the spot where a city called San Francisco would one day rise. Neither pueblo prospered, growing only to a population of 100 to 150 residents.[48] The locations of San Jose and San Branciforte conformed to the Law of the Indies, which advised colonizers to be very careful in selecting the site of a pueblo: it should be placed convenient to water, wood, good soil, and a mild and salubrious climate. The climate farther north on the San Francisco Peninsula, especially near the Golden Gate, was, as the Indians knew well, arid and windy; the land was sandy, and there were few trees. When it came to plotting an agricultural pueblo that would feed the Presidio soldiers, the local authorities looked to more fertile lands.

The rugged land near the entry to the great estuary was not easily molded into the shapes specified in Spanish imperial planning. So when Anza returned to Mexico, and the Franciscans lost political patronage, the Crown abandoned San Francisco Bay without building even a modest pueblo, much less that "most beautiful city" envisioned by the Europeans who first discovered the great estuary. The Spanish Empire did, however, leave behind the architects of another way of taking land and making space, the band of immigrants who ventured north from Sonora and Sinaloa in September 1775. Anza had recruited the flinty settlers who signed on for the dangerous and grueling expedition to San Francisco Bay by promising them land, cattle, and better prospects in Alta California.

By the time the Anza expedition departed for Alta California in 1774, the residents of Sonora and Sinaloa at points south were habituated to urban living, whether it was around the vast Zócalo, the main plaza of Mexico City, or in the small village plazas scattered throughout the colony. The first Spaniards to explore northern Mexico found that local Indians had also favored pueblo living. The Opata, for example, resided in dense enclaves of around two hundred houses surrounded by irrigated fields. By the third decade of the seventeenth century the Spanish had collected the natives of the provinces of Sonora and Sinaloa into eight Indian pueblos, each with a municipal government, its own *alcalde*, and a parish priest. A century later, the Bourbon reformers expelled the Jesuits and secularized the missions, opening up the pueblos to Mexican farmers and miners, who often intermarried with the Indians. Flourishing towns like Pitic (now Hermosillo), Villa Sinaloa, and San Miguel de Horcasitas became what one geographer called "enterprising, urban-centered society." It was in these pueblos of northern Mexico and Arizona that Juan Bautista de Anza recruited the pioneer families of San Francisco.[49]

The Anza caravan included 38 humble soldiers, 29 wives, their young children, and a few servants. Hoisting a cargo of agricultural supplies, and accompanied by 500 horses and 355 cattle, the immigrants braved an arduous and dangerous journey over 2,000 miles of desert, mountains, and hostile Indians. When Anza returned to Mexico, they stayed on to eke out a living in the ruins of the imperial project and planted themselves firmly and prolifically on the San Francisco Peninsula. The population that claimed Spanish or Mexican ancestry soon grew to 500 settlers scattered around the bay. As of 1830, over 80 percent of the non-Indian population had descended from the first families of 1790. San Francisco's founding generation was composed not of lonely pioneers, but of a rugged group of kinsmen, including couples as well as parents and children. Several children were born during the two years it took to arrive in San Francisco by land. The fecundity of the first couples of San Francisco was impressive. For example, José María Amador, the soldier from the Presidio, boasted that he had three wives and sired an unlikely thirty-seven children.[50]

The settlers who secured the headlands of San Francisco Bay for New Spain were neither aristocratic, nor Spaniards, nor overwhelmingly what US citizens would later come to call "white." A census of the first settlers taken in 1776 classified less than half of the population as *español*, a term that usually denoted Spanish descent but Mexican birth. Of the remainder, 31 percent were mestizos and 18 percent mulattoes, plus two Indians. A census of the

San Francisco Presidio taken in 1790 conformed to the Mexican standard by listing a racial classification, or *casta*, for the adult residents. Only three were called *europeo*. Thirty-six of the adults were classified as *español*, eighteen as mestizo, three as *coyote* (one-fourth Indian), five as mulatto, nine as its rough equivalent, *color quebrado*, and four as *indio* (a term usually applied to the native tribes of Mexico as well as Alta California). This mélange of ancestries mirrored the hegira through New Spain and up the Pacific Coast. The pioneer Castro family, for example, whose lineage would include one of the first California-born governors, appeared in the census of Monterey with the label mestizo.[51]

Whatever their biological descent, most of these immigrants came from small villages in the northern reaches of New Spain. Nearly two-thirds of those appearing in the Alta California census of 1790 came from the provinces of either Sinaloa or Sonora. Most of them had lived closely together, intermarried with local Indians, and established firm roots in American soil. Many came from the same villages, such as Villa Sinaloa. The European signature on the lands around the great estuary of the West was not written in the lordly hand of the Calverts or the Carrolls. In fact, it was not even legible. The majority of the early residents of the Presidio were illiterate. They can best be described as Mexican *pobladores*.[52]

Given the leveled social structure of the first Spanish settlement along San Francisco Bay, censuses subsequent to 1790 dispensed entirely with recording differences in *casta*. Instead, a single category, *gente de razón* (people of reason), served as a label for all those who had migrated from Mexico as well as their progeny born in California. This inclusive gesture, awarding people of mixed-race and humble origins such an august title, did not indicate, however, that racial distinctions had dissolved in the bracing air of San Francisco Bay. Quite to the contrary, as Barbara Voss has argued, based on her minute archaeological investigation of the Presidio of San Francisco, the *castas* were simply replaced by a blunter racial division. The pioneers of Alta California drew the line between superiors and inferiors, selves and others, us and them, not within the different ranks of colonists, but along a divide between themselves and the local Indians. In stark contrast to the frequency of intermarriage in the rest of New Spain, only two weddings between the migrants from Mexico and the Indians native to the Bay Area were celebrated at Mission San Francisco. Even Christianized Ohlone were classified as "neophytes" rather than *gente de razón*. The archaeological record of the Presidio, as uncovered and interpreted by Voss, indicates that the immigrants from northern Mexico disdained association even with the foods and handicrafts of the California *indios*; they ate beef and wheat off of Chinese or European pottery. Once they had set the native population apart as others, the colonists of the San Francisco Bay area recast themselves in the homogeneous image not just of *pobladores* but as *gente de razón*. Just as Jean Crèvecoeur's *Letters from an American Farmer* had announced the emergence of a new kind of man along the eastern frontier, the apparition of *un nuevo americano* was evolving in Alta California. Settler colonialists on both sides of the North American continent set themselves apart from both the Old World and the natives of North America in a place that was pregnant with inequities as well as opportunities.[53]

TAKING LAND AND MAKING A NEIGHBORHOOD

Along the northern Pacific coast, this new breed of Americans would come to be called *Californios*. The ruins of the Presidio and the Mission left few clues as to just what shape they would give to the land around San Francisco Bay. The *pobladores* proceeded to make space in their own independent manner. The first implementation of the official land policy was recorded in a grant of land to Manuel Buitrón in 1784. Buitrón was an adventurous pioneer who was eager to make his mark on the New World. Born in Orihuela, a city in southeastern Spain, he migrated to Mexico and then joined the first colonizing party en route to San Francisco Bay. Somewhere along the way, up the inland route to San Francisco, Buitrón took an Indian wife named Margarita who was twenty years his junior. The census of 1790 listed his age as fifty-four and cited Margarita's birthplace as Alta California. She may have been a California Indian, but probably not an Ohlone, for her first child had been born fourteen years before, around the time that the first colonizing expeditions set out from Mexico. Manuel Buitrón petitioned the comandante of the Presidio, Don Fernando Rivera, as follows: "I Manuel Buitrón, a soldier in the Army, at your feet earnestly supplicate that you may be pleased to grant me my discharge, and permit me to remain in this Mission, giving that which His Majesty allows to every settler." Buitrón presented the petition in a deferential manner, but he was also crafty about improving his social and economic position. He expected an appropriate reward for his service as a soldier: "a piece of land pertaining to said Mission, of the length and breadth of one hundred forty varas, in the form of a perfect square, where at present I have planted corn."[54]

117

The precise request for a tract of land "assigned to me and my descendants" revealed that Buitrón was well informed about imperial policies and determined to make use of them. He petitioned for land not in his own name but "in the name of the Indians," and by right of marriage to an Indian, "daughter of the mission." The success of his strategy was due to his understanding of both protective Bourbon policy toward Indians and the power exercised by the head of California missions, Junípero Serra. Buitrón made his petition to Padre Serra, and he presented it "in virtue of the right of his wife Margarita," and "in accordance with the Royal orders; that they shall not be able to sell, donate, alienate the same to others beyond the children or descendants of said Mission," all this in the name of "royal Justice." Thus the first individual land grant in Northern California went to a Spanish soldier, with an Indian wife, who carefully navigated his way through imperial and ecclesiastical regulations.[55]

Manuel and Margarita projected a new and independent way forward into California's future. This way, however, would take them away from the future site of the city of San Francisco. They chose a land grant to the south, nearer the sunny and fertile shores of Monterey Bay. Only a handful of those first to arrive at the Presidio and the Mission secured official land grants during the Spanish era, and most of them were higher-ranking officers in the military, whose *casta* was reported as *español*. This fortunate cohort, the Bay Area's founding ranchers, the Peraltas, Argüellos, Amadors, and Castros, took up huge estates, all at a considerable distance from the Presidio and the Mission, in the North, South, and East Bay. The whereabouts of most of the more humble, mixed-race *pobladores* are not well documented. Evidence of the first land-taking near the future site of San Francisco did not surface until half a century later, when some of the men and women who had once resided at the Presidio and the Mission were summoned to testify before the United States Land Commission, meeting in 1851 to adjudicate the Mexican claims to territory in the newly conquered State of California. A witness named Francisco Sánchez, who was born at the Presidio in 1808 and had lived there ever since, reconstructed his own census of the local population. He estimated that only 10 or 12 settlers and their families remained at the Presidio "when the Americans came." He knew, in addition, about 150 people scattered along the San Francisco Peninsula. The rest of the *gente de razón*, approximately 500 people total, resided across the bay on the eastern or northern shores.

Another first family, that of a common soldier named Marcus Briones and his wife, Isadora (both classified as mulatto), also settled far from the

Presidio and outside the mission walls. Most of the Briones' children took up residence across the bay or far down the peninsula, in what is now Marin County in the north, Contra Costa County in the east, and San Mateo County in the south. Of the eight Briones offspring, only two remained within the limits of what is now the city of San Francisco, and neither of them resided on the grounds of the Presidio or the Mission.[56] In 1820, one of the daughters, Juana Briones, married an *indio* soldier stationed at the Presidio named Apolinario Miranda. After the wedding, which took place at Mission San Francisco, the Briones y Miranda family left the Presidio behind. A decade later, when the Republic of Mexico began making official land grants, Juana and Apolinario were living about a mile outside the old fort, in a place called Ojo de Agua. The couple made their home and raised a family in this pastoral valley; according to testimony in the hearings, they "continued to occupy the place, had fruit trees there and cultivated all the ground and so remained there until after the war and the Americans came." Another family that descended from the first settlers of the Presidio, that of Paula and Candelario Valencia, followed the Mirandas' path a short distance away from the Spanish center of settlement. They planted vegetables, dug a well, built a house, and occupied it for decades. Their homestead was not near the Presidio, however, but just outside the Mission. The Valencias appropriated the orchards of the Mission as well as a segment of the old missionary quarters. Another long-term resident of the peninsula, named José Erández, called Candelario Valencia's residence "an apartment he actually occupies in the ruins of the Principal House" (that is, the former priest's quarters). The Valencias' stake in the land was bequeathed to a third generation in the name of their son José Ramón Valencia and his wife. Another man, who had lived at the Presidio as a child, corroborated this pattern of occupying space near the Mission, testifying that the *pobladores* made their homes adjacent to Spanish structures that were "all in ruins."[57]

Some families had appropriated small plots of fifty to one hundred square varas just outside the Mission and near streams, springs, and lakes. Others poached on the outlying grasslands where cattle could forage. A witness named Juan José Bojórquez, born around 1806, described his livelihood as taking care of the horses and cattle that his father pastured "around the vicinity of San Francisco." Another early Presidio resident, José Cornelio Bernal—whose family was identified in the Spanish census alternately as mulatto and mestizo—took up land where the Mission once corralled its mules and cows. José de la Cruz Sánchez testified that Bernal had long allowed his cattle to roam near a small brook along the road to San Jose, where he built his house. According to Bernal's widow, Carmen, a priest at the Mission had originally awarded these grazing rights to her spouse. She also averred that they had occupied this tract some time before they petitioned for a formal land grant; their request was for a much larger tract, one that extended across twenty leagues of the San Francisco Peninsula, out as far as the neighborhoods now called Potrero Hill and Hunters Point. The Valencia family also took land in this informal manner without registering any concern about legal propriety; they were already "farming it when they petitioned for it."[58]

Few of those who stayed on after the Spanish abandoned their outpost near the Golden Gate held formal titles to the lands on which they lived and raised their families. They failed to mark off the terrain with deeds and boundaries. When pressed to provide proof of title and the exact dimensions of their parcels, Spanish-speaking witnesses before the US Land Commission resorted to general phrases, such as, "I knew because I saw it," or "because I lived there . . . I was familiar with all the locality about San Francisco." If marked at all, boundaries were recognized by natural features—a hillside, a mesa, or streams, arroyos, springs, and trees—as well as scattered manmade landmarks—gardens, corrals, houses, decaying mission buildings, and an occasional fence. As late as the 1850s, old-timers, such as José de la Cruz Sanchez, were unable to locate the places of their youth on the map of San Francisco. When pressed by the Land Commission to translate their local knowledge of the landscape into legal technicalities, the *pobladores* responded in the language of their everyday experience. Paula Valencia, for example, defended her land title as follows: "I thought it was the Mission land as there was no other Rancho about there except that of Carmen Bernal. They were government lands, land for all the neighbors."[59]

Paula Valencia, whose parents had made the long trek from Sonora to San Francisco Bay along with Juan Bautista de Anza in 1775, had seen the land pass from the Ohlone to Spain, and then to Mexico. In 1855, US federal officials called upon her to defend her right to live out her lifetime on the small plot that she, her father-in-law, her husband, and their children had farmed and made their own for three generations. Paula Valencia had only a hazy understanding of the principles that the Spanish had devised and updated for the occupation of their colonies in California. She seemed to have no knowledge of the *Reglamentos* of Governor Felipe de Neve, or of the *Nueva Recopilación* issued in Spain in 1812, which had reserved mission lands for Christianized Indians. As she saw it, the land had been opened for

———

the secular use of families of Spanish or Mexican origin; *solares* of fifty to one hundred square varas became kitchen gardens; and *propios* and *ejidos* remained as "land for all the neighbors." The dividing lines between family parcels were not clearly marked, and much of the vast landscape was free range to roaming cattle.[60]

These boundaries would not become rigid and distinct until the 1820s, when the Republic of Mexico began to write the rules of private property upon the land of Alta California. For the time being, the Californios were occupying land in their own informal way. Legally, all this land was still under the title of the Spanish king. As with that grant to Manuel Buitrón, it could be used only on condition of "royal justice." The constraints imposed by distant monarchs did not, however, stop men and women like Candelario and Paula Valencia from putting the land of San Francisco to use in their own distinctive ways. The *pobladores* were either blissfully oblivious to the laws of nations and the authority of Spain or they chose to ignore or defy them. They abandoned the Presidio and converted the Mission into their homesteads. They plowed under the native grassland to plant orchards and fields of beans and chili peppers, and they tended those two hundred cattle that had been driven north from Mexico until they became a vast herd. Disregarding the claims of the Crown and the church, they began selling the hides of the cattle to merchant ships docking on the bay. They converted the Ohlone catchment into fields and pasturage, and then put the hungry Indians to work as their peons.

In other words, they took the land in a decisive manner and put it to private uses. The growing population dispersed to more fertile agricultural and pastoral sites to the north, south, and east. In the process, the farmers and grazers of the San Francisco Bay area slowly began to convert the Ohlone's littoral habitat into land for the production of commodities coveted in New Spain and in Europe—not the Chesapeake's tobacco, but the hides and tallow first manufactured by the Franciscans.

After half a century of European occupation, the first Californios had drawn a pattern of settlement on the San Francisco Peninsula that differed from Mesoamerica as well as Spain. The colonizers of Alta California failed to establish the formal pueblos that had become a fundamental spatial formation in those parts of Mexico that had been settled by the Spanish centuries earlier.[61] The Mexicans who ventured into Alta California late in the eighteenth century took up land in an expansive and untitled—but not amorphous—manner. The *pobladores de Alta California* were pioneering an open, dispersed, sprawling, decentralized, and informal use of space. The vast acreage that the Spanish granted to the Peraltas, or that José Cornelio Bernal occupied—without bothering to petition for a land grant—signaled some consequential changes upon the land. The Spanish landing in San Francisco Bay cleared the land not just for cattle, but also for the Californios, who would venture far out from the Presidio and the Mission. In this it seemed that the land was taking men and women rather than the reverse, luring them across the bay, out along its wetlands and streams, and up the fertile hillsides, much as it had once led the Ohlone. It might be said of both the Ohlone and the *pobladores* that they were the land's before the land was theirs—to paraphrase a famous line of the poet Robert Frost (who, despite his New England pedigree, grew up in San Francisco and played as a child on the Pacific shore).[62]

The *pobladores* were not solitary, isolated frontiersmen, seeking "elbow room" and shunning common social space. They produced a pattern of settlement according to a political logic of their own derived from habit, memory, necessity, and some vague understanding of the concept of sovereignty. As far as the eleventh century, the peoples of the Iberian Peninsula had exercised a kind of local citizenship that had entitled those who settled permanently in the same place to such privileges as sharing a common pasturage and having a voice in local governance. This community status inhered in the relationships between neighbors, or *vecinos*. Historians of Spain and Mexico have called this informal method of creating political space *vecindad*. Much like the chartered towns of England and the British colonies, the Spanish pueblos had secured certain guarantees of self-government from the Crown; these were sometimes formalized in a contract from the king or lord called a *fuero*. By the fifteenth century, these customs had become well-established local practices for the people who made their living on contiguous pastures and neighboring gardens, and who walked to their fields from a cluster of homes around a plaza. When the members of the Anza expedition left the pueblos of Sonoma and Sinaloa, they carried similar expectations to the shores of San Francisco Bay. The *vecinos* of San Francisco Bay enacted a kind of vernacular popular sovereignty when they honored the borders with their neighbors' land, shared common pastures, and gathered for worship, weddings, baptisms, and festivals at the old Mission chapel. The *vecinos* of San Francisco fashioned an informal polity out of their quotidian relations with one another.[63]

For the time being, however, it would take a huge stretch of imagination

---

to see the men and women who left Mexico to colonize the shores of the San Francisco Bay area as potential city-builders. Soldiers, peasants, and their families, they were not intent on creating an international port, or on plotting out a grid of commercial streets. Some of them may have been aware of the Spanish principles of town planning, and most had a passing acquaintance with the pueblos and plazas of Mexico and the Southwest. They did not, however, implement the exacting standard of urban planning promulgated by Spain; nor did they take up the land in the manner of zealous English property owners. Contemptuous of the natives, they helped themselves to large swaths of the land the Ohlone had carefully managed for centuries. In their willingness to ignore the Old World and make use of the new land without bothering to secure a title, the Californios might have been the most quintessentially American pioneers. They occupied the shores of San Francisco Bay in an expansive, neighborly, ethnically diverse, and yet racially restrictive way. They created a polity out of their quotidian relations with one another. As the shadow of the Spanish Empire began to recede from Alta California early in the nineteenth century, two significant patterns emerged in particular: first, the movement east of the Presidio by Apolinario Miranda and his wife Juana de Briones y Miranda, and second, the convergence of settlers on small lots around Mission San Francisco.

As of 1820, the *pobladores* remained within the loose political orbit of the Spanish Empire. Well before that date, however, squalls of independence began to waft through the Western Hemisphere. Latin America would become a virtual *laboratorio constitutional* in the first decade of the nineteenth century after Napoleon invaded Spain, spawning local resistance, spreading liberal ideas, and stirring debates about sovereignty and popular restlessness under the authority of local elites as well as the Spanish. Republican movements thrived in the vacuum created by warring Europeans. Hegemony over the North American continent was very much in dispute early in the nineteenth century. Indeed, in assessing the state of North America as of 1800, the historian John Tutino concluded that "Spanish North America flourished, extending into Texas, consolidating in New Mexico and building California, while the United States remained a young nation of conflict and uncertain opportunity." A dozen years later, a decisive battle in the struggle for control of the hemisphere was fought in a place called Baltimore, to which we now return.[64]

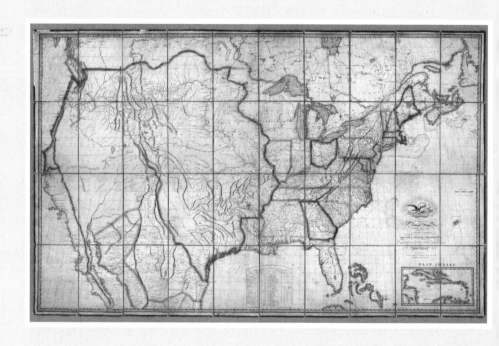

John Melish, Map of the United States with the Contiguous British &
Spanish Possessions *(Philadelphia: John Melish, 1816). Courtesy of the
David Rumsey Map Collection, Stanford University.*

PART II

MAKING THE MUNICIPALITY

The City and the Pueblo

The lines upon the map of North America became finer and clearer early in the nineteenth century. A whole flock of cartographer-businessmen based in the city of Philadelphia drew detailed portraits of the United States extending as far as the Mississippi. One of them, John Melish, looked toward an even wider horizon. In 1816, he drafted a map and accompanying book titled *A Geographical Description of the United States, with the Contiguous British and Spanish Possessions*. Although Melish's map showed that the United States occupied only a fraction of the continent, and that Spain claimed the largest segment of North America, his geographic imagination leapt all the way to the Pacific, where he saw "at a glance the whole extent of United States Territory from sea to sea." The strokes of Melish's pen rushed toward "an agreeable resting-place on its western limits," leaving thousands

---

of miles blank until he arrived at a range of "snowy mountains" not far inland from the Pacific shore. A tuft of feathery lines suggested the topography of an alpine elevation, or perhaps an ocean tide. Melish recognized that Russians had poached upon the northern border of the Pacific, on land coveted by Spain and Britain as well as the United States. To the south was a province of Mexico called an "intendency" in the Spanish constitution of 1813. Melish named it New California and made note of six settlements there, including the capital at Monterey and a place called "St. Francisco"; the other place names proved to be ephemeral or phantoms of Melish's imagination.[1]

Melish did not invest the boundary between the infant republics of the United States and Mexico with much authority. He subscribed to the principle that full title to land should be granted only to those who fertilized it with their own labor. Seeing only Indians or a few Spaniards west of the Mississippi, Melish opined that it "never was intended by Providence, that two or three hundred men should claim and hold a vast space capable of supporting millions." He claimed the Far West as homesteads for industrious Americans, "to the thousandth generations." He supported this voracious land grab with something more than Yankee hubris: he had the force of the US government behind him. The law of the land was "calculated to enable every industrious citizen to become a freeholder, to secure indisputable title to the Purchasers, to obtain a revenue AND ABOVE ALL TO SUPPRESS MONOPOLY." Two decades before the proclamation of "Manifest Destiny" beckoned American citizens westward, Melish invited his readers to take up land all the way to the Pacific. He summoned pioneers with the slogans of Jeffersonian democracy: anti-monopoly, republican virtue, and the principle that "the people enjoy in the fullest extent the sovereign power."[2]

Much of the historiography of the early national period and

———

Jacksonian democracy fits within the ideological frame of Melish's map: a firmament of American identity, western expansion, and popular sovereignty. The national map fails, however, to reckon with the contentious and consequential production of space that was under way in two other quarters, the new towns and cities of the United States and the pueblos and provinces of Mexico. Part II of *Taking the Land* narrows the lens of history to the local scale, even down to the streets and pavements of Baltimore and the clusters of adobe ranch houses on the San Francisco Peninsula. Chapter 4 follows the inhabitants of a town along the commodious bend in the Patapsco River as they formed themselves into the "Body Politic" of Baltimore City in 1796. Chapter 5 finds *pobladores* from around San Francisco Bay marking off the rough boundaries of a pueblo near a cove around the corner from the Golden Gate. In the process, the former colonists of Britain and Spain created a propitious form of political space, the municipality. By coming together to exercise sovereignty at the local level, the citizens of Baltimore and the *ciudadanos* (citizens) of San Francisco also conducted political and economic experiments that would have lasting consequences.

CHAPTER 4

ERECTING BALTIMORE INTO A CITY

Democracy as Urban Space, 1796–1819

W hile the *vecinos* of San Francisco Bay were reshaping the land in their own way, without fanfare or any apparent unified plan, the townsmen of Baltimore were building the scaffolding for commercial prosperity: streets, roads, docks, and a harbor from which merchant vessels could sail the Atlantic. In the 1790s, the growth of the Baltimore economy was still hobbled by political constraints. The townsmen found their power to organize space limited by higher authorities, no longer by the British Empire, but now by the State of Maryland. The merchant leaders of Baltimore bridled under state authority and repeatedly petitioned to secure the right of self-rule. A Maryland statute dated November 1796 recorded their final success: "Be it enacted by the General Assembly of Maryland, That Baltimore-town, in Baltimore county, shall be and is hereby erected into a city, by the name of The City of Baltimore." The delegates to the Maryland Assembly did not bother to define just what it meant to be a city. Largely planters and slave owners, they were reluctant city-makers, fearful of those urban vices that Thomas Jefferson called "pestilential." When townsmen and state legislators spoke of the city, however, they had something more in mind than the sheer size and contentiousness of the population that had aggregated near the mouth of the Patapsco. The leaders of Baltimore made their intentions in requesting a city charter clear: "The good order, health, peace and safety cannot be preserved or the evils and accidents to which they are subject, avoided or remedied without an internal power, competent to establish a police and regulation, fitted to their particular circumstances, wants and exigencies."[1]

In seeking a charter, the leaders of Baltimore expressed their determination to govern themselves independently of either the leaders of the State of Maryland meeting in Annapolis or the federal government assembling in the new District of Columbia just a few miles to the south along the Potomac. The charter granted by the State of Maryland was a legal guarantee that the local inhabitants would have, within certain clear limits, the authority to act together in their own collective interest. They would use that authority, that "internal power," to speed forward the project of reshaping the land around the Chesapeake port. Having converted the shoreline into parcels of private property, the leaders of Baltimore took on the collective task of knitting together the aggregation of private lots into an urban public. Formerly a town, still a part of the county, and legally subservient to the state of Maryland, the city incorporated as Baltimore was granted its share of sovereignty. The municipality was empowered to supervise a major project of spatial production, "erecting a city."

Under the "peculiar circumstances" of Baltimore between the 1790s and 1825, city-making turned out to be an extraordinary historical enterprise. The task of erecting a city set the people of Baltimore on a vertiginous course of economic growth and political transformation. In three decades the fledgling city would careen from urban crisis to civic celebration, a course that would become known locally as the ascent from "mob town to monumental city." When the dust had settled by the third decade of the nineteenth century, Baltimore was the third-largest city in the United States, with a booming economy and a boisterous popular democracy resting on a distinctive urban landscape. But as the breathless pace of this chapter will suggest, arriving at this sanguine moment in urban history was never guaranteed.

ERECTING AN URBAN CORPORATION: 1797–1808

What could it mean to *erect* a city? Certainly the gentry gathered in Annapolis did not intend to take a hand in hauling the lumber, molding the bricks, hammering the nails, and paving the streets, the arduous physical labor required to build a city as a physical place. A more accurate notion of what the Maryland Legislature intended was conveyed by the phrase that followed: to "*incorporate the inhabitants*" of Baltimore. The language of incorporation was familiar to eighteenth-century ears. The General Assembly regularly passed acts of incorporation, sanctioning a variety of public and private projects: building such things as churches, turnpikes, market halls, towns, and now a city. That is what the members of the Maryland General Assembly had in mind when they ruled that "the city of Baltimore, and inhabitants thereof constituted a body politic and corporate, by the name of the Mayor and City Council of Baltimore." The charter issued by the General Assembly created a public corporation and authorized the members of the corporation to act in concert for specified goals, in this case the practice of self-government at the local level. In place of town commissioners appointed by the state, the charter set up the procedures for the election of a bicameral city council. Under the charter issued by the State of Maryland in 1796, the mayor of the new city would not be popularly elected, but rather chosen by the city council, itself a quite patrician body. Each member of the first branch of the municipal legislature was required to own property worth at least $1,000; for members of the second branch, which appointed the first, this prerequisite was $2,000 in property.[2]

In "erecting" a city, the Maryland General Assembly relied on a time-honored English convention: they issued a charter of corporation to a select group of individuals, much as Elizabeth I might have done centuries before. The city-builders of Baltimore were making use of a widespread municipal tradition. From Amsterdam and London to hundreds of smaller places, European monarchs granted the members of a local corporation a bundle of privileges denied to the general population. Burghers and freemen exercised an array of those powers coveted by the inhabitants of Baltimore: the authority to set up markets, to tax one another, and to enact ordinances, for example. Whether granted by a European monarch or a colonial governor, a charter called a polity into being. By the seventeenth century, hundreds of municipal charters had been issued in England, and they soon spread to the colonies. John Locke's constitution for the Carolinas transcribed English corporate privileges as "all liberties, franchises and privileges required and useful." New Amsterdam secured its charter and established a kind of city council for Manhattan in 1653. Philadelphia secured its charter in 1701, and at about the same time Lord Baltimore granted similar privileges to both St. Mary's and Annapolis in the proprietorship of Maryland.

The municipal corporation proved to be an efficient mechanism of colonial settlement. It authorized the population that concentrated in port cities and market towns to take certain circumscribed public actions on their own behalf. The rights, liberties, and franchises of the corporation were exclusive privileges extended to only a minority of the local inhabitants cited in the charter. Throughout Great Britain and its colonies, towns and cities were closed corporations, restricting membership and office-holding to local elites. Those entitled to exercise the franchise could extend quite far down the social ranks, however, on to guild members as well as merchants, and in the case of fifteenth-century England, to the owners of land valued at as little as fourteen shillings. Maryland's state constitution restricted voting to owners of forty to fifty pounds' worth of property, and the original Baltimore charter permitted only the wealthy to serve as mayor or as members of the second branch of the city council.[3]

Having laid down a conservative rubric of representation, the General Assembly of Maryland instructed the City Council of Baltimore to hold its first meeting on the second Monday in February 1797 and "in every year thereafter." The first acts of the municipal legislature were small and prosaic, ranging from licensing chimney sweeps and regulating the size of bricks to supervising harbor navigation and opening streets. Most of the civic tasks enumerated in the city charter had been performed by the town commissioners previously, and all remained subject to review by state authorities. Still, the infant city government swiftly mobilized wide citizen participation. In 1808, for example, a small band of unemployed sailors "marched in regular order, colors flying," to the Mayor's Office, where they begged "your honor to assist us in this our distressed situation."[4]

The legislators of Baltimore City took avidly to their jobs and soon were meeting weekly to enact a basic program of municipal housekeeping. At its first meeting, the city council passed a spate of ordinances. First on the agenda, predictably, was traffic control. The councilmen ordered that bells be placed on horses to warn of their approach, set up stations for carters and drivers, and effectively banned double parking around the market and major hotels. The council also used its new authority to remove animal obstructions from the thoroughfares, issuing a fine of a dollar a day for odiferous hogs left to roam in the streets and a two-dollar fee for depositing "stable

—

manure" in the streets. With mundane acts like these, the city council was acting decisively to shape a dense collection of people into a city. At its April meeting of year one, the Baltimore municipality assumed the authority to "go into the property to assess things as they appear to them will promote the general advantage and prosperity of said city." Confident of their authority to intrude onto the private property of the inhabitants of Baltimore, the councilmen delegated a variety of powers to the appointed board of street commissioners. "Five persons of known integrity, discretion and knowledge" were authorized to "consult together respecting what streets, or parts of streets, lanes or alleys, are or ought to be paved." In a very palpable way, by patrolling the spaces of the city and penetrating into the everyday lives of the citizenry, the elected leaders of Baltimore were crafting an independent, self-governing, if not entirely autonomous, municipal polity, all this within a few weeks of being granted a charter by the State of Maryland.[5]

By the dawn of the nineteenth century, the city government was at work deepening the harbor, building a public wharf, placing hundreds of lamps upon the expanding network of paved streets, and building a new market hall, with offices for the mayor and council members on the third floor. Such projects brought the cost of city-building home to the citizenry in the black-and-white figures of the municipal budget. Appropriations for the year 1800 included $3,000 for the harbor, $11,000 for lighting the streets, and $2,000 for street cleaning and the elimination of nuisances. The municipality collected revenue by a variety of means: a $10,000 lottery for general city expenses, a special assessment to abutting owners of repaired streets, and a tax on merchant vessels to be used for deepening the harbor.[6] Another routine source of income came to the city through fines and licenses. That urban amenity, "a copious and permanent supply of clean wholesome water," was delivered by way of another standard method of urban improvement, a private-public partnership. The city contracted with private companies and authorized them to perform municipal services for a price. Finally, there was a bottom line to the cost of building a city, direct taxation of the citizens, which accounted for 27 percent of the city budget. The Baltimore tax collector assessed movable as well as real property, carriages as well as building lots, churches as well as private mansions, even libraries and wine closets. The tax rate was high in the third decade of the nineteenth century, second only to the city of Boston, 75 rather than 82 cents per $100 of property.[7]

The elite leadership of the city corporation operated as ally and analogue of private associations. Both the Mayor's Office and the city council were presided over by prominent merchants accustomed to using acts of incorporation to do both public and private business. Members of the Mechanical Society monopolized the mayoralty and dominated the council. The roster of city officials was flush with the directors of banks and insurance companies, all issued corporate charters by the State of Maryland. When it came to meeting vital public needs like dredging the harbor, lighting the streets, or supplying water, the elite members of the council resorted to the same legal mechanism, teaming up with a private corporation to do the public business. The public and private corporations were legally homologous, and their membership was overlapping. Both were tools for molding the land and waters along the Chesapeake into an urban network that carried goods from the port to the hinterland, keeping the arteries of commerce open and flowing with profits.[8]

Public merged with private in the elite city corporation, and it was difficult to disentangle one from the other either spatially or economically. The integration of the two sectors became concrete and visible at one particular place on the map of the city, the public market. The founders of the port along the Patapsco built the first marketplace even before they had secured a city charter. Within a few years of incorporation, the city had spawned two more public markets and remodeled the first into an elegant three-story structure strategically located near the intersection of the Basin and Jones Falls. Marketplaces were established according to the collective initiative of citizens and neighbors. Farmers brought perishable foodstuffs to the city and sold them at the public markets, where shoppers purchased them and carried them to nearby homes. As the population spread out from the harbor along the public streets, neighbors began sending petitions to the city council, with page after page of signatures, begging for new markets closer to their places of residence. By 1820, Baltimore boasted no less than seven market halls. The public market provided a spatial anchor of social life, routinely bringing people together as they procured the most basic sustenance of life. The Central Market was one of the fondest artifacts in the memory of Baltimore's premier city booster, John H. B. Latrobe; his watercolor of the Central Market pictured the city as a colorful amalgam of brightly dressed people, of white and dark complexions, all pressed up against one another in a narrow commercial but public space.[9]

The city fathers of Baltimore assumed that private commerce would be funneled into these public and regulated marketplaces. One of the first city ordinances specified that all trade should take place in this circumscribed

—

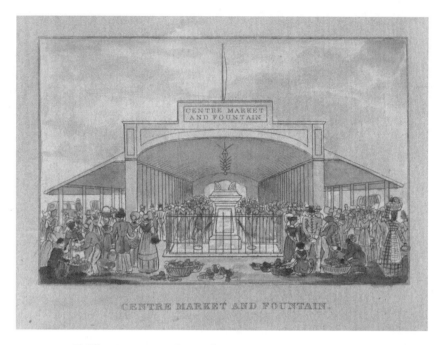

Fielding Lucas Jr., Baltimore's Centre Market, 1836, colored by
John H. B. Latrobe, 1842. Courtesy of the John Work Garrett Library,
Sheridan Libraries, Johns Hopkins University.

territory, along rows of stalls, lined up together, bounded by intersecting streets, and rented out by the city. The municipal statute read simply and categorically that goods brought into the city could not be sold "at any other place but at or in one of the aforesaid market houses, under penalty of $5 fine." Municipal control of commerce entailed licensing for nearly every vendor in the market and the inspection of nearly every commodity that passed through the city. The city corporation regulated the sale of a staggering volume and variety of local consumer goods: meat and fish, pork and herring, potash and coal ash, butter and lard, sweet potatoes and limes, plaster of Paris, turpentine, hay and tobacco, beans and hides. Inspectors stationed at the docks put the city seal on the grain shipped abroad. In sum, the public markets of Baltimore followed in the Anglo American tradition of municipal regulation long ingrained in the mercantilist economies of city corporations.[10]

The City of Baltimore enforced regulation outside the market halls as well. The municipal records expressed this principle of political economy as the necessity of monitoring the relations of "buyers and sellers." The quint-essential municipal regulation was the assize of bread. The 1802 statute set the standard size of a loaf at "1 lb. 8 ounces, unadulterated." Should a baker be found cheating, he would be fined twenty dollars, half of which went to the informer, the other half to the city. Not everyone in Baltimore honored this relic of the moral economy. As early as 1803, the city council heard reports that "the ordinance to regulate the sale of bread I fear has been evaded by many of the bakers." In 1808, the city bakers formally petitioned the mayor for a modification of the assize of bread, citing the more liberal practices of other cities. In response, the mayor wondered whether "a better system [might] be adopted which may not infringe the rights of the Trade, and may at the same time protect the purchaser of this essential article of life from imposition." In all probability, the mayor and councilmen listened carefully to the bakers' petitions; their trade association was a prominent city constituency, one that marched proudly in the parade that celebrated the US Constitution in 1789. Bakers and councilmen squabbled over the assize of bread for the next thirty years, but the first and the second branches of the council could not agree to suspend it. With its population steeply rising, the city simply appointed more and more bread inspectors, and increased their visits from once a month to once a week.[11]

Long after the institution was moribund in New York and Philadelphia, Baltimore's public market maintained its central place, both as a physical space and as a tenet of political economy. The merchants at the helm of the city corporation may have been a small elite, but they strove to keep market forces under strict public control. Citizens as well as leaders adhered to the principle of public regulation of the relations between buyers and sellers. One citizen invoked this principle when a soap and candle factory sent noxious odors into his neighborhood. He presented his grievance to the city council in these words: "I consider your laws protecting me from evil." The active citizenry of Baltimore held one another and their representative to the standard of the commonweal, what the first meeting of the council heralded as "the general good of the inhabitants," their "general advantages and prosperity."

Municipal governance would seem to be on a sound footing in March 1801 when the city council appointed commissioners and authorized them to begin assembling the materials and hiring the workers to construct a place for itself on the urban landscape, a city hall. To defray the cost, the council authorized a fifteen-shilling increase in direct taxation and specified that it

---

would extend year after year until the whole project was complete and the city budget was in the black. In the meantime, the city commissioners were instructed to "procure a suitable house" in which the councilmen could meet. A cryptic passage in the minutes of the city council suggested that some of their constituents were reluctant to make a civic investment as extravagant as building a city hall. The council dismissed this protest, asserting, "It must be well known that procuring out-door signatures, to petitions or other papers, does not always show the sense of the majority being frequently obtained more through personal influence of those handing them about and [more] from their industry and exertion than from a deliberative view of the subject matter contained in them." The Baltimore City Council resisted such citizen protests, holding to the "deliberative view" of municipal government, best conducted within the elite chambers of the municipal legislature. Nonetheless, the city council's ambitious plans were stalled: the ordinance to fund a city hall was rescinded in 1807, leaving the city council to meet in rented quarters until after the Civil War. This and many other projects were delayed at least until certain questions about the proper political foundation for erecting a city had been resolved.[12]

The original charter laid a conservative foundation for city government. By the second decade of the nineteenth century, the members of the municipal corporation, most of them merchants meeting in their borrowed quarters, had supervised the building of a physical platform for rapid urban growth: the streets, bridges, wharves, harbors, and marketplaces that would support the growing city. They had done so without many substantial public institutions or much coercive governmental power. The ad hoc, voluntary practices of the town—the citizen-soldiers, the voluntary firefighters, and vigilant citizen oversight along with a private water company—continued to provide the modus vivendi for keeping order and providing public services. The small scale of the city government gave an immediacy and accessibility to urban affairs. Citizens of modest means found easy access to their elite representatives: each councilman was a neighbor in one of the city's eight wards, serving approximately 3,500 people. Ordinary men and women flooded the Mayor's Office and the city council chambers with their petitions, opinions, and demands for representation. Engaged in the common project of building a city, they became practiced in civic initiative. Erecting a city on the land taken from Algonquian tribes and British colonizers was a daunting but also an energizing political experiment.[13]

But not everyone endorsed the original terms of incorporation. In January

1794, an anonymous citizen expressed his objections to issuing a charter on the terms suggested by the city elite. The widely circulated broadside, signed "Fellow Citizen," spoke "to the Citizens of Baltimore Town" in a new political vernacular. Fellow Citizen reprimanded the Maryland General Assembly for violating multiple republican principles: by entrusting Baltimore's affairs to appointed commissioners who served for life, they were showing indifference to "the rights of election and rotation in office" and assuming "power of so extraordinary a nature, as to excite astonishment." Fellow Citizen dismissed the conservative restrictions on office-holding in the proposed charter as a *"foreign precedent,* formed when the rights of representative government were little known, or but little regarded." In place of the aristocratic authority of government prescribed by the General Assembly, Fellow Citizen would install a municipal legislature "chosen by the people at large" and inclusive of "the merchants, as mechanic, to the honest man who lives by his labour as him who can live honestly without labour." These were precocious assertions of democratic principles, reaching beyond the staid republicanism espoused in Annapolis. Having exercised their political muscles by building a town and repelling the British, the workingmen of Baltimore were not about to withdraw from the public sphere. They became the mainstay of the first prototypes of partisan politics, called "Republican Societies."[14]

The ink was hardly dry on the city charter when the citizens of Baltimore began to assault its conservative clauses. After a decade of popular pressure, the elite leaders succumbed to the proponents of a more democratic polity. Conceding that the restrictions on political participation had proven "inconvenient in their operation and repugnant to the wishes of a great portion of the inhabitants of Baltimore," the city council forwarded to Annapolis a petition to end property requirements for holding public office. The Assembly reduced the cost of serving as mayor or council member by half and soon removed it entirely. The voting population became a larger and more diverse constituency when the Assembly ended property restrictions on voting and holding office. Catholics finally secured the right to vote with the Revolution. Were it up to the local citizens, Baltimore's capacious public sphere would have also opened the franchise and public offices to non-Christians; Baltimore began lobbying to grant full citizenship to Jews in 1802. When that right was finally conceded by the state in 1826, the city voters promptly elected two Jews to the city council. When the residency requirement was reduced from a year to a mere six months, the polling places of Baltimore filled up with the foreign born. On election day, voters filed into taverns

—

and onto street corners in each of the city's eight wards, where they could now cast secret ballots. Baltimore residents of African descent also claimed the right to representation, but a racial restriction on the right to vote was imposed in 1810, an omen that the path to democracy in America would not be open to all men, much less any women.[15]

DEMOCRACY ON TRIAL, 1808–1812

With the reform of the municipal legislature in 1808, city government began to emerge from the cocoon of the original charter and metamorphose into a more broadly representative political system. Democracy was far from pure, however, and translating the principle of political equality into just and efficient municipal practice was not so easy. Democratic governance is a formidable project under the best of circumstances, and Baltimore put it to a severe test early in the nineteenth century. The conflicting interests that conglomerated along the Chesapeake port—those of elite planters, powerful merchants, assertive mechanics and tradesmen, and the mass of laboring poor, slave and free—made Fellow Citizen's democratic project seem wildly utopian. The crowd that gathered around the mouth of the Patapsco in the 1790s was teeming, tempest-tossed, and culturally diverse. The official census figures registered some 8,000 persons in 1790 and counted well more than twice that number—19,269—ten years later, all of them crowded together on a few square acres hugging the shoreline. The ratio between newcomers and residents of just ten years' standing was so small that Baltimore became, to use another colloquial definition of a city, a world of strangers.[16]

The pioneers of Baltimore City were also socially and culturally estranged from one another; no one church, one language, or one set of traditions bound them all together. The first Baltimoreans came from many different parts: the pioneer merchants who hailed from Pennsylvania or Western Maryland jostled with land-starved sons and daughters from the country-side, runaway slaves from nearby plantations, and immigrants streaming in from across the Atlantic. Half of those who disembarked from Europe and arrived on Maryland's shores during the eighteenth century were either convicts or "redemptioners," or indentured servants, bound to labor for those who paid their passage to America. When the other Atlantic port cities were closed to shipping, first during the American Revolution and then in the Napoleonic Wars and a succession of federal trade embargos, Baltimore

Harbor became a major point of disembarkation for immigrants from the British Isles and Western Europe. The Haitian Revolution sent several thousand French speakers, black, white, slave, and free, to Baltimore.[17]

This mixed population was buffeted in the turbulent seas of international politics. Just as the first city government convened in 1797, Britain tightened credit, slowing trade along Baltimore's wharves and putting the city's three novice banks in jeopardy. The embargo imposed on the French a few years later threatened those merchants who were dependent on their Gallic commercial connections with bankruptcy. The Napoleonic Wars subsided, disrupting the livelihoods of those who had formerly profited from the suspension of European competition—merchants, local artisans, and the farmers who brought their wheat to the Baltimore markets. The volatile international economy inflicted misery on the Jack Tars of Fells Point. Two hundred and sixty-nine sailors petitioned Baltimore's mayor for relief in 1808. "By reason of the embargo" they pleaded, they were in "arrears to our Landlords [and] . . . incapable of gaining a support by any other way than by our profession as Seamen."[18]

Strained relations between the people of Baltimore and the newly formed federal government added to the urban tensions. The civic consensus expressed so jubilantly in the parade for the Constitution in 1788 began to dissolve once that document became the actual operating manual for a federated government. The policies of US Treasury Secretary Alexander Hamilton pitted debtors against creditors and domestic manufacturers against international merchants. The Alien and Sedition Acts, and the efforts by the administration of John Adams to drastically increase the time to citizenship, did not win favor among those recently arrived in Baltimore from other shores. By the time Baltimore received its long awaited charter, the citizens of the new nation were divided into two partisan factions, the Federalists and the Jeffersonian Republicans.

Baltimore acquired a reputation as the most strenuously partisan city in the country. It quickly became a stronghold of the rudimentary Jeffersonian party. The Jeffersonian Republicans and their Jacksonian successors would win the majority in nearly every election after 1800. Their newspaper, the *Baltimore American and Commercial Advertiser*, summoned the electorate to barbecues and polling places and berated their Federalist opponents as aristocrats, monarchists, and tyrants.[19] The Federalists, for their part, did not quietly withdraw from the partisan fray. Their presses continued to issue pamphlets warning of "The Evils of Democracy" and fearing that the "uninformed and misguided" citizens would usurp the authority of "the most wise, sensible and discreet of the People." They mourned the loss of the "republican virtuous and experienced Senate" maintained by high property restrictions on the membership in the upper chamber of the city council. The Federalist faction continued to call unapologetically for the retention of this aristocratic element of self-governance, a necessary counterforce to democracy. To an emerging Jeffersonian faction, however, an elite senate or private cabal was an offensive relic of a tyrannical past: "The people desire not an aristocracy nor the appearance or shadow of one," wrote the local republican editor. "They wish for a senate taken from their own body, acquainted with their wants, and willing to provide for them."[20]

Taken to the streets of Baltimore, these ideological differences became virulently personal. The *Federal Gazette* ridiculed Republicans as "respectable maniacs and other citizens making buffoons and laughing-stocks of themselves, merely to gratify the ambitions and flatter the vanity of General Smith." The Smith in question was Samuel Smith, a hero of the Revolution and a onetime Federalist who championed Republican workingmen and rose to the office of US senator. But to the Federalists, he was one of those "pitiful demagogues" who performed "monkey tricks" to win the votes of the "mob," and worse. Smith had "prostituted the dignity of a senator to feed [his] avarice by a dishonorable traffic with the enemy of [his] country." To the Federalists, that enemy was France, with whom the Jeffersonians had allied, thereby making them "Jacobins." The name-calling reverberated through the local press and fervid campaign rallies; the Republicans tarred the Federalists with the label "Tories" and raised their glasses with icy toasts to their opponents: "May the enemies of France be defeated in all their attempts and may thinking brave men of other nations, where monarchy reigns, follow their examples."[21]

Two decades after the Revolution and a dozen years after Baltimore was "erected into a city," fellow citizens were still waging an internecine struggle and defining their political positions in relation to Europe. These disagreements were not just matters for erudite discussion. They were aired in the partisan press and soon spilled out into the streets. In the October election of 1808, the *American* enjoined the "Republicans of Baltimore, to turn out and vote to a man. Arouse yourselves in your might: let your voice be heard across the land and your power be felt at the polls." Newly empowered Republicans were sent to the polls with the warning to be wary of the "tricks of the English faction." Four years later, the partisan rhetoric had only grown shriller. The Republican press threw epithets like "savage," "bloodthirsty," and "Barbarous" at the Federalists, and called the campaign techniques of their rivals "systematic Assassinations of reputation." The Federalists slung mud, and worse, at the Democratic Republicans. They called Senator Smith "the pimp of power" and reduced those who voted for him to harlots. The Federalists likened themselves to the pure and virtuous "Columbia" besieged by a "hideous faction."[22]

By the summer of 1812, this war of words had escalated from bloodthirsty rhetoric to actual bloodshed. Two politically charged deaths on the streets of Baltimore awarded the city its dubious title "mob town." The violence in Baltimore was the first volley in the war that James Madison was about to declare against the British. The prospect of a war with Great Britain outraged the editors of the *Federal-Republican*, whose offices were located on Gay Street just up from the Basin in the Republican stronghold of Baltimore City. When the Federalist press published an editorial opposing the war, the mobilized electorate called them Tories and taunted them with a reference to the revolutionary practice of tarring and feathering. On the evening of June 22, a group of thirty or forty men and boys enacted their political loyalty by systematically dismantling the offices of the *Federal-Republican*. The editors retreated to the countryside and set up shop in a more sympathetic location, the village of Georgetown, but not for long. On June 27, they defiantly returned to Baltimore and installed their presses in rented quarters in the center of the city at 45 Charles Street. They had more than words in their arsenal. The editors were led by the Federalist firebrand and revolutionary general Light-Horse Harry Lee and trailed by a cartload of muskets and a full contingent of armed defenders of freedom of the press. The provocation was too much for the politicized citizenry: a crowd gathered outside the fortified newspaper office taunting and intimidating the occupants. One round of blank cartridges issued from the Federalist fortress did not deter the crowd; a popular leader, an apothecary by the name of Gale, charged the Federalist fortress and was repelled with live ammunition. As Dr. Gale died in the street, the crowd attempted armed retaliation with a "field piece." The revolutionary war was not yet over in Baltimore City. The street warfare would continue through the night. While the body of the ringleader of the belligerent Republican crowd was carried off, the armed band of Federalists suffered their first fatality: the revolutionary war general James Lingan died of a beating he received near the city jail, where he and his comrades had been taken for protective custody. Editor Alexander Hanson and General

Lee survived the mob's assault on the jail but were said to die later as martyrs to the lost Federalist cause.[23]

The hostilities ended after this night of ferocious partisan conflict, but the political fallout would linger for months. The battle resumed in the press, in pamphlets, and in government reports. General Lee seems to have recovered sufficiently by 1814 to issue "A Correct Account of the Conduct of the Baltimore Mob." He opined that the conflict was provoked by "Jacobin Democracy" and abetted by President Madison. Lee's description of the assault on the Baltimore jail reads like partisan pornography. The mob threatened castration, poked at the eyes and the private parts of their partisan protagonists, and threatened to ignite their flesh with hot oil. All these events were accompanied by the taunts of a "band of assassins from Fells Point," who were shouting, "I can kill you."[24] A committee of the House of Delegates promptly mounted an investigation of the riot of 1812 and assembled evidence to support the account of General Lee. In the opinion of the state legislature, the Baltimore riot was the work of the urban rabble of "men, women, boys," "laborers, apprentices, and some craftsmen and sailors," with a good representation of the Irish and the French. Witness after witness came forward to cast the rioters in the image of Baltimore's unruly plebian population that was now intent on purging the city of Tories. By contrast, the defenders of the *Federal-Republican's* bastion on Charles Street presented themselves as "young gentlemen, some from the country, most from the town, of intelligence, good character and devoted to the discharge of a duty to which they were called and in the discharge of which they seemed to glory."[25]

The committee appointed by the Maryland Assembly laid responsibility for the Baltimore riot on the municipal government. They charged city leaders with having coddled the urban rabble and accused the head of the local militia, General John Stricker, and his second-in-command, Major William Barney, of giving their permission to a murderous course "by acting with Great Mildness, patience and forbearance when the offices of the Federal Republicans were first sacked." Major Barney was portrayed as the sniveling abettor of the mob, posing as "their personal and political friend" and pretending "to protect life and property . . . and prevent violence." The leaders of the local militia were accused of shirking their military obligations and preferring to "consult with the people, as they impiously denominated the mob."[26]

The mayor of Baltimore, Edward Johnson, a wealthy brewer who maintained a house in the country, was not so quick to indict his constituents for what he termed "the late unhappy occurrences by which the peace & harmony of our city have been destroyed." He summoned a joint committee of the two branches of the city council to issue a rejoinder to the reprimand from Annapolis. The city's official report presented its case in antiseptic language and lingered over the efforts of the civilian authorities to curb the violence.[27] The elected leaders defended their temperate response to the volatile street scene as the only prudent course in a democratic city. England might have a riot act, they advised the General Assembly, but in the absence of such a statute in Maryland, Major Barney had no right to disperse a public assemblage that had not broken the law. The mayor and the local militiamen relied on time-honored and quintessentially urban tactics of keeping order. According to Mayor Johnson, the proper first response was to "walk among the people" attempting to "quiet their anger." When an irate man raved against "the murdering scoundrels who have come from Montgomery [County] and slaughtered our citizens," the mayor politely introduced himself and informed his fellow citizen of his civic duty "to assist" in keeping public order. The mayor circulated through the crowd, urging restraint and more judicious protest. When the disorder continued late into the night and the next morning, he took more decisive action: he requested that citizens assemble at the office of the city council to form a posse. But neither his call for local assistance nor General Stricker's final activation of the militia brought a sufficient number of men forward to defend the beleaguered Federalists.[28]

In the end, the mayor of Baltimore used customary if ingenious ways to keep urban order. First he arranged to transport the Federalists to jail for protective custody. The crowd agreed to grant safe passage to the jail, but only after exerting their class consciousness by forbidding the haughty gentlemen from riding in carriages. The mayor managed to summon enough responsible citizens to surround the prisoners in a human shield. He took other precautions as well, such as ordering members of the cortege to remove the provocative insignia of the haughty, Federalist-affiliated Society of the Cincinnati from their garments. Mayor Johnson then stepped inside the "hollow square" surrounding the prisoners, exposing himself to "the fury and indignation of an incensed populous." The leaders of Baltimore shunned military tactics and preferred to use old-fashioned ways of keeping order on the city streets. When the state investigative committee asked Baltimore's legal counsel, John Purviance, about the wisdom of calling up the state militia, he demurred, in deference to republican suspicion of a standing army, what he described as "the jealousy, which the spirit of our government constantly inculcates, of the interference of the military with civil authority."[29]

The Federalist opposition was not so scrupulous about the use of force. They brought "plenty of buckshot," along with muskets, bayonets, and "good pistol," to the office of the rival newspaper. General Lee "armed [his men] with muskets" and ordered them "to fire on the rear of the mob." "Rather than be taken in an ignominious way," he said, "they should use the few pistols in their possession to take the offense." In sum, Harry Lee, a staunch Federalist, who had led the faction's campaign against other popular movements, including the Whiskey Rebellion in Pennsylvania, and who traveled to the defense of the *Federal-Republican* from his home in Virginia, was clearly still fighting a war against ideological opponents who had established themselves in Baltimore City. If history had stopped along the shores of the Chesapeake in 1812, the future of democracy in Baltimore might have been forestalled: either dissolved in urban chaos, checked by militarized federalism, or devolving into the tyranny of the majority. Neither the old culture of deference to elite leaders nor the intimacy and solidarity of the republican town could contain the furious partisanship and conflicting class interests that roiled Baltimore on the eve of the War of 1812. Neither the comfort of hindsight, nor a complacent faith in the US Constitution, nor historical bromides—such as "era of good feelings"—were yet available to calm the political strife. It might seem that the experiment in urban democracy was about to come crashing to an early and ignominious end.[30]

Events in the city of Baltimore in the summer of 1812 exposed a raw and tattered seam in the constitution of the infant republic of the United States. The 1812 riot pitted two levels of sovereignty, state and municipal, against one another, each with a very different constituency, the planters in the Maryland House of Deputies, and the obstreperous electorate of the city of Baltimore. As for the "General Government" based in Washington, DC, it played an offstage role, fanning the partisan flames of opposition between Federalists and Jeffersonian Republicans. Furthermore, the volatility of governance in the city along the shore of the Chesapeake Bay played out in turbulent international waters. There was no certainty that the war that James Madison declared against Great Britain in 1812 would stabilize the young republic of the United States.

DEMOCRACY IN TRIUMPH: FROM MOB TOWN TO MONUMENTAL CITY, 1812–1825

In the summer of 1812 there was little time to contemplate the conundrums of multiple sovereignty and national integrity. When war broke out with

Great Britain on the eve of the Baltimore riot, the battle lines were drawn within a few miles of the scrappy city astride the Patapsco. In August 1814, the White House, the United States Capitol, and other federal buildings were in flames. President Madison had taken flight, and only a thunderstorm saved the rest of the nation's capital from the conflagration. The British had every reason to expect that the small city of Baltimore would fall as well, and what's more, they had a strategy to ensure that it did. They set off on a two-pronged attack on the city, one flank coming by land and the other advancing up the Chesapeake.[31]

In this time of emergency, the local militia came with alacrity to the nation's defense. Samuel Smith accepted the commission to head the state militia, and John Stricker commanded some three thousand soldiers called up to repel the British land forces approaching just to the north of the city. Aided by a bullet to the commanding British general and a drenching rainstorm, the Baltimore regiment stalled the British land attack. The defense against the Royal Navy was to require a more complex municipal mobilization. Already in February 1814, Mayor Johnson of Baltimore had penned a testy message to Washington bemoaning the failure of the federal government to provide funds to defend the city. The mayor had proceeded to form a Committee of Public Supply composed of seven men, who in turn called for the election of four delegates from each ward. That broadly representative body had voted unanimously to borrow $500,000. They accompanied their resolution with the request that the state "impose an equal and general tax on all real and personal property" to meet the national and local emergency.[32]

When Annapolis did not accede to the request, Mayor Johnson, taking direction from the grassroots of the wards, requested assistance from local bankers. He was pleased to report that "the several monied institutions of our city, with liberality highly honorable to them, have offered to loan any reasonable sum, that the present exigency may require." (The liberality did not extend to forgiving the substantial interest on that loan.) Fifteen hundred city residents endorsed the pledge of the Committee of Public Supply to repay the loan, expecting that the federal government would eventually reimburse them and the city. These dutiful citizens were said to include many wealthy individuals who would suffer an especially onerous tax burden in order to defend Baltimore City. Less affluent citizens lent their labor rather than monies to the city's defense; all able-bodied males not in arms, including slaves and free persons of color, were ordered to work on the construction of fortifications, designed by Samuel Smith. Local musicians held benefits to raise additional funds, while women rolled bandages and sewed colored bunting into the large flag that would wave over the ramparts of the Chesapeake at Fort McHenry (it measured forty-two by thirty feet). The mayor congratulated the people of Baltimore for their civic exertions, proof that the partisan rancor of 1812 had been "swallowed up in a sense of the common danger," adding, "There is a public spirit and vigor existing in our citizens which will cause them to endure privations, to submit to every sacrifice which may be required to enable them to meet and repel any attempt of our implacable foe."[33]

The militia stopped the British advance up the Chesapeake on September 12, 1814, and the city of Baltimore has basked in the glory ever since. Francis Scott Key, who watched as the militiamen withstood the twenty-four-hour bombardment of Fort McHenry, wrote some stanzas to commemorate that night. They were set in type by a local printer, put to the music of an English drinking ballad, and sung in taverns around Fells Point and the Basin. The anthem that debuted at Baltimore's Holiday Street Theatre soon became a national chorus and began to drown out memories of "mob town." The people of Baltimore made haste to memorialize their civic triumph not just in sonorous words but also in towering marble. Within a year, they had laid the cornerstones for two lofty monuments, one dedicated to George Washington and the second to "the brave men who fell at Northpoint . . . Forgetting all party dissension and private animosities, discarding all feeling but those of patriots, husbands, fathers and brothers."[34]

The civic effort that turned mob town into "the Monumental City," as President John Quincy Adams would dub it, began immediately after the conclusion of the War of 1812. On July 4, 1815, the city gathered to break ground for the nation's first monument to George Washington. A few weeks later, on September 12, the first anniversary of the Battle of North Point, the citizenry assembled just a few blocks away to lay the cornerstone of what they called the Battle Monument. The first monumental project was initiated in 1809, just after the city remodeled its charter in a more demo- cratic fashion. To raise a statue of Washington was a retaliatory gesture, honoring a Federalist icon. The ceremony that broke ground for the Wash- ington Monument had a rather patrician air. It was designed to champion virtue and sobriety and to "let the citizen remember, that our chief bowed to the supremacy of the laws, and gloried in rendering prompt obedience to the voice of constituted authority." A member of the board of managers of the monument committee, John Comegys, injected a more prosaic theme into the ceremonies. He envisioned Washington's marble embodiment presiding over the "improvement of agriculture; to the extension of commerce, who now spreads her sails over every sea and from the outermost parts of the earth from Baltimore harbor."[35]

The invocation of commerce spreading out from Baltimore Harbor was not far from the minds of those who campaigned to erect the Washington Monument. Of the twenty-three managers of the monument who can be identified, fourteen were merchants, three were attorneys, one an artisan turned wealthy manufacturer, and another a ship captain who claimed the title of "gentleman." Of the remainder, only three were humbler storekeepers and craftsmen. Most of these elite citizens had business addresses on the wharf or along Baltimore Street and demonstrated the associated financial acumen. They were not philanthropists, however; they did not contribute their own funds to monument building. Rather, they incorporated as a lottery company and sold shares, which were in rather large denominations, costing a minimum of $10. The investment tempted customers as far away as New York City to purchase as many as $50,000 worth of tickets for resale at a profit.[36]

While some of the same elite Baltimoreans promoted the Battle Monument, the second civic project was managed in a more popular manner. The broadly representative Committee of Vigilance and Safety that had defended the city in 1814 initiated the monument campaign. Its membership reached down into the ranks of manual workers, all self-proclaimed partisans of "honest homespun democracy." The Baltimore City Council contributed what remained in the war fund to the project. Rather than organizing a lottery, the overseers of the Battle Monument solicited contributions from their fellow citizens and to that end sent agents into every ward and precinct of the city. The ward representatives included a cordwainer, a saddler, a tanner, a grocer, a watchmaker, a coppersmith, a carpenter, a cabinetmaker, and several bricklayers. This relatively plebian group came up with a strategy for building democracy into the very foundation of public sculpture. They specified that no contribution should exceed $5. The Republican press made the intent of this condition clear: the Battle Monument was not to be "an ostentatious memorial, for wealth will not be allowed to exert its prerogative of superior liberality; but . . . the proudest and patriotic proof of unanimity of sentiment, which united all in a duty so solemn, so pleasing." Accordingly, the subscription book, a copy of which was buried in the cornerstone of the monument, listed each contributor by name, including that of Charles Carroll

—

himself, valued at no more than $5. The democratic spirit was performed as well as documented. Subscribers were invited into the Mayor's Office to make their contributions and sign the registry, bringing women as well as men into the seat of local government. Once the cornerstone was laid, the subscribers were invited to march in procession through the streets of the city.[37]

Two monuments, put forward by different factions and grounded in different political philosophies, projected competing civic identities on the city skyline. Land was broken for the first work of public art on July 4, 1815. The orator of the day imagined a massive column surrounded by classic deities bowing down before the figure of Washington, who would be "muscular and robust . . . the fierceness of his countenance inspire[ing] Despotism with terror." The design of the monument was delegated to a young architect of Charleston, South Carolina, who won a competition sponsored by the monument managers. Robert Mills puzzled over how to best memorialize the nation's first president. His first draft for the monument planted a statue of Washington atop a pillar raised high above the urban landscape, but he did not stop there.[38] He envisioned a whole retinue of ordinary Americans scaling the classic column: a blacksmith, a preacher, domestic servants, Indians, and a slave. Letting his political imagination run far beyond the conservative limits of the monument's sponsors, Mills etched the figure of a slave receiving "a written grant of manumission, inscribed, Freedom," presented by Washington "with his own hand." Mills's capacious vision of American citizenship also welcomed the common people within the space of the monument itself. He designed a stairway inside the column that would permit citizens to rise to the top, wind around Washington's pedestal, and view the chronicle of popular democracy sculpted there. Representations of such diversity threatened to overwhelm the Apollonian icon of Washington. By 1815, Republican sentiment and symbolism had insinuated itself even into the plans to erect a monument to the Federalist idol.

As one might expect, the architect chosen for the Battle Monument would give even more play to democratic symbols. The commission to design the memorial to the soldiers who defended the city in 1814 went to a French-born architect, J. Maximilian Godefroy, who offered his services without charge. Like the members of the Democratic-Republican Societies of Baltimore, Godefroy maintained his allegiance to the French Republic. A refugee from Napoleon, he was not a fan of monumental sculptural homages to chiefs of state; there would be no equestrian statue like those in Paris's Place de la Concorde atop the plinth of the Battle Monument. Godefroy chose neither

Robert Mills's illustration of the Washington Monument, Elevation of the Principal Fronts, *1813. Courtesy of the Maryland Historical Society.*

a single figure of authority nor a lofty column as the way to commemorate Baltimore's triumph in the War of 1812. Instead he designed a rusticated Egyptian base and inscribed it with scenes from the Battle of North Point, including the death of General Robert Ross, which was guaranteed to please the Anglophobes of Baltimore City. Above this patriotic base Godefroy raised a squat, sturdy pillar, a symbol of civic solidarity. At the top he posed a classic female figure to represent the city itself. The locals soon dubbed it Lady

Design for the Battle Monument, engraved by B. Tanner, after Maximilian Godefroy, architect, 1828. Courtesy of the Maryland Historical Society.

Baltimore. The most inventive and startlingly democratic feature of the Battle Monument was the one wound around the pillar: bands of marble bearing the names not of kings, presidents, or generals, but of the ordinary men who died defending the city in the War of 1812. Not until after the Civil War would other cities memorialize ordinary American soldiers in marble.[39]

Hardly a year after war's end and three years after a brutal fratricidal battle in the city streets, the united citizens of Baltimore had broken ground for two impressive civic apparitions. Lady Baltimore was installed at the top of the Battle Monument in 1822. The marble Washington was lifted up to its perch in 1829, a simple column, cleansed of Mills's elaborate representations of democracy found in his first sketch. It was the Battle Monument that the people of Baltimore took into their hearts. The City Council christened that precocious symbol of civic democracy, and not the lofty column honoring Washington, as the official Baltimore Monument, and embossed its image on the seal of the city. (Today it is plastered on everything from police cars to recycling bins.) Godefroy's monument also won pride of place in urban space. The Washington Monument was erected outside the city limits, on the private plantation of John Eager Howard. The Battle Monument was placed in front of the courthouse in the heart of the city, where it would anchor the municipality politically as well as symbolically. The space around the Battle Monument, formerly known as Washington Square, was renamed Monument Square; it served as a regular place for the population to gather for town meetings, election rallies, and public celebrations. Democracy took a stand in the streets and squares of Baltimore, subduing aristocracy and dissolving municipal warfare in proud celebration.

While the citizens of Baltimore would bask in the glory of their monuments for the next decade, they also displayed their civic spirit in more routine but also more costly ways. The city's revered citizen-soldier, Samuel Smith, begged the federal government, to no avail, to reimburse Baltimore for funding the defense of the city and the nation in the War of 1812. Municipal expenses did not subside after the war. As the bill for lighting the city and paving the streets rose to six figures, the city had to borrow from Baltimore's infant banks to pay its debts. The specter of increasing municipal debt did not detour the mayor or the city council from the path of "improvement." In 1818, when the State of Maryland acceded to the city's request to raise the tax rate, the council levied an increasing burden of taxation on all propertied citizens in the city. Setting the tax rate was the first order of municipal business each year, and the city council regularly added additional assessments: the school tax, the poor tax, and appropriations for special projects. If city leaders are to be believed, the pioneering generation of Baltimore taxpayers bent relatively easily under this burden. Mayors regularly praised citizens for both their generosity and the "cheerful" manner in which they paid their tax bills. The Finance Committee, newly created by the city council in order to cope with the increasing volume of revenue streaming in and out of the treasury, expressed confidence that a tax increase

> will be cordially approved and cheerfully paid by our constituents. A liberal
> and enlightened community does not require to be told that multiplying

---

and increasing concerns of a populous and enterprising city cannot be carried on, its peace and safety faithfully protected and its interest and prospect wisely promoted without the expenditure of considerable sums.[40]

The committee report placed only two conditions on the proposed tax increase: "It is sufficient our constituents should be satisfied, that the imposition of taxes is as equal as circumstances will admit and the proceeds thereof are fairly and honestly applied." The pioneer leadership of Baltimore rushed to exercise the municipal prerogative of taxation by imposing hefty assessments on property owners, including themselves. Though not a progressive tax per se, Baltimore's system of generating public revenue exempted the propertyless and exacted particularly large sums from the affluent. Exemptions from taxation on real or personal property were hard to come by: in early Baltimore, the tax collector visited private clubs, even churches and charities. All told, the tax bill for Baltimore property holders came to a tidy sum.[41]

THE STREETS: THE MUNDANE SPACES OF DEMOCRACY

The erection of a city along the Patapsco required civic investment in spaces more prosaic than the new monuments. The lofty sculptures embellished the more mundane process of building urban infrastructure. To call the site of the Battle Monument a square was something of an exaggeration; it was just a slightly swollen section of Calvert Street between Saratoga and Lexington. In fact, the ordinary street is a more apt spatial synecdoche for the rise of democracy in Baltimore. The complicated process of opening, paving, and repairing streets began immediately after the incorporation of the city and continued uninterrupted through the American Revolution, the riot of 1812, and long after. It helps explain why the erection of the Battle Monument was not an anomalous expression of democracy. Streets, lanes, and alleys served as the essential physical infrastructure on which a democratic political culture was built, block by block, in the late eighteenth and early nineteenth centuries.

The shape of the city—both its boundaries and its interstices—was unclear when the city received its charter. Then, within weeks of securing a charter, the city council took determined action in order to shape the contours of the municipality. They commissioned "a correct survey" that "would be a great security for the property of the inhabitants." The council's ambitious intentions to survey the city with the accuracy of a compass and "the ascertainment of a meridional line" would not come to fruition for more than a quarter century. In the meantime, citizens appealed in vain for a survey that would firmly establish the basic coordinates of their property. As one petitioner put it, they awaited the "opportunity of seeing the situation on the maps of the city, and of ascertaining prior to . . . improvement if the location [of his property] was correct and if there were conflicting claims."[42]

Some years later the City Council did commission a rough municipal map. It was drawn by Jehu Bouldin, who did a brisk business platting private lots and marking off the prominent intersections of Baltimore with stones placed along the waterways, or by reference to the names of nearby property owners. His sketch of the city featured straight lines up from the harbor, along the Jones Falls, and crisscrossing the city at odd angles. He pictured nine turnpikes jutting out from the Basin that oriented Baltimore in

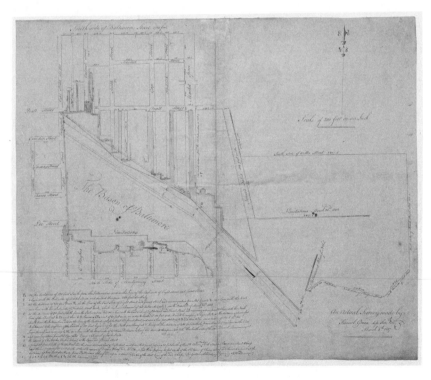

Jehu Bouldin, Plat of the Basin, ca. 1817. Cartographic Records, BRG 12-4.
Courtesy of the Baltimore City Archives.

---

relation to other towns and cities: Havre de Grace, Philadelphia, Frederick, and Washington. Baltimore's master surveyor described the focal point of his map as "commencing at the center of a stone placed at the end of [a] line drawn magnetically North one mile and half from the Centre of Baltimore and Calvert Street as on the south side of which stone is the following inscription: act to enlarge the city in 1817." Bouldin left the territory within these blunt lines a vast open space, interrupted only by a small hatch mark along the shore of the Patapsco. In another map, he filled in the nucleus of the Chesapeake hinterland with a sketch of streets that stretched into wharves at the Baltimore Basin. Bouldin finished off this map with a flourish of blue watercolor.

These rather fanciful surveys were not replaced with anything resembling an urban plan until 1822, when the surveyor Thomas Poppleton presented the council with a drawing of a grid of streets that filled in the open space within the boundary lines Bouldin had drawn. The "Poppleton Plan," enlarged and expanded, would provide the major blueprint for the development of the city as late as the 1880s. In 1836, the street commissioners informed the city council of the "great importance to the city" of Poppleton's map, adding the somewhat wistful admission that it was "the only guide for the commissioners in the establishment of boundaries."[43] To call Poppleton's handiwork an urban plan, or even a proper survey, was an exaggeration. In awarding the $900 contract to Poppleton, the city council had bypassed the experienced surveyor Jehu Bouldin and his sons, Alexander and Owen, who had been measuring out parcels of the bay shore by metes and bounds for decades. These discreet measurements, identified by the name of a single property owner, or sometimes "authorized by the city commissioners," were the primary ways of giving a composite shape to the city in its formative years. Poppleton's plan grouped these urban fragments together into one rather misshapen diagram.[44]

Before there was a town or city, the scattered parcels and plantations mapped by individual surveyors like the Bouldins were linked together by the natural tissue of the shoreline and the creeks and rivers—"runs" and "falls" in the local vernacular. Late in the eighteenth century, the Maryland General Assembly authorized the construction of the roads sketched on Bouldin's maps, the rare public arteries that would link the scattered private properties with one another. The state assembly passed an "Act relating to Public roads" in 1794 and taxed property holders three shillings for the service, payable in labor as well as currency. As was customary, the property

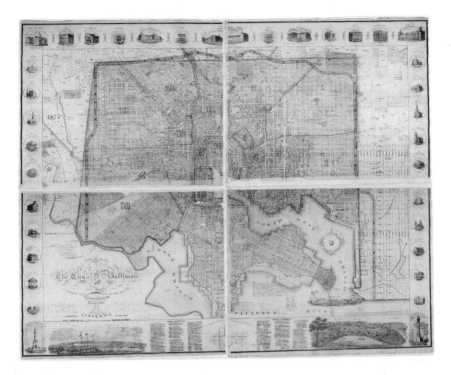

The Poppleton Plan, first drawn around the lots near the Patapsco shoreline in 1822; it was still the basis of plotting urban expansion into the 1880s. Baltimore City Sheet Maps Collection. Courtesy of the Sheridan Libraries, Johns Hopkins University.

owners would retain title to the land midway through the road. If roads provided a transportation link through the agricultural hinterland, the street was the characteristic integument of the city. The only references to "streets" in the catalog of the Acts of the Assembly were in reference to Baltimore, first the town and then the city. The General Assembly regularly authorized the first town commissioners to lay out specific "Streets, Lanes, Lotts and Alleys" to form a "Correct Platt."[45]

What would ultimately hold this assemblage of properties physically together was Baltimore's fabled network of "streets, lanes and alleys," three conjoined words that echo through the municipal records to this very day. Once the city charter was granted, the Baltimore City Council immediately appointed its own street commissioners, whom they "authorized and required" to assume the "full power and authority" to ascertain "the lines of any

---

of the streets, lanes and alleys, or any boundary of any of the lots with the said city." The new street commissioners took to the assignment with gusto. In the year 1801–1802, fully thirty of the forty-two city ordinances were devoted to the subject of streets, lanes, or alleys. The founders of Baltimore marked off commercial arteries on water as well as land. One atlas drawn up by the port wardens extended the line of streets leading to the Basin into the water along a parallel set of wharves. Another map laid out streets along the Jones Falls in straight fifty-foot-wide thoroughfares. Surveyors aligned the streets around individual properties, including such quaint landmarks as "William Ross's new brick Kitchen," or "forty seven feet nine inches from the front of John Carrere's three story Brick House."[46]

Laying out a street was the quintessential act in the creation of urban space along the Chesapeake. Rural Maryland was a loose web of natural landmarks, private parcels, and plantations. The colonial towns along the Patapsco—Jonestown, Fells Point, and Baltimore Town—were composed of little more than an aggregation of lots drawn and numbered by land speculators. Erecting the city of Baltimore was another kind of spatial production. As recorded in the municipal records, it was the achievement of countless property owners who gave up their private land to create "a public Highway, for ever." To open a street, as a typical document in the records of commissioners phrased it, was to agree to "convey to the City of Baltimore as a public Highway forever all the aforesaid piece or parcel of ground . . . for the use of the City."[47]

The text accompanying a ruling of the city commissioners that opened a street between Franklin Lane and Jones Falls in 1799 made the stakes of the enterprise explicit: "And the streets shall ever thereafter be deemed and *taken*, and are hereby established and declared to be public streets of the city of Baltimore" (emphasis mine). Another record put the process of street-making in the words of the property holders: "We the subscribers Proprietors of a Piece of parcel of ground, situated, lying and being in the City of Baltimore, Do hereby *give up all our right, Title, Interest and claim to the said piece of ground,* known by the name of Union Alley, unto the corporation of the said City as a public Highway, for Ever, agreeably to the annexed Plat" (emphasis mine). To open a street like Union Alley required citizens to surrender their property in order to create public space. The amount of property forfeited may have been minuscule, but the meaning was historic: it was a matter of giving back rather than *taking* the land.[48]

To make a street was a complex and collective process. By ceding a small fraction of land in front of their households to the street commissioners, the unsung inhabitants of Baltimore created those ribbons of public space that joined plats of private property into a functioning city. These mundane city-builders might be as august as Charles Carroll or as humble as those who signed their petitions with a mark. Together they wedged public space between the lines of private homes, creating places where all sorts of people could come together for all sorts of purposes. The border between public and private so elusive to political theorists, and murky as a point of law, acquired a decisive, legible, and material form on the streets of Baltimore early in the nineteenth century.[49]

The property owner's responsibility did not end once a street was opened. Those whose property lined the newly opened streets were also held liable for their repair and paving. The city charter foisted two-thirds of the cost of street maintenance onto the abutting neighbors. This procedure, and this ratio of costs, was a convention of Anglo American city corporations, and before that the practice of London burghers. Activated in the new cities of the American republic, it had the effect of endowing the streets themselves with democratic possibilities. The civic project of street paving bloated the municipal record books with long, complicated ordinances and tedious regulations. The street commissioners were required to make the times and places of their meetings public and give extended notices of their decisions. After meeting onsite with the citizens who petitioned for street improvements, and hearing any objections to the project and its cost, the street commissioners were admonished to proceed "in such manner as may be in their judgment and opinion the most likely to promote equal justice between the parties concerned." Street ordinances, in sum, instructed both citizens and city officials in the politics of consent, collaboration, accountability, and "equal justice."[50]

A modest map drawn up by Bouldin in 1807 exemplifies these unwieldy procedures. He labeled his handiwork the outcome of an act of the General Assembly intended "to quiet the possession and fix the lines of the lots of ground fronting the west side of Philpot streets between Wills Street and Thames Street." The property owners, four men and six women residing near the docks in Fells Point, agreed to his survey, and had most likely initiated the process. Two years later Bouldin registered another survey drawn along Philpot Street. It was endorsed by the signatures of men and women who expressed their "agreement and ascent to the said Lots and parcels of ground being held in the Manner located on the Plat made out at the instance of

———

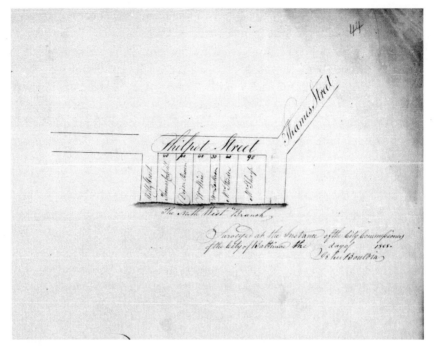

Street commissioners' map of Philpot Street, 1807. Cartographic Records,
BRG 12-2-2-18. Courtesy of the Baltimore City Archives.

the said Commissioners." Finally, the collective process of street-making
was entered in the "Register of the City of Baltimore there to remain in
perpetuity." The opening and repair of every street, even one as humble as
Philpot Street, convened a segment of the public into being and compelled
neighbors to form a consensus, most often a two-thirds majority. The collective decision was often contested by the minority, such as one angry citizen
who wrote to the city council in 1804 "aggrieved by the Tax for opening
Second Street," and another who protested being "taxed and made liable for
a sum of Money surpassing any advantages or conveniences which we have
derived from them." The aggrieved property owners, their protest heard,
were obliged to submit to majority rule.[51]

While the franchise of the streets extended only to property owners, the
tiny lots along Philpot Street did not come at a great cost. Some editions of
the ordinances invited tenants as well as property owners to be consulted

—

about street paving. The wishes of the illiterate were counted as equal to those of their educated neighbors. Signatures on petitions to the street commissioners were often signed with a mark. The democratization of the streets advanced apace with the expansion of suffrage, and in some ways went beyond it.[52] Unlike access to the electoral franchise, there were no blanket and explicit racial or gender exceptions to property rights. Therefore, widows and other women who held title to even a small plot could represent themselves before the street commission. The ranks of African Americans assessed a property tax included carpenters, laundresses, cooks, and draymen, and they all shared in the rights and obligations of street-making.[53]

Nor did the politics of city-building stop at the curbstones. Abutting owners were liable for the full cost of keeping the footways in front of their domiciles in good repair. If they failed to comply, the commissioners would undertake the task and charge the property owners with the full cost, plus a penalty of a quarter-dollar per linear foot. Any property that fronted a waterway or wharf was also subject to the authority of the street commission. The city council received petitions to straighten not just the streets but also the unruly creeks and waterways that bordered private lots. In 1817, property owners along Harford Run applied for public assistance in taming the watercourse that ran along their lots. A year later, owners of lots along Jones Falls petitioned the city to bridle the rampaging river by "walling off its sides." The web of civic relationships that made a city extended beneath the surface of the streets as well: private property owners petitioned the city for permission to dig wells and pump water from beneath their property. Maintaining the urban infrastructure, be it along, above, or beneath the streets, forged a taut relationship between property owners and the municipality. In the case of Harford Run, the city council held the line against the petitioning property owners: "Although they [did] not consider it reasonable that the city be burdened with the whole expense of such an improvement," the council expressed its "willingness to aid and contribute thereto by making such appropriates from time to time as the work progresses." Having carefully compared the private benefits with the public welfare, the city council left the walling of Harford Run to the "personal interest in this improvement of said streets."[54]

The bargain that the councilmen struck with the residents along Harford Run was typical of their agile balancing act between public and private interests. The council, like the other institutional participants in the enterprise of street politics, the commissioners and the Maryland General Assembly, saw its role as supervisory and supplemental to citizen initiatives and private financing. The method of funding street paving, generally labeled as special assessments, was a fundamental method of city-building and a strategic division of municipal responsibilities. While abutting property owners shouldered the cost of paving the streets in front of their doorsteps, the city funded the entire cost of the intersections. Moreover, citizens played the critical initial role in laying down those streets that gave form to the urban core of Baltimore: they ceded a fragment of their property to the public, funded the bulk of the cost for paving, and complied with a majority vote of their neighbors. Street-making was, therefore, something more than a complicated duet between private citizens and city officials: it was a practical lesson in democratic citizenship, habituating city people to the practice of collaborating with one another and taking an active part in municipal self-government. In sum, the routine practice of making streets conditioned the people of Baltimore for more illustrious democratic actions, such as reforming the charter, fighting off the British in 1814, and building those lofty monuments.

After the streets were opened and paved, the municipality lined them with modest amenities. The street commissioners took it as their responsibility to light the city with lamps, often having them mounted on sturdy iron poles. They carefully placed hundreds of them along the streets above the legions of pumps and wells that drained the soggy pavements. In addition to making these piecemeal investments in infrastructure, the city council relied on a large compendium of municipal regulations to keep the streets open and presentable. A spate of ordinances was enacted to clear the streets of "offensive smells," "noxious effluvia," and those "nauseous Liquors or offensive matters that may annoy or incommode inhabitants of the city." Such infractions usually brought a hefty twenty-dollar fine. The depredations of animal life on city streets were the perpetual scourge of the city council. The councilmen were forever monitoring the movements of swine through the streets, weighing the balance between the nuisance of porcine pedestrians and their serviceability as scavengers removing the offal left in the streets by other species. Frustrated by their inability to control wandering dogs, the councilmen went so far at one point as to license shooting them on sight. In the euphoric civic climate following the victory at North Point, city officials went further than opening and ordering the streets: they took steps to shade and beautify them. The city council was hesitant to take action in 1816 when one of its members proposed that the city streets be ornamented with trees. By 1819, both branches had agreed to launch the greening of the city, a project that is still ongoing among the citizens of Charm City.[55]

The city fathers who had worked so indefatigably to get a city charter approved were not satisfied with such piecemeal and parsimonious public improvements. A major impetus for becoming incorporated as a city was to secure the authority to undertake more ambitious projects of urban development, such as maintaining and enhancing the waterways so central to the local economy. The only item in the city budget rivaling the cost of maintaining and lighting the streets was the allocation to the port wardens, which was expended on building wharves, clearing marshes, and dredging the Basin. Another expensive project was one of particular local pride. In 1816, the city council moved "to light the streets, squares, lanes and alleys of this City, in a more effectual manner, and with more safety, convenience and beauty," by means of "carburetted hydrogen gas." The councilmen signed on to a plan proposed by Rembrandt Peale, of the renowned family of painters, who was the proprietor of another municipal landmark, the Baltimore museum that bore his name. The council contracted out this public service to Peale's private corporation, which dispensed its services on the usual condition of citizen consent, "as may be agreed upon between the company and the owner or occupier of such house or houses." In exemplary fashion, Baltimore became the first US city to provide systematic street lighting.[56]

By 1816, it had become customary for the municipal government to contract with private companies to provide public services such as lighting the streets or carting away the detritus that accumulated in them. The model for such a project was the Baltimore Water Company. In 1799, the city approved a plan to pipe water from Herring Run or Gwynn Falls into the city. It was a contract between one corporation and another. The private water corporation pooled the resources of the "very eminent artist" Benjamin Latrobe as well as of prominent local businessmen, such as William Patterson, John O'Donnell, and John Eager Howard. These merchants and landowners, whose fortunes would rise with those of the city of Baltimore, made a complicated deal with the municipality. In exchange for their services, the city granted the water company loans and cash payments as well as a monopoly over this profitable business. The company directors came regularly before the council to renegotiate the terms of their partnership.[57]

Meeting basic urban needs, such as a supply of water, was a matter of negotiation between citizens, the city council, and private corporations. While the water company put its own business and engineering acumen to work piping water beneath the city streets, it was left to the municipality to create public spaces where citizens could quench their thirst. Maintaining the springs, small oases dotting the streets where citizens stopped to refresh themselves, took modest appropriations from the city council. In 1810, for example, the city invested the sum of $7,000 to refurbish the space around the Calvert Street Spring. Public funds garnished the watering place on the top of Calvert Street with a bench, some greenery, and a fountain. In February 1814, when the British were about to march on the city, the mayor took the time to attend to the matter of dispensing water to his fellow citizens. He called on the city council to provide "another useful and ornamental decoration of the city." In an unusual act of largesse, the city council built "spring houses" around these sites of mundane public service and employed "keepers" to ensure their proper functioning. These small recesses from the busy streets won the affection of city residents and captured the imagination of the nephew of Benjamin Latrobe, the distinguished British-born architect employed by the water company, whose buildings graced Philadelphia and the national capital and included Baltimore's Catholic Basilica. John H. B. Latrobe illustrated a whimsical guide to the city of Baltimore in the

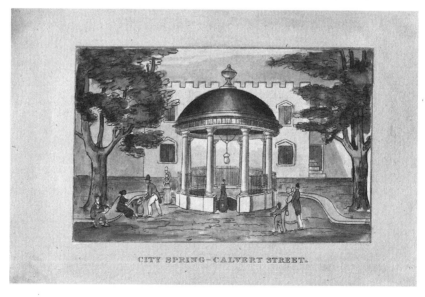

Fielding Lucas Jr., City Spring—Calvert Street, *1836, colored by John H. B. Latrobe, 1842. Courtesy of the John Work Garrett Library, Sheridan Libraries, Johns Hopkins University.*

1830s. It featured an elegy to the Calvert Street Spring, which he depicted as a sylvan retreat graced with a cupola and bathed in the soft shades of his watercolors. To ordinary citizens, the nearest public spring served the mundane purpose of supplying a basic necessity. But it also became the site of urban pleasure, courtesy of the mayor and city council, and funded by the taxpayers. The quotidian public life of the city flowed through the streets, where one occasionally found refreshment under a cupola beside a spring, just footsteps from the pavements. The councilmen, street commissioners, and taxpayers of Baltimore were a frugal lot, but they took care to beautify as well as open, pave, and repair their streets.[58]

CIVIC LIFE ALONG THE STREETS

Baltimore City was erected along the spine of its streets. People coming together on those streets, beside the public spring or beneath a monumental sculpture, helped nurture a civic identity. Private homes were aligned along those streets in a way that further solidified the fellow feeling of Baltimore's residents. The city's fabled row houses of one to three stories, some of wood and a few of logs, nearly half of them in sturdy brick (as required by municipal ordinance), joined rich and poor along the same dense thoroughfares. The most elite addresses of the early republican city, such as the city residence of Charles Carroll, were three-story row houses ringed by slightly smaller homes but of similar style, all pressed together and lined up flush with the street. Triumph in the War of 1812 was celebrated by building other handsome rows of housing garnished with classic trim not far from Monument Square. Robert Mills designed a block of attached residences up Calvert Street, a private counterpoise to his Washington Monument. Rising to three and a half stories and ornamented with marble and iron railings, they sat tightly together, anchored to the streets and elevated just four steps above the public pavement. Those marble embellishments were actually added on the recommendation of the city council, which was concerned that the municipal investment in the surrounding infrastructure should have aesthetic as well as real estate value. Mills's stately row of houses turned out to be too palatial for the place and time of their construction, between 1817 and 1819. Given the name Waterloo Row, his investment soon went the way of the Napoleonic Empire. The typical Baltimore house was more modest than those on Waterloo Row. The streets around the harbor and in Fells Point were lined front and center with smaller versions of Mills's speculative

---

row houses. Some, especially those nestled in the alleys, were as small as ten feet six inches wide and only one and a half stories high, but even these often boasted a bit of classical trim.[59] A few places for formal public assembly could be found within this tight web of private lots. Mapmakers interrupted the monotony of the urban landscape by zooming in from the streets to focus on a few select places. For example, the fanciful piece of cartography published by Warner and Hanna in 1801 pictured a tidy grid of streets up from the harbor surrounded by vivid patches of greenery. Only one place on the map was given a close-up view, the Assembly Rooms, a site for genteel dancing and amusement, located right in the public market near the Basin and along the fashionable row of residences built by Thomas McElderry and Cumberland Dugan in 1796. A few years later, the Warner and Hanna map affixed a list of a dozen other important urban sites to their map: six churches (one Catholic, five Protestant, and one German Reform), two banks, the courthouse, the jail, a customhouse, the observatory, and the Merchants' Exchange Building, all crowded together on a narrow grid of streets.

By the time the prominent local printer Fielding Lucas Jr. issued his imaginatively embroidered plan of Baltimore in 1822, the volume of streets had expanded geometrically along with the population. The city's sixty-two thousand residents crowded into thirty-two churches, including three "African Meeting Houses." They shopped in seven public markets, banked in eight different institutions, worked in eight factories, and were educated at two different colleges. The list could go on and on, to include places of entertainment, including the Peale Museum and two theaters, plus four inns, a library, and such notable philanthropic institutions as the Female Orphan Asylum, a dispensary, fifteen voluntary fire houses, and four springs. Crowning it all were the two monuments, one in the heart of the city, the other under construction astride the Howard plantation. Like the Washington Monument, most of these landmarks were the product of private initiative, emblematic of how civil society had grown up and thrived along the public streets of the city.

This array of places for public assembly gave the Baltimore skyline a distinctive profile. It was represented in one lauded engraving, called the *Constantinople View of Baltimore City*, that pictured at least four prominent domes on the horizon above the harbor. Latrobe designed two of them—the Baltimore Basilica and the Merchants' Exchange Building. Maximilian Godefroy created another for the Unitarian Church, and the local architect

———

Charles Varlé, Warner and Hanna's Plan of the City and Environs of Baltimore, *1801, Baltimore City Sheet Maps Collection. Courtesy of the Sheridan Libraries, Johns Hopkins University.*

Robert Carey Long covered the College of Medicine of Maryland (now the University of Maryland School of Medicine) with the same type of impressive structure. This architectural motif, the domed rotunda, might seem Byzantine or evoke the image of Jeremy Bentham's panopticon, with all the disciplining and punishing meaning Michel Foucault attributed to it. Marc Leone, a historian of Maryland architecture, sees a different political meaning in the domes of Baltimore, however. Rather than serving as a vantage point from which to monitor the movements of incarcerated men and women, as in Bentham's concept, the rotundas that rose up over the streets of Baltimore brought assemblages of citizens together of their own free will to worship, read, deliberate, trade, and care for one another.[60]

Those elegant domed buildings also reflected the diversity of the city's population. Within a few feet of one another stood the domes of the Baltimore Basilica—which was America's first Catholic cathedral—and the Unitarian Church. A few blocks away, the red brick spires of the German Lutheran Reformed Church (now Zion Lutheran) framed the belfry that

———

165

kept public time and alerted the citizenry in case of emergency. Most of the thirty-two churches of 1822 were topped with modest steeples. Scattered along the streets slowly rising from the harbor, they further embellished the architectural character of Baltimore. Gathering places for different social segments of the cosmopolitan city—Catholic, Protestant, and Jewish, of English, German, Irish, and African descent—they displayed the multiple facets of civil society that coexisted within the corporate city and testified to the voluntary and collective efforts of private citizens working with elected officials to exercise municipal sovereignty. Like the two monuments, the domes and steeples began as private initiatives but rose above the skyline as symbols and reminders of a composite civic identity. Like the paved streets that snaked through the city, they bespoke the investments that citizens made in shared urban space. And like the covered marketplaces, they convened a public together on an everyday basis, outside but near their homes.

One building was still notably absent from the Baltimore skyline: a city hall. The city council declined to build so much as a modest hall for the people, preferring to rent secondhand quarters for the mayor and council. This was a rational decision: after all, the city did not require much office space; there was no need for bureaus, given the paucity of municipal bureaucrats. The building and maintenance of the small city seldom required the direct exercise of municipal authority. Assessments to abutting owners funded basic urban infrastructure; public services were contracted out to private companies or corporate monopolies; health and sanitation were monitored by licenses and regulations. The few city employees—licensed inspectors, watchmen, keepers of fountains, and market clerks—did their work out on the streets, in the neighborhoods and public spaces of the city. Representative government, by its very nature, could not be contained within four walls. The place of the elected leaders of the city was with their constituents and among the neighbors who shared the eight wards of the city, each small enough to permit routine encounters between a councilman and those who voted him into office. When the mayor and council needed to raise money to provide fuel to warm the poor and homeless during a particularly cold winter, or to recruit laborers to fortify the harbor against British attack, they called up the citizens to meet in the wards and take the appropriate action. Larger assemblies met outdoors in central public spaces, especially beneath the Battle Monument. No barriers blocked admission to these public spaces.

The public life of the streets was open and available to most of the men and women who settled in the Monumental City. Residents of every creed and color joined together in the separate voluntary associations that composed civil society. Access to the formal institutions of municipal sovereignty, however, was another story. With the passage of time, the social limits of the municipal public became clearly articulated. The electoral franchise was officially declared a white male privilege in 1810. Soon, access to the streets became subject to ominous restrictions. Men and women of color would be required to present a passport issued by a respectable white citizen in order to travel through the city at night. The appearance of African Americans in the municipal record of active citizenship was eerily rare, and it worsened with the passage of time. When they were acknowledged in the official public sphere, it was usually as petitioners or as objects of municipal suspicion. Black refugees from Haiti were regarded as a public eyesore; they were said to bathe naked in Jones Falls and to sell spoiled foodstuffs on the streets outside the public markets. The casual, everyday movements of African Americans through the city streets sometimes provoked suspicion and surveillance. A petitioner to the city council dated March 28, 1817, asserted the right to remove black vendors from the city streets, saying simply, "Your petitioners would respectfully solicit the passage of an ordinance restraining and prohibiting the practice in the future." Aside from such rare appearances on the back streets of municipal politics, African Americans entered the public record only to be consigned to the almshouse or the city jail. The spotty records of both institutions show the "colored" to be drastically overrepresented.[61] Ominously, with hardly any forethought, the citizens of Baltimore drew a decisive line of exclusion around their fledgling democracy, most emphatically around those of African descent.

For African American women, the freedoms of the city were even more illusory. They had to battle desperately for a place in the public sphere, and their major point of entry to the public record was through the city jail. This was in fact one way that women could become public figures. Matilda Hawkins, a free woman of color, made a reputation for herself by regularly appearing before the justice of the peace. She was the perpetrator of a forceful attack on public authority in 1821, when she was charged with the "assaulting and battering of Joshua Willis Constable while in the discharge of his official Duty in Quelling a Riotous disorderly mob of Negroes." Hawkins had an accomplice in this assault, one Eliza Hawkins, who reputedly held Constable Willis down while her kinswoman delivered the beating.[62]

Republican politicians did not appreciate such boisterous appearances of women in public. The Federalists had a very different role in mind for the ladies. It was expressed in a lurid verse commemorating the 1812 riot, "A Poem in Three Cantos," penned by David Longworth and published in New York in 1813. The poet gave female allegories an important supporting role in his political elegy. The chief villain, a mob leader named Mumma, a man, was known to have some female associates, for "On Brothel walls the harlot penn'd his name." If harlots inspired Republicans to sedition, the Federalists claimed a "virgin" as their muse, but one with certain seductive qualities in the poem, including "lovely shoulders bare" and a "snowy bosom" that "throbs" and "shudders with affright" at the excesses of urban democracy. Although these stanzas did not become enshrined as a national anthem, they did omen a campaign to usher women away from the public sphere, off the streets of Baltimore and out of the minds of the municipal leaders.[63]

At least one woman reader struggled to make her way through this thicket of gender ideology and find a place on the margins of the public sphere. Mary E. Ellicott, the daughter of an affluent miller and grain merchant, kept a scrapbook filled with eclectic political keepsakes. Although she welcomed "a day without party please," she also pasted clippings from both the *Federalist Gazette* and the *Republican Patriot* into her scrapbook. In the privacy of her journal she revealed some liberal sentiments, such as this opinion: "The Jews in a Christian country are entitled to a free participation on all our civil rights."[64] Mary Ellicott joined a coterie of the wives and daughters of the Baltimore elite who did more than consign their political imaginations to scrapbooks. In 1811 they founded a benevolent society "for the purpose of employing and relieving widows and educating orphans under the direction of Managers appointed by the members of the society." They gave their association a unique title replete with political meaning: "The Humane Impartial Society." The managers of the new society presumed to elect their own president and follow the example of their menfolk by forming "a corporation and body politic." They took on the role of "building, selling, leasing and conveying, land and tenements, goods and chattels and other property real and personal." These financial ambitions were supported by "capital" in an amount not to exceed $40,000, which the managers put in the bank under the corporate name of the Female Humane Impartial Society. These women grasped the opportunity to open a public place in the city for the members of their sex. They also embraced the diversity of their urban habitat with a liberality rare at the time. The charter of the Female Humane Impartial Society proclaimed that "each religious persuasion of the city of Baltimore shall be represented; that is to say one of each of the following societies:

———

168

Baptists, Presbyterians, Episcopalians, Swedenborgians, Catholics, Friends and Methodists." The members of the society broke a promising path to civic service and would soon erect their own landmark on the streetscape, a handsome home for orphans and widows and a workshop employing needy seamstresses.[65]

The philanthropy of the Female Humane Impartial Society exposed another restrictive clause in the constitution of municipal government—the inability of many citizens to exercise the rights and freedoms of the city due to their limited economic resources. The beneficiaries of the charity and others like it, and a large portion of the rest of the city population, were exiled from the republican polity on the grounds of poverty. The difficulty of earning one's living denied countless men and women, of whatever faith or color or origin, the full rights and freedoms of the streets. Until 1825, debtors were carted off to prison by the hundreds, scores of them for owing no more than five dollars. Visiting Baltimore from Washington in 1823, the journalist Anne Royall was appalled to find six women imprisoned for debt, all huddled in cells without as much as a blanket. Those who could not eke out a living in the city of Baltimore were liable to surrender their freedom and enter the almshouse. The conditions in Baltimore's poorhouse were at least better than those of the jail, or of slave quarters. The poor tax was a regular item in the state budget, and Baltimore took pride in the fine eleemosynary edifice constructed on its outskirts to accommodate the poor. A committee composed of the most illustrious citizens paid an annual visit to inspect the facility, and reported that the poor were well cared for. They could even report that the poorhouse larder was stocked with a ration of chocolate. But, as the historian Seth Rockman has powerfully demonstrated, a sizable portion of the inhabitants of Baltimore, black and white, had a very difficult time "scraping by." If not so desperate as to be consigned to the almshouse, neither did they secure a commodious and honored place under Baltimore's republican rotunda. For many—indeed the majority, composed of women, African Americans, and the poor—the republican city was but a faint and distant promise of equality for all.[66]

For the majority of the men and women of Baltimore, making a living required hard manual or menial labor in exchange for paltry wages. Only a tiny minority of those who found their way to the port along the Patapsco early in the nineteenth century ever rose to political office, or to the top of the economic order, or even made a personal entry into those unusually garrulous papers of the mayor and the city council. A vexing contradiction was lodged

—

at the very foundation of the embryonic urban democracy. The people of Baltimore had erected a city upon the foundation of private property, on land taken up in irregular portions and distributed unequally among the citizenry. Early in the nineteenth century, the city was apportioned into lots and leases of relatively equal size, and this arrangement created the material conditions for the expansion of the franchise and the sustenance of democracy. That foundation could, however, be easily eroded by economic changes, especially if the mercantilist constraints on the market economy were relaxed and the full force of unrestrained capitalist growth was unleashed. When that occurred, as will be seen in a later chapter, another fault line opened in the urban political economy. The wide distribution of private property served not just as the foundation of democratic expansion, but also as the source of public revenue. Property taxes were a major source of municipal funds in the city of Baltimore, and assessed at a high rate compared to other cities.[67] It would not be long before complaints about the tax burden would expose the contradictory impulses of citizens: they enjoyed the privileges of property ownership, but came to resent paying for the maintenance and improvement of the urban landscape beyond their doorsteps. Such grievances were not paramount, however, as the city of Baltimore reveled in the triumph of the War of 1812 and the rapid economic growth that followed it. It was at this time that Baltimore entered the pantheon of early American cities.

For the time being, men and women, native and foreign, black and white, enjoyed unusual if unequal opportunities in Baltimore City. Tenacious citizens of moderate income found their way from the street into the papers of the mayor and city council. One such group appealed to the municipality in May 1816 to permit them access to stalls as vendors in the public market. They identified themselves as "poor, necessitous and indigent women chiefly burdened with young and helpless children for whose subsistence they have not means whatsoever save only their own personal industry." Poor, necessitous, and indigent they might be, and often widowed, but they were not without resources. They had the energy and political savvy to draft a petition to the mayor, boldly sign their own names, and collect added signatures from neighbors, both male and female. The market women upheld their occupation, describing how they "gained a support by going out into the country, and buying Vegetables to Sell again in the Market at a small profit. We generally buy from those who would not bring to market what we buy. We humbly pray of your Honors to permit us as heretofore to sell Vegetables in the Market." These hardworking women, "hucksters" in the vocabulary of the marketplace, objected to a municipal regulation that exiled them to the "footways near the corner of the market space." In some ways, the women hucksters took a political position on the vanguard of liberalism: they asserted their right to make their living on their own and in defiance of the regulated municipal economy. More pragmatically, they simply sought their fortunes in public spaces: in and beyond the market hall, along the street and the footways, or by collecting signatures on petitions to the city council. A solitary woman by the name of Catharine Oliver had the audacity to charge the mayor and city council with violating her right to operate her oyster house on Sundays. Asserting that she held a license to practice her trade, she convinced the municipal authorities to reverse their decision in her case. As late as 1830, a few women could beat city hall, especially if they had a stake in the regulated urban economy, be it a license to sell oysters or a stall in the public market.[68]

The streets of Baltimore also served as the public stage on which slaves and free blacks claimed their rights and freedom. The first public speech attributed to an African American woman was delivered in Baltimore. Maria Stewart urged the women of Baltimore to better the condition of their race and gender by converting their houses into storefront businesses—that is, to exploit the opportunities available along the streets of the city. African American men used the city streets to assert their liberty in a variety of ways. A black militia company could be heard drilling in the streets as late as 2:00 a.m. Two hundred years ago, Daniel Coker, restive under white religious leadership, founded an independent congregation, African Bethel Church, on an alley in South Baltimore. Although Coker himself chose to depart Baltimore for Africa in 1820, most of his brethren found spaces in the republican city to oppose both slavery and African colonization. The most fabled individual journey from slavery to freedom commenced in the narrow streets of Fells Point. Frederick Douglass recalled that he first glimpsed the meaning of freedom by observing indentured Irish boys on the city streets: "I would sometimes say to them, while seated on a curbstone or a cellar door, 'I wish I could be free, as you will be when you get to be men.'" The education was mutual. Douglass reported that he "had no small satisfaction in wringing from the boys, occasionally, the fresh and bitter condemnation of slavery." A season in Baltimore led Douglass to write: "A city slave is almost a free citizen."[69]

As long as race, gender, or poverty left the majority of the people of Baltimore only "almost free" citizens, the first city of the American republic

—

fell far short of its democratic promise. Still, that time, that place, and the extraordinary collaborative project of building a city, almost from scratch and in the wake of the American Revolution, opened up new public spaces and hopeful political possibilities. In Baltimore between 1797 and 1819, the forces of history aligned in an extraordinary if not exceptional way. Political ties to the Old World were severed, calls for equality rang out on the streets, and enterprising people converged from all directions. The weight of the past was relatively light upon the newcomers who made their way to the premier port of the Chesapeake in the late eighteenth and early nineteenth centuries. At the mouth of the Patapsco they found both the space in which to make a city and the incentive to do it collectively. Under these unique conditions, the peoples of Baltimore established the balance between individual initiative, collective effort, and relatively equal access to the levers of power that nurtured urban democracy.

Meanwhile, the same international currents that fostered democracy in the Chesapeake port were also stirring up republican aspirations in Latin America, and even reaching Spain's far northern imperial outpost on San Francisco Bay. It would be some time before a city as large and well organized as Baltimore would be erected in California, but, as the next chapter will attest, the settlers scattered around the San Francisco Bay were also beginning to craft an independent polity in the ruins of the Spanish Empire. At a time when the nation-state was a relatively weak institution throughout North America, the assertion of municipal sovereignty in Baltimore and along the shores of San Francisco Bay had political consequences of transcontinental dimensions.

———

CHAPTER 5

SHAPING THE SPACES OF CALIFORNIA

Ranchos, Plazas, and Pueblos, 1821–1846

A t the time that Baltimore was being erected into a city, settlement remained sparse and scattered along the shores of San Francisco Bay. By 1822, however, Mexico—and the Californios—had declared their independence from Spain, and invented new ways of living together on the shores of the great estuary. Under the flag of the Republic of Mexico, the settlers of the province of Alta California and their descendants created a new and distinctive landscape, one that extended out into ranchland, came together around a plaza, and acquired the political legitimacy of a pueblo. In 1835, by order of the governor of the province, the local *alcalde* walked off the boundaries of San Francisco's first official municipality. The *alcalde* was named Francisco de Haro, and his comings and goings along the San Francisco Peninsula would subsequently illustrate the vernacular practices that shaped a distinctively Californian urban space.

The spotty records of Mexican San Francisco chart Haro's role in the taking and shaping of land around the bay. Sometimes called "Citizen Haro" in the Mexican records, he came of age with the territory of Alta California.

—

The account book of the merchant William E. P. Hartnell locates him in the general area of San Francisco Bay in 1826, when he purchased a plow. In the 1830s, Haro dutifully requested permission to graze his cattle on the pasturage once belonging to Misión San Francisco de Asís. A decade later, he assumed a public position, the office of *alcalde*. In that capacity, he played a critical role in drawing his neighbors together into a small nucleated settlement, called a pueblo, in the Mexican glossary of urban places. By the 1840s, Haro and his sons had extended their agricultural holdings substantially; they were pasturing cattle on more than two thousand acres near Lake Merced, to the southwest of the old Mission. It was not until 1843 that he applied for a formal title to a small *solar* of one hundred square varas that the Republic of Mexico had confiscated from the Franciscans. Haro's titles to land around San Francisco Bay record how that Spanish landscape had been literally reconstructed. As one of his neighbors testified, Haro made his home out of adobe salvaged from the walls of the Mission.[1]

Through a series of agile steps, Haro made the transition from the Spanish Empire to the Mexican Republic to a California pueblo. In the process he also took ownership of substantial property. The vast tract of ranchland that Citizen Haro acquired in 1837 was not a simple grant of the Mexican government, but a cash purchase. He struck quite a bargain with a retired soldier from the Presidio, acquiring some two thousand acres at a cost of one hundred cows plus an estimated $25. Royal titles and Indian trusts had given way first to Mexican grants and then to the transfer of land between neighbors in exchange for cows or small sums of cash. Francisco de Haro enters the land records again in the year of his death, 1847, when he sold a small lot near the ruins of the Mission for $28. By then, his outlying ranchland had grown far more valuable. He was grazing a large herd of cattle and selling hides and tallow on an international market, incurring a debt to the merchant house of Guillermo Davis for some $2,000.[2]

The path that Francisco de Haro and his neighbors took through time and space also traversed major changes in the history of the world economy, in republican politics, and in the urban landscape. First of all, the Californios converted the San Francisco Peninsula into parcels of private property, freed from both the ecclesiastical control of the Franciscans and the mercantilist constraints of the Spanish Crown. Second, Haro and other men like him, and at least one notable woman, would write the lines along which generations of San Franciscans were destined to walk. Haro's signature can be found on at least three iconic features of the California landscape: the rancho, the

---

vecindad, and the harbor that would one day become the center of a city called San Francisco. Finally, like the townsmen of Baltimore, Francisco de Haro and his neighbors—*vecinos* now invested with the full status of citizen in Iberia and New Spain—joined their private property together into a polity in which they could begin to exercise municipal sovereignty.

This chapter will show that the Mexican *pobladores* were not simply swept up by global economic forces or traipsing into urban modernity on a path set by the cities of Europe or the northeastern United States. The shapes they built on the land were not the result of imperial edicts, or transcription of classic Spanish town planning; nor did they bear much resemblance to the instructions for town governance issued by either Mexico or the State of Maryland. The first urban spaces along San Francisco Bay were local inventions, created in response to local exigencies and opportunities. Through their resourceful management of land and people, the *pobladores* prepared the foundation for a distinctly Californian organization of space.

MEXICAN SOVEREIGNTY AND THE TAKING OF RANCHLAND

Francisco de Haro, along with his family and his neighbors, took land and shaped spaces very much under their own initiative but within the broad parameters laid down by the Republic of Mexico. After winning independence from Spain in 1821, the Republic of Mexico enacted a sequence of reforms in the structures of government. The first Mexican constitution, in 1824, and a second, in 1836, created structures for governing at the local, provincial, and national levels. The federal authorities in Mexico City issued a spate of directives about the political organization of the northern territories, yet the central government was never able to enforce its policies with enough consistency and diligence to override local practices in Alta California. At the same time, liberal principles, especially as they relate to land, circulated through the provinces of the Republic of Mexico as far as the San Francisco outpost. Eschewing the trappings of the Spanish Empire, the documents of the republic suspended the language of decrees of "royal justice," addressed *ciudadanos* in a spirit of "Razón y Justicia" (Reason and Justice), and closed with an homage to "Dios y Libertad" (God and Freedom).

The central government did not grant San Francisco a city charter like the one secured by the City of Baltimore, but it did transmit an array of designs for organizing political space to the leaders of Alta California. These communications had begun under the reign of the Spanish Empire, when José de Gálvez

—

had divided Mexico into twelve regional governments, called *intendencias*, each divided into local *ayuntamientos*, overseen by elected officials, *alcaldes*, *regidores*, and justices of the peace. These units of government multiplied and acquired new powers when Napoleon invaded Spain in 1808. The municipality of Madrid called for those loyal to the Spanish monarch to form rebel governments throughout the empire. The result was the proclamation of a constitutional monarchy in exile in the city of Cádiz in 1812. Delegates to the Cortes de Cádiz were elected by local governments from across the Spanish Empire, including the *intendencias* and *ayuntamientos* of Mexico.[3]

The formation of the *cortes* triggered political mobilization across Latin America and would lead to the creation of independent nations, including Mexico. In the words of one historian, the nations of Latin America were created out of "un conjunto de pueblos—reinos, provincias, ciudades" (a combination of pueblos—kingdoms, provinces, cities). When Mexico severed its relationship with Spain, it created a framework of government reflective of these multiple sites of sovereignty, a "república representative popular federal" (representative, popular, federal republic). Like the young republic to the north, Mexico was a federation composed of multiple layers of sovereignty, from the local *ayuntamientos*, to nineteen provinces, or *intendencias*, to the Supremo Gobierno (Supreme Government) in Mexico City. The Mexican constitution of 1824 made Alta California a *territorio* within the Mexican federation and invested it with a representative body, the Diputación (the deputation, or legislative council). Under a new constitution enacted in 1836, the territory of Alta California was divided into different regional governments, creating a northern district called "el partido de San Francisco." From the start, the politics of Alta California were practiced in local and regional units of government. Like the townsmen of Baltimore, the Californios operated in a multilayered political system and enjoyed relative autonomy from any centralized state.[4]

This dispersal of sovereignty made for a complicated and volatile political geography in Mexico and in the territory of Alta California. For the native-born sons of the first Mexicans to come ashore in San Francisco, it afforded capacious political space in which to practice self-government. The Diputación de la Jurisdicción del Partido de San Francisco was their base of operation. The Californios rose quickly to leadership over the regional legislative body, which began meeting as early as 1832. They were joined in the Diputación by members of a new party of colonizers sent north from Mexico in 1833. The leaders of the expedition, José María Padrés and José

María Híjar, carried liberal notions to Alta California, including some radical ideas that had germinated in the long struggle for Mexican independence. The armed rebellion led by Padre Miguel Hidalgo y Costilla, for example, championed the abolition of slavery, the rights of Indians, and the elimination of racial distinctions among the citizenry. This wave of Mexican reform also installed José Figueroa, a mestizo, as governor of Alta California. Figueroa, who presided at the capital in Monterey, authored the first book to be published in California, *The Manifesto of the Mexican Revolution*, which laid out the basic liberal creed: "I defend the justice, liberty, security and property of citizens; my cause is that of the people and the laws."[5]

After finishing the task commissioned by the Republic of Mexico, driving the Russians from Alta California, some members of the Padrés and Híjar expedition lingered around San Francisco Bay, where they formed alliances with the local residents, including the largest landowners of the region, who held seats on the Diputación: Juan Bautista Alvarado, Mariano Guadalupe Vallejo, and José Castro, for example. All three represented a second generation of *pobladores* who assumed major civilian and military positions in the regional government of San Francisco. Alvarado had a reputation as a republican firebrand and was said to have mounted a cart in the Mission's courtyard to champion the land rights of Indians. Vallejo was an admirer of Jefferson, the proprietor of a vast rancho north of San Francisco Bay, and the architect of an especially grand public plaza in Sonoma. These were the founding sons of California. Vallejo and Alvarado were both thirty-two years old when they joined the Diputación. At one time or another, all three would rise to the station of governor of Alta California, a position formerly reserved for émigrés sent from Spain or north from Mexico City. [6]

The central government in Mexico sent its emissaries to Alta California, governors like Figueroa as well as the Híjar-Padrés colonizing party, with instructions to relieve the Franciscans of civil authority and secularize the missions. The policy of secularization, first propounded by the Spanish, was renewed by the Republic of Mexico in 1824 and finally completed in 1836. The initial intent of secularization was to confiscate mission lands and redistribute it to Christianized Indians. Figueroa pleaded eloquently for this policy, saying that the fertility of the mission lands was a direct product of Indian labor, and thereby earned the natives of the Bay Area a stake in the Mexican Republic. In 1833, the republic authorized the distribution of Indian land in the following order: first to the Indians, second to the local residents who were landless, third to soldiers and military officials, fourth

—

to the new settlers sent north from Mexico, and lastly to foreigners. Notably missing from this list were those elite Californios who had already occupied large tracts of ranchland.

This policy provoked immediate opposition from the rancheros who happened to preside at the Diputación of San Francisco. In Los Angeles, it resulted in a full-scale revolt against Governor Figueroa and prompted the hasty return of Híjar and Padrés back to Mexico. The Californios defied the federal government in Mexico City and enacted its own secularization policy, which would consist of issuing titles to large grants of the former mission lands under their own authority. Virtually none of them went to the indigenous population.[7]

The leading Californios used their political power for one purpose above all others: expropriating the land once tended by the Indians and then overseen on their behalf by the missionaries. Any further references to Indians near the future site of the city of San Francisco would consist primarily of peripheral views, glimpses of women washing wool near the ruins of the Mission, or scattered *rancherías* in the East or North Bay, where farm laborers lived off paltry wages, paid in beans rather than mussels. Northward, in today's Sonoma County, one tenacious Miwok clan did secure a Mexican land grant from Governor Figueroa in 1835. A portion of the northernmost California mission, San Rafael Arcángel, this replica of an Indian pueblo was a ghost town a decade later. Governor Alvarado laid claim to the land, saying he had purchased it from the Indians in 1844. Although the Indians did not retain ownership of this ancestral domain bordering an ancient shell mound, they continued to return there for ceremonies and to feast on clams, quail, and blackberries.[8]

By the mid-1840s, the missions as well as the Indians had become casualties in the advances of the land market. The public announcement was terse: "There will be sold in this Capital, to the highest bidder, the Missions of San Rafael, Dolores [San Francisco], Soledad, San Miguel, and La Purísima, which are abandoned by their neophytes." The records of the Diputación showed that Mission San Francisco was sold "to the highest bidder" on October 28, 1845.[9] Only a lone Indian *temescal* (sweat lodge) still stood on the northwest corner of the San Francisco Peninsula, near a cove called Yerba Buena: it was a ghostly landmark overshadowed by some warehouses under construction by foreign merchants, immigrants from Europe and the United States.

Once the republican leaders of Alta California had dispensed with issuing land titles to Indians, they unleashed liberal principles of political economy. Mariano Vallejo issued a full-throated call for economic development, exhorting the *ciudadanos* of the region to embrace "progress by all the advantages lying within the orbit of its capacity." To Vallejo and his compatriots in the Diputación, a "happy aspect of success" would begin with the conversion of the land into private parcels. As members of the provincial legislature, the Californios enacted policy on a variety of subjects, including agriculture, finance, and police, all the while liberally issuing land titles. The committee on agriculture emphatically proclaimed its commitment to private property. It pronounced that "nothing more beneficial can be done in favor of Agriculture, than to procure, to the owners of land a peaceful and secure possession thereof."[10]

The conversion of the San Francisco Peninsula into private property was not left entirely to the free market. According to Spanish precedents and Mexican law, land-taking was a complex political process. It began with a petition to an officer of the local government, the *alcalde* or justice of peace. The local officials compiled a file of documents, called an *expediente*, that established the legitimacy of the request, and then forwarded it to the governor. The prospective landowner might then sketch out the location and size of the grant, but could not claim it until a final document was issued and signed by the governor of Alta California. To occupy his land, the new owner was required to meet the three qualifications attached to Mexican land grants. The first stipulated that the owner take up the parcel within the year, constructing a house or otherwise improving the land by planting orchards, building corrals, or digging irrigation ditches. Second, the grantee was required to pledge to abide by the *policía*, the regulations of the municipal authority, the *ayuntamiento*. Finally, the grant was made conditional on complying with the first two provisions; without compliance, the land could be repossessed.[11]

It was not until the 1830s that the inhabitants of the San Francisco Bay region began to make the effort required to secure formal title to the land they occupied. Between 1832 and 1840, approximately twenty grants were issued annually; the number nearly doubled in the 1840s. The largest grants were located at a considerable distance from the entry to San Francisco Bay. The Peralta family's Rancho San Antonio set this geographical pattern. Corporal Luis Peralta was one of the more elite members of the colonizing party that had left Sonora in 1774. The recipient of one of the few land grants issued by the Spanish government, the senior Peralta chose a large tract across the bay extending from present-day Berkeley south to San Leandro, amounting

---

to 11 leagues, or approximately 50,000 acres. Most grants of this size were laid out after 1821 under the authority of the Republic of Mexico, but they retraced Peralta's giant footsteps, aggrandizing massive tracts of pasturage and dispersing the *pobladores* far from the Presidio and the Mission.

The conversion of mission lands into pasturage speeded up at the midpoint of the 1830s. José María Amador, that fierce Indian raider from Chapter 3, received his reward from the Mexican government in 1834 in the form of 16,517 acres on the east side of the bay called Rancho San Ramón. Mariano Vallejo took his reward for military service in the form of 175,000 acres on the northern periphery of San Francisco Bay in Sonoma. Vallejo converted his land grant into an industrial-sized ranch and a factory for the production of hides and tallow. Vallejo's fellow governors and other provincial officials took up their portions to the south: Alvarado acquired 54,000 acres, and Castro secured multiple grants, totaling 100,000 acres. This land boom just happened to coincide with the grantees' tenure in the elite offices of Alta California, including governor, member of the Diputación, and local *alcalde*. Like other astute rancher-politicians, Vallejo hastily augmented his holdings in the 1840s when it became apparent that time was running out on Mexican hegemony in California.[12] The rough dimensions of these land grants were

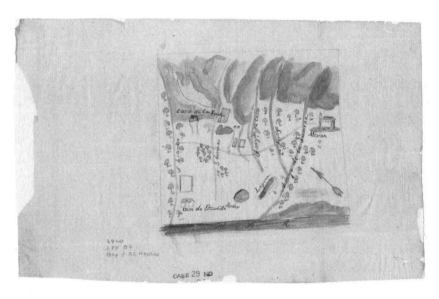

Diseño del *Rancho San Leandro. Land Case Map A-59, not dated.*
Courtesy of the Bancroft Library, University of California, Berkeley.

---

documented, if at all, not by a formal survey but by an impressionistic, often picturesque, drawing, a *diseño*.

Land grants as lavish as Vallejo's were small compared to those amassed by Southern Californians like Governor Pío Pico, whose holdings amounted to some 500,000 acres. Grants located closer in to the old Presidio and Mission of San Francisco were typically diminutive by comparison, a few square varas, or at the very most one league (4,000 odd acres). Whatever their size, Bay Area land grants represented a new scale of land-taking distinctive to California. Privately owned tracts of agricultural and pastoral land around San Francisco Bay were called *ranchos*, a Spanish term denoting something larger than a farm, or *finca*, but more modest than the *haciendas* or *estancias* found in Latin America. The ranch, the iconic space of California, was the creation of astute pioneers who had determined that the local climate and topography, so similar to Extremadura or Andalucía in Spain or the Sonora coast in Mexico, were best suited for pasturing the offspring of the cattle brought north by the Spanish. They were a remarkably fecund herd: the cows of Alta California were counted at some 6,000 in 1785, ten times that number in 1802, and 400,000 by 1834.[13]

It was not a taste for beef that drove the cattle-mania of Alta California, but the value of commodities that could be traded on an international market, tallow and hides. Hides became known as "California bank notes" and served as the chief currency among ranchers and missionaries seeking goods from Europe, South America, or China. At their peak, the rancheros of Alta California traded millions of hides and thousands of tons of tallow on an international market that heated up during the Napoleonic Wars. The ranches of Alta California trafficked in transnational commercial agriculture, not unlike the tobacco plantations around the Chesapeake. The rancheros, like the southern planters, relied heavily on servile labor, that of the displaced Indians who eked out a living toiling on the pastures and in the butcheries and tallow and soap factories of Mexican California. Although they were not rewarded with a modern wage, this Indian labor force was often highly skilled and trained for service to the global economy; thousands became skillful *vaqueros* (cowboys), butchers, and tallow makers. The descendants of the Ohlone had become essential to the cattle economy.[14]

THE FIRST LANDLORDS OF THE SAN FRANCISCO PENINSULA

For all their prominence on the cultural landscape of California, the largest

———

ranches were peripheral to the formation of the central city that would bear the name San Francisco; they spilled out all around the bay, far to the north, south, and east. The rancheros traded their produce with ships anchored offshore not far from their pastures. Until the upsurge of Mexican grants late in the 1830s, the care of the northern tier of the San Francisco Peninsula rested in the hands of the first Mexican settlers, many of them veterans of the Anza expedition. These founding families seldom received a land grant from the Spanish, yet they survived, dug roots, multiplied, and replenished the earth. A handful of soldiers and their families grew into a small community of subsistence farmers. Apart from Manuel Buitrón, who chose to locate his parcel near Monterey, and Luis Peralta, with a vast rancho in the East Bay, not one of these founding families had secured a land grant before 1833. When they, their children, and grandchildren came before the United States Land Commission to defend their rights to the family land in the 1850s, they made modest claims. Almost three-quarters of the properties they claimed were four hundred square varas or less. The most common land allotment around Mission San Francisco was 100 square varas, roughly the size of a *manzana*, or city block, in much of Latin America. A rare few solicited half a league, over two thousand acres. near the southern border of what would become the County of San Francisco.[15]

This did not mean, however, that the San Francisco pioneers remained wards of the Presidio or the Mission. Soon after they arrived from Mexico, and without political sanction from the Spanish governors, the *pobladores* relocated outside the confines of the Presidio. When in the 1820s the Mexican government began to issue land titles, the first settlers and their progeny acted quickly to secure formal ownership of the land that they had long occupied and made fruitful with their labor. Nearly 60 percent of the first families ultimately acquired title to lands of their own. For property-less migrants from northern Mexico, many of them mestizos, and most of them illiterate, this was an auspicious start on a new life in California. A few examples of their spatial strategies will adumbrate this distinctive pattern of taking the land.

The first petition for a title to land near the top of the San Francisco Peninsula is dated 1833. It bore the name of an Indian, though not a member of a tribelet native to the Bay Area. He was Apolinario Miranda, a descendent of the "Indio" couple listed in the Spanish census of 1790. Miranda would come of age in Mexican rather than Spanish California and take advantage of new opportunities to work his own land. At Mission San Francisco in 1820,

—

THE MAKING
OF BALTIMORE AND
SAN FRANCISCO,
SEEN SIDE BY SIDE

Although Baltimore and San Francisco developed at their own pace and in their own distinctive styles, the citizens of each city accomplished the task of building a modern urban space by the midpoint of the nineteenth century. This gallery of images, Baltimore on the left and San Francisco on the right, illustrates this parallel, if not simultaneous—but hardly uniform—civic accomplishment.

Chesapeake Bay, satellite image. United States Geological Survey (see page 26).

San Francisco Bay, satellite image. United States Geological Survey (see page 27).

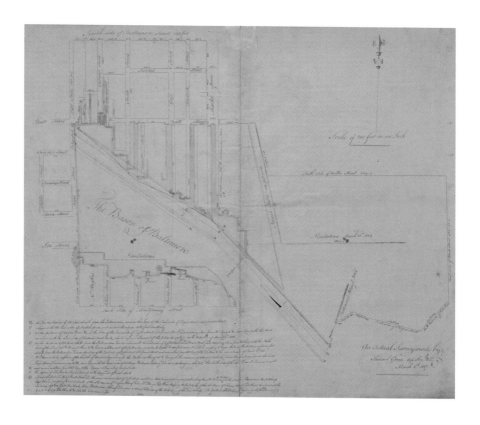

Plat of the Basin, Jehu Bouldin, ca. 1817. Cartographic Records, BRG 12-4.
Courtesy of the Baltimore City Archives (see page 153).

Mission Dolores. Louis Choris, Danse des habitans de Californie à la
mission de San Francisco *(Dance of the inhabitants of California at
the Mission San Francisco), ca. 1815, fG420.K84.C6. Courtesy of the
Bancroft Library, University of California, Berkeley (see page 105).*

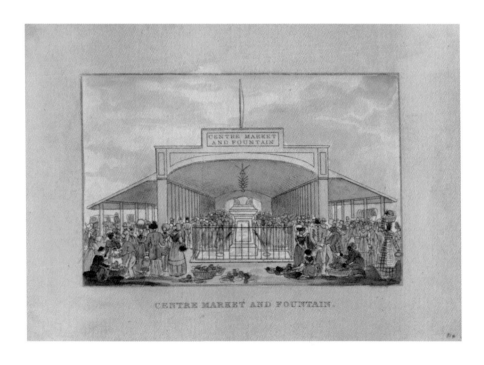

*Baltimore's Centre Market, Fielding Lucas Jr., 1836, colored by
John H. B. Latrobe, 1842. Courtesy of the John Work Garrett Library,
Sheridan Libraries, Johns Hopkins University (see page 134).*

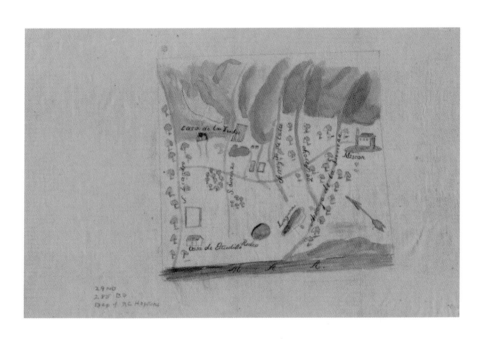

Ranches scattered around the bay. Diseño del *Rancho San Leandro, Land Case Map A-59, not dated. Courtesy of the Bancroft Library, University of California, Berkeley (see page 180).*

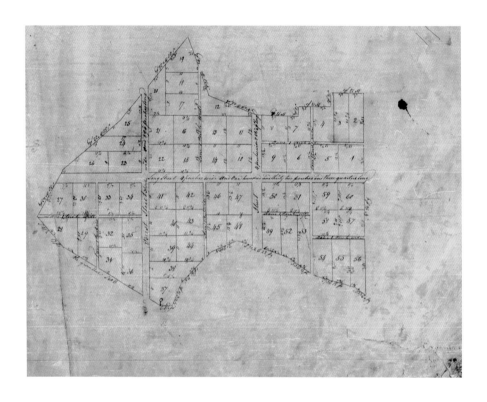

The lots of Baltimore. Jehu Bouldin, plat of original Baltimore Town, ca. 1729. Cartographic Records, BRG 12-2-1. Courtesy of the Baltimore City Archives (see page 69).

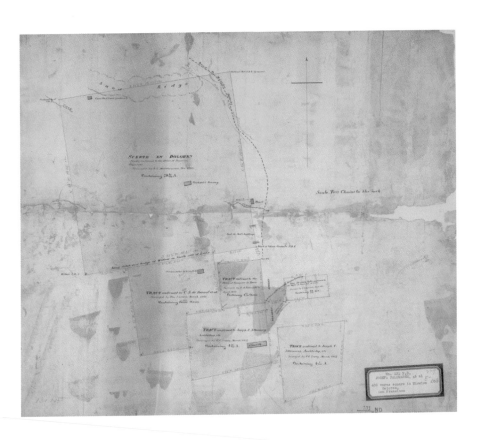

The suertes *of Establicimento de Dolores. Survey, "400 Varas Square in Mission Dolores" [1862?]. Land Case Map D-913A. Courtesy of the Bancroft Library, University of California, Berkeley (see page 191).*

Baltimore's street grid. Charles Varlé, Warner and Hanna's Plan of the
City and Environs of Baltimore, *1801, Baltimore City Sheet Maps Collection.
Courtesy of the Sheridan Libraries, Johns Hopkins University (see page 165).*

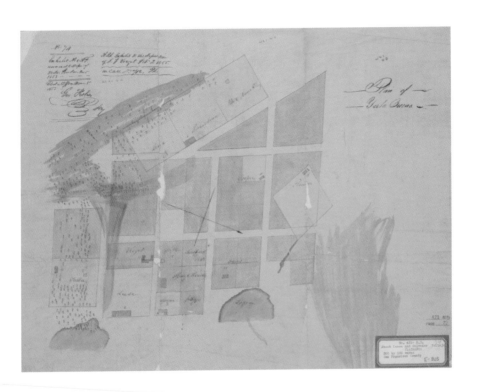

Diseño *with Plaza San Francisco. Unknown artist after William Richardson,* Plan *of Yerba Buena, California, 1835 [redrawn 1860?].* Land Case Map F-919. *Courtesy of the Bancroft Library, University of California, Berkeley (see page 208).*

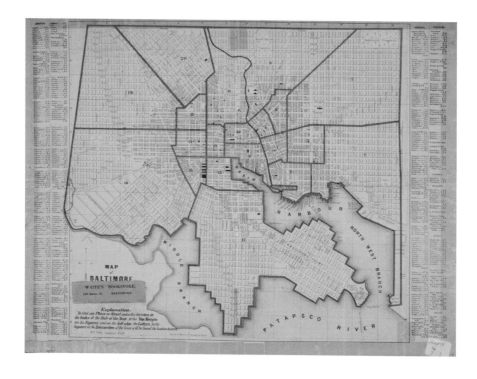

Map of Baltimore, *1859. Baltimore City Sheet Maps Collection.*
Courtesy of the Sheridan Libraries, Johns Hopkins University (see page 332).

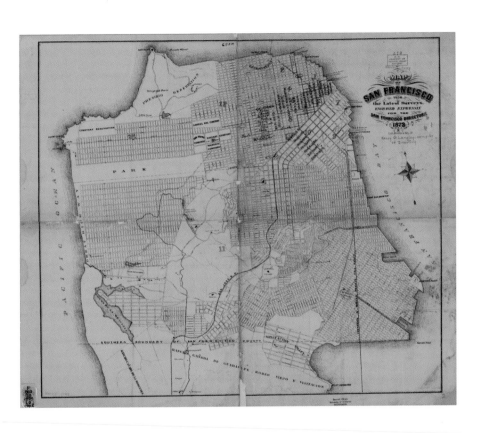

Map of San Francisco from Latest Surveys Engraved Expressly for the
San Francisco Director, Bancroft's Official Guide, *1873. Courtesy of the
David Rumsey Historical Map Collection, Stanford University (see page 333).*

Baltimore Street. Edward Sachse, Baltimore Street Looking West from Calvert Street, *1850. Courtesy of the Maryland Historical Society (see page 250).*

Sansome Street, San Francisco. William Hahn, Market Scene Sansome Street,
San Francisco, 1873. *Wikimedia Commons (see page 347).*

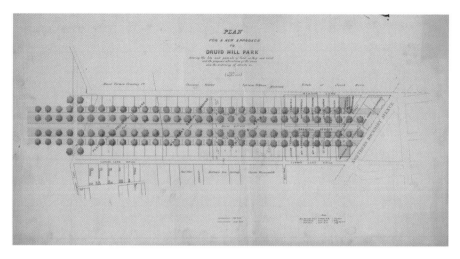

Baltimore's tree-lined streets. Plan for the street to Druid Hill Park, ca. 1860.
Courtesy of the Sheridan Libraries, Johns Hopkins University (see page 355).

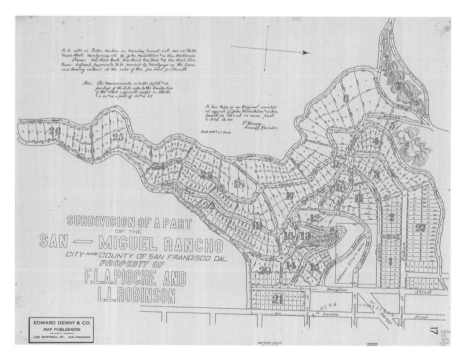

Curving landscape atop San Francisco. Subdivision of San Miguel, 1867. Courtesy of the
Earth Science and Map Library, University of California, Berkeley (see page 354).

Apolinario wed Juana Briones, who had been born down the peninsula in the village of Branciforte. She was the grandchild of a mulatto and a mestizo. By the time he applied for land thirteen years later, Miranda had sired five children. Someone in the household had been cognizant of California land policy, for Apolinario petitioned the *comandante* of the Presidio for a piece of land, one hundred varas square, at a place known as Ojo de Agua de Figueroa. The petition asked for this small parcel in the name of "favor and justice" and covered all the legal bases for receiving a land grant: it recognized that the *comandante* had the power to grant *solares*, expressed Miranda's desire "to Establish myself and for his family," and begged a reward for service at the Presidio. Miranda added that he had already erected a house at the site.[16]

Years later, the neighbors of Apolinario Miranda and Juana Briones de Miranda recalled that the family had occupied the Ojo de Agua before 1833, having planted a garden there and built a corral for their cattle. Carmen Bernal testified that Miranda continued to "occupy the place, had fruit trees there and cultivated all the ground and so remained there until after the war and the Americans came." Lacking a land title, Miranda did not establish formal boundaries or draw up a cadastral map to mark his ownership. He counted on the testimony of his neighbors to provide legitimacy for his claim. The witnesses plotted out the Miranda land by reference to a spring, rough-hewn fences, and the reassurance that the boundaries were "generally well known." "I think," said one neighbor, "this a fair representation of the lots this green spot and the Southerly side of the map . . . 50 varas from the spring branch to the fence on either side." Testifying retrospectively before the US Land Commission, another old-timer, named Charles Brown, sited Miranda's land about a mile east of the Presidio. Another located it in a place called "Yerba Buena." The measurement and the jurisdiction may not have been exact, but the reality of life on the land was without dispute. Without any legal sanction, from either the church, or the Crown, or the Republic of Mexico, a family of ten had taken up the land on which to make a living and maintained it into a third generation.[17]

Carmen Bernal, who testified in support of the Miranda title, was also summoned to defend her own right to land before the Land Commission. The widow and her deceased husband, José Cornelio Bernal, had been assigned the mestizo *casta* in the census of 1790. In 1835, they applied for title to a tract of land near Mission San Francisco, arguing that this *solar*, or house lot, had been promised to them by the priest as compensation for José's service to the church. Governor Figueroa denied this original request

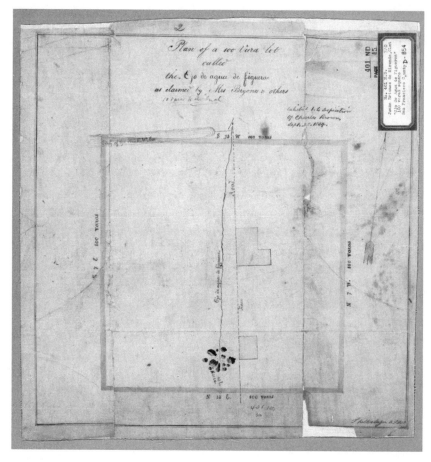

Plan of a 100 Vara Lot Called Ojo de Agua *[1854]. Land Case Map D-854.
Courtesy of the Bancroft Library, University of California, Berkeley.*

on solid Spanish principles. They were poaching on the land of the Mission, the "property of the town of San Francisco de Asís which it deserves as the common land for cattle." The governor would permit Bernal to graze his cattle there, but not to take ownership of part of the public weal. Bernal returned to the *ayuntamiento* in 1839, after the missions had been fully secularized, with an inflated request, for a full ten leagues, over forty thousand acres. In keeping with his rising expectations, Bernal was scrupulous in following the procedures for a land grant. His petition to the justice of the peace, Francisco Guerrero, began, "Whereas Don José Cornelio Bernal has for his own personal benefit and that of his family, asked for the place called 'Rincon de las Salinas' and 'Potrero Viejo.'" Although he was the son of an illiterate mestizo, Bernal was well informed about Mexican policy. In the words recorded in the case, he expressed his desire to enjoy his property "freely and exclusively, making such use and cultivation of it as he may see fit," and agreed that "within one year he shall build a house and it shall be inhabited," and that "he shall ask the respective magistrate to give him judicial possession in virtue of this dispatch, by whom the boundaries shall be marked out" by such natural landmarks as "some fruit, or useful forest trees." Bernal's compliance with Mexican land policies secured him a title to the sprawling ranch called Rincon de Salinas y Potrero Viejo. In securing his grant, he also wrote his name indelibly on the map of San Francisco, in the neighborhoods now known as Bernal Heights and the Potrero.[18]

Bernal would later testify before the US Land Commission that he had lost the original map, or *diseño*, that had accompanied his petition. He relied instead on the testimony of neighbors to support his claims. They readily obliged, stating that the boundaries of Bernal's ranch were "definite and well known," or "generally, publically and notoriously known." José de la Cruz Sánchez, who had been born at the Presidio and was a one-time *alcalde*, recalled that Bernal had built a house at the Rincón long ago, planted a garden (of one hundred varas), and tended milch cows. Soon four hundred head of cattle were "roaming widely" through Potrero Viejo. Bernal marked off the rancho's borders by "a small brook or spring branch which is called La Precita, along the main road to San José." Another witness marked the western boundary of Potrero Viejo as "along the edge of the bay." When the United States threatened to advance into Alta California in the 1840s, Bernal worried about defending his land with such impressionistic evidence and employed a French Swiss surveyor to measure his southern boundary more precisely. Jean Vioget's mapping technique was primitive: he measured Bernal's rancho in Castilian varas using rawhide ropes that had a tendency to expand and retract with the weather. It would take some time to standardize the measurement of the vara (and establish a rough equivalence with 33 inches). Bernal's patrimony would be put in jeopardy once US land agents took command of California territory. During the Mexican period and among his neighbors, however, his property was secure.[19]

Bernal's large ranch, located down the peninsula, and Miranda's modest farm site, farther north, were only two examples of the vernacular spaces created by the first Californios. The Mexican land grant awarded to Candelario

---

and Paula Valencia in 1840 typifies a third way of occupying the shores of San Francisco Bay. The Valencias dutifully petitioned the *alcalde* Francisco Guerrero for a small *solar* of one hundred square varas. Candelario was a descendent of a Presidio soldier, an *españolo* by *casta*, who had served a term of ten years and four months when he petitioned to be released from the cavalry of San Francisco. In all probability, he had occupied and made use of that land while he was still a soldier in the service of New Spain. His petition claimed that he had "lived there ten years before the grant and planted potatoes, beans and other things for his family." It was not until 1839, however, that he initiated the legal procedures to obtain a title. Candelario petitioned the *alcalde* "in consideration of the services he had rendered" and asked that "his large family" receive "the ruins of a house called de las Lugas." Another document, submitted for the approval of Governor Alvarado, reported that Candelario was asking for a title to "the apartments I actually occupy and its ruins to the W[est] of said house for the principal house." The house in question was the former residence of the Franciscan padres.[20]

The Valencias had constructed their homestead within the walls of the Mission, literally atop the Spanish past. They did not mark off their land as a mathematical portion of the earth's surface. The boundaries of their *solar* were established by agreement with their neighbors and confirmed by intimate, local knowledge. Candelario said he had "built a house on it that year and Enclosed the Lot and planted it with vegetables." His family "lived in the house, and . . . continued to occupy it till the present time[,] and . . . [had] dug a well on the lot." The land was improved with the fruit of family labor, claimed as an inheritance from the past, and held with the consent of the neighbors; in the words of one San Francisco pioneer, the Valencia land was framed by "some old and abandoned fruit trees belonging to the orchard, and bounded by the Lot of don José Antonio Galindo." The tracts of land taken up by the Valencias and by their neighbor José Galindo were one hundred and two hundred square varas. This was larger than a standard house plot and large enough for gardens, a corral, and a few head of livestock, but it was too small to be called a rancho. The land grants around the old missions were spaces for the sustenance of families rather than for the grazing of herds of cattle whose hides might be traded on an international market.

José Galindo's testimony on behalf of the Valencias' claim reveals that these spaces served a larger purpose as well. The space "in the ruins of the mission" had become a node of social bonds dating back at least a generation. According to local practice and in keeping with Mexican policy, the land once managed by the Ohlone was to pass on to the settlers' progeny, both sons and daughters. Upon his death, Candelario's wife would aggressively defend their title to the ancestral land. Twenty years later she would support a petition for her sons to retain ownership of the family homestead. Estagno and José Ramón Valencia went before the United States Land Commission testifying that they were "natives of the place under your control . . . not having any other industry than that of tiller of the ground we implore you for our benefit and that of our parent and large family to grant us two hundred square varas." Candelario had conveyed the land to his children in "consideration of natural love and good will."[21]

Devoted largely to subsistence agriculture, the patches of family property near the Mission were defined by social and familial relations. Neither these small tracts nor the ranchos spread around the bay were measured and bounded in a very precise fashion. According to local recollections, "There were no marks for the boundaries" of the Valencia tract, just "the orchard of the mission . . . on the north[,] and the fences marked the other sides. The claimants were fencing it in when they petitioned for it." Another witness, Manuel Castro, was unable to support his endorsement of the Valencia claim by finding it on a map of the area. "I do not know the names of the Streets," he said. "It was on [the] Street which ran in front of the Church." Confused by maps and not accustomed to recognizing street names, the descendants of San Francisco's first settlers knew their land in immediate and personal ways. The spatial terms scattered through the records of the US Land Commission in the 1850s nonetheless suggest that these pioneers were building a distinctive space of their own. Near the Mission, but not part of it, a hodgepodge of small farms formed a latticework of neighboring dwellings, gardens, fields, and pastures.[22]

MAKING DOLORES: THE NUCLEUS OF THE *VECINDAD*

When the pace of issuing land grants heated up in the 1840s, new migrants came to settle in the area around the Mission. Several of these newcomers, José Jesús Noé, Francisco de Haro, and Francisco Guerrero among them, helped to give new definition to the surrounding land. Haro arrived, probably from Monterey, sometime in the 1820s. Noé came up from Mexico with the Padrés and Híjar expedition. Guerrero also arrived with the Mexican colonists. All three of them became local leaders, at one time or another assuming the position of *alcalde* or member of the Diputación. Noé and Haro made it their business to take and shape the land at the heart of historical San Francisco. Noé, a landless soldier, stayed on in California after Híjar and Padrés went back to Mexico. He took the opportunity to become a landowner in 1839. Noé's *informe* justified his ownership on the customary grounds: "He solicits from your Honor the grant of the Camaritas . . . that he may erect a house thereon and cultivate some vegetable gardens for the support of his family." José Castro, in the capacity of justice of the peace, granted Noé's petition on the customary grounds: "The petitioner is an honest man having a large family, and is now in the most indigent circumstances." Governor Alvarado approved Noé's petition.[23]

Noé was hoping to secure something more than a plot that would support a house and garden, the typical meaning of a *solar*. He went on to explain that he was "obliged to remove from the Ranch of 'Las Pulgas,' where he and his family now reside," because it was "a place very retired in itself and where they may be exposed to some mishap as it is quite isolated." Finding the rancho too remote from local society, Noé sought a home site closer to his fellow Californios. The place he chose was "near to the creek and landing of the Ex Mission of San Francisco."[24]

Noé's neighbors came before the US Land Commission bearing witness to the authenticity of Noé's claim to land near the former mission. Candelario Valencia stepped forward to testify that he had known the land since his youth. He reported that Noé had complied with the Mexican rule of landholding by building "a small house of wood" and a corral there within a year of the grant. When the garrulous old Presidio soldier José de la Cruz Sánchez testified to the authenticity of Noé's claim, he invoked his own crusty credentials: "I lived there, I was in a manner raised there and was well acquainted with the ground." José Castro plotted the location of Noé's grant on another spatial matrix, giving it a definite place name, the Establecimiento de Dolores (settlement of Dolores). Today, the site of Noé's homestead can be identified by a house number along Mission Street in the city. In 1840, its coordinates were a spring, and the road that went from the Mission to San Jose. The place called Dolores had become a distinctive social settlement by the 1840s, a cluster of properties close to the old Mission but not named for San Francisco de Asís.[25]

By 1843, José Jesús Noé recognized the value of this emerging concentration around the old Mission. He refused the first survey of his property and went back and had it measured again, to make sure that his three hundred square varas were of the proper size and in the optimal location. Over the

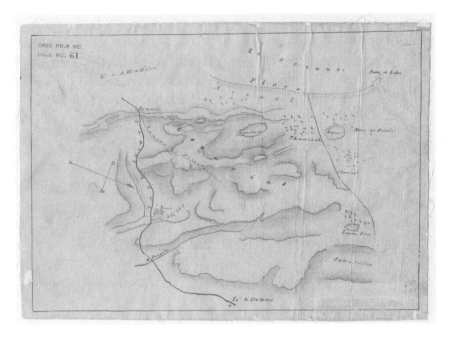

Diseño *of Rancho San Miguel, 1845. Land Case Map B-9.*
Courtesy of the Bancroft Library, University of California, Berkeley.

next few years, Noé's understanding of land values would grow, and he would become more perspicacious about the procedures for establishing owner-ship. In 1845, the once impecunious soldier petitioned for another grant, this time before Governor Pío Pico, capitalizing on Mexican largesse on the eve of the Mexican-American War. He asked this time for one league of former mission land, and he took care to have it surveyed according to the reliable Yankee measurement of chains. Governor Pío Pico granted Noé's request with a curt reference to "razón y justicia." Noé named his new land in the style of the Californio elite, Rancho San Miguel. The parvenu orbited through the landscape of San Francisco, moving from the social center to remote ranchland on an upward pathway of social mobility.[26]

Although Noé's route through the lands around San Francisco Bay was rather circuitous, it was not solitary. He was hardly alone in tracing a full cir-cumference of the San Francisco Peninsula, petitioning for land both at the center and on the periphery of the original Spanish sites. Perhaps the most adept navigator of the space between the ranchos and the Establecimiento

---

de Dolores was Francisco de Haro. Like Noé, Haro secured multiple land grants, including one in Dolores and one on the border with Noé's Rancho San Miguel. Haro purchased Rancho Laguna de la Merced from the heirs of the first settler José Antonio Galindo in 1835, at the going price in pesos, American dollars, or cows. Five years later, he petitioned the *alcalde*, Francisco Guerrero, for a one-hundred-square vara *solar* in consideration of his growing family, "conforme a justicia" (according to justice). In 1843, he was awarded an additional fifty square varas for his service to Mexico, and because he already occupied the house. When he died in 1847, Haro left seven children, including the two sons who, along with his widow, would be called upon to defend their title to the family property before the US Land Commission.[27]

The Land Commission was skeptical of the claims of the heirs of Francisco de Haro and originally rejected their title to the grant of one hundred square varas because the "description [of the premises] is too vague and indefinite." Indeed, it would be difficult to align the Haros' grants with the standard American streetscape, but Spanish-speaking witnesses who testified for them had no doubt about the spatial contours of the places where they had made their homes "before the Americans came." Residents from miles around rallied in support of the Haros' Mexican land title. The witnesses, who all claimed long-term and intimate knowledge of Haro and his land, included elderly men who had resided at the Presidio and the Mission as children, such as Tiburcio Vásquez and José Fernandez.[28]

All these far-flung occupants of the shores of San Francisco Bay concurred in several particulars about Haro's grants and those of his sons and his neighbors. Their plots were lined up around the Mission, but not for a religious purpose. Francisco de Haro and his neighbors had expropriated the Mission for domestic and secular use. They had made their homes in the Spanish ruins, the former quarters of the padres, the guardsmen, the majordomo, even the oxen. Other depositions relied on such landmarks as the former soap factory, a mill, a grease boiler, the ateliers for making cloth and blankets, and the shops of the blacksmith and the carpenters. The memories of Indians had not faded from the cognitive map of the residents of Dolores; they also sited Haro's property in relation to the *monjerío*, where "the Indian nuns of the Mission were shut up at night," and two rows of Indian houses that ran parallel to the walls of the Mission. Most of these landmarks were "now in ruins." Some witnesses dated their demise to 1840. References to a few natural features, such as the gardens and the "acequia

---

[irrigation ditch] which flowed on the North side of the mission crossing the road to the Presidio," were scattered amid the adobe walls, patios, and gardens of the *establecimiento*.[29]

The Haros and their neighbors were not seeking elbowroom à la Daniel Boone. Not content out on their expansive ranchland, they sought a central gathering place and remodeled the grounds and buildings of the Mission for that purpose. Petitions for these small land grants of fifty to four hundred square varas used the Spanish terms *solar* and *suerte* interchangeably, not distinguishing very carefully between house lots and fields. By routinely requesting a plot of one hundred or more square varas, they exhibited an appetite for house lots that were larger than those of either a Mexican pueblo or an Anglo American town, spaces large enough for a corral and a garden as well as a domicile.

The fact that the Mexican land grants near the former mission were

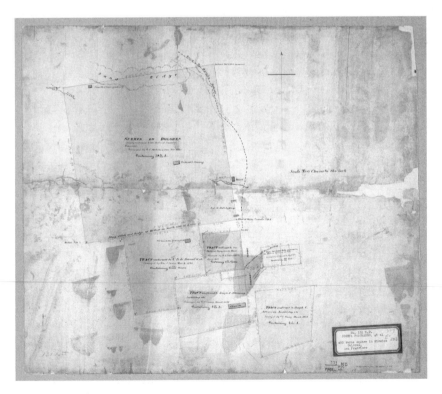

Survey, "400 Varas Square in Mission Dolores" [1862?]. Land Case Map D-913A. Courtesy of the Bancroft Library, University of California, Berkeley.

—

measured in square varas further substantiates the impression that the Californios were constructing a nucleated urban settlement, or at least an ad hoc village, at the place they called Dolores, formerly the site of Misión San Francisco de Asís. They did not, however, align their small parcels of land along a street grid. Francisco de Haro lived and died in the majordomo's house on "the corner of what was formerly the plaza." Another neighbor located the Valencia tract in the general whereabouts of the church, along roads and a space he called a plaza. He described the dimensions of this public space as "a lot of straight lines longer one way than another, a rectangular quadrangle." Dolores was not just any village; it had configured space in a loosely Hispanic style around an unpretentious plaza, much like the pueblos of Sonora and the southwestern United States. Haro's petition for a *suerte* of fifty square varas in 1843 clearly demonstrated that a Mexican American—Californian—space had grown up around the ruins of the Mission. He located his small land grants "en el Establecimiento de Dolores . . . en frente de la calle principal y plaza"—that is, at the settlement called Dolores in front of the main street and the plaza.[30]

Acknowledged in the legal records compiled by the local *alcaldes* and the governors of a Mexican territory, the *vecindad* of Dolores was exercising vernacular sovereignty. With their rights to private property now sanctioned by the Republic of Mexico and certified by local officials, the people of the Partido de San Francisco and the Establecimento de Dolores were something more than *vecinos*: they assumed the status of *ciudadanos*. It was by formally and legally taking land, not by securing the franchise, that the Californios became active citizens of a Californian republic.[31]

If there was a discernable concentration of Mexican citizenry on the shores of San Francisco Bay, it was probably near the former Mission. A German visitor in the year of the Gold Rush, 1849, took the three-mile journey from the Port of San Francisco to the site of the Mission and found some commercial amenities there: two taverns, a dancing room, a drinking and gambling saloon, and a brewery operated by his countrymen. By then Dolores had acquired a cosmopolitan air. After the death of Francisco de Haro and just "before the Americans came," his house "in front of the plaza" became the residence of his son-in-law, Charles Brown. Brown was one of four sons-in-law named as heirs to Haro's lands. They included Andrew Dennison, who occupied a house along the same wing of the former mission, and two other sons-in-law, by the names of Fisher and Jameson, who resided farther down the road. The fourth son-in-law, Francisco Guerrero, was the most notable figure in the extended family, rising to the status of large land-owner, local *alcalde*, and prominent figure in the Diputación. As *alcalde*, Guerrero signed off on one of Haro's original grants. Coincidentally, he had a small lot in Dolores in addition to five leagues, over twenty thousand of remote ranchland in Solano and San Mateo Counties.[32]

The Haro kinship chart is worthy of notice for a number of reasons. First, it demonstrates that the Establecimiento de Dolores had become an entrenched social space, two to three generations deep and encompassing a dense network of people. Second, it exposes certain incestuous political practices at work in Dolores, including rampant nepotism in the granting of land. Haro not only relied on his son-in-law to acquire a land title, but also returned the favor when he rose to the status of *alcalde* himself. The family patriarch held that office in 1844 and received his grant for Rancho Merced in 1845. The surnames of Haro's sons-in-law attest to a third characteristic of the neighborhood. The vested familial interests that laced through Dolores were not ethnically exclusive. By 1840, Californio families such as the Haros were regularly intermarrying with Europeans and Americans. Charles Brown, an American sailor who jumped ship onto the northern shore of the San Francisco Peninsula around 1829, took a job with the Hudson Bay Company, subsequently opened a mill, and ultimately secured two parcels of land, a ranch in Napa as well as the property in Dolores. Not coincidentally, Brown also won the hand of Francisco de Haro's daughter. As he recalled it, he wed "a daughter of the country" and "thus became one of the natives." Brown's intimacy with the Californios began immediately upon his arrival in San Francisco Bay; he debarked near a sparsely inhabited cove where only one structure offered him shelter. It happened to be the farmhouse of Juana Briones de Miranda, who, as you will recall, had migrated east of the Presidio to the riparian valley of Ojo de Aqua de Figueroa. Asked to state her place of residence before the Americans arrived, she answered neither the Presidio, nor the Mission, nor Dolores, but a place called Yerba Buena, harbinger of another San Francisco place, and representing another innovation in the taking and shaping of the land.[33]

MAKING A PLACE CALLED YERBA BUENA

The northeast corner of the San Francisco Peninsula did not become a beacon to settlement until several millennia after humans first arrived at the shores of the great bay. The Ohlone did not establish a village there, and neither the Spanish nor the Mexicans found it fit for colonizing. The terrain along the shore varied from "a high precipitous rock bluff" to sand hills and swampland. As late as 1820, only a few Russians trading in the pelts of sea otters made use of the shore of San Francisco Bay as a commercial landing place. Approached by sea as late as 1838, the harbor of Yerba Buena appeared to be just a "pretty sandy beach" with "a rough shed up the hill and the house of the city laundress lady Doña Juana Briones." The closest thing to an official imprimatur for occupying this space was the Mexican grant to Apolinario Miranda, the spouse of Juana Briones de Miranda, located to the east of the Presidio at Ojo de Agua.[34]

Juana Briones was the most prominent descendent of the Anza expedition to take up residence in proximity to the center of what would one day become the city of San Francisco. By 1840, she had discarded her husband's name and acquired a reputation as the most enterprising occupant of the north beach. Juana supported herself and her children by gardening, by dairying, and occasionally by serving as a healer, a midwife, or a hotelier. From her perch along the north shore, she also dispensed hospitality to passing ships and runaway sailors. Her guests included one Robert Ridley, who would marry her daughter Presentación, and William Richardson, an English renegade from a passing ship. Richardson struck up a fast friendship with Juana Briones and assisted her in building a larger house farther to the east, at a place now called Washington Square, but known in the Mexican era as Washerwoman's Cove, after yet another of Juana's business enterprises. If anyone deserves the credit for founding the city of San Francisco, it would be this international pair: Juana Briones and William Richardson.[35]

Richardson called the beachhead of San Francisco "an anchorage"; the Californios called it *un punto* (a point) or *un puerto* (a port). Whatever the term, this embryonic settlement was born of the sea rather than the land and grew with the trade along the Pacific. Soon after washing up on the north beach, William Richardson began operating two schooners that transported the rancheros' produce to the growing numbers of merchant vessels sailing the Pacific. He wedged his way into Mexico's maritime politics, becoming a naturalized citizen in 1822, and married the daughter of the *comandante* of the presidio. Rechristened "Guillermo," Richardson was soon trading along the coast as far south as Los Angeles, where he persuaded Governor Manuel Micheltorena to award him the office of captain of the Port of San Francisco. Richardson was also awarded a small land grant, of one hundred square varas, just above a cove called Yerba Buena, after the fragrant local foliage that Juana Briones purportedly brewed into a tea.

Like Juana Briones and "Guillermo" Richardson, the early land-takers of Yerba Buena Cove had commerce, not agriculture or pasturage, on their minds. Richardson determined that the *embarcadero* the Spanish had originally sited near the Presidio was vulnerable to furious winds and an inauspicious location for an international port. With authorization from the Mexican governor, he moved the anchorage to the more peaceful cove just south of the eastern corner of the peninsula. At the time Richardson was assessing the commercial potential of Yerba Buena, the only inhabitants of the cove were a small band of Russians hunting sea otters. At about the same time, a British cartographer affixed the name "Yerba Buena" on his map and gave the port on San Francisco Bay a place on the international maritime chart.[36]

The tentacles of global capitalism had penetrated as far as Yerba Buena Cove by the 1830s. Governor José Figueroa worried about "the many adventurers, native and foreign, who, like meteors on a tempestuous night, are on every side crossing among us."[37] Citizens of the Mexican Republic were not shy of such interloping *empresarios*. Mariano Vallejo, *comandante* of the Presidio, saw this corner of San Francisco Bay as an ideal place to conduct lucrative international trade. He formed a strategic alliance with Guillermo Richardson and convinced Governor Michelterena that Yerba Buena was the best place to collect duties on the foreign goods sold to the rancheros. The governor granted permission to move the Mexican customs office north from Monterey.

The settlement in Yerba Buena Cove was one small inconspicuous stop on the route of nearly one thousand ships, representing twenty different nations, that were circling through the Pacific in the years before the Gold Rush. By the late eighteenth century, European traders had converted the littoral world of American Indians into waterways of international commerce. To the mariners who trolled the Pacific coast, the shoreline of California was the eastern border of a vast oceanic trade route, what historian David Igler defined as "an intricate set of overlapping borderlands linked by some very treacherous seas." In 1800, the San Francisco Bay was one quiet way station in the vast commercial network that spanned the Pacific. The floodgates to international commerce were opened in 1821, when the Republic of Mexico suspended the tariffs that Spain had imposed on international trade. The British merchant William E. P. Hartnell was one of the first to tap the market

---

for European goods among the rancheros of San Francisco. Under the corporate charter of McCulloch, Hartnell and Company, he sailed up from Peru to San Francisco and on to Honolulu. Hartnell was joined by a cohort of Boston traders, the likes of William Heath Davis and Thomas O. Larkin. Although 45 percent of the ships docking in Pacific ports flew the US flag, merchant capitalism Pacific style was a cosmopolitan enterprise conducted by ship captains of diverse nationalities operating out of multiple ports.[38]

When the tide of oceanic commerce lapped into San Francisco Bay, it left the small Port of Yerba Buena in its wake. Hartnell unloaded shiploads of manufactured goods destined for local consumption: sewing needles for the missions, gold-leaf booklets for the office of the *alcalde*, handkerchiefs for Guillermo Richardson, and sundry other items destined for the *habitación* of Francisco de Haro. Perhaps the most intrepid merchant in the Jurisdiccíon de San Francisco was Thomas O. Larkin. After going bankrupt in Boston, Larkin sought a second chance among the Mexicans of Alta California. "If I go to Monterey I shall do as the people do," he wrote. "And if I chose to marry there I should do it, providing I had any (say a little) love for the Lady." Commerce did not conquer love entirely. Larkin married an Anglo-Protestant like himself who was already the mother of his illegitimate child. He would, however, curry the favor of the Californios by baptizing his children as Catholics. Larkin maneuvered agilely through the loose web of Mexican land policies and would soon secure twenty-eight thousand acres, including numerous lots in Yerba Buena.[39]

The port of Yerba Buena Cove grew slowly at first. The pioneer merchants, from Russia, Britain, and the United States, traded in the pelts of sea otters. Managing the fur trade could be a desolate and lonely business. It ended in suicide for one employee of the Hudson Bay Company, who was lured into making dangerous arms sales during one of the military coups that plagued the Republic of Mexico. Not everyone was as plucky as Guillermo Richardson. A native of Ohio, Jacob Leese, conducted a flourishing business in the exchange of hides and tallow at Yerba Buena. Leese traded all along the Santa Fe Trail, from New Mexico to Los Angeles and San Francisco. He secured the title to a lot of one hundred square varas next to Richardson's, where he built a warehouse and stocked it with commodities from around the world destined for local ranches. In the late 1840s, Leese picked up cargo in Hong Kong and incurred debts in London amounting to $4,600.

By this time, Leese faced stiff competition from merchants like Guillermo Davis, who did a steady business with rancheros like José Castro, who piled up a debt of over $1,000 for such things as cherry brandy, silk handkerchiefs, china trunks, tablecloths, shawls, and sugar. As long as the cattle business flourished, the Californios could afford such luxuries. Castro had credit with Davis and Company in the amount of $4,000 for tallow and fowls. Haro owed Davis $1,994 for such purchases as *aguardiente*, brandy, silk stockings, handkerchiefs, shawls, and gloves; the debt was offset by credit for one bull at $1,964.[40] The account books of another local merchant, William A. Leidesdorff, transcribe an itinerary that circled the continent before docking at Yerba Buena. Leidesdorff, who hailed from the Danish Caribbean, sailed his bark, the *Julia Anne*, from New Orleans and around Cape Horn to San Francisco, where he amassed a fortune in land as well as dollars. Leidesdorff made contracts with Richardson, counted the Peraltas among his customers, and lobbied the *alcalde*, Francisco Guerrero, and Governor Pío Pico until he obtained the post of commissioner of customs for Alta California.[41]

Yankee visitors to Yerba Buena saw the commercial potential of the harbor, yet had only passing knowledge of those who had resided nearby for two generations. When Richard Henry Dana docked there in 1835, he found "a newly begun settlement, mostly of Yankee Californians, called Yerba Buena, which promises well." Foreign observers such as Dana did not have the demography of the small settlement quite right. Yankees did not constitute the majority of inhabitants of Yerba Buena. Edward Kemble, who arrived at the late date of 1846 in the company of a boatload of Mormons seeking a new colony, formed a slightly more accurate impression of Yerba Buena, albeit one that was both bigoted and distorted by hindsight. Kemble recalled Yerba Buena as a "half-breed babe—the half Mexican and half 'foreign' prodigy whose infant ligaments are scarcely recognizable in the stately San Francisco."[42]

Reconstructing an exact ethnic profile of Yerba Buena is an impossible task. A sketchy census, dated 1842, listed three Americans, three Englishmen, one resident of Dublin, one from Holland, and one from the apparently sovereign nation of Boston. Another census, supplied by John Henry Brown and dated 1846, registered a German baker, a shoemaker with his Indian wife, a Mexican, an Irishman, and "a half-bred Indian and wife" as among the first settlers. Brown himself added to this cosmopolitan medley. Born in England, where he had been apprenticed to a sailing company, he had docked in Havana, Philadelphia, New York, Cincinnati, and somewhere among the Cherokees before landing in Yerba Buena. The itinerary that took William Leidesdorff to Yerba Buena began in the Danish Caribbean, where

———

it was rumored that he was a bastard and a mulatto. A final item on Brown's census of Yerba Buena registered "a few Mexican families whose names we will omit [who] usually spent the winter months in the city." A housing survey conducted in 1844 depicted a similarly heterogeneous built environment, consisting of thirty-one frame houses, twenty-six adobe buildings, and twenty-two shanties. Local Indians still outnumbered the combined ranks of Mexicans, Europeans, and Americans in the population of Alta California by an estimated ratio of five to one. All that one can conclude from this scattered evidence is that the population beginning to concentrate on the northeast corner of the San Francisco Peninsula was tilting decisively toward those of non-Hispanic origins. The majority, however, were not members of the tribe calling themselves "Americans."[43]

If one wished to give Yerba Buena an ethnic label, it would best be called a mestizo town, its population a mélange of Mexicans, Europeans, and Americans. When the adobe customhouse was erected just up the hill from Yerba Buena Cove in around 1843, it anchored a rustic international port town under a Mexican flag. When asked to name the pioneer residents of the port, Guillermo Richardson later recollected that the premier merchant had been Jacob Leese; other pioneering businessmen went by names such as Juan Cooper, Juan Fuller, and Guillermo Davis. Richardson also gave Juana Briones a prominent place among these founders. Although San Francisco Bay was under the tenuous political control of the Republic of Mexico, commerce at its major port was conducted by immigrants, mostly from Europe: Peter (or "Pedro") Sherreback, native of Denmark; Jean ("Juan") Vioget, from French Switzerland; and Robert T. Ridley, "a regular English cockney," for example. Many of the settlers became naturalized citizens of Mexico; one, Guillermo Hinckley, would even serve as *alcalde*. The evolving settlement of Yerba Buena reflected the cosmopolitan aura of the population. In recognition of the demographic mix, the *ayuntamiento* began to issue its edicts in English as well as Spanish.

The households as well as the businesses of Yerba Buena were mestizo institutions. "Jacobo" Leese followed the example of Charles Brown, "Guillermo" Hartnell, and "Guillermo" Richardson, making a strategic marital alliance with a California family. He wed the sister of Mariano Vallejo. Four of Francisco de Haro's heirs had non-Spanish names: Brown, Harrison, Dennison, and Tissot. The Hartnell family business mastered this marital strategy: Hartnell wed the daughter of a client in the Port of Honolulu, while his son wed into Rancho San Leandro. The founding mother of Yerba Buena,

Juana Briones, also sanctioned mixed marriage as a commercial strategy. One of her daughters would marry the cockney tavern keeper Robert Ridley, and her adopted daughter wed a merchant, John Cooper, a kinsman of Thomas Larkin.[44]

The California wives of Anglo merchants brought a variety of assets into their marriages, including their own property. Spanish law was more accommodating to women than English common law as codified by William Blackstone. Wives and married daughters were permitted to hold property in their own right, accounting for the frequent appearance of women in the land records of Alta California. After her marriage to Apolinario Miranda at the chapel at Mission Dolores in 1820, Juana Briones resided with him on the small plot for which he acquired a title in 1833. Then, three years later, while Apolinario was still living, Juana was granted the first of six lots she would claim in her own name, all located in her place of business, Yerba Buena. Juana Briones maintained her residence in the village of Yerba Buena throughout her life, but her land lust did not end there. She also purchased a ranch of her own, named La Purísima, in Santa Clara County. Yet her title to property did not grant her release from patriarchal authority. As long as Juana lived with Apolinario Miranda, the father of their eight children, she was subject to abuse. She took her husband to court twelve times accusing him of domestic violence before she was finally granted a divorce.[45]

The women of Alta California who married European adventurers found that their privileges under Mexican law could be unreliable. Rosalía Vallejo is a case in point. Her claim to the substantial property of her parental family no doubt sweetened the courtship for Jacob Leese, but it was a risky wager for Rosalía. She sued Leese for divorce after he squandered her dowry. While women did appear frequently in the land records of Alta California, they usually did so as widows certifying the ownership of the lands claimed in the name of their husbands, sons, or sons-in-law. When three female heirs to the Peralta lands sued for a fair share of the family property, they were rudely and doubly rebuffed. First, the California courts honored their father's will, which bequeathed all the ranchland to their brothers, and then, in 1859, the US Supreme Court upheld their disinheritance. After the death of Francisco de Haro, his sons-in-law waged a legal battle over the division of Rancho Laguna Merced, in the process denying the wives of their rivals their rightful inheritance. Juana Briones's tenacious hold on those lots in Yerba Buena and the ranch to the south in Santa Clara is testimony not so much to the generosity of Hispanic law as to her own exceptional talent and

---

determination. Not even the driving enterprise of Juana Briones, however, could secure the privileges to which her father, sons, brothers, and abusive husband were entitled by birth. When a municipal government was installed on the shores of San Francisco Bay, men alone became *ciudadanos*. By virtue of their gender, men alone would be granted the political authority necessary to shape Yerba Buena into a viable pueblo.[46]

MAKING POLITICAL SPACE: FOUNDING A PUEBLO NEAR SAN FRANCISCO BAY

A motley crew of pioneers came together from around the world to determine the location of a future city along the shores of San Francisco Bay. They were not authorized or directed by any single, centralized authority. The location of the yet unnamed city of San Francisco was marked out without the approval of the Spanish Crown or the Mexican Republic. Until the 1820s, the *pobladores* produced a pattern of settlement according to some logic of their own: habits, memories, necessity, ambition, and some vague understanding of the rules of political sovereignty. They were not, however, without knowledge about how to fashion a local polity. Dating back as far as the eleventh century, Spanish *vecinos* had exercised a kind of municipal citizenship that entitled those who settled permanently in a certain locality to such privileges as common grazing land, rights to water, and reserves of public space, as well as a voice in community decisions. By the fifteenth century, these customs had become well-established local practices. They were part of the everyday habits of the people who made their living on contiguous land, adjoining pastures, and neighboring gardens. The *vecinos* of Dolores and Yerba Buena exercised vernacular citizenship when they defended their family plots, grazed livestock on common land, and shared the water of Dolores Creek and the bounty of the bay. Such informal, mutual, and consensual government was commonplace through much the world until the nation-state began to assume firm boundaries in the sixteenth century.

The vernacular political practices that created the Establecimiento de Dolores or the port at Yerba Buena did not, however, provide sufficient fortification for the Mexican Republic. They were not a strong bulwark against the Russian colony north of San Francisco Bay or a barricade against American trappers and farmers approaching from the east. In the 1830s, therefore, the central government of Mexico instructed the *pobladores* of Alta California to form themselves into a formal municipal government, a city, a villa, or a pueblo. The Mexico City press rejoiced in the proliferation of "new towns which are perhaps destined one day to change the face of this continent and direct the attentions of the civilized world to places now entirely unknown." The smallest unit of local sovereignty, according to Mexican specifications, was the pueblo, with a minimum population of one thousand inhabitants.[47]

In the 1830s, it would be hard to choose a single site along San Francisco Bay at which to erect a pueblo. By then the original settlers had scattered far and wide around the bay. The *pobladores*, joined by a few new Mexican colonists and some transient Pacific merchants, had laid out a superfluity of rudimentary spaces on the northern tip of the San Francisco Peninsula—the Presidio, the Mission, the ranchos, the Establecimiento de Dolores, and Yerba Buena. These settlements went by a variety of names, of which Yerba Buena and Dolores were only two disputed monikers. Various place names, including San Francisco de Asís, Mission Dolores, Dolores, Yerba Buena, Yerba Buena Cove, and simply San Francisco, were prefixed by sundry generic categories of political space: *partido, puerto, punto, pareja, establecimiento, municipalidad*, even *corporación*.

Identifying a central pueblo within this linguistic and political haze took some doing. According to Governor José Castro, his predecessor José Figueroa had first proposed marking off a town along the bay in 1834. After Figueroa's death, Castro endorsed the plan, and in 1837, under order from Governor Alvarado, the pueblo began to materialize as "a town in the place called Yerba Buena." Castro and Alvarado happened to be the first native-born governors of Alta California and members of the Diputación, but neither of them lived near Yerba Buena Cove. Only a small fraction of the scattered residents of the San Francisco Bay area clustered around the small harbor. Therefore, Governor Castro's call to elect an *ayuntamiento* for San Francisco was directed to the regional government, the *Partido* of San Francisco. The summons to elect *alcaldes* and *regidores* for the new pueblo reflected the loosely drawn and expansive boundaries of the Californios' political geography. Beginning in 1836, residents of Dolores, Yerba Buena, the east side of the bay, San Mateo to the south, and Sonoma to the north all attended the meetings of the *ayuntamiento* called San Francisco. The political geography of the ayuntamiento was capacious but imprecise. The *alcaldes* summoned "todos los vecinos de la esta Jurisdicción de San Francisco" (all the neighbors of the jurisdiction of San Francisco) to meet to elect their leaders. But the location of their annual elections fluctuated.[48]

The precise location of the meetings of the pueblo varied. In December 1835, the body politic came together for an election "in the Plaza of said

Pueblo," cast 108 ballots, and elevated eight of their number to public office. Sometimes the *ayuntamiento* met in Yerba Buena, sometimes at the Mission, occasionally at the Presidio. The 1837 election was held in the "sala principal" (main room), presumably of the old Mission. In 1844, the electors met "en la sala juzgado de la Misión" (in the judge's chambers of the Mission), but only ten of thirty-eight voters listed their residence as "Dolores." Thirteen came from the ranches, thirteen from Yerba Buena, and two from the Presidio. This itinerant location of the *ayuntamiento* caused some confusion, inconvenience, and contention. In 1835, several of the rancheros who had migrated some distance from the Mission and the Presidio (including the Peraltas, Castros, and Bernals) petitioned to change their affiliation to San Jose. Those who lived closer to the old Mission also grumbled about the expansive geography of the San Francisco polity. It was rumored that a number of families from the Establecimiento de Dolores objected to the influence of the "foreigners" in Yerba Buena, and had begun agitating to form a separate pueblo.[49]

In legal terms, the creation of a pueblo on the San Francisco Peninsula was a policy of the Mexican Republic to be implemented by the governor of Alta California, but it was local residents who mapped it out upon the land. Governor Castro told the local landowners that, in calling for a pueblo in Yerba Buena, he was acting "in keeping with your desire for progress and . . . your untiring efforts for the Enlightenment and greatness of your country and of our fellow citizens." When it came to actually drawing the specific boundaries of a town, Castro did not call on one of the largest landowners or most powerful merchants of Yerba Buena. He turned to Francisco de Haro of Dolores to map out the center of a pueblo near the cove. Haro, as *alcalde*, took his assignment very seriously and abided by the strict procedures for forming an *ayuntamiento*. Before undertaking this major spatial and civic responsibility, he insisted that the *regidores* meet to endorse his plan. As Guillermo Richardson remembered it, it took two days to summon the *ayuntamiento* together from their far-flung ranches. The *regidores* acceded to the creation of a pueblo at Yerba Buena, but neither they nor the *alcalde* nor the governor ever specified its shape, borders, or dimensions. The pueblo at Yerba Buena was a vague and labile political space. Drawing citizens together from a wide and sparsely settled territory, it convened in various locations in order to ascertain and pursue unspecified common interests.[50]

Within this eccentric space, the citizens of the district of San Francisco maintained a functioning *ayuntamiento* for what would be the last decade of Mexican sovereignty in California. Although the meetings of the municipal government were infrequent, the *alcalde* and the justice of the peace effectively preserved and advanced what they saw as *los bienes públicos* (the public good). The efforts of the *ayuntamiento* to serve the general welfare are documented by a few remaining records of the Partido de San Francisco. Their municipal agenda was not that dissimilar from that of a small English borough or early American town. The local governor set up a number of police regulations: for example, sales of liquor after nine o'clock were prohibited, one was not permitted to enter the pueblo with firearms, and working on Sunday was forbidden. At a time when the supply of specie or currency was very limited, the typical punishment for such offenses was one to eight days of labor on the public works, or, in the case of serious crimes, arrest and deportation to jail in Monterey. The justice of the peace mediated and adjudicated civil disputes. The Spanish-speaking justice of the peace (*juez de paz*) was called upon to resolve the commercial disagreements that arose among and between the European and American merchants of Yerba Buena—people such as Richardson, Leese, and the merchant Nathan Spears from Boston, for example. "Roberto" Ridley lodged a complaint against his employer, the Hudson Bay Company. More modest tradesmen brought relatively trivial matters before the magistrates; the shoemaker Pedro Sherreback, for example, accused his neighbor of pilfering a frying pan, and Juan Davis asked to be compensated "con interés acostumbrado" (with the customary interest) for a stolen cow.[51]

The personal disputes that came before the *ayuntamiento* most often arose in the denser settlements of Yerba Buena and Dolores. Two spots near the port were particularly troublesome: Jean Vioget's tavern and the household of Juana Briones, which served as a kind of groggery and inn. In 1841, Guerrero, the justice of the peace, mediated a dispute between José Cornelio Bernal and John Fuller that took place in Vioget's home at Yerba Buena. Bernal, of Potrero, stood accused of insulting Fuller of Dolores "with offensive words." Fuller had retaliated with a blow to Bernal's arm and neck. The justice of the peace brokered a reconciliation without the aid of a jury. A tumult at Señora Briones's home involved as many as twenty rowdy "hijos del país" (sons of the country) who disturbed the peace with their dancing, shouting, and insolent behavior. Juana herself brought the charges, signed with a cross. Although she was illiterate, Briones knew how to use the local government to both keep the peace and protect her own domestic space. Briones was not the only wife to come before the *ayuntamiento* charging her husband with physical abuse. Another witness testified that "everybody knows" that Rafael Chaco beat and stabbed his wife. Chaco was incarcerated for spouse abuse in March 1846, but he was soon released for reasons of domestic economy: his wife had "completely recovered from the wound which he inflicted upon her; and it was time to plant corn."[52]

The legal arm of the *ayuntamiento* operated with a light and neighborly touch, making small interventions in the private affairs of the citizens, and enforcing modest regulation of the economy. Fines rather than taxes met the minimal budgetary needs. The only evidence of government interference in economic affairs was an attempt to supervise the branding of cattle and grading of leather. The efforts of the Republic of Mexico to control and tax international trade at the Port of Yerba Buena, or to encourage enterprise and capitalist development, were largely ineffectual in the far north of Alta California. The Port of San Francisco became a free trade zone by default. Still, despite the lackadaisical governance of the flimsy and elusive pueblo, the scattered residents within the jurisdiction of San Francisco had fashioned a serviceable political space around the great estuary.

PLOTTING A CALIFORNIAN URBAN LANDSCAPE

Despite instructions sent from Mexico City, the *ayuntamiento* of San Francisco did not make urban planning one of its municipal responsibilities. The first Mexican governor had prescribed lots of seventy-five square varas in size and recommended that mission buildings be converted to schools and town council chambers. Híjar and Padrés came north with orders to lay out city blocks of one hundred square varas, streets that were twenty varas wide, and a profusion of public squares: "at least after every 10 streets, besides the main square, which is to be in the center of town." Alleys were prohibited. The Diputación of San Francisco paid lip service to this methodical urban planning. It advised the local governments that in forming streets and squares and "in making concession of building lots it should be in an orderly manner . . . as required by the locality of the place."[53]

The *ciudadanos* of San Francisco had shaped their pueblo in haphazard ways, by slowly aggregating their *solares* and *suertes* in Dolores and Yerba Buena. They dutifully complied with the directive from Mexico City and plotted a pueblo near Yerba Buena, mimicking a few Hispanic principles of urban design, but using their own local compass. Something of the public spirit of Spanish urban planning was reflected in occasional references to *ejidos* and *propios*, the prohibition of the private ownership of the waterfront, and colloquial references to plazas, at both the Establecimiento de Dolores and Yerba Buena. Individual land-holding was still imperfectly private. Most land was distributed according to the public procedures of *informes* and *expedientes*, and encumbered with the restrictions set by the *ayuntamiento*. Although the Mexican government permitted the private sale of land as of 1837, business was slow and prices were moderate. A fifty-square-vara lot near Yerba Buena could be had for twenty-five pesos.[54]

It was by measuring off varas of land, piece by piece, that the *ayuntamiento* of San Francisco shaped an urban landscape. Governor Castro stipulated that lots in "el paraje nombrado Yerba Buena" should be limited to fifty square varas. The first land grant sited in "the place of Yerba Buena" dated from 1838. The office of the *alcalde* issued more *expedientes* in the 1840s, most of them for small parcels of fifty square varas. This was the standard size for a lot in a pueblo or commercial town, but substantially smaller than the parcels of land claimed by the residents of Dolores, which could be as large as four hundred square varas. For example, the *alcalde*, Haro, processed a grant of one *solar* to Joaquín Estudillo in 1835. It measured two hundred square varas. Haro exercised a bit of independence by defying the rule set by Governor Castro.[55] He also acted as a local intermediary and consultant in matters of land allotment. He advised his illiterate neighbor Candelario Bernal, among others, about the legal technicalities of the *informe*.

The embryonic landscape of San Francisco had been cobbled together from these piecemeal and irregular land grants without the ordering matrix of surveys and plans. Transportation around the bay went primarily by water routes or along pathways cut by individual ranchers traveling on horseback. As late as 1839, the only access to the *embarcadero* at Yerba Buena was by way of a narrow trail worn by "travel and use." About that time, Jacob Leese employed a single laborer who worked for seven or eight days to cut a second trail to the shore. The Russians were more diligent: they reportedly took two and a half months to open what were termed two "broad cart paths" toward their dock near the cliffs at the northeast corner of the peninsula. The pioneers of Yerba Buena did not bother to overlay the Port of San Francisco with streets, the signature of commercial rationality along the Chesapeake. Describing how Yerba Buena looked in 1846, John Henry Brown had to take some liberty with the local cartography: "There were not streets in those days," he later recalled, "but in order to locate the people and their houses in a more satisfactory manner, I will call the streets by the names which they now bear."[56]

Had Brown looked more closely, he would have found at least the semblance of one street on the map of Yerba Buena. In 1835, Guillermo Richardson had sketched a vague, unofficial plan to stake out a settlement near the shipping port of Yerba Buena. He drew two straight lines across the surface, commencing at the customhouse, and labeled them "Calle de la Fundación"). Not just another road, or *camino*, the term *calle* connoted a city street and spoke of a more deliberate attempt to create urban space on the shores of San Francisco Bay. As one might expect from the adopted Californian of British origin, however, Guillermo Richardson's rough sketch of Yerba Buena bore little resemblance to the ideal of Spanish urban planning or the Mexican plans to colonize its northern territory.

It fell to a conscientious *ciudadano* of Dolores to draft an official map of a pueblo in the Jurisdicción de San Francisco. As Guillermo Richardson remembered it, Haro came "to my tent and told me he was ready to lay out the village and needed my assistance in so doing." The specifications were few and imprecise, chiefly to reserve two hundred square varas along the beach opposite the anchorage as public space and to select a lot of one

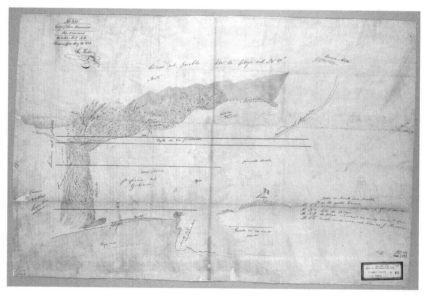

Unknown artist after William Richardson, Plan of Yerba Buena, California, 1835 [redrawn 1860?]. Land Case Map F-919. Courtesy of the Bancroft Library, University of California, Berkeley.

hundred square varas for Richardson himself. Fortunately, Haro could call upon a trained surveyor who was then residing in Yerba Buena for assistance. Jean Vioget was a well-known personality around the cove, renowned for his hearty laugh and the ruckuses he hosted in his tavern and billiard parlor. He remembered the first mapping of Yerba Buena in some detail. His instructions, which he said came from *alcalde* Guerrero rather than Haro, directed him to "regulate the grants already made, and so as to have a regular plan for future grants—I mean by regulating the grants already made, that I should make my plan to accommodate the lines of the streets and blocks as far as practical so as to embrace the Lots already granted within that plan. . . . I made no more streets because I saw no necessity of them."[57] The surviving copies of Vioget's original map show a very rough survey. It featured that one street, Calle de la Fundación, which ran diagonally toward the northwest along lots reserved for Richardson and Leese. Another lot bore the name of Vioget. A strip along the shoreline two hundred varas wide was reserved as public space. There was another conspicuously vacant space near the center of Vioget's map, an open rectangle slanted to the southwest at a short distance from the beach. Although it bore the label *plasa* in one early copy but not another, its shape clearly suggested the central public space of a Spanish or Mexican pueblo. Under interrogation before the US Land Commission in the 1850s, Richardson maintained that the pueblo of Yerba Buena extended only a few varas up from the beach. Vioget etched the words "Linderos del Pueblo" (Boundaries of the Town) on the periphery of his map, suggesting the modest scale of town planning near San Francisco Bay.

The first map of Yerba Buena was a curious piece of cartography: it was initiated by a Mexican citizen of English descent, drafted by another Mexican citizen, of Swiss-French origins, and supervised by the *alcalde* of a Mexican pueblo. It was part cadastral map, with a vague impression of a street grid, but set in a picturesque natural landscape graced with such prominent natural features as a sinuous blue lagoon, hazy sand hills, rocky cliffs, and the curving shoreline of the bay. Vioget's map—done without benefit of a compass, drawn at imprecise angles, sectioned into *solares* and measured in varas—was more like a Mexican *diseño* than either a Spanish urban plan or a Baltimore street grid. Vioget was not surveying ranchland, however. He measured commercial spaces—lots for the warehouse of Richardson and Leese, for example—and reserved other spaces for public purposes, such as two hundred varas along the beach and that suggestion of a plaza. This was mestizo cartography.

———

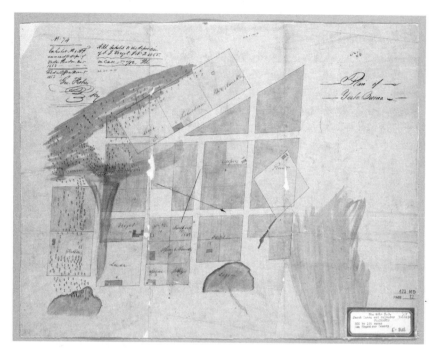

Jean Jacques Vioget, "Plan of Yerba Buena," 1839. Land Case Map D-913A.
Courtesy of the Bancroft Library, University of California, Berkeley.

Vioget's map of Yerba Buena was the closest thing to a representation of urban space produced along the shores of San Francisco Bay before the American conquest. For two generations, under the minimal supervision of the Spanish Empire or the Mexican Republic, a hearty group of settlers managed to shape the land into a livable social and political space, with a vague resemblance to Spanish urban planning and reminiscent of the pueblos and plazas of Mexico. Early San Franciscans used the terms *pueblo* and *plaza* regularly, particularly when they testified before the justice of the peace, called a local election, or appeared before the US Land Commission. In fact, San Francisco was profligate in the plotting out of these classic Hispanic spaces. Occasionally, someone would cite the Presidio as the point of origin for a pueblo and a plaza. This much is clear: the population concentrated in at least two places on the western side of San Francisco Bay, and each met the general requirements for a town or pueblo. Both Yerba Buena and the Establecimiento de Dolores adapted the *reglamentos* issued from Spain and Mexico to their own local conditions. A distinctly Californian way of occupying the land created two vernacular pueblos, each with an embryonic plaza, one near the old Mission and the other several miles to the northeast near Yerba Buena Cove. The locations of these two distinct social spaces were common knowledge to local residents and to those merchants who anchored their trading vessels on the shores of San Francisco Bay.

But no single plaza or clearly bounded pueblo exerted a centripetal force within the constellation of Spanish and Mexican spaces scattered around San Francisco Bay. Yerba Buena and Dolores were but two spots within sprawling ranchlands and a sparsely occupied expanse of earth. The colonizing expedition organized by the Republic of Mexico in 1833 began as a project of town-building but soon dissolved into the dispersal of the new settlers. Governor Figueroa reluctantly terminated the policy of town-building in the far north of the Mexican Republic. He ordered "that the colonists be free to establish themselves at a place agreeable to each individual within the limits of the Territory, where they will be assisted according to the resources available to me." Most of the members of the Híjar-Pádres expedition returned to Mexico, and the few who remained went elsewhere; they did not settle in Dolores, Yerba Buena, or anywhere on the San Francisco Peninsula. They were more likely to migrate north, to what would become the town of Sonoma. Mariano Vallejo laid out a new town near Mission San Francisco Solano, which featured a giant plaza of 800 acres, set in a street grid and accessible through a road measuring 110 feet in width. The extravagance of Vallejo's town plan might seem to inflate Hispanic planning to the dimensions more characteristic of modern America—a plaza resembling a central park and a street the size of a highway.[58]

Such traces of a Hispanic landscape, some of which can still be found scattered around Northern California, were not the product of coherent urban planning, however; nor were they anchored in one central place. The concept of the town or pueblo does not fully encompass the distinctive shape that the Californios had written on the land around the San Francisco Estuary. The human ecology of the Bay Area was contained within looser political boundaries. The jurisdiction of the Diputación of San Francisco spanned the vast bay area and incorporated two separate urban nuclei. The Californios freely adapted notions of pueblo and plaza to their local needs and the unique topography of the bay. In the process they created a kind of multilocal polity, with centers in both Dolores and Yerba Buena and extending many miles away into the ranchlands. Not as dense as the port towns growing up on the Atlantic, centered in plazas rather than channeled along streets, the municipality of San Francisco Bay embraced the pastoral hinterland. It was not set apart from the outlying plantation economy as in Baltimore.[59]

For two critical generations, a small aggregation of settlers, of diverse origins and ethnicities, had worked to produce a rudimentary but distinctive urban space on the San Francisco Peninsula, and they had done so with little regard to any superior political authority. They had driven the Ohlone from the land and waters that the natives had tended for centuries, and they had put most of the arable land to agricultural and pastoral use. On their own initiative, the steadfast migrants from Sonora and Sinaloa had claimed a vast acreage of hundreds of square miles as their individual properties. They also had given those spaces the distinctive shape and style that would become the signature of California. The *pobladores* dispersed out to distant ranchos and mapped the boundaries of their land with the swirling lines and green borders of their *diseños*. But at the same time, the rancheros also plotted a course in a roughly centrifugal direction, to a social center near the old Mission, and to a commercial nucleus where they traded hides and tallow for European and Asian goods. The Mexican settlers of San Francisco Bay established two unique urban spaces: Dolores, a *vecindad* that would one day become a barrio, and Yerba Buena, a commercial port that would later become known as downtown San Francisco.

Just as these spaces took on their distinctive Californian shape in the 1840s, world history caught up with the remote settlement on the shores of San Francisco Bay. Signs of change were apparent from within the pueblo of Yerba Buena. The land once granted by the largesse of the Republic of Mexico was being marketed for cash, albeit in small sums. One new arrival to Yerba Buena boasted that he could obtain a lot for the price of a flask of brandy. Jacob Leese estimated the cost of a lot measuring fifty square varas at $6.25, plus 25 cents for each additional square vara. Juana Briones, the exemplary California *empresaria*, managed to acquire a sum of $3,000 to purchase an entire rancho in San Mateo County. José Jesús Noé sold off Las Camaritas and made a more promising investment in a lot in Yerba Buena. Humble farmers could no longer expect to be granted homesteads of their own and access to common pasturage. Big-time real estate deals came to San Francisco in 1843, when Governor Micheltorena sold two large tracts, carefully carved out from between the two settlements of Yerba Buena and the Establecimiento de Dolores, to the European shipping merchant José Limantour. Limantour made his claim upon the peninsula of San Francisco with a bluster and extravagance yet to be seen in the frontier outpost. Aware that Micheltorena was conducting a military campaign, and desperate for cash and arms, he offered the governor $40,000 in exchange for the largely barren tract between Yerba Buena and the Mission that the locals shunned as an arid wasteland.[60]

Limantour represented a new breed of conquistadores advancing toward San Francisco Bay, some of them arriving by land rather than by sea. Pío Pico, who would be the last Mexican governor of Alta California, warned that armies of American farmers were approaching from across the Sierras. Alarmed by these intruders, the Mexican government imposed restrictions on the entry of foreigners into its territories. Among those captured in the roundup of "foreigners" was Robert Ridley, despite the fact that he was a naturalized Mexican citizen and married to the daughter of Juana Briones. The Yankee threat soon materialized in a notorious attempted land grab, prologue to the Mexican-American War. A band of thirty-four American settlers living in the area laid siege to Mariano Vallejo's rancho in Sonoma on June 14, 1846, and proclaimed an independent republic, raising a flag picturing a grizzly bear and a red star—the "Bear Flag." A loquacious leader of the marauders, William B. Ide, declared the government of Alta California a "despotism" that had reneged on a promise of "lands on which to settle their families." He would, by force of arms, put in its place "a Republican Government which shall encourage virtue and literature, which shall leave unshackled by fetters, agriculture, commerce and mechanism." Ide set notions of republicanism and the free market against the outmoded type of political economy practiced by the Californios.[61]

This episode in the history of "manifest destiny" looked more like a farcical frontier romp than a republican revolution. The men behind the Bear Flag Revolt celebrated their conquest by emptying Vallejo's wine cellar, insulting his wife, and committing a brutal murder. Charles Brown remembered the revolt as the work of "fiends of Hell." The men gratuitously slayed the twin sons of the former *alcalde* Francisco de Haro and left their bodies to decompose on the beach. The "California Republic" fizzled in less than a month; the American conquest, however, which began while the Bear Flag Revolt was still in progress, would be achieved quickly, when, on July 8, the US Navy entered San Francisco Bay on a ship called the *Portsmouth*, and the Californios ceded the San Francisco Bay without a fight. On July 9, the

—

Yankees marched into the plaza of Yerba Buena and raised the Stars and Stripes on the flagpole in front of the adobe customhouse. They celebrated a belated Fourth of July in the plaza of Yerba Buena. Then, in October, the Californios graciously ceded the Partido de San Francisco to the Americans. Mariano Vallejo joined General Robert F. Stockton in a procession from Yerba Buena to the Mission and entertained the Yankees with a "collation." As a military operation, the conquest of Mexican California was a simple and decisive achievement. The Americans evicted the six families still living in the Presidio, and the United States maintained it as a military base until it was finally converted to peaceful uses at the end of the Cold War.[62]

The Americans dispensed with Indian claims upon the land with dispatch. The editor of the first California newspaper expressed support for waging a "general and exterminating war" in order to "remove from our most fertile soil the most degraded race of aborigines upon the North American continent." Captain John B. Montgomery, skipper of the *Portsmouth*, was less bellicose than the editor, but no less effective in exerting white supremacy. He ordered that any Indians found to "wander about the country in an idle and dissolute manner" would be "liable to arrest and punishment by labor on the *Public Works* at the discretion of the *Magistrate*."[63] In the 1850s, the California Land Commission met with hundreds of tribes and ceded significant territory to the Indians, but the US Senate never ratified the treaties, once again denying the Ohlone title to their former hunting grounds.[64]

It would take more time and considerable effort to dislodge the Californios. The shapes they had written on the land—pueblos, plazas, ranchos, and the "partido de San Francisco"—would not quickly or completely fade away. They bequeathed a distinctive notion of urban space to their *vecinos* in North America and augmented the range of possibilities for taking land and making towns and cities. Be it in Yerba Buena, on the outlying ranchland, or at the Establecimiento de Dolores, Californios posed an alternative to the orthogonal grid of streets and townships six miles square that were gobbling up territory as the "Americans" marched westward. Above all, the California frontier set an example of how local inhabitants could produce space in their own fashion, and make the municipality, even an urban space as small as the pueblo of Yerba Buena, a lever of historical change on the North American continent. As late as 1847, the western flank of North America could still be called "los Estados Unidos de Méjico." Tucked on the far margin of that map was a bay named San Francisco and a pueblo labeled Yerba Buena.

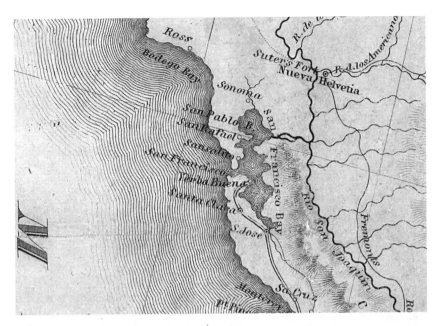

John Disturnell, Mapa de los Estados Unidos de Méjico *(Map of the United States of Mexico), 1847. Courtesy of the University of California at Los Angeles, Library Special Collections, Charles E. Young Research Library.*

D. Griffing Johnson, Johnson's New Illustrated County Map of the Republics of North America with the Adjacent Islands & Countries *(New York: A. J. Johnson, 1859). Courtesy of the David Rumsey Map Collection, Stanford University.*

PART III

MAKING THE MODERN CAPITALIST CITY

By the 1830s mapmakers had devised ways to visualize the complex sovereignty of both the United States and the Republic of Mexico. American schoolbooks depicted the states, counties, intendancies, and provinces of North America as brightly colored, roughly geometrical blocks, the prototypes of the jigsaw puzzles still found in American toy stores today. Early in the 1840s, mapmakers used this same pictorial geography to differentiate British, Mexican, and US claims on the land of North America. At the conclusion of the Mexican-American War in 1848, however, two antithetical maps were on the table during the negotiations that led to the Treaty of Guadalupe Hidalgo. While the Americans drew a blunt border along the Rio Grande, a map of los Estados Unidos de Méjico drew the borders of Mexico east beyond the Rockies and north to the Oregon border. When the American cartographer

—

D. Griffing Johnson drew a bold red line between Mexico and the United States along the national border, it may as well have been written in blood rather than ink.

The boundaries internal to Mexico and the United States were equally contentious and precarious in the middle of the nineteenth century. Those interlocking states and provinces were joined tenuously together to form the two federated republics of the United States and Mexico. The conventional maps of North America failed to recognize the turmoil along the border of the Mason-Dixon Line in the United States or the violent resistance to centralized authority in Mexico. Most myopically, national maps papered over the issue that was dividing North America: slavery, and its legitimacy, morality, and tenability in a capitalist society. Maps of North America such as Johnson's, published on the eve of southern secession in 1859, colored over the sectional crisis with cheerful pretentions of indivisible national sovereignty.

American mapmakers occasionally sketched an urban image on the margins of their charts, the Capitol Building in "Washington City," for example, or perhaps the street plan of the far larger city of Baltimore just up the Chesapeake. Cartographers were slow to spy the seedlings of a city that were sprouting along San Francisco Bay, despite the desires of the British, the Spanish, and increasingly the Americans to acquire a port there. Such urban places took up only tiny portions of land, but the history to be made there would roil the whole continent in the middle of the nineteenth century. The political ingenuity and economic energy accumulating in Baltimore, San Francisco, and a growing network of cities thrust capitalism back and forth across the continent, from the warehouses of the B&O Railroad to the dock of the Pacific Mail Steamship Company in San Francisco.

Chapter 6 will take account of the continuing municipal effort and increasing private investment expended in shaping Baltimore into a modern capitalist city. Chapter 7 details how the Mexican-American War opened a vast swath of land to American investors, provoking a municipal imbroglio over the title to the ranchos of Alta California and the pueblo of San Francisco. When the Gold Rush opened the Puerto de San Francisco to a flood of immigrants, Hispanic and Anglo American ways of taking land and making cities squared off one against the other.

CHAPTER 6

———

MAKING BALTIMORE
A MODERN CITY, 1828–1854

W hile the Californios were slowly shaping a municipality near San Francisco Bay, Baltimore was brandishing its reputation as the Monumental City. When gold was discovered near Sacramento in 1848, some of Baltimore's proud citizens rushed to the West Coast, bringing with them a token of their civic pride. Members of the Mechanical Company of Baltimore arrived aboard the clipper ship *John Marshall* with a steam-powered fire engine in tow. Renaming their company the "Monumental of San Francisco," they paraded the engine through the primitive streets around Yerba Buena Cove to advertise the advances of industrial production and the accomplishments of municipal sovereignty in the Chesapeake city. That newfangled machine also announced that the modern economic forces that had transformed the city of Baltimore would soon inundate Dolores and Yerba Buena.[1]

The arrival of modern capitalism in Baltimore was heralded in a novel vocabulary of municipal finance. One term in particular was heard with increasing frequency and volume beginning in the 1820s. Mayor Jesse Hunt

———

resorted to it when he announced his intention of "inducing men of capital enterprises to locate among us." One of Hunt's successors, Mayor James Law, used the same word when he accused the city council of "deprecating the labor of those whose industry is their only capital." A committee of the city council joined the chorus and gathered much of the urban population under the mantle of "capital." "In a great commercial community like this," the report read, "the different classes of capitalists, salesmen, draymen, carters and laborers are necessary to each other, and each equally indispensable to the welfare and property of the whole."[2]

In Baltimore, capitalism was not just the enterprise of private merchants, bankers, and entrepreneurs; it was also the work of mayors and city councilmen. A whole litany of new terms—"stocks," "bonds," "sinking funds," "dividends," "auditors," and "finance"—came trailing "capital" into the lexicon of urban government. They had become counterpoints to the traditional mercantilist language of urban economics, which used terms such as "regulation," the "assize of bread," and "the general welfare." Baltimore embraced the modern form of industrial capitalism with a remarkable municipal act in 1828. In that year, the city corporation went into partnership with a private company to finance America's first long-haul railroad, the Baltimore and Ohio. The city council voted to purchase stock in the private corporation, investing taxpayers' money in a project calculated to speed up the progress of American and world capitalism. The relationship between the public and private sectors was strained from the first, and the city council would never receive the anticipated return on its investment. Another institution emblematic of capitalism, the Bank of Maryland, met with full-out popular fury. The bank's failure in 1835 provoked such animosity toward the bank directors that their homes near the Battle Monument were encircled by a pillaging mob.[3]

The partnership between the city and the capitalists was off to a rocky start. Baltimore had no sooner recovered from the local bank crisis than it was struck by the international financial panic of 1837, followed by a prolonged period of painful economic recovery. Civic pride and the city economy had rebounded, temporarily, by midcentury as capital overflowed the city limits, moving slowly westward along the iron tracks of the city's namesake railroad. This chapter will follow the project of building the modern city until the midpoint of the 1850s, when the mayor "invited capital to mingle with your soil and build itself under the protection of your laws." The whirlwind of municipal capitalism, despite all its risks and vicissitudes, had shaped a

———

modern urban landscape and demonstrated the national and global significance of city sovereignty.[4]

BUILDING MUNICIPAL CAPITAL, 1825-1835

The currency of the term "capital" early in the nineteenth century is not
particularly worthy of remark. Most historians date the rise of capitalism
from the acceleration of global commerce in the sixteenth century, and agree
that it was the appropriate classification for the American economy in the
late eighteenth century. In the vernacular of early Baltimore, "capital" meant
something more specific than simply the market economy and international
trade, however; it denoted the large-scale investments necessary to promote
urban "improvement" and ensure prosperity. Capital had become indispensable to local economic growth by 1820. The individual effort and personal
connections that built the Port of Baltimore were not enough to make the
city competitive in the expanding regional and world economy. The modern
capitalist city required major investments in industrial production and
mechanized transportation. The amounts of capital necessary to open factories and build railroads could not be acquired though personal networks of
credit or conveyed by exclusive state monopolies. The economy relied on new
tools of accumulation, such as stocks and mortgages, and more powerful
financial institutions, including banks, insurance companies, and especially
private corporations. The voracious appetite for capital in the region of the
Chesapeake would soon overreach the limits of mercantilism and municipal
regulation. By fits and starts, capital flowed ever more freely, voluminously,
and turbulently through Baltimore City.

This story of capital is not just a business history. It is set in the chambers of Baltimore's mayor and city council. The merchants, professionals,
artisans, and shopkeepers who held public office in Baltimore devised new
procedures to manage the flow of capital early in the nineteenth century.
First, they appointed a commissioner of finance, and later, a Ways and
Means Committee. In 1821, anxious to control their rising expenses, the
councilmen created a sinking fund, a financial device that would permit the
city to use future taxes to finance improvements while slowly paying off the
municipal debt. By 1823, the council and mayor were acting like advanced
municipal capitalists, issuing stock certificates paying 6 percent interest to
fund a municipal debt of $26,000. By 1839, the mayor Sheppard Leakin

was peddling the stock to what he called the "finest Houses of Europe" and promising returns in pounds sterling.[5]

The municipal economy of Baltimore operated in an advanced and enterprising fashion. Over the next two decades, with the municipal debt steeply rising, the Maryland General Assembly would hear, and usually accede to, the city's appeals to increase levies. In 1832, Mayor William Steuart went to Annapolis begging permission to tax the property owners of Baltimore. He pointedly reprimanded the stingy General Assembly for "restricting the Mayor and City Council to an amount of taxation less than their expenses, without making any provision for the magnificent Public Works, the City of Baltimore is patronizing." The mayor called for the repeal of limits on municipal taxation, pledging that the "city authorities of Baltimore will never increase the tax so as to render it oppressive to their fellow citizens."[6] The city began relying less on lotteries and licenses and supplemented special assessments with taxes on all propertied citizens in the city. Pressed for revenue in the 1830s, some city councilmen would propose, unsuccessfully, taxing salaries, income, and banks.

A pastiche of financial strategies—an alloy of taxation, an occasional lottery, borrowing, and issuing stock—carried the city forward into the 1830s and through some troubled times. In the middle of the third decade of the nineteenth century, it became clear that Baltimore had weathered the Panic of 1819, and the end of the crisis revived the city's civic spirits. By 1824, the city was ready to launch a capital project on a qualitatively and quantitatively different scale. In January of that year, Mayor Edward Johnson reported that the municipal budget had finally recovered, congratulated the city council for keeping expenditures down, and then, without skipping a beat, proposed an ambitious program of urban improvements: new bridges, improved waterways, more street openings, the repair of wharves, and the expansion of public markets. The city made a critical investment in human capital in 1825, when it created a rudimentary public school system. A few years later the press gleefully announced that a town meeting had endorsed another ambitious and costly project by agreeing "to impose new duties upon us in our corporate capacity." The object of this public magnanimity was the construction of a network of canals that would link the Chesapeake to the Susquehanna River. The town meeting relayed the proposal posthaste to the city council, which appointed a three-man commission that would put the municipality in the regional transportation business.[7]

———

Taking up the challenge presented by New York State, which had funded the Erie Canal, Baltimore's municipal government, determined to compete for the lucrative trade in Western foodstuffs, came up with an innovation in transportation more daring than roads, turnpikes, and canals. Heretofore, transportation beyond the city limits was either a private initiative—often chartered by the state, such as the local turnpikes—or a rare expenditure of federal capital, such as the National Road. Now, only six years after a devastating demonstration of the risks of engagement with capitalist markets, the City Corporation of Baltimore jumped eagerly into debt to finance a costly scheme to boost the local economy. This audacious leap forward into highly capitalized municipal economics was registered as a simple city ordinance, dated March 20, 1827, when the mayor, Jacob Small, and the city council resolved to invest the sum of $500,000 "in the capital stock of said Rail road company, as soon as the subscription books shall be open for that purpose." The railroad in question was the Baltimore and Ohio, a private corporation with which the city corporation would be wedded, and not always harmoniously, for much of the remainder of the nineteenth century. Ultimately, over $5 million of the taxpayers' capital would go to the B&O.

On July 4, 1828, the people of Baltimore were invited to a festival celebrating this union between public capital and a private corporation. At sunrise, three cannon shots set in motion a procession of over five thousand people—a host of artisans, women workers from the Union Cotton Mill, the Freemasons, and a full cohort of young men of the middling sort, the likes of John H. B. Latrobe, who now became a lawyer for the B&O. Contingents of the manual and the merchant classes joined one another at the Centre Market, where the representatives of both the municipality and the private corporation—the members of the city council and the "company directors"—led the procession out to the railroad construction site. After a march of four hours, the parade reached its destination, a platform erected on an open field at the western outskirts of the city. The honored places on the podium went to the city's founding generation, Samuel Smith and Charles Carroll; the latter broke the earth for the "cornerstone" of the Baltimore and Ohio Railroad. The *Baltimore American* estimated the crowd at between fifty thousand and seventy thousand men, women, and children: "Virtually everyone in Baltimore had turned out, either as participants or spectators." For the next few years, the railway inched slowly beyond the city limits while the city paid off its portion of the stock subscription in tax funds and borrowed money.[8]

At the outset, the relationship between the railroad and the municipality

---

was relatively seamless and cooperative. P. W. Thomas, the first president of the railroad, posed the enterprise as a union of the two incorporated bodies, one public, one private. Thomas was deferential to the city corporation "as the direct representative of the people, and the immediate guardian of the public interest." The railroad president clothed himself in democratic and egalitarian principles, confident "that [the] benefits of this great work, in the promotion of which all parts of the city have liberally cooperated, should be generally diffused." Shortly thereafter, in a letter to Thomas, Mayor Hunt granted the railroad permission to construct a track through the commercial heart of the city, "all the way down President Street to the water," believing it "would be beneficial to the interest of the city, that it should remain permanently a thoroughfare to the water." The mayor signed this private communication "respectfully your most Obedient Servant." Careful not to show bias to one class of special interests, the mayor also paid his respects to a less illustrious constituency by accepting an invitation to join "the Mechanics and Working Men's Procession in celebration of the anniversary of the victory in the War of 1812."[9]

The partnership between the city and the railroad was not to remain untroubled or equitable for very long. The city was never granted more than a small minority membership on the board of directors of the B&O, receiving just one representative for every two wards, far fewer than the city's share in B&O stock would warrant. It would be a mistake, however, to credit the launching of the Baltimore and Ohio Railroad to the work of private capital. A literary celebrity of Baltimore, the novelist John Pendleton Kennedy, framed the collaboration between the city and the business community more accurately. Following an 1836 meeting, when the B&O managers came before the city requesting more municipal capital, he wrote, "It is the public who should furnish the money, in their corporate character, not private stockholders." He offered four sound reasons for this method of generating capital. First, the railroad should belong to the public; second, private capital was insufficient to fund so large a project; third, private companies were guided by profit motives; and finally, the public was a better and more reliable source of credit.[10]

Kennedy was right on all counts. And the public entity, the City of Baltimore, indeed would be a major source of the capital (second only to the State of Maryland) fueling the Baltimore and Ohio Railroad as it moved slowly toward the markets of the West. The private corporation, by contrast, proved to be an untrustworthy public investment. Even as Kennedy wrote, the halcyon era of municipal capitalism was drawing to a close. In March 1834, the Bank of Maryland closed its doors without explanation, ultimately robbing hundreds of small depositors of their savings. It was the first local tremor in another international financial downspin that would last nearly a decade. The creditors of Baltimore's banks would lose over $2 million in deposits before the financial crisis was over. The city remained remarkably calm over the next eighteen months. Citizens addressed the banking crisis in the time-honored way, by gathering in the central public space. On March 3, 1834, the local presses published "an official notice for a public meeting of the citizens of Baltimore in Monument Square at 4 o'clock to-morrow afternoon to receive the report of the Washington committee and adopt such proceedings on the occasion as the public exigencies may require." On March 21, they assembled again in Monument Square to hear another report of a delegation they had sent to Washington to present their grievances. Month upon month, orderly but angry citizens gathered in Monument Square to express their grievances with the bank managers, but they received no satisfactory explanation of why they lost their savings. Reports that the directors of the Bank of Maryland had defrauded the depositors and escaped with their own profits gained more credibility. By July 1835, the people of Baltimore were running out of patience; the town meeting tottered on the brink of riot.

Popular fury welled up around Monument Square in the first week of August, erupted into violence on Wednesday, August 6, and raged on for five nights. One broadside circulated through the city summoning the "Citizens of this republic and of this City" to the square with a scurrilous challenge: "Will you suffer your friend to be molested—will you suffer your beds to be polluted—will you suffer your pocket to be rifled and your wives and Children beggared?" The anonymous firebrand indicted the "sly speculators" behind the bank closing by name, singling out the bank director (and later US senator) Reverdy Johnson. Then he issued an incendiary charge: "Let the war hoot be given from the corner of every street. Liberty, Equality, justice or death." While hundreds of citizens lent their passive support from the sidelines, a gang of men and boys heeded this inflammatory call to action. The crowd proceeded to Johnson's residence, which fronted on Monument Square. It was rumored at the time, and has been confirmed by historians, that Johnson and other bank directors had drawn excessively on the bank's funds, reinvested them, made a profit, and then withdrawn their own inflated deposits before the run on the bank. But Johnson had left town,

Jack Downing, The Bank of Maryland Affair, *1835. Notice the Battle Monument being taken away by a demon. Courtesy of the Maryland Historical Society.*

eluding the tarring and feathering that would have been his fate in decades past. His property bore the brunt of the crowd's anger: the mob took furnishings, wine, and books from his library to compensate themselves for the lost deposits, and moved on to the residences of other bank directors, cursing the "damned aristocracy," the "stockjobbers," and "the moneyed aristocrats." The rioters systematically dismantled the marble portico of Reverdy Johnson's mansion on Monument Square.[11]

Both the Washington Monument and the Battle Monument floated futilely above the tumult in the streets below, impotent symbols of the former civic harmony. The mayor, the same Jesse Hunt, a saddler who had solicited funds for the Battle Monument twenty years before, relied initially on the old informal techniques of pacifying the crowd. After walking among the people urging restraint and promising to respond to their grievances, he convened a "town meeting" that passed a resolution asking that the bank records be opened to the public. Given the anger surging around Monument Square, the town meeting was relocated to the more elite and cloistered quarters of the Merchants' Exchange. When all else failed, and under a threat of intervention from the state militia, local authorities took more forceful action. A band of volunteers armed themselves with sticks, poles, and guns. Under the command of the venerable old hero Samuel Smith, they assembled a staging ground in Mount Vernon and marched into Monument Square to confront and subdue the crowd.[12] The local authorities finally managed to restore order to the streets of Baltimore, but the divisive force of finance capital had been unleashed. Hezekiah Niles, a local newspaper editor and publisher, feared that an "awful political outcry is about to be raised to rally the poor against the rich." The banking crisis had ripped apart the bond of reciprocity between the public and private interest and undermined municipal sovereignty in the process. Fort McHenry became the site of a less than star-spangled event in August 1835, when the United States stationed armed federal troops there, ready to enforce order in the streets.[13]

The trauma of the Bank Riot did not dissuade the mayor and the city council or suppress municipal investment for very long. Jesse Hunt bore the onus of civic failure and was replaced in the next election by the revered senator Samuel Smith, who reassured the citizenry and promptly initiated another series of public projects. Alarmed by the threat that Pennsylvania rail lines and the archrival city of Philadelphia would beat Baltimore to the Ohio and capture the western markets, Smith called another town meeting to generate support for the "public works now in progress." Smith assured the citizens of Maryland that despite recent signs of economic downturn, this was an ideal moment to invest further in long-distance transportation. The country was at peace and basically prosperous; its public treasury was "over-flowing," and its credit "unlimited." "That credit," the mayor believed, "may be used to bring to her citizens a considerable amount of foreign capital," notwithstanding "the manifest want of banking capital in the State."[14] John Pendleton Kennedy chimed in to warn his fellow citizens that if they did not invest now, their "day of prosperity [was] gliding by."[15] This combination of threats and promises sparked action. Both branches of the city council voted to wager a full $3 million of the city's credit to expedite the advance of the Baltimore and Ohio Railroad toward the West.

Even in the aftermath of the Bank Riot, the mayor and city council assumed the role of investors of last resort. It might seem that the public sector, embodied by the sovereign municipality of Baltimore, was a leading edge of economic development, a major source of capital, and the responsible party when the private sector failed.[16]

———

FROM CAPITAL TO CAPITALISM, 1835–1850

Despite the city's continuing support for the Baltimore and Ohio Railroad and other transportation projects, municipal capital was becoming a worrisome method of public investment. The partnership between the City of Baltimore and its namesake railroad realigned the time-honored relationship between government and private enterprise. Heretofore, Baltimore's economic growth had been promoted by prominent merchants, but managed largely from within the city corporation and under the oversight of a popularly elected city council, in which merchants dominated, but small tradesmen and artisans were well represented. Through the first decades of the nineteenth century, politics and economics operated hand in glove, through the associated actions of the leading merchants, who assumed public office as well as direction of the local banks, insurance companies, and chartered corporations. Furthermore, political decisions were vetted in public spaces, in the town meetings regularly held in places like Monument Square.

The scheme to build a railway to Ohio was presented to the public in the customary manner. The debut of the B&O was announced in the press with a call to a town meeting, whose proceedings were published, along with the names of the elected officers and the text of several resolutions that were ratified by those present. In reality, the meeting that drafted the act of incorporation of the Baltimore and Ohio Railroad Company had been conducted in a private mansion and attended by a small group of the most affluent merchants, manufacturers, and landowners. The site of that gathering of the directors of the railroad company, in an affluent residential district up the hill from Monument Square and in the shadow of the Washington Monument, augured a growing estrangement between the private corporation and the body politic or public corporation of Baltimore.[17]

Soon after the municipality had hitched its fortunes to the B&O, the city was wracked by the international financial panic of 1837, which left both the railroad corporation and the economy of Baltimore traumatized well into the 1840s. As the railway made its way as far as Virginia, well short of the promised terminus at the Ohio River, the value of B&O stock steadily declined, and city credit plummeted apace. Worried councilmen confessed that they lacked the expertise to understand arcane matters of railway finance, and considered an assortment of strategies to lessen their financial burden: demanding dividends from the railroad, selling off the city's B&O stock, buying up the railroad wholesale, or resorting to "hypothecation" (a scheme that would use the city's stock as collateral for more borrowing). On occasion, the

—

city even issued its own money. When the supply of small currency dried up after President Andrew Jackson issued the Specie Circular, reducing the supply of soft money, Baltimore printed its own scrip to be used for tax payments or in local commerce. The city eased the money supply again in 1841, when it accepted stock orders of the B&O as local currency.[18]

The consequences of the city's railroad investment were recorded in the municipal budget. For more than two decades, the mayor and councilmen anguished over how to provide basic city services and at the same time manage the mounting funded debt. The bulk of that debt had accrued through investment in the Baltimore and Ohio and other improvements in regional transportation, including the Susquehanna Tide Water Canal, the Chesapeake and Ohio Canal, and the Baltimore and Susquehanna Railroad. Year after year, the mayor's annual message began with an accounting of "interest on the city stock and other internal improvement stocks." Interest on the debt alone amounted to an astounding $303,000 in 1842. The municipal budget was colored a bleak red through the 1840s. In 1848, for example, Baltimore had one of the highest tax rates in the nation, amounting to over $1 per each $100 of property; of this sum, 66 cents went to payment for internal improvements. Earlier in the history of Baltimore Town, tax dollars had funded the city's internal improvements—the basics of repairing and lighting the streets, maintaining the harbor, building market halls, staffing public schools, and meeting the relatively small expenses of city administration. After 1835, budget priorities were reversed: According to one economic historian, "interest on the funded debt became the dominant expenditure and formed from one-half to one-third of the ordinary net annual outlay." Basic city services were being forfeited to the debts incurred by investing in private corporations.[19]

Anxiety about funding the debt began to consume the annual message of the mayor. Funds for everything else—courts, schools, the jail, the poor tax, and the care of the streets—were put in jeopardy by a regimen of municipal belt-tightening. Mayor William Steuart called the alarm in 1832. Facing the inflated cost of the railroad and a growing budget deficit, he sent an irate message to the state government lamenting its stingy contribution to those "magnificent Public works the city of Baltimore is Patronizing." Steuart's successor, Jesse Hunt, met the increasing cost of the debt with calls for a "strict system of economy" in other municipal affairs. Two years later, Hunt was still cajoling the council to make the effort to support those local projects that "public interest requires." He cited such mundane expenses as paying the mechanics who installed the pumps that kept the streets from turning into raging rivers and swampland. Meanwhile, Hunt commended beleaguered taxpayers for "cheerily" paying their assessments and formed a committee to investigate how to make the tax code more equitable.[20]

But city councilmen, mayors, and taxpayers began to wonder whether any benefit would ever come to the city from the B&O. One petition to the city council, dated 1840 and signed by hundreds of citizens, complained outright of "paying interest on the multimillion dollar B&O monopoly." A dissenting councilman proposed that the board of directors appointed by the city demand a reduction in the pay of the B&O officers. He was overruled.[21] The city stumbled on under the weight of its debt. In 1842, when Baltimore was still suffering from the Panic of 1837, Mayor Solomon Hillen Jr. reported that "notwithstanding the commercial agitation of the country, and the trials of which both public and private credit has been exposed, the corporation of Baltimore has met its heavy obligations fully and promptly." A year later, the mayor vetoed a bill that would permit the B&O to run locomotives across Pratt Street. He charged the company with the "Stealthy progression" of "privilege and Power" and allied himself with the "life and property of the humblest of our fellow citizens, as a price too dear to be paid for any amount of corporate emolument." The city council overturned the mayor's veto. But the municipal corporation of Baltimore would be paying off its debt to a private corporation until the 1890s, and this less than equitable alignment of public and private institutions produced regular grumbling in the backbenches of the city council. One councilman resorted to a rustic trope to convey his resentment about municipal funding of another branch railway, likening the role of a taxpayer to that of a "packhorse . . . called upon to bear the heavy burdens of taxation to meet constantly accruing claims of interest on the debt."[22]

By the fifth decade of the nineteenth century, the responsibility for civic welfare had been redistributed: while private companies single-mindedly pursued profits for themselves and their shareholders, the public corporation was charged with funding basic but costly public services. While the B&O made its way toward the Ohio, the city of Baltimore was left to dole out its tax revenues in ways that were something short of monumental. Mayor Jacob Small's annual message in 1830 left the people of Baltimore to ponder more mundane local matters, such as the price of bread, the condition of the streets, and the fact that "the manure is of much better quality than formerly." Small also took pains to recommend that the intersection at Light and Pratt Streets be cleaned, and a "chasm on Charles" be filled in. The pothole had become the bottom line on the modern municipal budget.[23] Baltimore's ambitious experiment in capital investment was leading to municipal impoverishment. The city met the crisis of capital with a policy of general municipal austerity, or what was called at the time "retrenchment." The anxious calls for belt-tightening became louder and more frequent after the Panic of 1837; in 1843, the city council went so far as to create a separate "retrenchment committee."

The growing divide between the public and the private corporations was also written into state and federal law. With the passage of general corporation laws in a number of states, including Maryland, private partnerships and joint stock companies proliferated, overtaking the scale of the public economy. Nine new banks and sixty-nine new corporations were granted state charters in Baltimore in the 1830s. By the 1850s, there were four hundred directors of private corporations based in the city. The general incorporation laws simplified the process of forming a limited liability corporation through which private companies could raise capital and share the risk among numerous stockholders.[24]

At the same time, a sequence of rulings by the Supreme Court began to define municipalities as public corporations, denying them some of the protections and privileges enjoyed by private companies and subordinating them to the authority of the states. In the US Supreme Court case *Trustees of Dartmouth College v. Woodward* (1819), Chief Justice John Marshall wrote a majority opinion protecting the right of private contract from state interference while denying city corporations the same immunity. In *Charles River Bridge v. Warren Bridge* (1837), Justice Roger Taney reinforced the legal distinction between private and public corporations. Taney (a native of Frederick, Maryland, who was well known in Baltimore) noted in passing that public restrictions on private corporations would retard ongoing improvements in transportation. In the 1850s, these precedents would justify further legal restrictions on municipal autonomy, among them a ruling in 1857 by a state court in New York that a railroad corporation could not be subjected to municipal interference without the approval of the state legislature. Municipalities, once the special beneficiaries of the corporate charters issued by monarchs and colonial legislatures, were now subordinated to the states and denied the privileges of private corporations. The distinction between public and private corporations had become, in the words of one legal authority, "of a piece with a city's legal powerlessness."[25]

———

The power of the city relative to other levels of sovereignty was ebbing in the middle of the nineteenth century. In the case of Baltimore, that decline, and the relative vitality of private enterprise, was symptomatic of a spatial realignment as well. The new geography was already apparent in the public ritual that celebrated the "cornerstone" of the B&O in 1828. It took place outside the city limits of Baltimore, an omen that the private corporation was about to take public capital and seek its profits beyond the Chesapeake, out toward the Ohio and far from local control. Conversely, the devastating blows to the local economy in the Panics of 1819 and 1837 emanated from afar, from interruptions in the flow of capital out of London banks and restrictions on the money supply initiated by Andrew Jackson in Washington. As historian David Schley has demonstrated, private capital moved progressively outside the orbit of local government. His study of the Baltimore and Ohio details how the railroad corporation left its municipal sponsors far behind, threatening to reduce the city to "a mere place of transit."[26]

A new generation of business leaders steered this centrifugal movement. Men like John Garrett, Enoch Pratt, and Johns Hopkins were not stationed in the Port of Baltimore but made their start transporting dry goods and groceries from the hinterland; all of these men became renowned more for their private philanthropy than for participation in municipal government, and all of them pursued their fortunes in a national and international market. Baltimore's literary eminence, John Pendleton Kennedy, had a metaphor for the way in which the city became snared in this new economic geography: "Baltimore should imitate the spider and spread her lines towards every point of the compass, and lodge in the centre of them." Caught up in the enthusiasm of the railroad boom, Kennedy went on to offer some hazardous financial advice: "The present generation are able to pay interest: let the next generation pay the principal." Baltimore had indeed cast its fate to a distant point of the compass. In the process, as Kennedy seemed to intuit, the city risked its local capital, paying the interest on corporate debt and hazarding the principal, the tax dollars of its citizens. Early in the nineteenth century, Baltimore had become the third-largest city in the United States on the strength of municipal capital. In the 1830s and 1840s, partnerships with transportation companies, such as the deal with the B&O, put municipal capital at risk; the private corporations were moving beyond the city and depleting the municipal coffers in the process. Under state law and in the municipal budget, capitalism was increasingly seen as the province of private corporations.[27]

THE CHANGING STREETSCAPE

Meanwhile, the task of city-building lumbered along the old public byways, starting at the level of the street. An ordinance dated 1832 described Baltimore as a mature and crowded urban space, "thickly settled, built upon and improved," and overlaid with "the usual regulations of watching, or lighting or clearing of streets." Baltimore's street commissioners continued to shape the city lot by lot and block by block. They responded to citizens' initiatives with conscientious deliberation. On receiving a request to open a street running east and west from the Washington Monument, they dutifully replied: "Fully impressed with the importance of the matter committed to them, involving the right of individuals on one hand and the general welfare and convenience of the community on the other." The work of the street commissioners was not financed by municipal credit, stock issues, or general taxation, but by special assessments to abutting owners. A broad citizenry continued to participate in this collective, piecemeal municipal project of making streets. Even in depressed times, such as in the aftermath of the Panic of 1837, hundreds of lots were being leased to the small builders who constructed homes that were affordable for those of modest income. In the flush times between 1848 and 1852, for example, some two thousand new dwellings were constructed annually, most of them of modest size and unpretentious style. In recognition of the volume of these small parcels, the street ordinance was rewritten to make leaseholders as well as those owning lots in fee simple subject to special assessments.[28]

In hard times, owners of large tracts as well as small leaseholders complained about the burdens of maintaining the streets in front of their property. The revolutionary war hero John Eager Howard went before the street commission to protest the assessment for opening streets through his extensive real estate holdings. A few years later a humbler group of property owners, including five women and two men who signed their petition with a mark, repeated the parsimonious refrain. They pleaded that the improvement of the street outside their doorways would "operate oppressively on many poor individuals in that neighborhood and ruin others." The office of the street commissioners, once occupied by the proud stewards of urban improvement, was becoming a chamber of petty grievances. The commissioners routinely rebuffed appeals to open new streets. A garbled apology dated March 1824 was symptomatic of the painful financial calculations required to balance the overburdened city budget. The commissioners explained their ruling against one petition to extend a street as due not just to the opposition of the majority of the abutting property owners, but also "owing to the pressure of this time and difficulty of raising money" in the face of basic municipal needs.[29]

Homeowners as well as city officials vented their frustration with the street ordinances and increasingly questioned the principle of special assessment. One property owner grumbled that while he could "easily understand" the logic of being charged for street improvements that benefited him personally, he wondered "what article of law subjects them to payment where no benefits are given and where they [were] never asked for." The street-level common good could easily splinter into the different financial interests of quarreling neighbors. The city council made repeated attempts to alter or clarify the street ordinances and to abate the confusion and conflict they produced. Was a simple or a two-thirds majority required to initiate a repair? Did the two-thirds majority refer to the number of abutting owners, or to those individuals who owned two-thirds of the street frontage? The street ordinance first formulated in 1797 was revised in 1817, 1827, 1833, 1841, and 1846. As early as 1837, the resistance of property owners prompted the street commissioners to question special assessments as the best method for funding municipal improvements: the commissioners suggested that because "the streets are a public convenience opened and condemned as a public highway," the expense of maintaining them might best be a city-wide responsibility.[30]

Under siege from property owners, the commissioners increasingly proceeded in more bureaucratic ways. In 1841, the three appointed commissioners assumed greater initiative in opening new streets. By midcentury, the ordinance was laced with red tape: applications had to be made in writing and advertised for seven days in at least two newspapers. Assessed property owners were allowed as many as sixty days to protest the commissioners' decision. Although appropriations were initiated by a citizens' application, the commissioners became increasingly exacting in their specifications: the dimensions and sizes of materials were prescribed—stones for footways, for example, had to be five by seven inches. One owner of a substantial number of city lots felt it necessary to preserve a copy of the street ordinances in his private papers, so that he could reference them in his effort to comply with the complex municipal policies. Still, despite its cumbersome operation, special assessment would remain the standard method of paving and repairing streets. The municipal public remained grounded in landed property, aligned on the streets, anchored in private ownership, and overseen by a wide, if increasingly begrudging, citizenry.[31]

The juggernaut of capitalist city-building would ultimately overtake this piecemeal collaborative method of producing urban space. By the middle decades of the nineteenth century, the parcels of private property were becoming larger, more complex, and harder for the city to manage. The landholdings of the Baltimore and Ohio Railroad Corporation were a prime example. Even as the city was financing the railroad company to a tune of $5 million, the street-level relationship between the two corporations grew increasingly restive. In his annual message of 1832, Mayor Steuart welcomed the company to place tracks throughout the city "under certain conditions and restrictions," thereby making an exception to the standard procedures of the street commissioners, and "obviating the necessity of applying in each particular case for such permissions." Two years later, the city council overruled this exception and voted, by a small majority, to demand that the B&O "seek permission to lay any track, and restore whatever street they may have broken up in the process."[32]

In the years to follow, the city council was bombarded with angry petitions, each with hundreds of signatures, calling for the removal of those very tracks. In 1835, the councilmen ruled in favor of the railroad. They reasoned that to restrict the railroad corporation "would be injurious to the general interest of the community; in derogation of existing individual vested rights and prejudicial to the improvement of the city property and pecuniary resources." A dozen years later, Mayor Solomon Hillen Jr. expressed quite another opinion. He found that B&O tracks on Pratt Street had become an affront to civic tradition and to urban democracy itself. Hillen charged the railroad with violating the cherished principles of public space in "a community like this, where our streets are declared to be 'public Highways' for the equal accommodations of all." The mayor called the B&O an "imperious" presence on the city streets and said that "in stealthy progression" it was asserting its "privilege and power." Considering himself "a stockholder" in these "public works," Hillen maintained that the B&O deserved no more consideration than "the humblest of our fellow citizens." By the time Hillen spoke up, many citizens shared his perturbation with the B&O. They indicted the tracks as a "danger to wives and children," provoking the "shrieks of the females" and causing "noisy disruption of funeral processions." Above all, the B&O's outsized presence on the city streets was an affront to pedestrian culture. Proposals to tear up railroad tracks surfaced for the first time in the 1830s and occasionally won the support of one branch of the city council, but the idea would not win full municipal approval until the 1870s.[33]

Long before then, the B&O had affronted the culture of the street with something more than intrusive tracks and noisy locomotives. It was consuming large segments of valuable public space for its yards, depots, and machine shops. In its voracious search for land, the railroad company colonized the territory south of Pratt Street, generating yet more squabbles. Residents of South Baltimore came before the city council charging the B&O with neglect of their public arteries and with closing up alleys lined with low-cost housing. Passenger depots, whose dimensions took up several squares of the urban grid, began to encroach on long-settled neighborhoods and entrenched property owners. A joint committee of both branches of the city council, formed to consider the recurring problems of opening railroad tracks, ruled against the B&O's appeal to close Bare and Conway Streets. The closures would conflict, in the councilmen's judgment, with "the vested rights of property owners who had spent considerable sums opening streets," and who, what is more, would lose the right of way to their homes. The petitioners, who included substantial property owners, charged the railroad with "Oppressiveness and Injustice" and presented their case as a defense of an egalitarian urban culture. They argued that the rights of the street extended "down to the humblest colored man or woman owning property in the vicinity." The urban terrain may have been appropriated for modern industrial uses, but it still rested on the social and political foundation of a pedestrian culture.[34]

Railroads were not the only private corporations grabbing up larger chunks of land in the capitalist city. Other industries, including the steam-powered garment factories on the west side, the machine shops south of the Basin, and chemical and iron factories on the city margins, were expropriating ever larger patches of urban space. On the east side of the city, the Canton Company took an especially voracious bite out of the urban landscape, heralding a new scale of land-taking. The head of the O'Donnell merchant family formed a partnership with William Patterson, the manager of a contiguous parcel in the east side. Together they drafted a more ambitious plan for exploiting the shores of the Chesapeake. The O'Donnells' wharf, astride the northern branch of the Patapsco, anchored a trade route that extended as far as China. The Canton Company converted that shoreline into an industrial district, complete with a canning factory and blocks of worker housing. Its corporate charter, issued by the State of Maryland in 1828, authorized the company to lay out three thousand acres "within the vicinity of the city of Baltimore, or near to any navigable water . . . into lots, streets, squares, and alleys, and other divisions."[35]

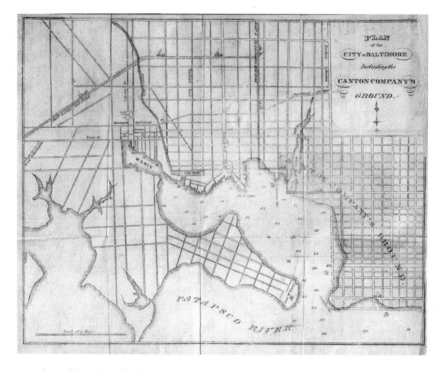

Plan of the City of Baltimore, Including the Canton Company's Ground, *1829.*
Courtesy of the Sheridan Libraries, Johns Hopkins University.

An industrial town was under construction just outside the Baltimore city limits. The Canton Company surveyed its own streets and lined them with factories and rows of tiny dwellings. A codicil of the corporation's charter from the State of Maryland authorized the company to "make such alterations in the course of the streets of the water line or wharf as the mayor and the City Council of Baltimore shall by ordinance passed by them assent to or approve." In 1836, the city agreed to extend certain public services onto the land belonging to the Canton Company. The city council agreed to became the purveyor of street improvement for the private company, but not without exacting some conditions, including "the assent in writing" of all the property holders on Fells Point. The municipality of Baltimore also asserted some control over the development process by insisting that any "reservoirs, sewers and other improvements constructed by the company be conducted under the supervision of the City Commissioners."[36]

Neither railroads nor factories, however, accounted for most of the spatial expansion of antebellum Baltimore. As in the port town before it, the modern capitalistic city grew outward by taking land on which to build houses. Geographer Sherry Olson has demonstrated that the economy of Baltimore lurched forward in step with the expansion and contraction of its land development and housing stock. Like Baltimore's industrial capitalists, its home builders made a major contribution to the big city economy. In the 1830s and 1840s, the prominent banker Joshua Gittings was quick to spy the profits to be gained by creating housing for the railroad and machine-shop workers in South Baltimore. Residential construction, hundreds of houses large and small, crept outward along the lines of the Poppleton Plan, stretching north, east, and west as well as south across the Basin. In the flush times between riots and financial panics, the columns of the city press were filled with laudatory reports of how the city was being reshaped one residential cell after another. To the editor of the *Baltimore Sun*, this amoeba-like urban growth was a routine process, a simple filling-up of the vacant "unimproved" land in the enterprising manner of the "takers-up" of yore. The expansion of the urban environment was itself a major capital project: a substantial private investment, the chief source of the city's tax revenue, and a stimulus to a flourishing market for consumer goods.

Unlike the railroad corporations or the steam-powered factories, home-building was still a small-scale operation, financed by minor increments of capital and advancing a few row houses at a time. The strategy employed by Ann Fell in the eighteenth century, leasing the land for a modest ground rent, continued to give builders with limited capital a way to construct houses at a steady pace and sell them at moderate prices. Those who built homes for the residents of the capitalist city were seldom men of great consequence or reputation; most of them came from the ranks of carpenters, and many of them were immigrants. Major builders seldom constructed more than one hundred houses over a lifetime. This pattern lasted into the 1880s; real estate development would not reach an industrial scale for at least another generation.[37]

Still, small-scale builders, taken collectively, reshaped the social geography of Baltimore. They laid out the land on which the industrial labor force and an increasingly diverse population of the capitalist city would live and share in some of the profits of urban growth. Land south of the Basin, once owned by founding dynasties like the Carroll and McHenry families, was converted into small residential buildings and sold to worker families residing near the railroad yards and mechanic shops. Working men, women, and children were packed densely together in row houses or pressed up against a small dwelling in the rear of the lot. These miniature alley houses provided homes for impecunious families, including large numbers of African Americans. An ethnic motif also wove through these working-class districts. By midcentury, Baltimore's population was one-quarter foreign born. A concentration of the Irish near the B&O yards, for example, led the Catholic archdiocese to build a church there. The construction of housing along these narrow streets had the effect of concentrating the working poor in separate quarters of the city and clustering immigrants in different ethnic pockets.[38]

At about the same time that the homes of workers and immigrants were being sorted into dense districts close to their workplaces and churches, another kind of residential district was being built just north of the old city center, near the site of the Washington Monument. At the time of its erection, the monument was outside the city limits, in the baronial territory of John Eager Howard. Howard's heirs began dividing the parcel into house-sized lots in the 1820s. On their appeal to the state, the city boundaries were extended into Howard's land. To make the properties more attractive to buyers, the heirs employed Poppleton himself to draw handsome plans for the grid around the Washington Monument. The blueprint enlarged the intersection of Charles and Monument Streets into avenues 110 feet wide with 30-foot promenades in between.

By the 1850s, this land development project had made a posh imprint on the landscape. The streets surrounding Washington's column were lined with mansions, whose frontages were almost double the size of a row house in more plebian districts. At least twenty feet wide and three stories high, each one housed a single family but boasted six times the volume of living space in the standard row house. It was the shape of the streets that framed these mansions that converted Mount Vernon into a unique urban landscape. The boulevards that radiated out from Washington's column at the intersection of Monument and Calvert Streets formed a cruciform of public space. Ornamented with marble bannisters and bronze sculptures, bordered in foliage and trees, and protected over the decades by preservationists and municipal ordinances, Baltimore's Mount Vernon became a masterpiece of urban landscape design. This elegant public artwork was not fashioned by a single architect or city planner but in the time-honored way of the Baltimore street commissioners, who wove public and private together along the city streets. The city council protected the ribbons of open

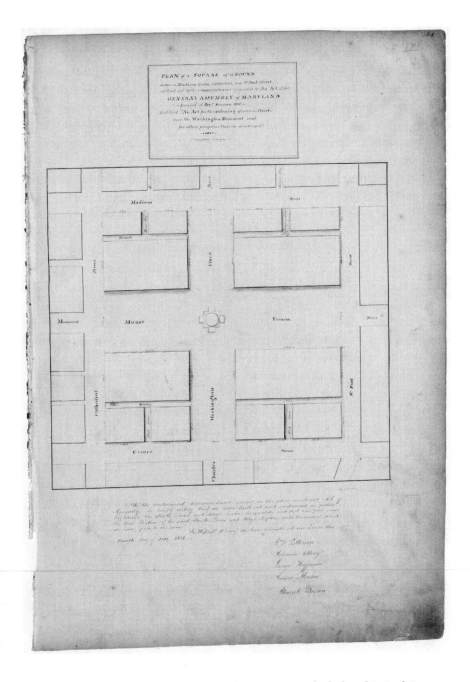

Plan of a Square of Ground Between Madison Centre, Cathedral, and St Paul Street, *1851. Cartographic Records, BRG 12-5-42. Courtesy of the Baltimore City Archives.*

space around the Washington Monument. They prohibited one resident from erecting a portico that would have obstructed the public view, and they passed ordinances regulating steps, porches, and "other ornaments to houses, fronting on Mount Vernon or Washington Place." In support of Poppleton's design for the Mount Vernon district, the street commissioners approved street closings as well as openings. In response to an application from affluent residents, they eliminated the alleyways that might lead to overcrowding in the genteel neighborhood.[39]

Located at the intersection of two wide streets beneath the Washington Monument, the Mount Vernon district portended two significant alterations in the urban landscape. First, it modified the time-honored practice of financing street openings with special assessments. The street commissioners granted more than $3,200 of general funds for embellishing the public space around the lots of Howard's heirs. The city contribution was a sizable inflation of the modest public investment required for a typical plain and functional city street. The developers of the Mount Vernon district reassured the city council that the investment would earn the city a substantial return in property taxes assessed on the surrounding mansions. Indeed, Mount Vernon was an early example of socially exclusive land use. A concentration of affluent homes, at a safe distance from the hubbub of Monument Square, remote from industrial nuisances, and unscathed by the alleyways where poorer inhabitants clustered, Mount Vernon became an elite enclave.[40]

By midcentury, affluent residential districts were sprouting up elsewhere in the city. City boosters in the daily press welcomed the "magnificent homes going up near the monument"; they were replacing the "mere shanties" of yore and the housing "rubbish" in the "central part of the city." Upon observing that the district north of the monuments was "sought after as a place of residence for persons of large means," a carpenter by the name of James Bromwell broke ground for eighteen substantial residential structures that would be three stories high and eighteen or nineteen feet wide. In June 1855, the *Baltimore Sun* reported that the "tides of Fashion" had also moved to the east and west of the monuments, raising the cost of real estate in the area. House by house and block by block, the energetic builders of Baltimore were reshaping the city in portentous ways, leaving smudges of inequality and exclusiveness on the city map.[41]

At this juncture, some influential citizens had second thoughts about the helter-skelter fashion in which the city was growing. The editor of the *Sun* ruminated on the subject at length, wondering if Baltimore had "lost sight of her true interest." He felt it necessary to add that "when we refer to her we include individual and aggregated interests." The editor captured the brisk but uncoordinated way in which the city had grown:

> The general idea is that landholders can dispose of their ground more profitably for building lots, and as a consequence they go to work and lease hundreds and hundreds of parcels of ground, twelve or fifteen feet by fifty or a hundred, at the low sum of one dollar per foot. Of these, small tenements are hurried up soon to dilapidate. We could point to scores of such streets as have been opened and built upon in this miserable manner. The eastern part of Baltimore abounds with them. They meet the view in the most indescribable irregularity, intersecting each other at all degrees of angles.[42]

The city council echoed the *Sun's* critique of Baltimore's chaotic homebuilding and gave some thought to revising the Poppleton Plan. Instead they only appropriated $500 to repair the tattered map, and wondered aloud if street maintenance should remain entrusted to abutting owners. But the problem would not go away. Two decades later, the city council was still bemoaning the "haphazard mode of establishing the grade of one and two squares at a time . . . a fruitful source of expenses to the city and property owners, occasioning tunnels and sewers at an immense cost in many instances which would have been unnecessary with proper system." Such challenges to the ad hoc way of shaping the city would be repeated many times before Baltimore, and American cities in general, devised more systematic methods of city planning.[43]

THE PUBLIC SQUARES

At the same time, private builders and public officials modified Poppleton's plan in unsystematic but significant ways. The *Sun*, joined by its rival daily, the *Baltimore American*, announced a campaign to reform the cityscape with a proposal for "Public Squares." The editor of the *Sun* made the following proposal for developing the cityscape: "Now let us suppose a different disposition had been made of these lands; that a portion thereof had been laid out in lots as demanded, and in part enclosed in a neat fence to protect the growth of the natural verdure, and a few trees planted therein." These verdant analogs of the city block should be "distributed at proper intervals among the streets of the City," overlaying the Poppleton Plan with a patch-work of greenery and gentility. The *Sun* called on the city to initiate this ambitious project by somehow obtaining "lots of a tolerable size in all the regions where desirable." The editor had to acknowledge a major obstacle to this reform, the fact that much of the land had long been taken; little open urban space had "not yet [been] seized upon by speculators."[44]

Although the city of Baltimore would soon sprout with a few "public squares," the local journalist cannot be credited with initiating this reform of the urban landscape. The *Sun* chided Baltimore for falling behind Philadelphia, New York, and Boston in this spatial innovation. There was, however, a local forerunner of the public square in the records of the city council dated 1829. Located on Hempstead Hill on the far eastern side of the city, it was first called a "Public Walk" and later "Patterson Park." This land, approximately the size of two city blocks, had been donated to the city by the park's namesake, William Patterson, in 1827. Three years later, the land remained unimproved, leading the mayor, Jacob Small, to propose that the city suspend further investment in the remote area. The land was still undeveloped in 1834, when William Patterson appeared before the city council once again requesting funds to grade the property he had donated to the public. He went as far as to proffer his own taxes for this purpose. The council rebuffed Patterson's ingenious self-serving scheme, and his park would remain unimproved until the 1850s, when the borders of urban development reached his property lines.[45]

The first successful proposal for a public square was at the initiative of neither abutting owners, nor a town meeting, nor the city council, nor the Mayor's Office, but rather, in response to inquiries from two land specula-tors from Delaware, James and Samuel Camby.[46] The Camby brothers came before the city council in 1839 begging taxpayers to fund the landscaping of a segment of the thirty-two acres that they had purchased and were develop-ing into a housing tract. Their scheme became the model for five spaces to be laid out in Baltimore before the Civil War: this one—Franklin Square—plus Union, Madison, Jackson, and Lafayette Squares. The Cambys offered the city a block of land to be "fore ever kept, and improved and embellished as a public square." In exchange, the city corporation was to pay the private developers a $10,000 subsidy, to be redeemed in the cost of laying out, grad-ing, paving, and ornamenting the square and abutting streets. Initially, the city council demurred. While the first branch of the council found the plan too expensive, a member of the second chamber found it a bargain, noting that the cost would quickly be returned in taxes. Such arguments mimicked those raised in the *Sun* extolling the "private as well as public advantages of public squares." The paper called it "vain to mention a slight increase in *taxation* as an objection. Taxation, with the *benefit* of the *taxed* in view is never to be dreaded." Based on such logic, the city council struck a bargain with the Cambys. They passed an ordinance that obliged the developers to line Franklin Square with three-story brick houses, each at least twenty-four feet wide, and therefore generating considerable tax revenue. On assurances that such a municipal investment in a private enterprise would rebound to a tax benefit for the public at large, the council voted fifteen to two to subsidize the housing tract around Franklin Square.[47]

Throughout the 1840s and 1850s, savvy land developers began to build public squares into their plans, calculating city subsidies for grading and landscaping into their budgets. The advertisements of carpenters, auctioneers, and "real estate agencies" boasted of prime locations near residential squares on both the east and the west sides of the city. This collaboration between the public and private sectors broke with and overrode the practice

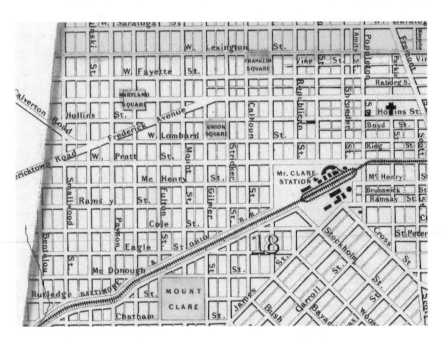

Westside Squares, 1857. Courtesy of JScholarship,
Sheridan Libraries, Johns Hopkins University.

---

of special assessment. Rather than delegating most of the cost of maintaining and improving the streets to the contiguous property owners who benefited directly, it subsidized large land developers, some of them, like the Cambys, from out of state. The appropriations for the new squares came from general citywide taxation, while the benefits accrued to just one—usually affluent—district. The precise arrangements, furthermore, were worked out between a land developer and the city, not initiated by a group of collaborating neighbors. The financing of the residential squares broke the pact that had once brought the owners of adjoining homes and shops together, taken them before the city commissioners, and given them a common stake in the public streets.

The city's investment in the residential squares produced a whole series of amenities not commonly found in the older and less fashionable parts of the city. Taxpayer funds were expended to grade a square of land, fence it, supply it with pumps and water, plant it with trees and foliage, and crown it with a fountain or a sculpture, sometimes with a new public school nearby. The expenditures could be costly. The appropriation for a fence around Union Square, made of iron and mounted on a foundation of "dressed granite," was $13,000. Prospective buyers were lured to Union Square with the promise of "fresh spring water" to be delivered at the city's expense. At midcentury, the city budgeted $9,000 for the railing at Franklin Square and $1,400 for the improvement of Mount Vernon. The developer of Jackson Square promised to erect a statue of Old Hickory at private expense, but begged the city to fund the octagonal pedestal on which it would stand. The developer also expected the city to level the steep grade of the land and stop the pooling of water in the low-lying sections of the square.[48]

The working relationship between the owners of the new residential tracts and the city officials was not always smooth and efficient. The Cambys were still petitioning for a proper fence around Franklin Square in 1850. The city council attributed the delay to the fact that the Cambys had not yet fulfilled its side of the bargain; they had not built the promised number of houses of sufficient value to redeem the municipal investment. The developers of Union Square, John and William Connell, complained that the city had not come through on grading the streets and enclosing the square, and asked to be relieved of their pledge to build houses around the plot of land they had surrendered to the public. The opening of squares in the 1840s and 1850s led the council to stretch and compromise the principle of special assessments. The press attributed an increase in annual taxation to the cost of improving

Washington Place and installing an iron railing at Franklin Square. The development of a fifth square, named for Lafayette, met with resistance in the mid-1850s. The mayor, Samuel Hinks, calculated the exchange in the old-fashioned way; he objected to funding an improvement that benefited only a select segment of the city.[49]

The proliferation of squares also invested municipal resources in the expansion and distension of the city's social fabric. The strain on the municipal boundaries began to register in a new vocabulary of urban geography, including increasing use of the term "neighborhood" and an occasional reference to "suburbs." The columns of advertisements for new housing situated squares in "improving neighborhoods," in "distant neighborhoods," in the "quiet and the peace of the neighborhood." The *Sun* spoke in 1858 of "blocks of new dwellings going up in the extreme western quarters of the city," and of "squares bordering the city." A real estate agent advertised that the housing around Madison Square was "in a neighborhood that was mostly improved," noting that it "combined the advantages of the country and the convenience to city business."[50] Omnibus lines carried those who could afford the fare out to Franklin Square and across town to a competing fashionable neighborhood, Jackson Square. The developers of these new neighborhoods also displayed a spatial imagination that was more rural than urban. They festooned the squares with trees and greenery and boasted a hilltop location that oriented the neighborhood toward the countryside, rather than toward the domes and monuments of the city. The domiciles on the outskirts of the city also differed from the rest of the city in architectural style and mode of financing. They were called "suburban cottages," not "row houses," and they were not leased, but purchased outright.

The people of Baltimore—now more diverse than ever—could no longer be joined easily together as a continuous progression of abutting owners. As a consequence, the city began to fracture into different spatial and social sectors. Only the relatively wealthy among the citizenry could afford to purchase the lots and the houses of the fashionable new neighborhoods. A home located right on Madison Square boasted 11 rooms on a lot 25 by 110 feet. Other fashionable rows offered marble trim on windows and doorways. A home in the upscale district on the west side, between Caroline and Eager Streets, had "all the modern conveniences" of gas and water. Unimproved lots around Jackson Square sold for over $1,000, ten times the cost of an alley lot a few miles south. A lot improved with four-story brick dwellings in the same neighborhood was priced at $8,500. A house advertised for sale

---

near Franklin Square did not list an asking price, but made it clear that it was "strictly a first class residence," distinguished by its brownstone front and an interior of "the best modern style in every respect with water and gas throughout the building." If less affluent men and women frequented these neighborhoods, they were likely to serve as cooks and servants, or perhaps as the "keeper of the square," employed by the city as caretakers of the genteel space.[51]

Only a narrow social strata reaped the benefits of the new urban spaces—walking the graded and paved streets that lined their expensive houses, relaxing in the green spaces that anchored them, and enjoying the quiet surroundings remote from the dense city center. The squares were bedecked with the symbols and associations of the middle class that was congealing around them. Above all, they honored a cult of domesticity. The residential square was advertised as a family refuge, a place of "innocent" recreation and the site of polite amusement. The promoters of squares promised homebuyers a place to retreat with their wives and children at the end of the workday. It was said that when residents gathered for musical soirées in the "aristocratic" district of Mount Vernon Place, the conversation flowed into separate gender spheres, the men talking of corporate stock and the women of romance and courtship. The districts of domestic opulence growing up at a distance from the old city center drew a divide of gender culture as well as class and race on urban space. Several residents of Franklin Square placed advertisements in the *Sun* seeking to employ "White" women only.[52]

A distinctive religious culture also clustered around the squares. The Camby brothers and other developers donated land to Protestant churches to lure respectable middle-class parishioners into the neighborhoods. St. Luke Episcopal anchored Franklin Square, and a Methodist congregation worshiped at Union Square. Parades of Sunday school students terminated in Mount Vernon; missionaries met in Union Square; and Franklin Square hosted a temperance celebration. The Cambys further increased the cachet of Franklin Square in 1852, when they offered free land to the Female Humane Impartial Society, which by then had become the favorite charity of the elite matrons of the city. Their charitable landscape now consisted of a home for aged females anchored by an architecturally notable building. The exclusiveness of the "public" square did permit some marginal groups with sufficient economic resources to take up residence. The developers of Union Square, for example, sponsored a German church in the neighborhood where Baltimore's celebrated journalist H. L. Mencken would grow up. The developers and homeowners of the fashionable new districts usually drew a scrim of Protestant exclusiveness around their squares. When the residents of Franklin Square had the temerity to request that the city close the gates of the square for a private charitable event, the councilmen declined, showing that there were some limits to the partitioning and privatization of public space. Working in concert, the inhabitants of residential squares were more successful in 1857, when the council allowed them to hold July 4 fireworks celebrations in their separate neighborhoods in Franklin Square, Lafayette Square, and Federal Hill.[53]

THE CENTER HOLDS

The dispersal of civic ceremony out toward the new residential districts was symptomatic of the changing shape of the city as a whole. The new urban spaces—the exclusive neighborhoods and the residential squares—had a counterpoint in the cognitive map of the older part of the modern city: the "central district." In part, this term simply acknowledged the growth of the city, now accommodating more than 150,000 people. As the population spilled out to the far reaches of the Poppleton Plan, the old city center seemed distant and apart from the new neighborhoods. But the term also raised doubts about the overall coherence of urban identity. If the press and disgruntled citizens were to be believed, the once-proud streets jutting up from the harbor had become offensive to the eyes, noses, health, and moral sensibilities of the upper classes. In 1846, one constituent informed the council that "there was enough blood and water on Wolfe Street to poison the whole neighborhood." A citizen of south central Baltimore complained of herds of pigs in the streets so menacing that he had contemplated uprooting his family and moving to the countryside. Another from the same area worried that the offal collecting near the curbsides would endanger the children who liked to play there. The children in the area that would later be called the "inner city" soon graduated into another type of street menace: the "gangs of bad boys" who stood on street corners, insulted innocent females, and harassed African Americans. By midcentury, the city had not yet found a solution to the oldest obstructions of the streets: sewage, garbage, roaming swine, rabid dogs, and the sight of human poverty. What did change, for the more affluent citizens, was the opportunity to take a carriage or one of the new omnibus lines out to more salutary quarters in a modern residential district or to one of the "suburbs" incorporated into the city map of 1853.[54]

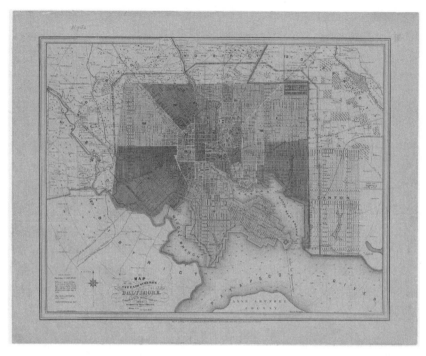

William Sides, Map of the City and Suburbs of Baltimore, *1853, Baltimore City Sheet Maps Collection. Courtesy of the Sheridan Libraries, Johns Hopkins University.*

Citizens, leaders, and newspaper editors all complained about the human occupants of streets near the Basin and Fells Point, portraying them as a caste of "beggars, vagrants and the disorderly." In his annual message of 1844, Mayor James Law issued a scurrilous indictment of the kind of people who tarried on the streets of the old city: "The reprobate loafer, whose moral depravity distills its poison into the body politics at will . . . the loathsome vagrant whose nature is so debauched by vicious excess." A member of the city council echoed the mayor's assessment of the urban crowd, calling them "drunkards and loafers both white and colored."[55] It was not race, but poverty, that assigned certain men, women, and children to the category of street rabble. To be found on the street without a home or a job labeled one a vagrant, subject to being rounded up and carted off to the almshouse.

A certain social and spatial sorting of the people of Baltimore was becoming visible on the map of Baltimore: the elite in their rural villas, the upper middle class around the remote squares, the new immigrants and railroad workers south of the Basin, the African Americans in the most crowded alley houses in Fells Point and Federal Hill. It was not necessarily a register of segregation and bigotry. The clustering of different social groups in different districts was sometimes a matter of choice and could give the expanding city a certain tensile strength, as it allowed the population to form small, cohesive communities without necessarily detracting from the solidarity of the whole. Demographic segmentation creates neighborhoods as well as ghettos. In Baltimore in the 1850s there was still a distinct possibility that the distances between the separate neighborhoods of the big city could be bridged as well as walled off from one another.

Everyday life in the city of Baltimore continued to flow through the common corridors of the streets arching down to the Basin. Blacks and whites, rich and poor, Protestants, Catholics, and Jews still resided relatively near one another, especially in the dense territory below the Washington Monument, and traveled the same streets from home to work. The tight weft and warp between the streets, lanes, and alleys, and the common commercial spaces of the public markets (which were still thriving long after their demise in other cities of the Northeast), wove the big city into a whole civic cloth. With omnibuses in their infancy and streetcars still in the offing, pedestrians had routine face-to-face encounters with the whole spectrum of the human multitude. More importantly, the separate wards still maintained a vital link to their representatives in the city council. While the streets near the harbor, those mundane cradles of urban democracy, may have lacked the "modern" embellishments found in the outlying squares, they were still a magnet for social mingling and political mobilization. And nearly every group and every cause found occasion to gather in that hallowed central space around the Battle Monument.

Some visitors to Baltimore had a more positive vantage point on the evolving urban landscape. Writing from the Barnum Hotel in Monument Square in 1850, a correspondent to the *Gloucester Telegraph* reported that Baltimore was "on the march to greatness and distinction, to take her place among the proudest cities of the land." He found the streets "very wide and perfectly straight, laid out at right angles and . . . adorned on each side with beautiful trees." This anonymous visitor to Baltimore, while especially appreciative of the "building blocks of Houses" in the "new parts" of the city, was most impressed by the central district, the domes of the Baltimore Basilica and the Unitarian Church, those two monuments, and the bustling streets downtown.[56]

Edward Sachse, Baltimore Street Looking West from Calvert Street, *1850.*
Courtesy of the Maryland Historical Society.

Citizens regularly came together at the slight dilation of Calvert Street beneath the Battle Monument. As many as fifteen thousand people gathered at the small but capacious space of Monument Square to deliberate about any number of questions, as big and consequential as "inalterable devotion to the American Union," or as particular as "an insult to the city by a visiting Englishman." During times of civic celebration, the "mixed multitude" marched with honored guests through a lineup of papier-mâché arches: if it was the funeral of a distinguished citizen, a cenotaph was erected in the center of the square near the Battle Monument. The square was the rallying place at election time, providing the platform for both Democrats and Whigs, sometimes simultaneously. Before the fall election in 1844, the rival parties scheduled rallies for the same evening, causing some concern about the incendiary possibilities. The dueling meetings went off without incident, however, as the Democrats set up a stand near the courthouse and the Whigs to the south, near Barnum's Hotel. Whatever the party or cause, it found a staging ground on Monument Square, a commodious place to gather to express an opinion, drape slogans and banners, or fill the air with the huzzahs of marching bands. Congregating in Monument Square was an act of urbane political integration. Separate political parties and different associations customarily gathered in different wards or neighborhoods before proceeding to march to the square.[57]

The central square of Baltimore occupies a distinguished place in the annals of American history and political theory. Reporting from Monument Square in 1831, a Mr. Finley provided Alexis de Tocqueville with key evidence for *Democracy in America*: "The Republicans, or the anti-Jackson party, chose me as their candidate," he said. "My opponent happened to be one of my best friends. We went together two days before the election to Washington Square where a platform had been erected for speakers at the town-meeting. I got up and began to explain to the audience—there were at least 10,000—the mistakes which General Jackson and the present administration had committed since they came to power, whereas my opponent made the case for the government." Finley acknowledged that catcalls sometimes drowned out the speakers, and "several men came to fisticuffs." On election evening, however, Baltimore was as peaceful as "Ash Wednesday in Rome."[58]

Still, Tocqueville was properly skeptical; he responded to Finley's political optimism with the retort, "You argue as a man who has never seen a people stirred by *real* and *profound* political passions. Everything with you up to now has been on the surface. There have been no large substantial interests at risk." Finley conceded, "That may be true; note that I only speak about us and about the present time." Tocqueville's skepticism was validated a few years later when Monument Square became the site of the Bank Riot. But the fact remained that as of 1831, even patricians like James Carroll and anti-Jacksonians like Mr. Finley saw fit to descend below the heights of Mount Vernon and the Washington column to engage the voters in the rough-and-tumble public space near the Battle Monument. In fact, Monument Square would be the magnet of civic engagement for decades to come. That public square accommodated major political changes as local, state, and national offices passed from one party to another, and then on to a new generation of citizens who had become accustomed to broadly representative government and sustained opposition between two political parties. The rivalry between the Federalists and the Republicans gave way to a second set of political combatants: the Jacksonian Democrats and the Whigs. The first national party convention, that of the Democrats, was held in Baltimore in 1831.

———

In 1834, both the Democrats and members of the newly formed Whig Party held rallies, parades, and national conventions in earshot of Baltimore's Monument Square. As of 1860, major political parties had chosen the city of Baltimore as the urban center at which to nominate their candidate for president thirteen times over.[59]

Monument Square would be the stage on which critical issues in the history of the city, the nation, and the world would be dramatized. Thousands gathered there to churn up bellicose energy for a war with Mexico in 1846. Monument Square was also capacious enough, on occasion, to bring capital and labor together. In 1851, striking workers gathered in the center of the square, while their employers met at Barnum's Hotel at the south end. In 1853, when mechanic shops throughout the city summarily reduced the wages of their employees, four thousand union members mobilized in Monument Square. Exhorted by the assurance that labor was the "real wealth and strength of the Nation," the striking men marched together to their different workplaces to demand a wage increase. The bosses made concessions to the workers, beginning with the managers of the Baltimore and Ohio Railroad.[60]

Monument Square was open to a whole world of people and causes. The revolutions in Germany and France inspired an expression of fervid support in Baltimore's central square in 1848. With an estimated thirty-six thousand immigrants now residing in the city, Monument Square welcomed increasingly cosmopolitan crowds. Immigrants and native Baltimoreans marched into the square to celebrate "republicanism in Germany and Europe generally." One thousand men organized themselves into different divisions and marched into the square to the music of Linhard's band. More routinely, German Americans, the city's largest immigrant population, held celebrations in the square under the banner of the Turnverein, the gymnastics associations that proliferated in US cities during the diaspora that followed the Revolution of 1848. The second major contingent of immigrants, natives of Ireland, also made Monument Square their own. On September 11, 1851, five thousand Irish Americans, who went by such names as Ryan, Kelly, O'Connor, and Cohen, gathered to petition for the freedom of their countrymen who had been imprisoned by the British.[61] At the midpoint of the nineteenth century, approximately half a century after incorporation, the capitalist city seemed capable of absorbing new and diverse peoples into its old and commodious public spaces.

At the same time, some Baltimoreans began to retreat from the cacophony of the central public square. The parade of the Protestant Sunday schools assembled not at Monument Square, but at the elite space of the Merchants' Exchange, and conducted its closing ceremonies in the polite neighborhood of Mount Vernon. Other Baltimoreans celebrated the Fourth of July either in the fashionable residential squares or by taking excursions out of town. More ominously, expressions of intolerance could be heard in the public squares. In 1851, a temperance meeting inspired a countermovement that provoked fisticuffs and pistol fire along the parade route during the election season. A small political faction called the Reubenites streamed out of their neighborhoods and into a procession that wound its way along the full extent of Baltimore Street, from Lexington Market on the west to Fells Point on the southeast. This band of partisans penetrated four miles into the western section of the city, where it set off cheers and fireworks at the homes of candidates and supporters. As the procession moved east and passed Christ Church, however, the Reubenites met "a party of men armed with pistol and stones." A handful of injuries and three or four arrests followed. The Reubenites quickly disbanded, but the incident was a harbinger of the divide soon to open up in Baltimore, and across the nation, between the native born and immigrants. Democracy was never easy, especially not in a city as rife with differences and as battered by change as antebellum Baltimore. A few years later, the city would nearly come undone when ethnic conflicts swelled, stirring up a short-lived political movement called the Know-Nothings.[62]

Until then, a better memorial to the maturation of Baltimore as a modern capitalist city would be a major civic achievement dated 1854: the founding of a public, municipally owned water system. This innovation came about as the result of a long campaign to make the provision of this vital resource a public rather than a private project, a general rather than a special assessment. Local officials had proposed taking control of the water supply from the private monopoly several times before, most notably in 1830, 1833, and 1835. The chief stockholders of the water company, which had been awarded a corporate charter for the job in 1808, had comprised a who's who of the founding elite of the city—Charles Carroll, Samuel Smith, John Eager Howard, and Robert Goodloe Harper, for example. Discontent with the private company had been mounting for many years, along with public awareness of the difficulty of allying public service with private profit. A committee on water formed by the city council in 1830 presented the conundrum of the capitalist city with pointed clarity: "The object of individuals, when they act by themselves, or when they act as a company, in investing money, is to make the most profit out of it that circumstances will permit them to make.

. . . If this is true, it follows of necessity, that the chief view of the Water Company was to make money out of the necessity of the people of Baltimore." It was not until 1852 that the city council acted decisively to resolve this conundrum. They appointed a six-man committee to investigate the practical possibilities of buying back the waterworks from the descendants of the founding stockholders.[63]

The committee members went about their work with scientific precision. They visited other city water systems, made exacting estimates of the amounts of water needed, calculated the cost of every element of the system, and commissioned engineers to investigate the best sources of chemically pure water. The ultimate decision to take public control of city water was not, however, left to a committee of experts. Nor was it entrusted to the city council and the mayor. The water committee decided instead to "let every man of this city speak for himself." The councilmen called for a plebiscite. They asked citizens to "assemble in their respective places of election" to decide whether to undertake this expensive project. The *Baltimore Sun* surmised that, given "the importance and necessity of an abundant supply of water for the present and for the future generations an affirmative vote upon this subject can scarcely be doubted." The result of the referendum was 9,727 votes in favor of creating a public utility and 304 opposed.[64]

This blending of the democratic franchise with modern governmental administration was a watershed in municipal history. The voters and their representatives who had inherited the practice of direct democracy devised in the early republic now carried it forward into modern times. One council member contemplated applying the old standard of special assessment, matching individual benefits to individual taxpayers. Surmising that wealthy districts had already installed pipes and secured water by private purchase, thus reducing the cost of completing a new system in their neighborhood, the councilman argued that they should be exempted from a water tax. His proposal was rebuffed. Special assessments might have been sufficient to meet urban needs on a small grid of relatively uniform row houses, but they fell short in the sprawling and diverse spaces of the capitalist city. To meet the common need for water, the municipality asked taxpayers to look beyond their front doors—and individual wells and the nearby spring—and invest instead in a modern, citywide public service. In 1854, a large majority of voters endorsed this reformulation of the obligations of citizens and property owners toward one another.

A number of urban historians have recognized this fundamental reorientation of urban governance dating to the mid-nineteenth century. They disagree, however, about just how to characterize and label it. Gary Browne's meticulous research in 1980 awarded 1850s Baltimore the title of "Public City" in recognition of the increasing centralization of the funding and management of municipal services. By transferring the responsibility of providing water from a private corporation to the municipality, Baltimore was clearly consigning a new public function directly to the government sector. Sundry other innovations a few years later, notably the professionalization of the fire and police departments and the expansion of executive power in the office of the mayor, support Browne's characterization of Baltimore's maturation into a public political economy. Browne's conclusions about city administration in the mid-nineteenth century have been seconded by other historians, including Hendrik Hartog writing of New York, Robin Einhorn on Chicago, and John Teaford on American cities more generally. The esteemed urban historian Sam Bass Warner Jr. saw it another way: in 1968 he titled his history of Philadelphia *The Private City*. More recently, writing in 1996, legal historian William Novak argued that "nineteenth-century America was a *public* society in ways hard to imagine after the invention of twentieth-century privacy."[65]

In Baltimore during the first half of the nineteenth century, there was something more complicated at work than an abrupt transition from a private to a public city (or vice versa). Building a city was a very complicated process in which public and private enterprise could not easily be disentangled. Although the municipality would not take up full direction of urban functions such as providing clean water until the 1850s, the erection of Baltimore into a city decades before was not a private effort. Building a harbor, erecting two monuments, laying out so many miles of streets, and financing a railroad required the assiduous associated effort of citizens and their elected leaders. The city could not be erected by private efforts alone; it had to be coordinated and legitimated within public institutions, including the increasingly democratic city council. One of the first actions of the Baltimore City Council was to regulate the private economy and assert authority over private affairs. In the decades ahead, private businessmen, corporate leaders, and the courts increasingly objected to this public meddling as they embraced the principle of laissez-faire economics, but all the while soliciting public subsidies.

Categorizing this complex political pattern as a simple transition from private to public (or the reverse) ignores the intervening political and social context. These innovations in municipal government coincided with critical changes in political institutions and leadership. The merchants who once presided over the local government from their posts around the Basin saw their public authority curtailed by representative government and questioned by a population schooled in the ways of both democracy and capitalist improvement. As urban democracy became more robust, diverse, and committed to free labor, rural legislators in the state capital at Annapolis curtailed the autonomy of the chartered corporation of Baltimore. The breach between the body politic of Baltimore City and the State of Maryland was fixed in law by the distinction between the public and the private corporation. At the same time, certain private interests, including those of the merchant elite, business corporations, and beneficiaries of patronage, found ways to forge advantageous relationships with the municipal sector. In the case of the B&O Railroad, the relationship between private interests and local government was at times troubled, but generally lucrative. Similarly, those enterprising architects of residential squares won public subsidies that contributed to their private profits. One result of this spate of changes in the municipal political economy was that it freed private businesses from public regulation. The increasingly voluble allegiance to the "free market" was another sign that modern American capitalism had come to Baltimore.

In sum, the people of Baltimore, acting through their representative institutions, were simultaneously unraveling and reweaving the border between their individual interests and their civic responsibilities. As private corporations claimed their private rights and privileges, the mayor, city council, and taxpayers were left with a growing burden of public responsibilities. In his annual message of 1853 Mayor J. Smith Hollins had to apologize for his failure "to reduce the taxes to the lowest possible amount compatible with a due observance of the city in its various departments." In a municipal report presented at the same meeting, the councilmen announced that there would be no dividend that year on the city's stock in the B&O. To secure its capital and simply make ends meet, the municipality had to exact tax revenue from increasingly stingy property owners. Municipal officials resorted to various strategies when they were squeezed between the complaints of taxpaying citizens and funding their debts to banks and corporations. In December 1853, the city council resorted to the stratagem of simultaneously lowering the tax rate and raising the level of assessments. More routinely, the city council resorted to a policy of retrenchment. To the private corporation went profits and limited liability, and to the city went the public responsibility and debt. The disequilibrium would bedevil American city politics from that time forward.[66]

Distraught but forward-looking members of the city council began to consider making major changes in the method of municipal finance. In his frustration with the city's dependence on special assessments, one member of the second branch searched for "some well digested system . . . carried out by the authorized agents of the city" to replace the disjointed individual assessments that were bloating the agenda of the city council. Others expressed a willingness to forfeit citizen initiative in order to install more efficient administrative machinery. One member of the council reasoned that the good of the whole would not be served if it could be stymied by the stinginess of two-thirds of the property owners aligned along a particular city block. Others became impatient with the hurly-burly sociability of the public market, denying petitions to open new neighborhood market halls and decrying the old stalls as the breeding ground of crime. These old ways of creating the urban public—special assessments, voluntary associations, town meetings, and elite stewardship—became insufficient as the city grew in size and complexity. The modern capitalist city could not be pieced together like a line of row houses along a small grid of streets. One member of a city council committee found an apt metaphor for this breakdown of the commonweal: "You can't beg off the road tax," he scolded, "because you only go by railway."[67]

Special assessments, voluntary associations, and other well-worn practices ultimately became too slow, inefficient, and ineffective for managing a complex urban economy in the age of capital. Yet there were costs as well as advantages to municipal modernization. The transfer of urban services to city agencies was not always an unalloyed improvement, for example. It put decision making into the hands of appointed and salaried officials instead of elected city councilmen, sacrificing democratic process for bureaucratic efficiency. Although special assessments could be criticized for distributing the benefits of the big city to specific taxpayers in sometimes inequitable ways, they had grounded civic identity securely in material space and routinely brought citizens together to care for and improve the environment they shared. In ways both small and large, the public spirit kindled in the shared spaces of the Monumental City might seem diminished rather than expanded in the modern capitalist city. The deflated civic pride could be gleaned from a city council resolution that barred hacks from parking around the Battle Monument on the grounds that "one of her public squares consecrated by a beautiful monument to the memory of the illustrious dead"

———

257

had been "desecrated as it has been for several years past, as a public stable." The public spirit of the Monumental City had not been entirely squelched by modern capitalism, however. Witness the major accomplishment of the plebiscite that had led to the public water system.[68]

The spirit of civic improvement was not moribund as the 1850s drew to a close. To some citizens of Baltimore, however, the scale of change was bewildering. It provoked a flood of nostalgia in the prose of the city's literary éminence grise, John Pendleton Kennedy:

> The growth of a city is a natural process which creates no surprise to those who grow with it, but it is very striking when we come to look back upon it and compare its aspect at different and distant eras. If I had been away during the long interval which separates the past I have been describing, from the present, I doubt if I should now find one feature of the old countenance of the town left. Every thing has changed as if there was not consanguinity of even acquaintance between the old and the new.

Kennedy's reminiscences provide an irrefutable firsthand perspective on the profound transformation of Baltimore between 1828 and the 1850s. Equating that transformation with natural growth, however, obscures the immense amount of thought, energy, and civic will that went into reshaping the city of Baltimore, its economics, its politics, and its spaces. Kennedy recognized that intensely political construction of the city with one telling example of land-taking: "Of all the functions of municipal care, the one that begins earliest and is the last to end in a thriving town is the opening and grading of streets. Corporate vanity finds its great vent in this exercise. The egotism of the young city runs into streets. It is the only department of government that seems to be animated with an intense foresight for the wants of the future."[69]

Kennedy can be forgiven for forgetting how the railroad was transforming his city and disrupting the everyday life of the streets. He was writing three years into the Civil War. The countdown to that war would proceed at a frantic and vertiginous pace in the late 1850s and would draw the citizens of Baltimore into the vortex of sectional and national politics. The issue that provoked that war was not the most pressing item on the agenda of Baltimore's municipal government. As one Yankee visitor put it in 1850, "The institution of slavery still presses with its benumbing and withering influence on Maryland, and is felt somewhat at Baltimore, although not to the same extent in the city as in the State. The African race abound, although few of them, we are glad to say, are held in slavery." Still, even as the slave population declined, the stigma of race remained. African Americans were concentrated in the poor districts and in the alley houses of Baltimore, and overrepresented in the almshouse and in the city jail. They were socially marginalized and politically ostracized: even in the almshouse, they were housed separately from their fellow sufferers. In that most exuberant and inclusive celebration of the capitalist city, the event kicking off the Baltimore and Ohio Railroad with the laying of a cornerstone, one contingent was notably missing—African Americans—despite the fact that there were now twenty-five thousand of them living in the city.[70]

The movements of African Americans through urban space became more restricted with the advances of abolitionism and fears of slave revolt. Racial curfews kept free blacks as well as slaves off the streets late at night, and excluded them from renting stalls in the markets. If the attention in the daily press was the sum of the African American place in the public life of the city, theirs was a dubious stature. Baltimore newspapers took notice when an African American woman known as "Old Hagar" made a "grotesque and weird" appearance on the streets of South Baltimore peddling herb remedies; supposedly she was frightening the small children. An African American named William Adams was allowed ten minutes to address the public—his podium was the gallows, where he was hanged for murder. (Whites who committed capital crimes were no longer punished and shamed publicly.) In the most extreme program of racial exclusion, Maryland became a center for the movement to send free blacks to Africa, the cause célèbre of a group of civic leaders that included John H. B. Latrobe, Charles Carroll, and John Pendleton Kennedy. Given the inequity, danger, and humiliation they faced in the public spaces of the city, African Americans sometimes chose to maintain separate places for themselves, their own schools as well as their own churches. A contingent of petitioners (all of them male) asked the city council to be excluded from paying the school tax, on the grounds that, denied access to public education, they maintained and paid for their own private colored schools. The transcript in the city council records read: "The undersigned Taxpayers of the city of Baltimore respectfully represent that the Coloured population of the City are Compelled to pay a Tax for the support of the Public Schools which your petitioners consider unjust." The predicament of these taxpayers exposed an abrasive contradiction in antebellum democracy: for those of African descent, membership in the municipal

———

public weal had become a financial liability rather than a cherished right. In sum, although slavery was becoming outmoded in the capitalist urban economy, politics in Baltimore had hardly become colorblind. The stigma of race conferred inequity not just on slaves but on freed men and women of African descent, projecting new patterns of exclusion, discrimination, and segregation on the urban landscape. This, too, was a mark of the modern capitalist city.

At midcentury, however, much of the political life of Baltimore still transpired on the local streets and squares; in open, outdoor spaces; and within the purview of almost everyone, including those categories of persons still excluded from the franchise: nonwhites, women, and very recent arrivals in the city. This basic political geography inspired a striking civic portrait painted by Richard Caton Woodville in 1848. The setting is the porch of the American Hotel, along a street that is dusty but graded. A sign on a smudged pilaster notes that the hotel also serves as a public post office. The focal point of the canvas is a young white man clutching an open newspaper. He is surrounded by seven others of the same sex and race, in varying ages, all in rapt attention, awaiting the latest news. On the fringes of the canvas, where the political drama spilled onto the street, Woodville painted the inhabitants of the most remote region of the public sphere. On the right, hardly visible but deeply attentive, is an aged white woman, who is said to have been modeled on one of Woodville's servants. Seated just downstage on the step of the hotel, but equally attentive, are two other figures, a dark-skinned man and a young girl, perhaps his daughter. Woodville's magical brushstrokes expressed the vitality and public accessibility of democracy in Baltimore and at the same time exposed its limits as reflected in the longing and chastening gaze of the three figures on the margins. While in full sight, in public space, they were barred from participation in the official circle of urban democracy. Woodville's rendering of his native Baltimore is titled *War News from Mexico*. The headlines from Mexico signal that the advance of urban capitalism, with all its imperfections, would soon be manifest around San Francisco Bay. It is the cue to return westward to the pueblo of Yerba Buena.

Richard Caton Woodville, War News from Mexico, *1848. Wikimedia Commons.*

CHAPTER 7

———

THE CAPITALIST "PUEBLO"

Selling San Francisco, 1847–1856

The news of war from Mexico was quickly forgotten in 1848 when gold was discovered on the land ceded to the United States by the Treaty of Guadalupe Hidalgo signed earlier that year. The news from El Dorado had spread as far as Baltimore by July 1849, when crowds gathered on the rooftops of Fells Point and waved farewell to a shipload of Argonauts departing for California. Among Baltimore's émigrés' was the merchant William Hull, who, arriving in San Francisco after the long journey around Cape Horn, admonished his fellow passengers to keep faith with "our own native city, where Morality and Religion prevail." He warned the Forty-Niners of the baleful "effect of gold upon the heart," saying it had "produced debauchery, and vice, and caused the soil of our new home already to drink of human blood." Once inside the Golden Gate, Hull's thoughts turned quickly to other matters. He observed that the harbor was already glutted with the wares of merchants like himself and worried about the inflated cost of everything from wages to water transport and rent. Like other Forty-Niners who departed Baltimore for the gold fields, Hull soon

———

turned his attention to money matters and other issues emblematic of the march of capital across the continent. A correspondent for the *Baltimore Sun* alerted readers to the commercial prospects of the San Francisco Bay region. With an estimated two hundred thousand immigrants flocking to the gold fields, the *Sun* anticipated that "the supplies needed from the Atlantic ports will be six millions of dollars worth of lumber—four millions of flour, and other articles to the amount of two millions."[1]

Shrewd merchants foresaw the economic opportunities awaiting them in California even before the Gold Rush. William Howard, a native of Boston, was already in business in Yerba Buena in June 1848. He acted quickly when he heard a rumor that some workmen at Captain John Sutter's sawmill near Sacramento had discovered gold, writing to warn his partner back East to "keep [the] secret as long as possible" to help him maintain an advantage over his competitors. To Howard, the financial promise of the Gold Rush lay not in mineral deposits, but in the enterprise of city-building. He invited the "best business men and capitalists" to partner with him in constructing a gasworks for San Francisco and ordered the necessary iron pipes from Baltimore. William Howard had clearly mastered the techniques of profiting from public service pioneered by such private corporations as the Baltimore Gas Company and the B&O Railroad. He expected to sell $500,000 in stock for his gasworks company, making it "the most profitable stock in existence in any part of the world." It would require, however, that he "obtain from the city the exclusive privilege of the city for a number of years." Howard had learned the lessons of municipal capitalism well; he moved west alert to opportunities to form a profitable alliance with the public sector.[2]

Other perspicacious businessmen saw the port of San Francisco Bay as a yet more fundamental opportunity for those with capital to spare. The San Francisco Land Association, based in Philadelphia, peddled $15 million worth of shares in the land adjoining the city, in denominations as small as $100. The company assured prospective stockholders that these parcels would yield profits equal to the real estate in booming cities back East, mentioning Baltimore as well as Chicago as examples. Another immigrant, named William Weston, wrote back to Maine in 1852 bragging that his investment had risen 150 percent in a single year: "To do as much with Capital, in Maine," he remarked, "would require 16 years." Weston was investing his capital not in gold mining but in real estate. The accounts of the wealthy landowner Thomas Hayes for 1857, the year after he completed his term as county clerk, indicate just how far and fast capitalism had advanced across the continent and beyond. His investments in the land along the shoreline of San Francisco Bay took him to London and Paris in search of capital.[3]

A very complicated land transaction was in the works around San Francisco Bay between 1849 and 1856. The transfer of national sovereignty from the Republic of Mexico to the United States of America was perhaps the simplest part of the unwieldy process. In keeping with international law and according to the Treaty of Guadalupe Hidalgo, the property rights of Mexican citizens were "inviolably respected," as was any public land in preexisting municipalities, such as any pueblo located near San Francisco Bay. During the transfer of sovereignty, furthermore, the institutions of local government were to operate as usual. They included the *ayuntamiento* of any existing pueblo, with its *alcalde, regidores*, and *juez de pais*. Until the territories ceded to the United States by the Republic of Mexico had been admitted as states of the Union, a series of ineffectual military officers served as governors of Alta California and prefects of the Partido de San Francisco. The first stage of the transition from Mexican to US rule, recounted in Chapter 5, had gone relatively smoothly; then the Gold Rush began, throwing the system of land tenure into chaos.

Establishing title to thousands of tracts of private property caused great confusion and controversy. The land of San Francisco would be crosshatched with blurry, ephemeral, fluctuating, and contested property lines, all drawn by a motley cast of characters who spoke both English and Spanish. Capitalists big and small—lawless squatters and righteous vigilantes, judicious lawyers and wily realtors—all competed to secure a piece of the Mexican pueblo. This chapter will recount their exploits at the jolting pace set by the times. The first stage of this land transfer, enduring until California was formed into a state and admitted to the Union in the fall of 1850, was particularly chaotic, as a series of ad hoc and half-legitimate municipal governments began to sell off the land and water with abandon. Next, the federal government, acting through an appointed land commission, attempted to bring order to the disarray of land titles, only to be ignored by the city government and overruled by the state courts of California. This last byzantine piece of jurisprudence went under the name of the Pueblo Land Case, and traveled through the courts under the title *San Francisco v. the United States*. On the eve of the Civil War, the approximate date when this chapter comes to a close, the ownership of thousands of acres would remain in question. On this jerrybuilt scaffolding, the city of San Francisco began to take its modern shape.[4]

THE POLITICAL ECONOMY OF THE GOLD RUSH

The languorous pastoral economy and weak *ayuntamiento* of Mexican California was a poor bulwark against the full-tilt capitalism that arrived with the Gold Rush. Yerba Buena was the beachhead from which to create what the historian Gunther Barth memorably called "the instant city." The rate of population growth was indeed faster than a New York minute. From an estimated one thousand residents in January 1849, the population rose to twenty-five thousand in less than a year, and to forty thousand by 1854. These static estimates of San Francisco's population did not include the tens of thousands who passed quickly through the city on their way to the mines. The flimsiest web of governance was all that held these thousands of people—overwhelmingly young men—together into a makeshift town. At its birth, the instant city was a political orphan. State and federal authority was ambiguous until the fall of 1850, when California was finally admitted to the Union. A sequence of improvised governments, one claiming the title of the "Ayuntamiento and Town Council," another calling itself the "Legislative Assembly," only added more turbulence to the dizzying pace of the Gold Rush. When rumors of vast fields of precious ore in the Sierra Nevada foothills were confirmed in May 1848, the population around Yerba Buena Cove plummeted temporarily, and even the fledgling town council absconded to the gold fields. Between January and August 1849, the council failed to raise a quorum for weeks on end. A rump meeting in April sent the sergeant-at-arms out to bring in members, whose absence those in attendance described, with consummate understatement, as showing "a lack of duty toward the people and disrespect to this body." For months and years to follow, municipal governance stumbled from one crisis to another: the membership of the council was doubled in hopes of securing a quorum, and council members resigned, were fired, were indicted, or disappeared.[5]

Amid the chaos, various municipal legislators struggled to provide basic city services. The first attempts at self-governance were primitive, to say the least. One ordinance enjoined all households to keep buckets handy to fight an epidemic of fires that repeatedly engulfed the tinderbox of tents and wooden shanties where San Francisco pioneers lived, profited, and gambled away their gold dust. To rid the streets of garbage and offal, the town council approved the purchase of two mule teams and some carts. In other ordinances, the council voted to banish swine to the outskirts, open a road to a cemetery, and purchase coffins for unfortunate Forty-Niners who would not make it home from El Dorado. The minutes of the Legislative

---

Assembly also recorded the purchase of sixty balls and chains to outfit the prisoners who were serving their time by laboring on the public works. For a jail, the councilmen commandeered a ship that had been left derelict in the harbor. As of 1852, San Francisco was hardly a manicured urban space. One newcomer, Samuel Brown, registered his shock at the panorama that rose up before him as he passed through the Golden Gate: such "mature and huge commerce," he observed, contained within "so primitive a city."[6]

Erecting a modern city on the shores of San Francisco Bay was a Herculean, if not Sisyphean, task. The costs of building the city were monumental, and the sources of taxation were paltry. The population heading for the mines or arriving without property rarely appeared on the assessor's ledgers; they were fleeting free riders on the municipal services. In a rare act of extravagance, the early town council made one major investment: it purchased the Jenny Lind Theater to serve as the quarters of the municipal government. This expenditure and others like it raised the ire of the overburdened taxpayers and served to tarnish the city with another mark of modern urbanism, financial scandal. The requisition of this first city hall deposited $200,000 into the coffers of the friend and business partner of David Broderick, a councilman and émigré from New York branded by his association with Tammany Hall. Broderick and the Democratic Party also were tarred by their association with a band of young men called "the Hounds," whose rowdy presence on the disheveled city streets in 1851 inspired the first outbreak of San Francisco's version of "mob town" vigilantism.

In some ways, San Francisco's recourse to vigilantism resembled the rough-hewn justice of other places in the American West. The crowded city was flooded with in-migrants and did not yet have basic city services such as police protection and a fire company. Under these circumstances, residents might feel justified in taking the law into their own hands. When Charles Palmer, who set out to California in 1849 intending to be a journalist, but quickly changed course when he grasped the commercial opportunities opened by the Gold Rush, saw his merchandise destroyed by arson and thievery, he blamed the Hounds. Like many of the men of his mercantile class, he saw vigilante justice as a reasonable response to the disorder of the frontier city. Although Palmer expressed shock at "the sight of two bodies, swinging 'twixt heaven and earth, and the hoarsely approving roar of ten thousand men," he had property to protect and judged vigilante action an "illegal but necessary organization of the people."[7] It would be simplistic, however, to reduce the first outbreak of vigilantism in San Francisco to frontier anarchy.

———

266

In some ways, it was symptomatic of an actual excess of government: those multiple town councils, the instant importation of partisan politics, and the expectation that the municipality would provide the extensive public services necessary to maintain a capitalist urban economy.

The champions of vigilante justice were reacting to an extreme case of those "embarrassments" to which nascent capitalist cities were prone. Essential investments in urban infrastructure had to be made "before taxes could be laid and collected." The costs of building a city above Yerba Buena Cove led to the familiar complaints from taxpayers as well as some particularly serious charges against the town council—the accusation, for example, that the government of San Francisco was shirking its "legal and moral obligations" by not honoring its debts.[8] Complaints about municipal debt and excessive taxation were endemic to the capitalist city. In San Francisco, as in Baltimore, they could lead to violent encounters in the very streets that the municipal government struggled to open, pave, and plank. The outbreak of vigilantism in San Francisco was an emergency method of bringing order to nascent capitalist space.

Some forty businessmen sent a petition to the state legislature that captured the frustration of building a city on the shores of San Francisco Bay in the era of Gold Rush capitalism. "It is hardly necessary to remind the Legislature," said their petition, "that the process of building a large city on a desert coast, and fitting it for the accommodation and uses of a large population and for the purposes of a commercial emporium—when this process is an immediate exigency, and the work of years is compressed into the labor of a few months—must necessarily, under the most favorable circumstance, be attended by extraordinary difficulties." The physical conditions around the great estuary of the West compounded the problems: "Sand hills had to be cut down, passage-ways through rocks to be made, mountainous places leveled, wharves constructed and marshes and parts of the Bay filled." These very material aspects of making a city along San Francisco Bay were foremost on the minds of the petitioners, who had contracted with the city to open roads up those "mountainous" hills and build wharves out beyond those muddy beaches. Unpaid for their efforts years later, they asked the state to bail out the municipality that had reneged on its debts. A decade after the United States claimed sovereignty over San Francisco Bay, the local government was bankrupt.[9]

The political institutions of the new American territory were too weak to accomplish what businessmen described as the urgent "demand for a commercial emporium." In this political vacuum a host of citizens and politicians hastened to erect facsimiles of the municipal governments that had matured in their home states and cities. The newcomers to San Francisco gathered in the old plaza to draw up their first state-sanctioned charter in 1850; they had updated it twice by 1853. The Forty-Niners instinctively entrusted representative government to a popularly elected mayor and a bicameral council. The democracy of all white men was never in dispute. Each charter gave priority to establishing electoral procedures: qualifications for voting, the organization of wards, the location of polling places, and a long list of municipal offices, many of them salaried and the source of patronage. A series of hastily assembled municipal legislatures organized committees on fire, health, prisons, ordinances, education, and, of course, streets. They set up the rudiments of a police force, a public hospital, a public school system, and a private water company, and even tidied up the Yerba Buena plaza a bit. The list of the powers of the San Francisco Common Council established in 1850 ran to over thirty items and included many archaic matters, such as regulating the "quality and price of bread," licensing pawnbrokers and "money changers," establishing a night watch, and sanctioning a public marketplace. San Francisco would never in fact enforce an assize of bread or build a public marketplace; these archaic practices of city governance did not survive the movement west.[10]

One component of local governance was quite thoroughly modernized as early as the charter of 1851, that of municipal finance. The City of San Francisco was instantly equipped with a sinking fund, a committee on accounts, a department of finances, a treasurer's office, a controller, a collector, and an assessor. Perhaps borrowing a lesson from Baltimore's troubled relationship with the B&O, the San Francisco charter stipulated that "the city shall not at any time become a subscriber for any stock in any corporation." Pioneer mayor John Geary admonished the municipal legislature to be frugal, advising that "in no case should a greater amount be drawn from the pockets of the people than is absolutely necessary for an economical administration of the government, and for the construction of such public improvements as are absolutely required to meet the necessity of the city and to secure its permanent welfare." At the same time, Geary imbibed the spirit of capital improvement. He singled out investment in the harbor, for example, as "a benefit to the country and of immense advantage to San Francisco."[11] At the same time that the city charter of San Francisco prescribed elaborate rules about city revenue, it placed constraints on taxation, limiting it to 1 percent of assessed value. In matters of municipal finance, the city seemed to be born modern, caught at the outset, within the contradiction of the capitalist political economy, between the Scylla of public expenses and the Charybdis of financial retrenchment.[12]

The municipality of San Francisco, however, enjoyed a public resource that was rarely available back East. The land around the Chesapeake had been parceled out into private property for over a century when Baltimore was erected into a city. The shores of San Francisco Bay were part of the newly acquired cession from the Republic of Mexico. This plentitude of apparently open land whetted the appetites of the American immigrants as well as the custodians of the bankrupt city treasury. Without hesitation or concern for international law, but in the spirit of frontier-style municipal capitalism, the elected officials of San Francisco began to sell off the public land to pay off the city debts.

SELLING THE LAND OF SAN FRANCISCO, 1849–1853

The Californios had begun preparing the land for capitalist development in advance of the Gold Rush. The Diputación of San Francisco had encouraged the advancement of private property in the district that included Dolores, Yerba Buena, and the surrounding ranchos. Beginning in the 1830s, with the encouragement of the Republic of Mexico, the *ayuntamiento* conveyed thousands of acres to private owners, encouraged trade at Yerba Buena Cove, and invited active participation in local government. Governor José Castro pronounced categorically in 1841 that "land not private or occupied by a pueblo may be divided." He stipulated, in addition, that lots in the pueblos be fifty square varas in size and placed along streets and squares "in due harmony." Those first private plots, *solares* of fifty square varas in the pueblo of Yerba Buena, set the cell structure of the capitalist city of San Francisco. Another native California governor, Juan Bautista Alvarado, was particularly energetic in converting the land around the bay into private property. Well before the Gold Rush, in 1842, he distributed sixty lots according to the Mexican procedures, each as a "grant by petition." Those lots would change hands repeatedly over the next twenty years as the prices rose, fell, and rose again, increasing a thousand-fold. Mexican citizens had set this baseline for the capitalist city "before the Americans came," to use the expression that the Californios employed to mark this watershed in the history of the American West. The naturalized Mexican Jasper O'Farrell first mapped out

269

a few ragged lots in 1847. By 1848, his inventory had grown to include thirty-six "beach and water lots," the valuable properties along the shore or in the tideland near the Port of Yerba Buena, as well as over one thousand small parcels inland.[13]

The sale of San Francisco land did not become a bonanza until an American municipality was founded on the shores of the bay. The shoreline, a public trust, according to Mexican law, was granted to the city by the military governor, Stephen W. Kearny. As the city's debts mounted, the ragtag town council of 1849 put the public land up for sale at auction. The American *ayuntamiento* of 1849 was particularly loose with the public domain. Scores of land and water lots were sold by *alcaldes* George Hyde and Thaddeus M. Leavenworth, and yet more by a justice of the peace by the name of G. Q. Colton. It was not hard to sympathize with Hyde and Leavenworth, the first a sojourner with the Mormon pilgrimage led by Sam Brannan, and the second a former Episcopal minister. With the town council fled to the gold fields, and in the absence of species, cash, or established banks, the municipal officials resorted to paying the bills using deeds to fifty square varas of the public domain as currency. Leavenworth reportedly paid the rent on his office with such surrogate money. In 1849, at the peak of the rush to the gold fields, two different municipal legislatures of questionable legitimacy presided in San Francisco. The enterprising justice of the peace, Colton, took the initiative and doled out the land for a "fee." Leavenworth executed fifty-one sales that year, and, like Hyde, soon became a pariah. He was hounded from office for squandering the public land and beaches. By one account, Leavenworth was threatened with hanging when he refused to turn over deeds to the grants he authorized.

Both Hyde and Leavenworth were driven from office for their financial perfidy, but the land sales continued, conducted at public auctions in the plaza. A public notice read that 250 lots, each fifty varas square, would "be sold at Public Auction on Friday the 10th instant." Handbills were posted throughout the town, with ten copies sent off as far as San Jose, Benicia, Sacramento, and Stockton.[14]

These plans were rudely aborted by authority of the territorial government of Alta California as exercised by Horace Hawes, serving as the prefect of the District of San Francisco, an office he inherited from Mexico. Hawes's first tangle with the municipal officials of San Francisco came in September 1849, when he vetoed a tax ordinance on the grounds that "people are very sensitive to the subject of taxes," the burden of which was particularly oppressive to those of "limited capital and resources." Hawes also looked askance at the other major source of revenue, the sale of land and water lots. He voiced his alarm with almost biblical fervor: "All that remains of the public property of the city is about to be swallowed up and sacrificed as effectively as if it were sunk into the bottom of the sea." Suspecting some chicanery in the town council, the prefect asked to be informed if any sitting members had purchased land or water lots. Six months later, Hawes produced a list of over one hundred lots that had been purchased by nine members of the common council.[15]

The prefect had a point when he said, "A man cannot be the seller and the buyer of property at the same time." But that is just what the council members had done. It would appear that some members of the city government had given in to what Hawes called a "temptation to fraud and collusion in the management of property held in trust." Hawes wreaked havoc in the common council with the announcement "that the sales of the lots above specified, and all other sales made by the *ayuntamiento* to any one of their own body, since the first of August last, are disapproved." Adding injury to insult, Hawes decreed that those who purchased said lots could not recover the purchase price.[16]

At least one councilman, Sam Brannan, who had abandoned his position as the leader of a Mormon colony to make his fortune in the Gold Rush town, seemed to take Hawes's ruling and his chastisement to heart. Consigned to the loss of a major source of revenue, he proposed that the city cut costs by such means as reducing the police force, denying health care to indigent foreigners, and suspending all unnecessary improvements of the land. His colleagues would have none of such austerity. They commissioned an attorney, A. C. Peachy, to review the legal record and rebut Hawes's argument that the sale of public land was illegal. Peachy consulted both Mexican and US precedents and made the case that, as agents of a former pueblo, the councilmen of San Francisco had the right to sell land to any valid purchasers. So fortified, the council defied Hawes's ruling and the authority of the territorial government. Declaring Hawes's decree a "high handed act of usurpation," they scheduled another sale of land and countercharged that Horace Hawes had illegally purchased lots from the impeached justice of the peace, Colton.[17] The next *alcalde*, John Geary, had a more savory reputation, but he was hardly frugal when it came to land sales. Alarmed that "we are without a dollar in the public treasury," Geary put 262 more water lots on the auction block for a "fee and town sale." This transaction was completed in a single public auction on January 3, 1850.[18]

—

When California was admitted to the Union in the fall of 1850, the State of California issued a new charter for San Francisco putting a popularly elected mayor and common council in charge of local governance. In order to put the infant city on a firm financial foundation, the new leaders promptly resorted to the same tactics used in capitalist cities like Baltimore: increasing fees and licenses, going deeply into debt, and even issuing scrip in an emergency. They also took advantage of the resources they had inherited from the Mexican pueblo and put more fifty-square-vara parcels of Yerba Buena up for sale. The lots of San Francisco had turned into political footballs tossed between the city, territorial, and state officials. In April 1850, Peter Burnett, who served a short term as territorial governor, at first supported Hawes's suspension of San Francisco land sales, but then he had second thoughts. "A much larger amount of municipal funds could be raised," he surmised, "if said lands were sold to the highest bidder." Burnett fired Horace Hawes and approved the resumption of a public auction of the land and water of San Francisco. In authorizing the municipal sale of the public domain, the governor hoped not only to shore up the city's finances but also to advance the growth of capitalism in California: "The uncertainty in which many of the titles are involved," he said, "has had the effect of late to prevent capitalists from investing money in real estate in the city and forcing many to invest in other places." Local authorities agreed. If the sale of the land and water around Yerba Buena was to continue, existing titles needed to be clarified. In the meantime, however, the sale of lots continued unabated.[19] The common council hastily updated O'Farrell's map of 1847 by commissioning a new survey by a proper American engineer named M. C. Eddy. Installed as the city engineer, Eddy divided all the space within the boundaries established by the charter of 1851 into 1,400 lots.[20]

Just keeping track of the frenetic process of selling off the city lots was a challenge to the flimsy bureaucracy of the instant city. Accordingly, the town council appointed a commission to review "all the property belonging to this city." One of the commissioners, Alfred Wheeler, compiled an inventory of the mounting municipal land sales. The task was an archivist's nightmare, requiring Wheeler to weed through books that he found to be "without any system or order, many of them being blotters of entries hastily made." The American records were no better than the Mexican documents: "The records of grants made after the change in government are almost entirely mere memoranda, oftentimes indefinite, with many alterations, erasures, interlineations and errors," wrote Wheeler. In 1851, after working for over a year,

---

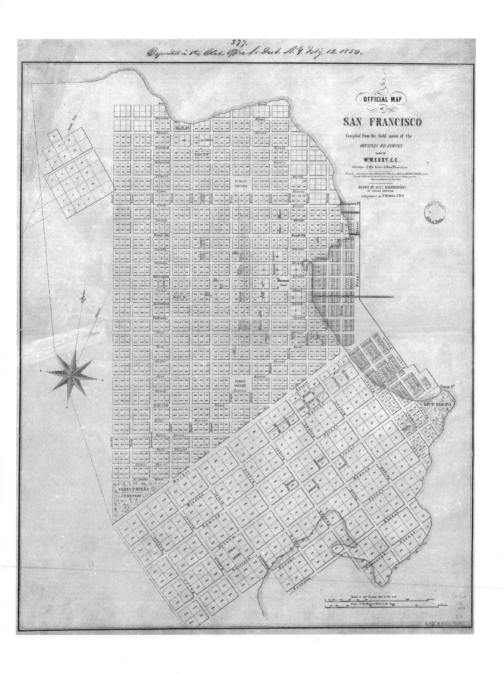

M. E. Eddy, Official Map of San Francisco, *1849. Courtesy of the Library of Congress.*

Map of Water Lot Property to Be Sold on Thursday, March 9, 1854, at the
Real Estate Sales Room of Selover & Sinton. *Bancroft Case C, G4364.S5G46.*
Courtesy of the Bancroft Library, University of California, Berkeley.

Water lots, 1850s. In G. R. Fardon, San Francisco in the 1850s:
33 Photographic Views by G. R. Fardon *(New York: Dover, 1977).*

Wheeler issued a report with the unwieldy title "Report on the Condition of Real Estate Within the Limits of the City of San Francisco and Property Beyond Within the Bounds of the Old Mission Dolores in Pursuance of an Ordinance of the Common Council of Said City." He had managed to reduce the chaos of paperwork dating between 1842 and 1850 to a list of 2,646 lots. Most of them marked off 50 square varas of land. A few were double that size, and 772 of them were plated on the waters of the bay. All this property, according to Wheeler, belonged to the "pueblo of Yerba Buena, or San Francisco." Wheeler's appendix would impress a quantitative social scientist today. It was organized into nine schedules, labeled A through I, and recorded over 2,500 land transactions made over an eight-year period.[21]

Schedule F, a graphic portrait of the fate of San Francisco's shoreline, illustrates the scale and the scandal of municipal real estate practices. What Wheeler categorized as "water lots" included a few Mexican land grants, dating from 1842 to 1846: 59 by Governor Juan Bautista Alvarado, 6 by Governor Pío Pico, and 11 by Justice of the Peace Francisco Guerrero. The selling of San Francisco had begun relatively slowly and prudently; money rarely changed hands, and even Pío Pico had proceeded modestly, in a last-ditch effort to preserve some Mexican turf from the advancing Americans. Subtracting these Mexican grants would leave the equivalent of 696 water lots unaccounted for when the United States laid claim to San Francisco Bay in 1846. Wheeler classified nearly all the land distributed in the American period as "fee town sale," indicating that the city officials had acquired monetary reimbursement for arranging a sale to private individuals. George Hyde accounted for 195 such grants in 1847. Defending himself in a letter to Thomas Larkin, Hyde said he had collected only $600 in fees. In the process, however, he had delivered a precious portion of the public domain into private hands. He had also casually overruled Spanish and Mexican restrictions on the privatization of the shoreline.

According to the records compiled by Wheeler, most of the "Grantees" of the shoreline had secured titles to only a lot or two; just a handful garnered more than ten, and only two more than twenty. The greatest single bounty— twenty-six lots—had gone to William Leidesdorff, who had built one of the first warehouses above Yerba Buena Cove and would go on to accumulate a fortune of $300,000 by the time of his death. Leidesdorff had returned some of his earnings to the treasury of the San Francisco *ayuntamiento* in the form of tax payments amounting to as much as $41,000. Like the other owners of multiple water lots, Leidesdorff was a political opportunist, taking advantage of his position as a onetime member of the American *ayuntamiento*.[22] At least eight of those fortunate Forty-Niners who secured a stake in the gold mine of San Francisco's water lots had served in municipal government. They included councilmen Parker, Brannan, Green, Bartlett, Eddy, Hyde, Ellis, and Price. David Broderick, the alumni of New York's Tammany Hall turned street commissioner of San Francisco and California senator, secured 13 water lots. H. W. Halleck, a member of the law firm of Halleck, Peachy and Billings, a partner of the council's legal adviser and author of the legal brief claiming the city had the right to sell off San Francisco Bay, secured 10 lots. Selling the 772 water lots, not to mention all those square varas of dry land, was a lucrative sideline for the founding fathers of American San Francisco.

One of the most ingenious practitioners of this enterprise was a physician by the name of Peter Smith. Dr. Smith found considerable work in Gold Rush San Francisco, where the mushrooming population was exposed to the hazards of mining accidents, inclement winter weather, and the alien bacteria of their new environment. He exploited this market by contracting with the city to provide hospital care for the town's indigent sick. His fee was $4 a day per patient. Because the economy of the instant city was also in an unhealthy condition, the city paid Dr. Smith in scrip. By 1850, Smith had accumulated a paper credit he valued at over $19,000, for which he demanded immediate payment in cash. With the municipal coffers bare, the council paid up with the only available resource they had, titles to land and water lots. In Wheeler's report "on the Condition of Real Estate in San Francisco," Schedule I was labeled "Peter Smith Sales." It recorded the sale of Smith's hospital lands along with five wharves and the grounds of city hall, all on a single day, July 15, 1850. Still short of the revenue to pay off the city's "funded debt," the city held another sale in September: sold at auction were forty lots of one hundred square varas each, fifty-five lots of fifty square varas each, and one water lot. A final sale put twenty more water lots on the municipal auction block. What became known as the notorious "Peter Smith sales" was only the most convoluted example of how San Francisco squandered its public domain.[23]

M. C. Eddy had completed his map with "neatness and dispatch" on January 28, 1850. But by 1851, the balance sheet of San Francisco land sales showed an untidy mess. When Thomas Larkin was asked to identify his real estate holdings in San Francisco, he responded with a barrage of unusual real estate terminology: "I had *Alcalde* Sales, Town Council Sales or Funded Commissioners Sales in all Sheriff's sales an execution against the city, and the sheriff's sales for taxes, in some of these in addition." Amid the confusion of titles, one thing was clear: the land around Yerba Buena Cove had been a great boondoggle for the first Americans to arrive in San Francisco, especially those savvy politicians and real estate speculators dubbed "water-lot gamesters." Prime among them was David Broderick, who accumulated lots that sold for as much as $16,000 apiece. The investments of attorney Frederick Billings yielded comparable sums. Adolphus Whitcomb purchased a single water lot for $342, and promptly "did expose the same for sale at Public auction" for a price of $15,000. Further inland, Thomas Larkin's early investments were paying off handsomely. A lot of fifty square varas that he had purchased for $500 in 1848 went for $10,000 in 1849; three weeks later, as the Gold Rush gathered speed, it sold again for $15,000. Still residing in Monterey, Larkin had given power of attorney to another old-timer, Jacob Leese, and instructed him to sell seven of his lots. These properties, numbered 11–14, 24, 28, and 30, were lined up on the far western border of the city on a spot now known as "Larkin Street." Larkin told Leese to offer his lots at the "market-price," to "be ascertained by means of References or Arbitrators." Larkin must have recognized some irregularity in the land deal, because he instructed his agent to "defend any action at Law or in equity which effect my rights or interest in . . . the peaceful, quiet and undisturbed possession and enjoyment of said property." Leese's own property, including a "solar" in the heart of Yerba Buena granted to him by Governor Manuel Micheltorena in 1839, proved the seed ground of another fortune. A survey of two city blocks conducted in July 1850 showed them already carved into narrow lots and affixed with the names of companies and partnerships, signs of a bull market in commercial real estate.[24]

Experienced merchants like Larkin and Leese, and shrewd politicians such as Broderick and Peachy, made a killing in downtown real estate, but they were not the only ones to capitalize on their knowledge of the local landscape. Californios were also sitting on the gold mine in Yerba Buena. The story of Roberto Ridgely's fifty square varas on the beach is a case in point. His lot was granted by the Mexican authorities in 1844 at no cost beyond his pledge to abide by the regulations of the *ayuntamiento*. Washington Bartlett, the first American *alcalde* of San Francisco, quickly confirmed Ridgely's grant. When the American invasion heated up the land market, Ridgely cashed out. He sold the lot, now known as number 139, to longtime Yerba Buena resident Leidesdorff for $2,000. (The executors of the Leidesdorff estate would sell it in 1855 for $27,375, with Halleck, Billings and Peachy overseeing the sale.) The value of José Jesús Noé's prime lot on the northeast corner of the plaza now known as Portsmouth Square also appreciated rapidly. The Americans called his *solar* on DuPont Street a real estate office. The purchase price for Noé's downtown property was said to mount as high as $70,000. Such figures were not much of an exaggeration at the time, given the rumors that a single hotel near the plaza went for $150,000.

Yet one foreboding question cast a shadow over all these glittering Gold Rush profits: Were any of the titles to real estate in San Francisco valid? Governor Peter Burnett's worry in 1850 turned out to be prescient. The titles to land were too ambiguous and contested to encourage investment, and thereby to supply municipal revenue. Furthermore, the city was rapidly running out of land to sell. Prefect Horace Hawes posed the financial predicament in his usual hyperbolic style. When the Americans took up the offices of the *ayuntamiento*, he reported, "The city was free of debt." But shortly thereafter, he added, "That body then disposed of 20 million acres of landed property within the short space of four years, and the suffering, the sacrifice of nearly all the rest within the city limits, have left us, as a slight token of remembrance, a debt to cancel of two million dollars."[25]

THE INTERVENTION OF THE UNITED STATES LAND COMMISSION, 1851 AND FORWARD

For nearly half a decade, various municipal governments sold off the land acquired from Mexico without much oversight or intervention from state or federal authorities. Preoccupied with the sectional crisis over slavery, Congress did not admit California to the Union until the fall of 1850, and did not formulate a policy about the lands ceded in the Mexican-American War for almost another year. This period of neglect allowed the impatient and land-hungry newcomers sufficient time to cover the San Francisco Peninsula with a tattered patchwork of conflicting claims. Then, in August 1851, the federal government, defying the Treaty of Guadalupe Hidalgo, pulled the legal rug out from under the real estate of San Francisco by requiring that everyone claiming land grants under the Republic of Mexico appear before the United States Land Commission to secure formal titles. This belated fiat placed in jeopardy not just the grants to the ranchos, the missions, and Yerba Buena, but also the lots sold by the American municipality during the frenzy of the Gold Rush.

———

In September, three land commissioners, all Whigs, hailing from the states of Vermont, Alabama, and New Hampshire, arrived in San Francisco to investigate the titles to Northern California properties. Accompanying them was William Casey Jones, the commission's agent charged with assembling documentation of the Mexican land grants. The commissioners worked with thoroughness and dispatch, going deep into Mexican and Spanish history. They collected reams of documents, examined the records of Alta California in Monterey, and tracked down "the great mass of old papers which were stored in the back room" of the *alcalde*'s office in Yerba Buena. The commission called scores of witnesses and subjected them to exhausting rounds of interrogation and cross-examination, in one case asking a witness no fewer than 172 questions.[26]

Most in dispute were the titles granted to individual rancheros by Mexican *alcaldes*, justices of the peace, or governors. The vast majority of those subject to the commission's scrutiny were Spanish-speaking Californios, many of them with limited education. Even the second *alcalde* of the American government, José Jesús Noé, was intimidated by the process. His lawyer recalled asking Noé, in 1852, "if he was afraid his title would not be confirmed—he answered that at the first he was afraid, for that when he first got his papers they were incomplete." Humbler clients of the law firm of Halleck, Peachy and Billings must have been even more anxious. Maria Soto, who signed her appeal to keep her lot with a mark, testified that she had dutifully complied with Mexican land policy, but now, "since the hoisting of the America flag," she was besieged by poachers on her property. She wrote to the *alcalde*, George Hyde, "that she has used every means in her power to have said lot improved but was prevented from doing so by her husband's illness . . . and the revolutionary state of the country which prevented her from being able to get workmen." Candelario Bernal was also befuddled by the commission's questions and pleaded ignorance of English. The language barrier was a two-way street; it also confounded Americans ignorant of Spanish. A testy former resident in the Bernal household named Helen Lowell accused her host of forging his title, but on cross-examination had to admit that she could not read the Spanish text.[27]

The communication gap was wider than a matter of translation. Californios and Americans marked off territory in fundamentally different ways. The favorite documentation of ownership used by land commissioners was a written record, chiefly a deed or a map. The Americans were obsessed with detecting forgeries and repeatedly asked witnesses to attest to the authenticity of signatures. Californio witnesses repeatedly demurred when asked to locate their land on a map. José de la Cruz Sánchez, called to testify before the Land Commission after living near San Francisco for fifty-seven years, could not convert his experience of the land into lines drawn on paper. As proof of the title to Las Camaritas, he could only offer his memory of "walking" the boundaries with Noé and marking them with a spring, an old road, and a few stakes. Pedro Chaboya, who had lived at the Presidio as a child, offered the Land Commission the same local knowledge. In response to the query "How does he know the boundaries of Bernal's rancho?" he replied, "I heard them called so and have been over them myself. Have had them pointed out to me and can point them out myself."[28] Candelario Bernal established his claim to Rancho Potrero Viejo by going out with Jacob Leese to "walk" the boundaries. When José Jesús Noé wanted to acquire the most fertile grounds for his rancho, he marked off the boundaries by traveling on horseback in the company of the *alcalde*, and confirming his borders in conversation with his neighbors. Ownership was a social and vernacular process established by recognition of neighbors, not a survey, a government seal, or a signature on a deed. Only after the Americans came did the Californios see a need to have their ranchos surveyed.[29]

The members of the US Land Commission usually affirmed the Californios' sense of place by accepting the testimony of neighbors when written documentation was sparse. Of some eight hundred California cases before the commission, more than six hundred titles were ultimately confirmed. This outcome was attributable to a number of factors, among them the professional integrity of the commissioners. The original commission that sat in San Francisco was appointed by a Whig administration that took the rights of private property very seriously, and searched assiduously for records of Mexican landownership. The Land Commission conducted a quite rigorous survey of archives, sending agent Jones to Monterey in search of *expedientes* and *informes*, and looking far back into Mexican and Spanish history for relevant precedents. Several commissioners had some knowledge of Mexican law, and if they did not, they enlisted local expertise. Guillermo Hartnell, who had been trading European goods at the missions and the ranchos for decades, was particularly skillful at translating between Californios and Americanos. Some even thought that Hartnell, like so many of the naturalized Mexicans of Alta California, had gone native. Apparently "white," speaking Spanish, married to a daughter of the country, and known to wear a blue serape and ride a Mexican saddle, his identity confused the immigrants from the eastern United States.[30]

Finally, American lawyers, including the ubiquitous Halleck, Peachy and Billings, helped to secure many Mexican land titles. The firm aggressively solicited Californio clients. They advertised their services in a printed letter, dated April 21, 1851. The first paragraph ended with a warning to act quickly to secure their titles: if not, it said, "las tierras deberán pasar al dominio del Gobierno de los Estados Unidos" (the lands would become territory of the government of the United States of America). The solicitors went on to announce that they had dedicated "todo su atención" (their fullest attention) to the "titulos de tierras en Californie" (land titles in California) and had acquired "una gran colección de libros de leyes españoles y mejicanos" (a large collection of Spanish and Mexican law books). The law firm boasted its local credentials: Halleck's knowledge of land law, Peachy's position in the "Ciudad de San Francisco," and Billings's experience in the California state courts. At the bottom of the page, the American lawyers listed twenty-five references, most with Spanish surnames and a few hybrids, including Guillermo Howard of San Francisco.

The firm soon took on a host of clients from around San Francisco Bay, including major rancheros, such as the Bernals, and those who resided on small plots in Yerba Buena, including Robert Ridley's widow Presentación. Whether the case was large or small, the firm did exhaustive research in the Mexican records. The file for Presentación Ridley contained a trail of records, from the original *expediente* signed by Governor Alvarado, to evidence of subsequent sales confirmed by Francisco de Haro, to a court order forbidding three Americans from illegally digging a road through her land. The Bernal file was even heftier. It included documents signed by two governors of Alta California—Figueroa and Alvarado—and excerpts from the Mexican laws of colonization (including a reference to recruiting "capitalists and farmers" to Alta California). The legal skill and obsessive documentation of law offices like Halleck, Peachy and Billings has to be counted among the reasons that the Land Commission initially confirmed most of the Mexican titles.[31]

The efforts of American lawyers were not altruistic. Remember Peachy's water lots in Yerba Buena, and consider the fact that his partner Frederick Billings had bought water lots 484–486 and sold them at a considerable profit. The commission agent William Casey Jones happened to be the brother-in-law of John C. Fremont, who laid claim to a huge tract north of

San Francisco called Rancho Mariposa. English-speaking newcomers such as Halleck, Peachy, Billings, and Fremont accounted for at least 20 percent of the claimants for Mexican land grants. They were not all citizens of the Republic of Mexico, but by the time the US government got around to sorting out the ownership of its new territory, they had acquired a major stake in the land around San Francisco Bay. Hartnell, of British descent, would win 74,000 acres, Larkin 28,000, his brother-in-law John Cooper 49,000. Henry Fitch, who registered his occupation with the Land Commission with just two words, "real estate," garnered 137,000 acres.

Something more fundamental than acreage was in contention before the United States Land Commission: the sacrosanct right of private property. To disregard Mexican titles would undermine a principle sacred to both North American republics, that of secure and unambiguous private ownership. Ruling in support of widow Bernal's claim under Mexican law, Land Commissioner James Wilson reiterated that fundamental principle: "The faith of the nation had been pledged to protect and maintain it," he wrote. "I do not perceive how the claim could be justly revisited. It would certainly be a strange sort of equity that would allow us to disregard the plain demand of justice, and sanction a palpable violation of the right of nations." To fail to protect the rights of property would be to regress to that antediluvian time before the land around San Francisco Bay had been taken.[32]

The Land Commission protected the titles of Californios, Americans, and Europeans, including the global capitalist José Yves Limantour. Claiming ownership to vast acreage immediately west of Larkin Street, Limantour sent his lawyers to the Land Commission armed with documents signed by Governor Manuel Micheltorena. The preponderance of evidence points to the legitimacy of Limantour's title, and so ruled the Land Commission, much to the alarm of the prospective land-takers of San Francisco. The value of the disputed tract had become considerably inflated by 1851. One local historian called the acceptance of Limantour's claim a "monstrous idea to the public." If it held up in court, the city would be denied a territory larger than the built-up area of the city. Accordingly, the newly incorporated City of San Francisco sued Limantour in the state courts to reverse the Land Commission's decision. The city's stake in this single case, number 424 in the land records of the northern district, was enormous. To the city, the Limantour claim meant tax revenue and land sales; to private investors, it meant a cornucopia of profit. But to an international tycoon like Limantour, Case 424 was small potatoes, and he withdrew his claim.[33]

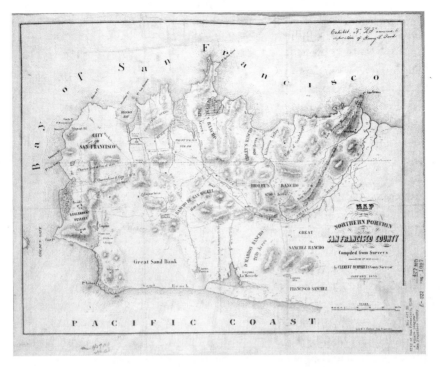

Map of the Northern Portion of San Francisco County, *submitted
by the city in the Pueblo Case. Land Case Map E-922. Courtesy of
the Bancroft Library, University of California, Berkeley.*

LAYING CLAIM TO THE PUEBLO

The City of San Francisco had an even bigger stake in another case on the
Land Commission's docket, number 427, popularly known as the Pueblo
Case. The map that the city presented to the land commissioners served
as a graphic representation of the city's predicament, but also projected a
solution. It showed that the corporate boundaries of the city were confined
to the top left quadrant of the San Francisco Peninsula. But beyond the city
limits, as set by the charter of 1851, lay an enticing hinterland. The territory
to the west, bordering the Pacific, labeled "Great Sand Bank," included the
Limantour claim. The land to the south included the ranches of Noé, Bernal,
Sánchez, and Haro. Mayor C. H. Brennan must have had those coveted
lands in mind when, in November 1852, he observed that, given the "present
condition of finances," it was urgent to secure the city's title not just to land

within the boundaries established in 1851, but to the space beyond, which he called "pueblo lands."[34] Those two words, "pueblo lands," signaled the most contentious and confusing episode in the whirlwind of San Francisco land-taking.

The city appeared before the United States Land Commission to claim title to all the territory allotted to a Mexican pueblo. The international law was quite clear: when territory was ceded by one country to another, as in the Treaty of Guadalupe Hidalgo, any public land within any established municipality remained under local control. Therefore, the first concern of the City of San Francisco was to establish that a municipality known as San Francisco preexisted the American conquest of 1848. Next, the city's lawyers sought to prove that this pueblo encompassed as much public land as possible. The original charter drew the boundaries of the city to the modest scale of Yerba Buena, its border extending to "a line two miles distant, in a southerly direction, from the centre of Portsmouth Square, and which line shall be parallel to the street known as Clay Street." When one of the city's lawyers, John Dwinelle, went before the Land Commission, by contrast, he staked out a colossal swath of municipal property: "to be determined by taking all the land included by the natural tidewater boundaries of the northern portion of the peninsula upon which the present City of San Francisco is situated, and proceeding with these natural boundaries south to a parallel latitude, which within these natural boundaries shall, when surveyed according to the Spanish and Mexican land, include the full quantity of four square leagues."[35]

Lawyers for the city defended their territorial claim by making an awkward and ironic legal maneuver: they deployed Spanish and Mexican law in order to justify converting the land of San Francisco into American real estate. The initial question might seem simple: Was there, according to Mexican law and Californio practice, a legitimate municipality that went by the name of San Francisco? To answer this question, one of the city's attorneys, Peachy, sent his partner Billings to make the first foray into the archives at Monterey in the spring of 1850. Billings came back armed with records of the actual meetings of the *ayuntamiento* held at Misión San Francisco de Asís. Peachy presented the councilmen with what he thought was prima facie evidence that San Francisco was a pueblo: "The Common Council has traced its origins to the *ayuntamiento* alternatively called 'San Francisco de Asís' after the old Mission, 'El Puerto de San Francisco' [the Port of San Francisco] and 'Establecimiento de Dolores' [the establishment of Dolores], or 'Paraje de Yerba Buena' [Clearing of Yerba Buena]." Although the council accepted Peachy's conflation of "San Francisco," "Dolores," and "Yerba Buena," the Land Commission was more incredulous. The commissioners heard counterevidence from a longtime resident of Yerba Buena. To the question, "Was any place ever known as the Pueblo or Town of San Francisco in California before the Month of July A.D. 1846?," Guillermo Richardson responded with an emphatic "Not any." He recalled that the annual elections of an *ayuntamiento* were sometimes held in Dolores, but never within the town of his residence, Yerba Buena. The name "San Francisco" was attached to the Mission, and the bay, or its far-flung surrounding ranches, but not to any single settlement or discrete plot of land, and certainly not a tract of four leagues.[36]

When John Dwinelle took his appeal on behalf of the city to the California Supreme Court, he came armed with more evidence. His office must have been bulging with paper, a portion of which was copied into the forty-five addenda to his argument in the Pueblo Case, published as *The Colonial History of the City of San Francisco*. Virtually a documentary history, Dwinelle's argument for the City of San Francisco concluded that, "by virtue of the ancient written laws of Spain and Mexico, [San Francisco] was vested in proprietorship, in trust for the habitants thereof, with four leagues of land, including the said PUEBLO or town, and the lands in the immediate vicinity of the same." Dwinelle cited chapter and verse from medieval kings, the Law of the Indies, the Bourbon plan of colonization, and arcane Mexican documents, such as the plan of the pueblo of Pitic in Sonora, all to prove that pueblos were both fundamental to the Hispanic organization of space and entrusted with vast reserves of public land, as much as fifteen leagues, in the case of Mexico City. Dwinelle went on to argue that the Mexican Republic had authorized dividing the pueblo into private properties, citing such examples as the grants to Noé in Dolores, to Guerrero in the southern ranchos, and to Vioget in Yerba Buena.[37]

To clinch his argument that the City of San Francisco was the direct descendent of a Mexican pueblo, Dwinelle made a crude translation of the Spanish and Mexican conception of municipal government. The *ayuntamiento* was a town or common council; *ejidos* and *propios* were "vacant suburbs"; the pueblo was not just "a hamlet or any other settlement; but in an exalted and specific sense, an organized town—a body politic and corporate." The plan of Pitic, for example, was "a perfect paraphrase of . . . an Anglo-American City Charter." Horace Hawes also saw the pueblo and the town as virtually indistinguishable. He posed the question before the US Land

Commission for the Northern District as a matter-of-fact question: "How then did towns grow up in Spanish countries?" He answered: "In the same manner as in the United States, by the union and the concentration of the population at some particular points, the establishment and natural increase of trade, commerce, manufacture. The citizens who want dwelling-houses, stores or shops, build them or buy them from the proprietor, whether he be the sovereign or some private persons, and the property is not changed in any manner by the formations of the town, or its erection into a corporation." Hawes's theory of urban development does capture the ad hoc and pragmatic way that towns and cities were formed in the New World. His history of city-building presumed, however, that the settlement of Alta California was propelled by the same commercial incentives that drove the development of cities in the East: "the increase in trade, commerce, manufactures," and the citizens' desires for "dwelling houses, stores or shops." Neither the Spanish Crown, nor the Franciscan missionaries, nor the *pobladores* of Dolores, nor the rancheros exactly duplicated the motives of those who headed west across the Great Plains.[38]

Nonetheless, the argument for the similarity of the town and pueblo has a certain merit. The settlement of the New World required that immigrants, be they from Spain, Britain, or Mexico, organize political spaces on their own terms with little surveillance or authorization from higher authorities. *Vecinos* as well as pioneers asserted sovereignty upon the land without consulting law books or awaiting instructions from a provincial or federal authority. As a matter of common sense and actual practice, town and pueblo could be read as near synonyms: both were political spaces produced by an exercise of local, vernacular sovereignty. The land commissioners thought as much and affirmed San Francisco's title to the public land that had once been a part of Mexico.

The pueblos of California and the towns of the Chesapeake were also alike in the alacrity with which they embraced the private ownership of land, whether plantations or ranches, *solares* or town lots. After 1848, converting the land around San Francisco Bay into private property proceeded with unprecedented velocity and voraciousness. Horace Hawes cheered on the Forty-Niners, encouraging them to take up land with abandon. He argued that Spain's Bourbon reforms had "destroyed the whole system" of pueblo land as of 1813. "In accordance with the new and wise polity," therefore, the lands around San Francisco Bay should "be reduced to private dominion as quickly as possible." The argument that San Francisco was a pueblo took a curious turn: it would establish a municipality, but only as a means to shatter the public domain into private fragments. There was little room in the American rendition of a pueblo for the public shoreline, shared pastures, or central plazas that the Californios had created and preserved on the shores of San Francisco Bay.[39]

Once the Land Commission ruled that San Francisco was indeed a pueblo, it still remained to determine the dimensions of the city's bounty. Yet again, the city's lawyers used Spanish and Mexican law as precedents in making a claim on a generous swath of Mexican land, a full four leagues (approximately 17,000 acres) of the San Francisco Peninsula. Neither the scattered ranches of the Californios nor the rudimentary and ad hoc pueblos of Dolores and Yerba Buena conformed to the prescription for urban space issued by either sixteenth-century Spain or contemporary Mexico. The settlement around San Francisco Bay did not extend out in an orderly fashion from one central plaza. There were at least three possible candidates for the center of the disputed pueblo of San Francisco: at the Presidio, at the Mission, or at Yerba Buena. Extending the pueblo out to the coveted four leagues from any one of these sites would land a surveyor in the bay or the Pacific Ocean. The meetings of the *ayuntamiento* convened by the Diputación extended the municipal boundaries even farther afield, drawing its members from ranches far across the bay.

The Californios never attempted to convert these vague and elastic boundaries into a precise geographical survey. The closest thing to a Mexican map for the pueblo was found in the testimony of Guillermo Richardson before the US Land Commission. Like the mental maps of the great ranchos, the boundaries of the pueblo of Yerba Buena were performed rather than measured. When asked by the land commissioners to define the borders of the pueblo, Richardson recalled accompanying the *alcalde* at the time, Francisco de Haro, on a walk around the landmarks scattered along and above the beach in 1839. Richardson drew a very tight boundary around the pueblo of Yerba Buena, just a few hundred square varas up from the cove. He knew that border as a line beyond which the pueblo had no rights to sell land: "I had applied for lots outside the limits of the town and never could obtain them," he testified, "and it was contrary to the Mexican Law. A simple magistrate had no authority to do it." The mental map of the mestizo pueblo was committed to parchment in the *diseño* that Richardson sketched in 1835 without benefit of compass. The map of Yerba Buena that Jean Vioget drew up some years later did not define the pueblo's limits much wider than

Richardson's *diseño* had. Both maps were entered into the records of the United States Land Commission, relabeled Exhibits 1 and 2, respectively.[40]

The initial boundaries of the American municipality were also modest. The text of the city charter drafted in April 1850 mapped the city's territory out from the plaza extending two miles, while a printing of the charter dated 1851 marked off the city limits at Mission Creek on the south and Larkin Street on the west. In the midst of the frantic sale of water lots, the municipal borders ballooned "over the water of the Bay of San Francisco, for the space of one marine-league [approximately four and a half miles] from the shore, and including the islands of Yerba Buena, Los Angeles and Albatros."[41] Those who argued San Francisco's case before the Land Commission in 1852 resorted to a creative form of geometry. Dwinelle "declined entering into the geometrical and arithmetical details" of Spanish regulations, but conceded that "the peninsula of San Francisco is of such conformations that the tide water of the ocean and Bay present natural obstacles in every direction except towards the south." Further, Dwinelle said that "the four leagues of the Pueblo must therefore be determined by taking all the land embraced in the peninsula north of such a parallel of latitude, as, with its tide-water limits, shall include four square leagues." The municipal officials of the American city of San Francisco operated on a pragmatic and inconsistent geography, adopting any tactic that would maximize the land under their control.[42]

The land commissioners pondered all this contradictory evidence, carefully parsing Mexican precedents and American practices. They concluded that there was a pueblo in San Francisco, but that it did not extend four leagues. Relying principally on the testimony of Mariano Vallejo, they drew the southern border of the City of San Francisco along a line from Mission Creek, bringing both Yerba Buena and a slice of Dolores together in one relatively compact pueblo. The municipal officials and business leaders of San Francisco refused to accept such a stingy donation of Mexican land and appealed the decision to the Supreme Court of California. Although the City of San Francisco won the first round in the legal battle before a more sympathetic tribunal, that decision would remain under appeal in the federal courts well into the next decade. The legal ambiguities did not stop the frenetic expropriation of the land around the bay. Dwinelle was still arguing the city's case in 1863, in hopes of "silencing the clamor and utterly and forever establishing the indisputable fact of the pueblo in such a manner as that whoever hereafter shall assume to deny it will render himself ridiculous." For the time being, however, much of the land around San Francisco was not completely taken. It was in litigation.[43]

The disputed boundaries of San Francisco's pueblo were of more than local interest. They were deeply implicated in federal land policy. While the US Constitution left to the states control of the public land within their borders, any territory outside those borders, including those lands ceded by Mexico in 1848, was under the jurisdiction of the federal government. The United States Land Act of 1785 authorized the federal sale of such public land in segments of 640 acres. While Federalists and Whigs regarded the sale of federal lands as a method of generating revenue for the national government, the Jacksonians saw public land as a popular resource and a method of opening the West to settlement. The Preemption Act of 1841 put land all the way to the Pacific up for sale in more affordable portions—only 160 acres, at a price of $1.25 an acre. It followed that any California lands that were not either the private property of Mexican citizens or within the boundaries of a municipality were available for purchase by US citizens on relatively easy terms. For those willing and able to migrate to the shores of San Francisco, the land outside the borders of the putative pueblo was still up for grabs.

Witnesses before the Land Commission, clients of the local law offices, and members of the municipal legislature translated the preemption law into a real estate proposition. In his private ruminations, William Peachy acknowledged that there was not much profit in the sale of the land set aside by federal statute: "Let us not be overwhelmed," he wrote, "by its magnitude[,] for its value to the US is only $1.25 per acre." One wag drew the disputed borders of the pueblo as the interface between city lots and preemption claims: "One acre within, or one hundred and sixty acres, without, the city suddenly becomes the property of every man, without deed, grant or idea of consideration." The divide between the pueblo and federal land was marked off with dollar signs: $1.25 an acre on the outlying public lands, and as high as $20,000 for a fifty-square-vara plot within the boundaries set by the 1851 charter. For one bewildered Mexican American who claimed "a piece of Land at the Mission," something more personal was at risk in the pueblo land cases: "all the Land I had in the world." For this son of the *pobladores*, the arcane legal arguments came down to this: His title to the Land was good "if that of the Pueblo was not good." For savvy pioneers—who were known colloquially as "squatters," and politely as "actual settlers," the federal

Preemption Act was a license to partake of the land boom around San Francisco Bay, provided they were not declared "pueblo lands."[44]

FROM PUEBLO LANDS TO REAL ESTATE, 1854–1856

The legal ambiguities did not stem the tide of land-taking. While *San Francisco v. the United States* made its way through the federal judiciary up to the Supreme Court, land-hungry Americans jumped with abandon into the market for California property. They arrived in San Francisco well practiced in the art of converting land into the modern capitalist commodity called real estate. Henry Fitch, who arrived in October 1849, spoke for a whole profession when he pronounced: "Making sales of real Estate was my principal employment." A competing firm, Thomas Payne and Company, placed this advertisement in the city directory of 1852: "Real Estate Business in all its branches, for the conducting of which they esteem themselves particularly qualified by having it their especial attention for over two years past."[45] Before the decade was over, tens of thousands of American acres had been surveyed and put up for sale with price tags that varied according to the condition of the local economy and the relative desirability of different urban districts.

Booms and busts, titles secure and titles fraudulent, fortunes gained and fortunes lost, and lots bought, sold, sold again, and yet again turned land-taking in San Francisco into a hysterical real estate spree that lasted through the 1850s. The land that Indians had tended for millennia, that Spanish missionaries had claimed for a Christian god, and that Mexicans had cultivated into ranches and shaped into pueblos was battered by a perfect storm of speculation in the middle of the nineteenth century. The most influential real estate agent in this frenzied market was the municipal government of the City of San Francisco. It was left to the mayors and members of the Board of Supervisors of the City and County of San Francisco to somehow control the whirlwind of land sales in the interest of the municipality, and often in their own personal interests as well.

By the mid-1850s, the inflation of real estate values had spread farther out from Yerba Buena, moving west beyond Larkin Street and south past the old Mission. The trail of deeds for Noé's property in Dolores, known originally as Las Camaritas, records the pace and magnitude of rising land values. One document, dated 1845, indicates that Noé virtually gave a lot away to one Vassault for only $5. Another indicates that the lot was promptly sold to a man named Hoffman for $400. By 1855, the 300-square-vara lot had exchanged hands at least seven times, reaching a peak value of $3,500.[46] Noé's Dolores neighbors, the descendants of Francisco de Haro, in contrast, tenaciously held onto their family plots near the old Mission. After the former *alcalde* died, his heirs appeared before the Land Commission to defend their titles to two properties, of 50 and 100 square varas, fronting on the Mission. The Haros' right to their family property was challenged from two sides: first by the Catholic diocese, which claimed the rights to the old Mission's grounds, and then by an Italian American immigrant by the name of Francisco Ruffino, who claimed to have been "a settler and actual resident on a portion of the said lands" for twelve years. Unless the Haros could prove prior possession of the plot, Ruffino felt justified in taking the land as his right under the law of preemption. Although the neighbors of the Haros supported the family's Mexican titles, the land commissioners were not convinced. They concluded that the testimony of long-standing residents of Mexican origin was "too vague and indefinite to define and segregate the property granted." The legacy of Francisco de Haro remained in jeopardy until 1860 when the US Supreme Court confirmed the family's title, but it was not formally entered in the federal record until 1882.[47]

In the meantime, the lands of the San Francisco Peninsula, particularly those located farther from Portsmouth Square, remained under double threat—from the city on one side and the squatters on the other. The squatters seldom summoned legal precedents or documentary evidence to support their claims. Rather, they poached on the land, invoked their entitlement as Americans, and sometimes backed it up with the threat of violence. The Haros had to defend their titles against John B. Polley, who identified himself as a "citizen of the United States and residing at the Mission of Dolores in said State of California." Polley proclaimed his right according to the federal Preemption Act: "That he is in actual possession thereof, and engaged in the cultivation and improvement of the same for his own benefit." He added an ideological flourish to his claim: "The large grants of land in this state made by the Mexican Government to individuals are incompatible with the spirit of our Republican institutions and deeply injurious to the growth and prosperity of the State and especially so when such grants are located within or near the limits of a large commercial city like San Francisco." The Bernal ranch was also under siege. A squatter named William Thompson who argued before the Land Commission boldly proclaimed: "I was a settler there at a very early time and think I am entitled." Other newly arrived

———

Americans took land by way of "shot gun sales." One plot near the Mission cost two deaths and five casualties. On Mission Street, near Haro's disputed land grant, a sheriff was shot trying to protect another title.[48]

As settlement spread outward from Yerba Buena Cove, the battle for pueblo land grew both fiercer and more sophisticated. The grasp of the real estate market reached as far as Rancho San Miguel, where José Jesús Noé was basking in his new prosperity in a home said to have cost him $30,000. Noé sold his ranchland to a merchant from New Jersey named John Horner, who had made a fortune by converting some 1,500 acres on the eastern shore of the San Francisco Bay into agricultural production. Horner paid $200,000 for Noé's property and rechristened the rancho "Horner's Tract." While Horner paid a handsome price for Rancho San Miguel, other astute entrepreneurs found more economical ways to grab outlying land. Called "big squatters," men with access to substantial capital began to take possession of the land beyond the charter line in large parcels, usually the 160 acres designated by the federal Preemption Act. Some of these enterprises, such as the aforementioned San Francisco Land Association, based in Philadelphia, were launched in the East. Philadelphia was also the home office of the California Land Distribution and Home Association, whose express aim was to acquire "desirable land in this state" and to distribute it "in subdivision among its members by allotment." The company assured residents of San Francisco or "elsewhere" that an investment of $2.50 a month would yield an annual income of $130 to $750. These promoters welcomed modest investments, and they advised "Persons of either sex" that "married women can, under the laws of this State, hold stock or land entirely under their own control."[49]

Other purveyors of pueblo lands put their names on large parcels to the west of Larkin Street, the contested Limantour claim. With questionable legal authorization, the sale of these large tracts, to become known collectively as the "Western Addition," were auctioned off at the dizzying pace of the capitalist urban frontier. The *Daily Alta California* announced an "Extensive Sale of Real Estate" in the Western Addition. The sellers addressed prospective buyers in the exuberant spirit of real estate capitalism, saying that "the attention of speculators and settlers is particularly called." Some sellers demanded cash, while others asked "10 percent cash, balance on delivery of deeds." An untold number of sales would end in default. The record of titles for Block No. 276 in the Western Addition is a good barometer of the real estate climate in the 1850s. The first entry described a 160-acre preemption claim, dated 1850, that was secured by one Merritt Welton. In 1851, the acreage was divided in half and sold for the sum of $500, supplemented with a mortgage, a pittance relative to the value of lots near the Yerba Buena Cove. In 1852, the property was in foreclosure, prompting a sale and quitclaim at $750. Divided again within the year, this quarter section of American public land became an unstable checkerboard of deeds, titles, defaults, sheriff's sales, and volatile prices. By 1856, this segment of the Western Addition had been sliced into portions of fifty square varas, many of them subject to defaulted mortgages, fluctuating prices, and forfeiture for unpaid taxes.[50]

The cooling of the real estate market in the middle of the decade was attributable to a host of factors, including the subsiding of the Gold Rush, a major downturn in the international economy, and continuing confusion about land titles. City officials began to despair, fearing that they would never quiet the claims and subdue the surging rivalries between squatters. While the legal battle for the land of the San Francisco Peninsula was being conducted in the California and federal courts, it was waged less civilly in the chambers of the common council. A councilman named Beideman, who claimed a large preemption tract, was accused at one point of having "struck a fellow alderman in the face." Another member of the municipal legislature, by the name of Sweeney, was struck with an ethnic blow—sarcastic comments about his accent. The battle over real estate on the western outskirts of the city also inspired an urban social movement of sorts. A band of citizens calling themselves the People's Party, or the Tax Payers' Union, made their own claims on this remote territory. They issued broadsides and called public meetings to advocate the sale of disputed tracts in order to pay off the municipal deficit. One pamphlet stated the problem bluntly: "Our citizens—as well those who now own property as those who hope to acquire it—are in debt to the tune of several millions of dollars." By selling off the public lands, the city could pay off "a considerable portion" of the debts incurred building the infrastructure of the instant city.[51]

Once again, San Francisco's plucky politicians took the initiative and assumed authority over the land around the bay. In 1854, James Van Ness— who was then on the common council, and would soon become mayor—put his name on an ordinance that converted thousands of acres of disputed pueblo lands into an extension of the city. The same municipal statute gave the long-disputed territory the name it bears today, the Western Addition. While the Van Ness Ordinance asserted the city's title to the north central section of the peninsula, it also conceded the futility of reducing all the conflicting titles to a rational and equitable order. Desperate to "quiet the claims," the common council took radical action. Section 2 of the ordinance read: "The city of San Francisco herby relinquishes and grants all the right and claims of the city to the land within the corporate limits to the parties in the actual possession thereof."[52] In essence, the Van Ness Ordinance made a blanket donation of land to the squatters, whether they were small farmers or stockholders from the East Coast. The only lands excluded from this concession were the Mexican grants, the *alcalde* sales, and sales for the funded debts. In return, the recipients of such municipal bounty had only to agree to pay their back taxes and assume the full cost of opening and grading streets. The common council, aware that a legal shadow still hung over the Western Addition, attached this proviso to the Van Ness Ordinance: "Nothing contained in this ordinance shall be construed to prevent the city from continuing to prosecute, to a final determination, her claim now pending before the United States Land Commission, for Pueblo land." Land-taking remained a major, if risky, municipal business. The Van Ness Ordinance, like the city's argument in the Pueblo Case, was a bluff in a game of sovereignty between San Francisco and the federal government. As long as *San Francisco v. the United States* was wending its way through the courts, the legal foundation of scores of city lots was tenuous, at best. Hedging its bet in the great land gamble, the common council changed the city charter once again in April 1856. The new charter formed the consolidated government of the City and County of San Francisco, reconvened the municipal legislature as the Board of Supervisors, and in the process moved the city limits far south, from Hunters Point to Lake Merced and on to the Pacific shore.[53]

SHAPING THE LAND INTO A CITY

Mere lots do not a city make. Molding all these units of private property into a cohesive and coherent urban place presented a formidable task to the leaders, citizens, and property holders of San Francisco.

Between 1849 and 1856, the various mayors, councilmen, and street commissioners used a set of rusty tools, mostly borrowed from the eastern United States, to reshape the mestizo pueblo into a city. In San Francisco as in Baltimore and most other modern American cities, the urban landscape was woven from the woof of the lot and the warp of the street, making the street commission the busiest municipal agency with the biggest budget. Article IV of the first city charter of San Francisco consisted of seven curt rules for opening, laying out, and improving the streets. Many of them could have been lifted from the ordinances of Baltimore. San Francisco property owners were advised that only one-third of the cost of grading and paving the street would be borne by the city. The increasingly stingy municipal financiers sometimes compelled the abutting property owners to assume the full cost of street improvements.

In February 1850, the city surveyor proceeded to "cut out the lines" of five streets down to the bay and vowed that "every street terminating at the bay was to be filled in" and lined up in parallel strips, mounting defiantly up the hills and over the sand dunes. Sleeping miners were rudely roused from tents to create primitive arteries through the congestion of arriving ships and departing miners. Obstructions like the old adobe customhouse had to go, as did the warehouse of William Heath Davis, once the main outpost of international commerce on San Francisco Bay. The town council ruled that "public convenience require[d] the immediate removal of the house" in order to realign the streets "according to the present plan of the town." Promptly, without ceremony, and seemingly without irony, the first streets were given the names of the politicians who had presided over the taking of the land around San Francisco Bay: not just the conquering US forces, Captain John B. Montgomery and Governor Stephen W. Kearny, but the members of the various town councils: Howard, Folsom, Harrison, and Brannan. The names of a score of other fleeting members of the town council—Turk, Davis, Tyler, Post, Green, Eddy, Ellis, Parker, Jones, Powell—were affixed to the streets of downtown San Francisco, along with those of the early *alcaldes*—Hyde, Bryant, and even the pariah Leavenworth. The street names of San Francisco were not the standard American litany of presidents, trees, numbers, or letters, but the signatures of the local politicians who had sold off the land to make a city. The street names around Yerba Buena Cove told a sobering story about how to build a city. Transplanted to the West at the time of the Gold Rush, the street became a financial instrument for building a bare-bones, boomtown version of the modern capitalist city.[54]

By the mid-1850s, the land surrounding Yerba Buena Cove had taken the rough shape of an American downtown, with rectangular lots lined up along streets and segmented into units called "blocks." Writing in his diary in 1851, Charles Palmer, a native of Connecticut, marveled at the nearly instantaneous transformation of Yerba Buena Cove: "How different—how vastly different . . . from June 1849!" The muddy cove was graced with the Central Wharf. The bare hills had sprouted trees. Clark Point, where Russians had once

---

hunted sea otters, was crosshatched with graded roads whose banks rose eighty feet high. Palmer commended the municipal leaders: "Everything that man can do has been done." City officials fought valiantly to tame the hostile environment as well as the unruly population. They planked the soggy shore and named it Montgomery Street. They built wharves hundreds of feet out into the harbor and marked some of them "dedicated to public use, as free public docks."[55]

If the pattern of streets above Yerba Buena Cove resembled the grid of a midwestern or East Coast city, its placement on the land of the San Francisco Peninsula gave it an aura all its own. The city engineer imposed the right angles of intersecting streets on hills and valleys seemingly heedless of the law of gravity. The effect was to create a riot of inclines and descents and breathtaking views of the bay. Critics were complaining about this defiance of the natural topography as early as the 1850s. Adding further whimsy to the landscape, the Americans did not have carte blanche to shape the San Francisco Peninsula according to the dictates of modern capitalism. They had to work within the lines set down before Montgomery sailed through the Golden Gate in July 1846. Mexican *pobladores* like Juana Briones, not conquering Yankees, had chosen the central space for the first city of the American Pacific, Yerba Buena Cove. Francisco de Haro had walked off the first streets of the premier city of California, leaving the Americans to trudge clumsily along in his footsteps. The Calle de la Fundación as drawn by Guillermo Richardson was the bedrock of the street the Americans would call Broadway.

The prominent features of the mestizo landscape did not conform to the North American way of marking the continent into 640-acre sections, each measured with chains and compass and placed along three meridians extending to the Pacific, one of them oriented to Mount Diablo. When the Americans came, they would have to situate their surveys in relation to pre-established boundaries and landmarks. The Californios had anchored the center of San Francisco above a muddy beach and below the surrounding sand hills. Furthermore, the axis of their map was oriented toward the old roads to the Mission and the Presidio. In addition to the pueblo of Yerba Buena, the Californios left two other obstacles to westward-wheeling capitalism on the San Francisco Peninsula: the ranchos and the Establecimiento de Dolores. The marks that the first Californians had made on the land around San Francisco would be hard to erase.[56]

The Americans had to adapt their land grab to a Spanish calculus measured not in feet and miles, but varas and leagues. When the Californios apportioned the *suertes* and *solares* into private grants fifty or one hundred square varas, they laid out the basic cell structure of San Francisco's urban landscape, a composition of lots and blocks in varas, segments roughly equivalent to thirty-three inches. While the small, standardized Mexican land grants of fifty varas square around Yerba Buena Cove easily melded into an American grid, the irregular shapes of outlying farms and ranchlands defied such uniformity. The *suertes* scattered around Mission Dolores, commonly measuring between one hundred and four hundred square varas, were out of scale with a Yankee townscape. Incorporating them into the urban fabric would require some modifications of the ubiquitous grid. As a result, San Francisco had not one, but three grids, all within a space of about three miles, each a relic of a different time and culture of land-taking. The first was Vioget's mestizo map of Yerba Buena; the second was drawn to the south of the old road to the Mission, where blocks were more generous in size, more like *suertes* than standard commercial tracts. Eddy's map pasted the first two grids together at the diagonal of Market Street. The third grid, the work of city engineer Milo Hoadley, plotted the Western Addition, reaching over the hills and out toward the ocean.[57]

On paper, if not in fact, each of the three grids was broken periodically by squares and plazas. The Van Ness Ordinance commissioned Hoadley to produce "a plan for the locations and dimensions of the streets to be laid out within the city lines, west of Larkin and southwest of Johnston Streets." The common council instructed him to reserve some land, not to exceed seventeen and a half blocks, for schools, hospitals, firehouses, and other properties "for the use of the city corporation." All else was to be carved into a grid of lots measured in yards and acres rather than varas and leagues, interspersed with a few "public squares, which shall not embrace more than one block, corresponding in size to the adjoining blocks." The resulting plan executed by Hoadley looked as monotonous as Chicago's relentless grid, but was broken at regular intervals by residential squares similar to those of Baltimore.[58]

The plan of the Western Addition had five rectangular public spaces, but they would not be rescued from the squatters for at least another decade. There remained, however, one classic public space preserved from the tyranny of the grid, the old plaza of Yerba Buena. The city's premier newspaper, the *Alta*, reported that the "Old Square" was "one of the most lively spots in California . . . the center of more events than any other in

——

297

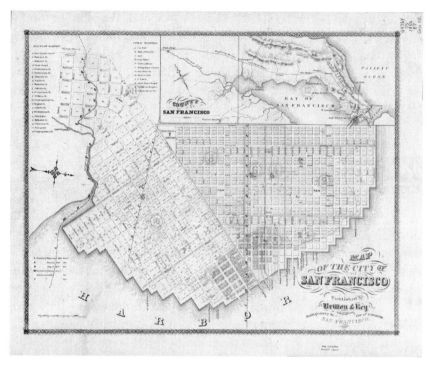

Map of the City of San Francisco, *published by Britton and Rey, 1856.*
Case XB, G4364.S5 1856 B7. Courtesy of the Bancroft Library, Univer-
sity of California, Berkeley. The Western Addition is represented in the
upper half of the map; Mission San Francisco is to the left.

California . . . tramped by vast numbers of people and city officials." The
capacious plaza did have its unsavory aspects. As the *Alta* put it, "this favored
spot seems the public charity box, where general benevolence makes its
deposits of all its thrown-off things." To some fastidious observers, the open
space in the center of the city was neither a plaza nor a square, but rather a
"pigsty," a "slaughter house," a "reservoir of deceased cats," and the habitat
of the "Goths and Vandals who crowd the thoroughfares of the commercial
metropolis." According to the *Alta*, "Squatters" were desecrating the city's
central public space by rallying there to claim cheap land within the bounds
of the pueblo. Eager buyers with more capital in hand assembled at the same
spot for an auction of the most valuable real estate of all, the water lots. The
Alta acknowledged that the plaza was in fact the beachhead of speculative

investment in private and public land. In March 1851, the editor reported that the red auctioneer's flag had been mounted atop an artesian well in the center of the plaza. He mockingly added: "Everything else in the city is subject to the auctioneer's hammer, why not the plaza?"[59]

Mayor John Geary had another idea. He began a campaign to bring San Francisco's central space up to date with East Coast landscape designs. His vision for reshaping the plaza might have been lifted from the plans for the squares of West Baltimore. He proposed that Portsmouth Square "be so improved that it will be made a favorite place of resort as well as an ornament for the city." Geary imagined grass, shrubs, walkways, even a fountain, to transform the disheveled Mexican plaza into a proper American public square, apparently mindless of the cost to taxpayers. The *Alta* joined the campaign to gentrify the small parcel of public space it had inherited from the Californios. The editor reimagined this space according to American standards of private property and real estate speculation. He appealed to citizens and officials to invest in fencing the plaza in order to "enhance the value of property around it." Coincidentally, that property included the *Alta* office.[60]

The physical transformation of the old plaza began modestly, with the erection of a redwood fence that was soon replaced by a more effective barricade against those "Goths and Vandals," an iron railing with a granite base. Once it was walled off, the plaza was filled in, not with public buildings, a taboo of Spanish planning that was not violated, but with vegetation and "shrubbery in the best style." In October 1854, the editor happily reported that workmen were "occupied in preparing triangular shaped beds for [the] purpose of planting grass and laying out gravel between each." A month later, a newspaperman went into ecstasies "on witnessing grass sprung up during the previous night in the plaza." A municipal investment of $30,000 on the part of the Board of Supervisors had remodeled the plaza to conform to the *Alta*'s ideal landscape form, that of "a pretty garden." Some city fathers proposed that the plaza be adorned with a monument to their civic accomplishments. Joint Resolution No. 346 pledged "to take early and suitable attempts for the erection of a monument in the City of San Francisco" that would commemorate "the adoption and maintenance of free institutions on the American continent, nowhere more signally and gloriously displayed than in the recent developments of American skill and enterprise on the Pacific coast."[61]

San Franciscans did not erect a facsimile of the monuments that rose over Mount Vernon Place or Monument Square in the city of Baltimore. They had

---

Portsmouth Square, 1850s. In G. R. Fardon, San Francisco in the 1850s:
33 Photographic Views by G. R. Fardon *(New York: Dover, 1977).*

more pressing matters to contend with. As one moved out from the old plaza and up the steep hills of the city, the streets were unpaved and un-planked; they roved through a shamble of crude wooden structures. The residents of the instant city, overwhelmingly young single men, were not about to invest in Baltimore's sturdy row houses or the single-family homes that sprouted in the city's suburbs. Only a few pockets of gentility could be found scattered through the city: the charming oval of South Park, for example, and the residential district nearby called "Happy Valley," laid out in 1849 by the pioneer city-builders Thomas Larkin, James Lick, and William Howard and festooned with prefabricated houses shipped from back East. The developers enjoyed the assistance of a $5,000 subsidy from the common council, on the wager that their real estate development was "an important movement toward advancing the prosperity of the town." In order to scale the hills of San Francisco, the city fathers employed a new technology called a "Steam Paddy," which was more efficient—and less costly—than a crew of brawny

Irishmen. Work had also begun on a street railroad. In 1854, a surveyor enlisted the prominent landlords John Horner, José Jesús Noé, and William E. P. Hartnell in a campaign to build a railway, which they optimistically called "the Atlantic and Pacific Railroad."[62]

The urban economy was not mature enough in the 1850s to begin erecting architectural testaments to either genteel domesticity or civic virtue on the shores of San Francisco Bay. The mark of modern capital, however, was written clearly in the brick and marble of San Francisco's downtown structures. By mid-decade, the tideland, where ships were once grounded in silt, and men and horses nearly drowned in the muck, had been transformed into Montgomery Street, and lined with the stately offices of banks, law firms (such as that of Halleck, Peachy and Billings), and auction houses (including those that hawked the lots of the Western Addition). Photographs taken in 1855 by George Fardon pictured San Francisco as a prosperous downtown with two-story stone and masonry buildings. The surface of the street, however, was rough and lined with refuse.

Montgomery Street, 1850s. In G. R. Fardon, San Francisco in the 1850s: 33 Photographic Views by G. R. Fardon *(New York: Dover, 1977).*

TROUBLE ON THE CAPITALIST FRONTIER

In the long term, investing in San Francisco land would yield a bonanza more bountiful than a gold field. In the short term, however, land grabbing was fraught with the risks of real estate capitalism. A Baltimore investor by the name of Charles Gibson wrote to a San Francisco attorney in 1855 saying, "I had better sell out by quit claim." The property in question was a piece of land that premier California businessman Thomas Larkin had described as very valuable. Six years into the Gold Rush, however, San Francisco real estate did not look like such a wise investment. Gibson's stake in San Francisco real estate had already cost him hundreds of dollars in taxes without reaping any profits, and his title was still under dispute before the United States Land Commission. Gibson was not the only nervous investor at the time he sold off his land. Stockholders in the San Francisco Land Association, meeting in July 1855, also had cause to wonder if their investments were as secure as the titles to Baltimore real estate. The association conceded that their land in the Northern District of California was also under a legal cloud, and liable to have a "speculative and fluctuating character." Still, the company hastened to assure stockholders that "there are peculiarities about the location of this city, which largely increase the value of our lands."[63]

The most experienced capitalists, from Baltimore or elsewhere, would discover that land-taking and city-building around San Francisco Bay could be a harrowing endeavor. Less than a decade after the Gold Rush, they learned a painful lesson about the vagaries of capitalism, especially when it came to matters of real estate. In April 1854, Thomas Larkin issued an ominous warning of an economic downturn: "The crisis I have so long predicted and which you were never willing to believe, is now at hand. I refer to the ruin of very many of your San Francisco merchants, and a great depreciation in the value of Real Estate." The business climate in the city by the bay was cyclic, alternately speeding up or spiraling downward. It careened through three periods of rapid deflation—one in 1850, another in 1852, and another in 1854—before the city descended into deep depression in 1858. The turbulence of the capitalist market battered the landscape of the infant city and left scars on the psyches of the Forty-Niners. The California archives are stocked with letters to family and friends back East that read like case histories of economic anxiety and financial trauma. William Weston's correspondence reeled from pride in his profitable investments to fear that his failures would "embarrass" his father and lead him to think "your Willy is a fool." Even savvy bigtime capitalists would bemoan the situation. Thomas

302

Hayes, who expended tens of thousands of dollars in capital to acquire land in the Western Addition on property that later became known as Hayes Valley, lamented the "gloomy aspect" of hard times and the difficulty of "keeping my head above water."[64]

Some of the most enterprising American capitalists met with failure. John Horner worried that "interest money, under California rates[,] [was] rapidly eating out my substance." Horner lost his tract on Rancho San Miguel in the Panic of 1857. In the same year, Hayes nervously pondered the real estate climate. Having sold only 40 of his 170 acres, and desperate to raise $75,000, he courted potential buyers with the boast that his tract was worth a million, and even more when a railroad would be completed up Market Street. At the same time, he fretted about the absence of a clean title to his tract in the Western Addition and complained of "litigation, so fruitful a source of annoyances and of expense in California." At the end of the decade, Hayes, who still had a large inventory of land, conducted a "great Peremptory Sale of 1000 Homestead lots in the Hayes Valley Tract." Although Hayes weathered 1857's financial panic, he died at sea off New York Harbor in 1868. His estate was still in litigation in 1896.[65]

For those with less capital than Thomas Hayes or John Horner, a depression could be especially harrowing. Charles Brewster, writing to a friend back in Boston in 1855, reported that "it is now nearly two years since this sad depression commenced and I fear the end is not yet come." He spoke plaintively for his peers: "Among our old friends . . . most have failed and have little or nothing. Our Youthful ambitions have become tamed, and sobered down in the stern realities of life." One Stark Smith, writing back home to his friend Sallie in the fall of 1853, provided another anxious economic forecast: "All the great fortunes that are made here now are made by speculating capitalists. Money begins to monopolize here as it does elsewhere." Smith had tempered his hopes of making a fortune by going west. He advised young men that jobs were scarce and arduous for workingmen, while "servant girls are in better demand . . . and can command readily sixty dollars per month." Stark's sober assessment of the local economy provided sound advice to the majority of hopeful argonauts, merchants, farmers, and realtors—and the rare "servant girl"—who ventured into the San Francisco Bay area between 1849 and 1857. Although a lucky few earned a fortune, almost everyone else found that the frontier version of capitalist economics was more capricious than they had expected.[66]

The story of George Hollingsworth, who left Missouri to join the Gold

Rush in 1850, is especially maudlin. By August 1852, he had lost hope of winning his fortune in the gold fields, and wrote home that "I feel like leaving the mines and hastening to the embrace of my wife and Children." By 1854, he had secured a stake in a preemption claim seven miles south of San Francisco. By then his wife's appeals to send money or return home had become more strident, but he pressed on in the pursuit of the California dream. He took hope from the homestead bill before Congress, and the rumor that a Pacific railroad would soon enhance the value of his land. In December of that year, however, George's brother wrote to inform Mrs. Hollingsworth that her husband had died. He added the consolation that he had been buried in a beautiful site on his own land.[67] A more tempered testament to the state of the local economy came from a former resident of Baltimore named Joseph Emery. He survived and prospered, but he did not escape the risks of modern capitalism by going west. "We have the Devil to pay here," he wrote back home in 1855. "For the last two weeks some 1/2 dozens banks have busted up in our city[;] some had assets only 1/4 of liabilities. These are the hardest times I have ever known here. Nobody pays and everybody owes."[68]

Just as in Baltimore, the vicissitudes of capitalism produced political conflict in San Francisco, both in city hall and on the streets. They led Joseph Emery, for example, to protest high taxes, to label Democrats "loud mouthed thieves," and to lend his support to vigilantism. The Vigilance Committee of 1856, a revival of the committee formed in 1851, was something more than a spontaneous expression of self-government frontier style. Charles Palmer described it as a respectable civic institution, a "body, selecting itself from the mass of the people and restricting its membership to the ablest and purest of the community." This second committee of vigilance was a political faction organized to usurp authority from the fumbling *alcaldes*, mayors, and town councils. The partisan undertones of vigilantism surfaced in the next entry in Palmer's diary, where he bemoaned the defeat of the Whig Party at the hands of what he called "the Democratic Squatter party."[69]

The vigilantes conducted two more hangings in 1856 and drove additional political rivals from the city. Most of the victims were affiliated with the Democrats and associated with their leader, David Broderick. As if partisan conflict were not enough, ethnic and religious antagonism was mixed into the lethal political potion. The victims of the vigilantes were often Irish Catholics, and the political faction that evolved from the Vigilance Committee was affiliated with the nativist Know-Nothing Party. The partisan and ethnic conflict that ravaged San Francisco in the 1850s also issued from the toxic bed of real estate speculation. Thomas Payne, the proprietor of a "real estate auction house," played a leading role in the Committee of Vigilance. Broderick was a purveyor of water lots and had been shouted down in the plaza for buying and selling off the public domain. He went on to higher office in Sacramento and in Washington, where he defended the rights of squatters, the nemesis of the Whigs and the vigilantes alike. Land disputes, in other words, were a potent if inchoate element in the mix of rival interests that surged, at times violently, around the old Mexican plaza during the mid-1850s.

When the fury of vigilantism subsided in 1856, the emerging social order of the American city came into focus. The Committee of Vigilance, rechristened the People's Party, became the paragon of respectability, winning elections and parading proudly through the city arrayed in garlands and banners. These decorative items had been crafted by other recent arrivals in San Francisco—increasing numbers of women, who brought with them the promise of a new order of domesticity and sobriety. Another parade took the bodies of the two men who had been executed by the Committee of Vigilance, James Casey and Charles Cora, to their last resting place, the Roman Catholic cemetery located at the chapel of the Mission. A monument now stands over Cora's grave; it was placed there by his widow bride, the former prostitute Annabel Ryan. (According to the inscription on the tombstone, her birthplace was Baltimore, Maryland.) Not far from that monument stands the grave of Francisco de Haro, ranchero and *alcalde*, who died soon after the Americans came.

Haro's death was said to be the result of his sadness after the murder of his twin sons at the hands of Fremont and the perpetrators of the Bear Flag Revolt. Another Californio, the mapmaker Jasper O'Farrell, rendered Haro family history as another kind of melodrama. His version of the Haros' story hinged on the rumor that Marino Vallejo had seduced Haro's wife and fathered her twin daughters. The threat to inform the daughters of "their mother's shame," O'Farrell confided to a friend, was used to blackmail Haro's heirs into giving up their land.[70]

Tales like these, set in the romantic ruins of the old Mission, offer one fanciful way of reimagining the transformation of Mexican ranchos and missions into American real estate. They don't tell the whole story, however. The taking of the land around San Francisco Bay should not be plotted as either a lurid crime story or a direct, wholesale transfer of property from Mexicans to Americans. Remember Noé's successful real estate ventures, and Juana Briones's enterprising ways. She not only held onto her land when the Americans came, but actually expanded it to multiple properties, including three lots in Yerba Buena and a ranch of over four thousand acres in San Mateo County. In matters of real estate, the denizens of the sleepy pueblo of Yerba Buena, whatever their ethnic or national origins, had been brought up to speed with the capital cities on the other side of the continent. One business report said that real estate now "passe[d] from hand to hand in a manner that would put to the blush any Lawyer who had been practicing the conveyancing business . . . in the City of New York."[71]

The city of San Francisco had overtaken places like Baltimore in the pace of buying and selling, booming and busting. In the West Coast city, furthermore, selling land was the preoccupation of the municipal government. The frenzy of real estate dealings in San Francisco had made land-taking the city's major business, and it was presumed to benefit the public as well as the private sector. As a consequence, the San Francisco landscape was overwritten with a pattern of blocks, lots, and an occasional public square that looked more complicated than Baltimore's Poppleton Plan. The city expanded relentlessly down the peninsula and out toward the Pacific shore, lot by lot and tract by tract. Yet the latticework of real estate had to accommodate the topography of the bay and the patterns written upon the land by the first Spanish-speaking settlers. While the financial practices of the municipality of San Francisco were the apotheosis of real estate capitalism, they did not replicate the grid, but inadvertently created a unique urban landscape with a character all its own.

The next decade would bring the Hispanic American and Anglo American ways of taking land and shaping cities into closer alignment with one another. But in the meantime, the cities along the estuaries went their own ways, exercising their municipal sovereignty so as to create two distinctive cityscapes. Both Baltimore and San Francisco were plagued by political conflict, some of it violent, between the 1830s and 1860, but their struggles were over matters of real estate and capitalism, not slavery, the issue that was driving a wedge between the North and the South.

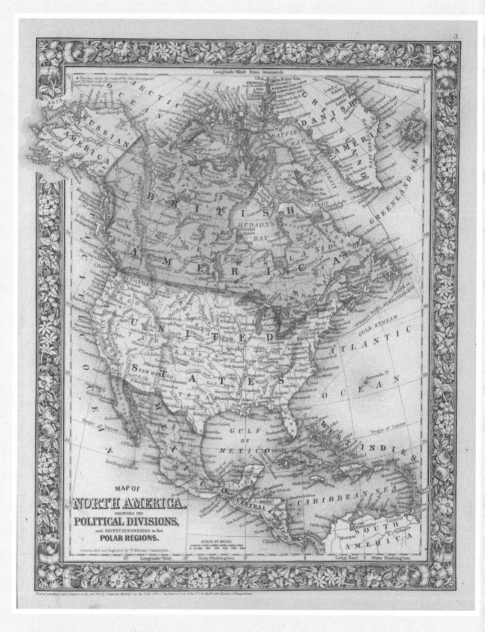

Samuel Augustus Mitchell Jr., Map of North America Showing Its Political Divisions, and Recent Discoveries in the Polar Regions *(Philadelphia: S. A. Mitchell Jr., 1865). Courtesy of the David Rumsey Map Collection, Stanford University.*

PART IV

THESE UNITED CITIES

If maps were history, the work of nation-building in North America would have been substantially complete before 1860. The land all the way across the North American continent had been marked off as US territory in 1848 at the conclusion of the Mexican-American War, and a clear border had been drawn with the republic to the south. By the time the Civil War ended, Samuel Mitchell of Philadelphia had been publishing maps of North America for over thirty years, specializing in those colorful checkerboards representing the subnational states of both North American republics. By contrast, a map drawn by his son, Samuel Mitchell Jr., in 1865 pictured the USA as one wide swath of pale yellow stretching across the continent, firmly bordered by similarly seamless national spaces: Canada on the north and Mexico on the south, each shaded in pink. Samuel Mitchell Jr. erased the signs of state sovereignty found in his father's maps, rendering them invisible, along with any scars left by the war between the Confederacy and the Union. His paper landscape was inscribed not with state borders but with the names of cities, scores of them, among which Baltimore and San Francisco were only two modest examples. At the end of the Civil War, the sovereign nation became the most prominent feature on the map of political sovereignty. At the same time that the nation eclipsed the states on Mitchell's 1865 map, the cities finally gained some cartographic recognition.

Part IV zooms in once again on the cities by the bays, taking a closer look at the municipal site of land-taking, political sovereignty, and modern capitalism. Chapter 8 will place the cities of Baltimore and San Francisco on the stage of the Civil War and follow them along two independent urban paths through national history. Both Baltimore and San Francisco resisted sectional polarization. They were too deeply invested in the capitalist economy—and too detached from the institution of slavery—to rush into the carnage of civil war. The real estate capitalists of San Francisco waged their battle not against the North or the South but with the federal land office. After a brief skirmish with Union troops on their way to mobilization in the nation's capital, the people of Baltimore begrudgingly submitted to Union authority. In 1861, both cities exerted a futile counterforce to the divisions rending the nation in two.

By the time the iron tracks of the transcontinental railroad reached the Pacific, the whole continent was ensnared in the web of capitalism being spun in Baltimore, San Francisco, and other major cities. Within their own municipal limits, the cities by the bays continued to take land, remake the city, and shape iconic urban spaces—downtowns, suburbs, and parkland. The people of San Francisco and Baltimore worked out their mutual welfare and civic identity within this complex of spaces, products of the continuing exercise of municipal sovereignty and urban creativity. Despite the structural similarities in the modern urban landscapes, the two cities along the estuaries retained the ineffable local differences that give each of them its special character and sense of place.

CHAPTER 8

BALTIMORE, SAN FRANCISCO, AND THE CIVIL WAR

n May 1860, the Constitutional Union Party unfurled the standard of national unity over the central public space of Baltimore, boldly, enthusiastically, and with all the hoopla that characterized urban partisanship. The delegates to a convention attended by representatives of eleven states, including Georgia, Kentucky, and North Carolina as well as Maryland and states to the north, met in Monument Square and adorned the stage with lavish electoral finery: "A grand stand, one hundred feet long, . . . spanned by an arch 36 feet high. Around the circle of the arch, on muslin, was painted the motto 'the Union, the Constitution and the Enforcement of the Laws.'" About six months later, on the eve of the presidential election, the Constitutional Unionists called another meeting. It reputedly brought 50,000 people to a rally in Monument Square, while 2,750 smartly dressed partisans marched through the surrounding streets. The patriotic architecture displayed on the south side of the square featured a life-sized portrait of George Washington and another of Henry Clay. As the *Sun* reported, "the whole stand was beautifully draped and festooned, and lighted by a number of gas

---

312

jets." The flickering portraits of Washington and Clay must have seemed like ghosts of Federalists and Whigs past, each party as moribund as the hopes for sectional reconciliation.[1]

John Bell, the presidential candidate of the Constitutional Unionists, would not poll well in the election of 1860. Monument Square was host to a cacophony of opposing voices during the campaign. The Democratic Party had held a fractious convention in Charleston, South Carolina; failing to agree on a ticket, the delegates had adjourned to Baltimore, where they nominated Stephen Douglas of Illinois. The dissenting southern faction nominated the proslavery vice president John C. Breckinridge. On the night of June 20, 1860, both factions held their own robust public meetings in Monument Square. Alexis de Tocqueville might have appreciated the scene. The *Baltimore Sun* reported that the rival Democratic camps had delivered no less than fifteen speeches from platforms that were spaced as close as thirty feet from one another: "The friends of one side or the other got not much benefit of the sentiments of the orators, their voices often mingling and with them their doctrines." Breckenridge supporters squared off against the supporters of Stephen Douglas. The *Sun* reported that the Democrats ceased their oratory about midnight, while "the speaking from the anti-Douglas stand was kept up to nearly 1 o'clock yesterday morning." Partisanship dissolved in song as well as oratory. At one point, the Breckinridge and Douglas factions serenaded their opposing candidates simultaneously but from alternate balconies, one on the Barnum Hotel and the other on the home of Reverdy Johnson.[2]

As the 1860 campaign season progressed, competition between the multiple and splintered political parties gained velocity, at times becoming violent. On June 23, "Douglas and Anti-Douglas stands" were erected in Monument Square, with nearly a hundred policemen on duty nearby. As "bands played from the balconies, swaying the throngs to and fro," one young man in the audience was stabbed in the back, causing a profuse flow of blood. Before the November election, the supporters of Breckinridge, Douglas, and Bell all mounted full-scale torchlit processions that circled the downtown streets and culminated in rallies in Monument Square. Partisans of the Republican candidate, Abraham Lincoln, also mounted a small procession as the election approached; it was interrupted by catcalls and at least one hurled brick, but no major injuries. Although the Republicans gained little support in Baltimore, the strong showing of Union Constitutionalists and Douglas Democrats enabled the city to resist the gravitational pull of the

North/South sectional axis. The tally of the November election would give Breckinridge a narrow margin of victory in Maryland, but in Baltimore, the combined forces of Bell and Douglas outpolled Breckinridge and held the militantly proslavery southern faction to a plurality of 49 percent.[3]

Off in California, the critical election of 1860 also blurred the lines between the sections and delivered a similarly ambiguous message about slavery. In San Francisco, the Constitutional Unionists garnered almost one-third of the vote, creating a substantial buffer between the Republicans and the Democrats. The California delegates to the Democratic National Convention endorsed not Breckinridge but Douglas, who went down to defeat in California, but by a small margin. In November, the state's final vote went to Lincoln, but with a very small plurality, 32.3 percent, compared to Douglas's 31.7 percent. Breckinridge trailed with a substantial minority, 28.4 percent. Read off the tally of votes in the cities that flanked the two great North American estuaries, the election of 1860 was a mandate for neither secession nor a war to abolish slavery.[4]

The history of these American cities therefore does not fit neatly into the national narrative of the 1860s. It cannot be plotted out along the familiar trajectory of sectionalism, civil war, reunion, and reconstruction. Yet the fates of the cities and the nation were bound tautly together through the 1860s, moving sometimes in unison, sometimes at odds, and according to a percussive rhythm. This chapter will unfold in a similarly staccato fashion, shifting back and forth between the two cities, each with its own local problems, changing prospects, and complicated relationships to section, state, and nation. The story begins with a brief sketch of the multiple and shifting scales of sovereignty in which the turbulent politics of the 1860s played out. It will show how both Baltimore and San Francisco maintained a cautious distance from the quarrel between North and South. Next, moving on to each city in turn, the chapter will demonstrate that both Baltimore and San Francisco were preoccupied from the late 1850s and through the 1860s with their own civic conflicts, local concerns that often set them at odds with the state governments of Maryland and California, respectively, as well as the federal government. The final section of the chapter will describe how, even amid the tumult of the Civil War, Baltimore and San Francisco continued to take land and mold the cityscape, and did so in ways that made them resemble one another more closely. In terms of urban space and municipal politics, East and West were coming together in the 1860s on the platform of an increasingly integrated capitalist economy. At the same time, these two inimitable cities emerged from the Civil War exhibiting something of the distinctive character they owed to their natural settings as well as to the different peoples and cultures who had been shaping and reshaping the land around the Chesapeake and San Francisco Bays for thousands of years.

MULTIFARIOUS SOVEREIGNTY AT MIDCENTURY

The history of the 1860s is almost always told as a face-off between North and South. Seen from the cities along the Chesapeake Bay and the San Francisco Bay, however, the political geography is more complicated and ambiguous. Maryland, located in an unaligned territory just below the Mason-Dixon Line and just north of the national capital, was officially neutral during the Civil War. The new state of California was a slice of US territory carved out of the Mexican concession of 1848; it extended over seven hundred miles along the Pacific coastline heedless of any Mason-Dixon Line. The California Constitutional Convention meeting in Monterey in October 1849 quickly dismissed a proposal to partition the state into northern and southern sections. To view US history from the vantage point of either Maryland or California is to see sectionalism through a blurry and distorted mirror.

Although Baltimore was located to the south of the Mason-Dixon Line, its relationship to slavery had become more complicated by the time of the Civil War; the city was increasingly out of step with the state of Maryland and the Confederacy. The proportion of slaves in the city had been steadily decreasing since 1820 and constituted only 2 percent of the population by 1860. Indeed, the high rate of manumission in the city had led to perhaps the largest population of free men and women of color anywhere in the United States; by that time, the majority of Baltimoreans of African descent had never been enslaved. Capitalist employers had calculated that it was more efficient and profitable to pay wages rather than to feed, clothe, and shelter their workers from childhood into old age. If there was money to be made from slavery, it was more likely to come from selling kidnapped slaves farther south. This was the livelihood of notorious Baltimore slave trader Adam Woolfolk as well as the captains of small ships departing from Fells Point, men willing to take on a human cargo destined for the New Orleans slave market.[5]

By 1850, even Baltimore's premier cotton trader, Brown and Company, with offices in Liverpool, Philadelphia, and New York, was closing down its investments in the slave South and specializing in international credit

---

exchange. The flow of pure capital was a surer source of profit than the cotton crop of the Deep South. The African Americans of Baltimore, for their part, had become accustomed to hiring out and living apart from employers. In an ad hoc, pragmatic way, Baltimore was conducting its own program of gradual emancipation. This is not to say that the citizens of Baltimore were allied with the abolitionists. The leading white critics of slavery, among them the local literati John Pendleton Kennedy and John H. B. Latrobe, were members of the Colonization Society, which was working to export people of color to Africa. Baltimore politicians weighted their conscience with pecuniary calculations. When Senator Reverdy Johnson finally came to endorse emancipation in 1864, for example, he felt it necessary to state that he was acting "not just upon grounds of political economy and public safety but on morality and religion." Political concerns and economic interests caused Baltimore leaders like Johnson to tread gingerly around the evils of slavery.[6]

Across the continent, in California, slavery was a relatively uncontroversial issue. The Republic of Mexico emancipated its slaves in 1829. The delegates to the California Constitutional Convention of 1849 quickly dismissed a proposal to institute slavery in the state. As a delegate to the convention, William M. Steuart, an immigrant from Maryland, reported, "a glance around the assembly would discover Southern men and Southern principles who had unanimously voted against slavery." For Steuart, a vote against slavery was a practical political calculation intended to "avoid in this convention those collisions which had proved so disastrous at home." Californians, like Marylanders, were hardly champions of racial equality, and showed no hesitation about subjecting California natives to peonage. Perhaps the most eloquent voice opposing slavery in San Francisco was that of David Broderick. When Broderick rose to combat the slave power in the US Senate, he, like Reverdy Johnson, spoke in the language of modern political economy. He pronounced that "slavery is old, decrepit and consumptive; freedom is young, strong and vigorous." To Broderick's mind, freedom was also white, however; his opposition to the expansion of slavery into the West was calculated to preserve a competitive advantage for white laborers. Opponents of secession, in both Baltimore and San Francisco, took pains to establish that they were not "Black Republicans." One San Francisco politician paid an underhanded compliment to Baltimore's most distinguished African American by accusing the Democrats of loyalty not to Stephen Douglas, but to Frederick Douglass. Governor T. H. Hicks of Maryland, who declined to call a state convention to consider secession, was decried as a "damned Black Republican."[7]

The political geography of the 1860s was refracted through a multifaceted prism of sovereignty. Historians of Canada and Mexico hasten to point out that there were at least three unstable fragments to the map of nations in North America. When, in 1867, the four colonial provinces of Canada were joined into one confederation, the map of North America assumed the familiar shape of three sovereign national states. The border between the United States and Mexico, however, remained an unstable boundary. The annexation of Texas and the Mexican-American War had shifted the border between the two nations southward and added to the national instability below the Rio Grande. Mexico was in a virtual state of civil war until 1867, as liberals and conservatives fought for control of the central government and then resisted the attempt by Napoleon III to impose Maximilian I as emperor. Meanwhile, marauding American filibusters repeatedly crossed the Mexican border.[8]

There were also at least three unstable pieces to the puzzle of nationhood within the borders of the United States: the North, the South, and the Western territory, only recently ceded from the Republic of Mexico. Even after Appomattox there were those who believed that the United States should be dissected further. William Gwin, a southern sympathizer from Mississippi and formerly a US senator from California, jockeyed to carve out a "Great Pacific Republic" after the Civil War. He was hoping that the new nation in the West would perpetuate slavery and poach on Mexican territory below the Rio Grande. Gwin's scheme had little chance of succeeding, but it was a reminder that the North American continent might have been dissected not just into the United States and the Confederate States, but into an even more splintered complex of nations.[9]

The shots fired at Fort Sumter announced one thing very clearly: the confederation of states north of the Rio Grande was hardly a unified site of national sovereignty as of 1861. But long before then, the highest federal authority, successive presidents of the United States, had been aggressively pushing to extend the fragile union all the way to the Pacific. The first attempt to acquire Mexican territory had occurred in 1825, when John Quincy Adams had approached Mexico offering to purchase lands in the West. In 1835, President Andrew Jackson had tried again to purchase California from Mexico. In 1844, President James K. Polk set his sights on Mexican

———

territory, and two years later, he went to war to secure that prize. Economic and diplomatic advantage was foremost in his mind when he plotted to acquire the territory of "California and the fine Bay of San Francisco." That westward destination became yet more tantalizing and reachable during the Gold Rush and in the age of rail. By the 1850s, no less than four plans were in the works to build a rail line that would span the continent. Both northern industrialists and southern congressmen, among them Jefferson Davis (who served as a US senator from Mississippi before he took the helm of the Confederacy), proposed different routes to the Pacific.

The westward expansion of the United States created a near lethal tension in the union between the states. The leaden steps in the long coming of the Civil War commenced with the compromise over slavery at the Constitutional Convention of 1787 in Philadelphia, hesitated at the border of the Missouri Compromise in 1820, then hastened toward secession as the admission of new states west of the Mississippi threatened to sunder the balance between free and slave states in the national legislature. After the Mexican-American War, the Whigs and Democrats who had gingerly bound the Union together since the 1820s tottered off the tightrope of compromise over slavery. The critical confrontation occurred in Congress in 1846, when President Polk requested an appropriation to fund treaty negotiations with Mexico. A relatively unknown congressman from Pennsylvania named David Wilmot introduced an amendment to the appropriation bill that would ban slavery in any territory acquired in the process. The bitter congressional debate that followed shattered the long-standing but precarious sectional compromise over slavery. Not even the legislative wizard Henry Clay could broker a compromise between North and South. Proposals to build a railroad across the continent went nowhere, and Stephen Douglas's invocation of the principle of popular sovereignty (permitting citizens to determine questions such as those about the future of slavery within their home states or territories) backfired, leading to the open warfare in "Bleeding Kansas."[10]

The compromise between the free and slave states ultimately eroded on the land of the western territory. The antislavery movement gathered rhetorical and ideological force in the slogan "free soil, free labor, free men." The soil in question was public land, especially the bounty of the Mexican Cession. The Preemption Act of 1841 had lured small farmers, large land developers, and some planters of the Deep South toward the West. The debate about slavery took a critical detour to Illinois in 1858, when it became the key issue in the campaign for the US Senate that pitted Stephen Douglas against

Abraham Lincoln. Lincoln's rejoinder to Douglas's argument of popular sovereignty was not just to issue the ominous phrase "a house divided against itself cannot stand," but also to ridicule Douglas's constitutional arguments as something called "squatter sovereignty," evoking "laughter and continuous cheers" from his Chicago audience. Lincoln railed against Douglas's strategy for containing slavery with a barrage of contemptuous language, calling it "insidious popular sovereignty," "do-nothing popular sovereignty," "everlasting popular sovereignty," and "humbuggery" that was "debauching public opinion." Douglas withstood Lincoln's slings by reiterating his allegiance to the exercise of self-government in the political space of the states and territories: "Let us recognize the sovereignty and independence of each state, refrain from interfering with the domestic institutions and regulation of other states, permit the Territories and new states to decide their institutions of themselves as we did when we were in their conditions." Lincoln had a rustic, crowd-pleasing retort: "Squatter sovereignty," he said, was like a "thin homeopathic soup that was made boiling the shadow of a pigeon that had starved to death."[11]

Whether it was called "squatter" or "popular," the doctrine of local sovereignty as expounded by Stephen Douglas was a last-ditch effort to defuse sectional acrimony about the expansion of slavery into the West and somehow hold the Democratic Party together against the onslaught of the Republicans. In 1858 in the state of Illinois, Stephen Douglas was able to paste the federal compromise together with an appeal to popular sovereignty. He won the senatorial election. Two years later, however, Lincoln defeated Douglas to win the presidency and provoke the secession of the southern states. That sequence of events unfolded in a political landscape that would have been unrecognizable to those who had drafted the Constitution of the United States of America. The nation now spanned the North American continent, was studded with booming modern cities, and had become enmeshed in a vast market of industrial capitalism. In that context, "squatter sovereignty" was more than a metaphor for local self-determination. It was also the nub of a political contest over the ownership to specific tracts of land in the West. As late as the Lincoln-Douglas contest of 1858, the lands of California and the West had served to stabilize the North-South standoff over slavery, despite even the provocation of the Fugitive Slave Act and the Dred Scott decision. The presidential election of 1860 swept away that ground for compromise. The plurality of votes won by Lincoln and the Republican Party owed much to their western strategy: a platform that not only opposed the expansion of slavery into the territories but also promised a transcontinental railroad, federal support for harbors and roads, and cheaper preemption lands. Lincoln assured voters that the West was reserved "for homes of free white people," and "God given for that purpose."[12]

The path to Civil War had taken a decisive turn toward the West beginning in the 1840s and gathered momentum in cities along the way. Reverdy Johnson, onetime Baltimore bank director turned Maryland senator, dated the descent into sectional warfare from the Mexican-American War, which he said had forced an ultimate confrontation about slavery that would "cause the union to totter on its very foundations." The establishment of an urban anchor of capitalism on the shores of San Francisco Bay further complicated the uneasy relations between the sections. It even led some observers to suggest that events in the former pueblo of Yerba Buena triggered the Civil War. Judge H. S. Brown of San Francisco blamed vigilantism for southern secession. By failing to suppress the Vigilance Committee (a task delegated to Lieutenant William Tecumseh Sherman, who was then serving in California), the military governors of the California territory had signaled to the South that they could defy the national government with impunity. Other observers contended that western expansion predetermined civil war. To Peter Burnett, a southerner who served briefly as the governor of the California territory, the coming of the war was presaged by the entry of California into the Union. Burnett argued that fears about toppling that fragile balance between fifteen slave states and fifteen free states caused the US Congress to delay admitting the western territories acquired from Mexico into the Union. By the summer of 1849, the stateless denizens of California had lost patience with what they called "the General Government." Burnett, along with members of the ad hoc municipality calling itself the "Legislative Assembly" of San Francisco, summoned residents of California to "assemble in their sovereign capacity" and demand immediate admission to the Union. Citizens of San Francisco, San Jose, and Sacramento gathered at "the largest public meetings ever held in California" to demand swift admission to the Union. These popular assemblies pressured the federally appointed governor, Bennet Riley, to convene a state constitutional convention. Delegates to that convention, mobilized in the former pueblos of San Francisco and San Jose, voted decisively to exclude slavery from the prospective state. To Burnett's mind, the path toward the American Civil War was nigh inevitable from that point onward.[13]

Another delegate to the California Constitutional Convention, William

Steuart, extended and seconded Burnett's interpretation of the coming of the Civil War. Steuart rose before the convention to thwart a plan to shift the boundaries of the new state so as to reserve more western territory for the introduction of slavery. "I think," opined Steuart, "that the proviso itself is calculated, above all else[,] to throw a firebrand into Congress." The delegates, including six native Californians, two Frenchmen, one Spaniard, and sundry immigrants from the eastern United States, defeated this second southern stratagem. The antislavery actions of California politicians ricocheted across the continent from the plazas of San Francisco and San Jose to the California Constitutional Convention meeting in Monterey and on toward Fort Sumter. Peter Burnett and the other San Franciscans who gathered in the plazas to demand statehood for California can claim a part in the complex of events that ultimately undermined the equilibrium between the northern and the southern states and shattered the congressional compromise with slavery. They exemplify how local actors can intervene in the national course of events by exercising political sovereignty in a particular place at a critical time. The critical blows against slavery inflicted by the territory of California in 1850 also owed something to the Mexican history of the American West, where slavery had been abolished over two decades earlier.[14]

CIVIL WAR COMES TO BALTIMORE, 1858–1865

That the United States of America survived the secession of the slave states and grew into a transcontinental nation is due in no small part to the history made in the cities, like those along the shores of Baltimore and San Francisco. It is also worth noting that the number of pioneers who went west was only a fraction of the number who left the countryside or crossed the Atlantic to populate America's cities. After 1820, America's population flow would move relentlessly in an urban direction. As the United States grew to become a powerful centralized state during and after the Civil War, the cities would continue to exert municipal sovereignty and shape the landscape in their own inimitable fashion. With their complex economies and diverse populations, cities like Baltimore and San Francisco charted a cautious course through the sectional quicksand of the 1860 presidential election. Sectional antagonism garnered support and gained velocity in the plantation South, while northern opposition to slavery came to focus on keeping the states and territories of the West free of the South's peculiar institution. As the champions of the North and the South squared off in Congress, the

———

cities beside the estuaries were fighting their own internal battles, complying with the platitude that all politics is local.[15]

The reluctance of voters in Baltimore and San Francisco to affiliate with either the North or the South was due in part to their preoccupation with local wars and land battles of their own. Different, if not unrelated, civic wars were under way around the polling places and on the streets of Baltimore and San Francisco in the 1850s. The battles commenced earlier but were resolved faster, and more amicably, than the American Civil War. The local combatants, furthermore, often battled against state rather than national sovereigns. Throughout the antebellum period, Baltimore quarreled with both state and national banks, while the Forty-Niners of San Francisco defied federal authority to form an independent state government in the Mexican territory. Election days in Baltimore had become dangerous affairs by the 1850s, with the torch-lit processions and rallies degenerating into street fights and fatalities around the polling places. The conflicts were largely between nativist gangs and immigrants. The creation of a professional police department in 1857 only exacerbated the violence of the elections of 1857 and 1858. The urban disorder provoked the State of Maryland to send troops into the city in 1859, which in turn led Mayor Thomas Swann to deliver an impassioned defense of local autonomy. (He tartly reminded the governor of Maryland that it had been the city of Baltimore that had saved the state and the nation in 1814.) In San Francisco, the vigilante hangings of 1851 were only the beginning of the civic warfare. With the revival of vigilantism in 1856, hundreds of civilians took up arms, trained in the plaza, and paraded through the streets as the military arm of the People's Party. After William Tecumseh Sherman failed to reassert federal authority, local sovereignty prevailed, leaving People's Party candidates to win municipal elections for the next decade.[16]

The militaristic season of urban politics late in the 1850s was a symptom of the collapse of the Second Party System that had maintained the equilibrium between Democrats and Whigs, North and South, and stilled the conflict over slavery since the late 1820s. Quixotic third parties, such as the People's Party in San Francisco, a City Reform Association in Baltimore, and the Know-Nothing governments in cities across the country, were symptoms of the frailty of this compromise. The disruption of the party system was particularly convulsive in Baltimore. The Know-Nothings were largely former Whigs, and their nativism was but one part of a larger platform. Local party leaders typically believed in a strong national government, had Union sentiments, were uncomfortable with the institution of slavery, and supported a bevy of municipal improvements. The Know-Nothing administration of Thomas Swann came into office with the help of bellicose nativists patrolling the polling sites, and ended with the demise of his party. On September 5, 1859, the *Baltimore Sun* posted a notice for a town meeting in Monument Square signed by a large number of "our most esteemed, active and eminent citizens." The call to the public meeting was urgent. It summoned "good citizens, irrespective of party, and every class of society" to repel a plague of "rowdyism, fraud, knavery, outrage, corruption and the general degradation of the time."[17]

As many as ten thousand people responded to the call to "be present in the Square." Addressing this "Great Gathering of the People," George Brown (the son of Alexander Brown, a cotton merchant and finance capitalist) proclaimed that "old party animosities had been buried. . . . Democrats and Whigs have come together in friendly union for a common purpose." In the customary fashion, the mass meeting broke down into ward caucuses in order to nominate delegates to a convention that would select a reform candidate for mayor. In the weeks ahead, the Know-Nothings countered the "Reform Movement" with more rallies and ward meetings. The campaign proceeded without any major outbreaks of violence and ended calmly with the election of the reform candidate, George Brown, as mayor. Baltimore's civic war had ended in an election that was far less traumatic than the previous two had been. The citizens of Baltimore had taken time-honored political steps—from public meetings to municipal elections—to resolve the internecine conflict of the late 1850s. Baltimore's City Reform Association would ultimately merge with the Democrats and maintain dominance in local and state elections for generations to come. But that would not happen until after the city had endured the Civil War that raged around it.[18]

Although Baltimore's local political warfare subsided in the fall of 1860, the toxic institution of slavery was not expunged from the state of Maryland. As the tide of bellicose sectionalism kept rising outside the city limits, Mayor Brown made a valiant effort to keep peace in the city. He would later report that he had been devising a method of gradual emancipation before "the growing hostility between the North and the South rendered the plan wholly impracticable." In the heat of the secessionist moment, he resorted to logical contortions in hopes of placating both Unionists and Secessionists. Addressing the city council in January 1861, Brown assured one side of the impending conflict that "Baltimore is a southern city. The great lines of internal

—

improvement upon which she places her chief reliance, have been projected upon southern soil." Then he turned about-face to address "our Northern brethren" and express his hope for "a speedy return to those fraternal relations which can alone ensure confidence in the future, and prevent danger to that cherished union under which we have so long prospered, and which Baltimore will be the last to forsake."[19]

Even in the face of Lincoln's election and after other slave states had seceded, Baltimore, Maryland, straddled the deepening divide between North and South. Mayor Brown, joined by Governor T. H. Hicks, held a postelection rally in Baltimore and pleaded the cause of peace. When South Carolina called a convention of secessionists, Governor Hicks took evasive action. Since the Maryland Legislature was not in session at the time, Hicks simply failed to call up the General Assembly to consider withdrawing from the Union. When the tattered fabric of compromises between Confederate and Union states ripped apart at Fort Sumter on April 12, 1861, Baltimore found itself in a painfully vulnerable position, caught between the nation's capital and the Mason-Dixon Line and on the essential railroad connection for transporting Union troops to the South. There were no casualties at Fort Sumter, although two Union soldiers died during the evacuation. So, ineluctably, Baltimore would become known as the historic site where "the first blood of the American Civil War was spilt" one week later. A stanza of the Maryland state anthem would memorialize that event as the "patriotic gore / that flecked the streets of Baltimore."

There is lore as well as gore in the standard accounts of what happened in Baltimore on April 19, 1861. Local historians remember the events with tales of both mayhem and heroism—of loyal southerners championing the Confederacy, on the one hand, and of benevolent ladies soothing the wounds of Union soldiers, on the other. Neither a regression to mob town nor a reincarnation of the Monumental City, the advent of the Civil War in Baltimore unfolded in the time-honored manner of street politics. The trouble began with the news that the 6th Massachusetts Voluntary Militia would pass through Baltimore en route to Washington. There is no doubt that many residents of the city were fiercely loyal to the Confederacy and determined to strike a blow against the advancing Yankees. On April 19, Confederate zealotry condensed in the headquarters of the Democratic Party, located in the customhouse just northeast of the President Street rail station. Eyewitnesses depicted a rowdy and foul-mouthed band of Confederate sympathizers streaming out from the customhouse and down to Pratt Street, where they welcomed the Yankees to Baltimore with catcalls, racial slurs, bricks, stones, an occasional musket shot, and their favorite epithet, "sons of bitches." The local rancor was forceful enough to accomplish something that had not occurred at Fort Sumter: it provoked one frightened member of the Massachusetts militia company to fire into the hostile crowd, causing the first of those appalling seven-hundred-thousand-odd fatalities of the American Civil War. Retaliation farther down Pratt Street left two Union soldiers dead on the urban battlefield. When the battle ended, the fatalities were estimated at twelve civilians and four Union soldiers.[20]

Pratt Street was something more than the inert setting for the first armed conflict of the Civil War. Its role in the sectional conflict had been scripted by decades of municipal history. The stage for the Pratt Street Riot was set in the first instance by the city's precocious place in railroad history. The Baltimore and Ohio rail lines provided the most efficient method of routing Union troops quickly through Washington and on to the southern battlefields. By 1861, however, the increasingly hostile relationship between the city and the railroad corporation had placed a serious obstruction along the route through Baltimore. The Baltimore City Council, in response to citizens' concerns about the danger and inconvenience caused by locomotives speeding through their streets, had ordered the steam trains to deboard passengers and cargo at the eastern depot of President Street and proceed down Pratt Street to Camden Station on foot or by horse car. Accordingly, the Union troops could not reach their destination without making a provocative and vulnerable appearance on the streets of Baltimore. The prosaic politics of the street had first set the stage for the first bloodshed of the Civil War and then assembled the necessary ammunition. It so happened that April 19 found city employees performing the most basic task of municipal government, repairing the pavement on the central thoroughfare of Pratt Street. When the Union soldiers arrived in the city, they were at work between the President Street Depot and Camden Station and armed with what one witness called "a splendid lot of paving stones." The construction site blocked the path of some troops advancing east after the original outbreak of violence. Confederate sympathizers ambushed the Union troops and attacked them with a fuselage composed of the materiel of street repair: bricks, sand, paving stones, and "ankers" (possibly anchors for telegraph poles).[21]

The same local political practices that incubated a riot on Pratt Street ultimately prevented the outbreak of a full-scale municipal war in the city of Baltimore. When the shots went out at Fort Sumter, Mayor Brown cautioned the citizenry to refrain from "harshness of speech." When news of the tempest on Pratt Street reached his office, he went quickly into action. Mayor Brown, like his predecessors during the riots of 1812 and 1835, went to the streets himself, cautioning calm, subduing the crowd, and accompanying the soldiers on their march to Camden Station. The forces of order at the mayor's disposal in 1861 were more formidable than those that had been available in the early republican city. In addition to the professional police force, which was now armed with pistols, the city was fortified by powerful connections beyond its borders. When Mayor Brown negotiated with President Lincoln about routing troops through Maryland, he had an influential industrialist at his side, John Garrett, president of the Baltimore and Ohio Railroad. Above all, the iron bonds of the national and increasingly global economy account for Baltimore's de jure neutrality in the Civil War and de facto support for the Union. George Brown, scion of a dynasty of cotton merchants turned international financiers, conceded as much some years later. He explained the role of Baltimore in the history of the Civil War as follows: "There was an underlying feeling that by a sort of geographical necessity [the city's] lot was cast with the North, that the larger and stronger half of the nation would not allow its capital to be quietly disintegrated away by her secession." As the mayor of a modern capitalist city, George Brown could ill afford to cast his lot with the secessionists.[22]

The citizens of Baltimore came to a similar conclusion and withdrew from the sectional fray. The evening of the riot, they assembled in Monument Square to listen to pacifying addresses from the mayor and the governor. Their speeches were interrupted by only a few rebel yells. Calm returned to the city within three days of the Pratt Street Riot. In a month, the "national flag" was flying over a Union rally in Monument Square. The pacification of Baltimore was secured by Lincoln's declaration of martial law on April 27, and punctuated in May by the abrasive tactics of General Benjamin Butler, who mounted six cannons on Federal Hill. With one of those weapons aimed directly at Monument Square, Baltimoreans went sullenly about their business for the remainder of the Civil War. By 1864, Baltimore was amenable to inviting Abraham Lincoln into the city, and entertained him and Mrs. Lincoln at a Sanitary Fair conducted at the Maryland Institute. Even a few months after the Pratt Street Riot, on September 12, 1861, when the Union military authorities jailed Mayor Brown, and on June 27, when they arrested George Proctor Kane, the city's marshal of police—both without trial, on suspicion of conspiring to undermine the Union—the city turned its other cheek.

One Maryland politician, a close associate and onetime resident of Baltimore, did raise a pointed objection to this assault on civil rights and local autonomy. He was the same Supreme Court justice whose decision in the Dred Scott case was one of the most fatal, irreversible provocations to the division of the nation between Yankees and Rebels. In 1866, Chief Justice Roger Taney journeyed to the center of Baltimore to deliver a ruling in the case of *Ex parte Merryman*. Taney excoriated Lincoln for suspending *habeas corpus*, subverting the authority of Congress, and permitting military authorities to violate individual rights of life, liberty, and property. By this time, Taney had become expert at operating all the levers of sovereignty, the local, the state, and the national. At his post in the federal judiciary, he invoked the US Constitution first to defend slavery based on the principle of state sovereignty, in the Dred Scott decision, and then to uphold the constitutional protection of civil liberties, in the Merryman case. With multiple ties to the state of Maryland and the city of Baltimore, Roger Taney was adept at navigating through the complicated political geography of federalism.

THE CIVIL WAR IN SAN FRANCISCO: SOVEREIGNTY OVER THE LAND

Slavery was not the only issue that provoked conflict between the different levels of government during the 1860s. City residents had other gripes with both the state and federal governments, some of them about issues almost as aggravating as those that divided the southern states from the North. To the people of San Francisco, the critical constitutional issue during the 1860s was not slavery, but control of the land acquired during the Mexican-American War. Their struggle to claim private property around the bay was waged not on the battlefield but within the different levels of the judicial system—the state, district, circuit, and federal courts. Those who happened to claim property as citizens of the former Mexican territory had reason to chafe at their subordinate place in the federal judicial system. After being summoned to prove their property rights before the San Francisco meetings of the United States Land Commission, scores of Californios received this alarming notice: "Cited and admonished to be and appear at the Court of the United States in Washington." Ironically, such commanding assertions of federal authority often bore the signature of the states' rights champion, Chief Justice Roger Taney. From the perspective of those whose titles were suspended, and countless others who coveted tracts of public land around the bay, this was the decade's most galling exercise of federal sovereignty.[23]

One resident of the town of Santa Rosa, just north of San Francisco, traveled all the way to Washington in 1863 to apprise Abraham Lincoln of what he thought was the most important sectional and constitutional issue of the time: the high-handed operations of the US Land Commission. George Fox Kelly later boasted that he had gained admission to Lincoln's chambers by offering a doorkeeper a five-dollar bribe. The unlikely interview began with the commander in chief politely asking him, "Mr. Kelly, what can I do for you?" Kelly assured Lincoln that he had not come to Washington on a matter of "personal or sectional" interest, but to relay a mounting concern "all over the state." To Kelly's mind, "The deathly struggle . . . between Democracy and Despotism" was not the one being waged by secessionists and abolitionists, but the one perpetrated by the rampages of "the land stealing department of San Francisco." Larding his protest with analogies to homeless children, rampant prostitution, and Romans selling their daughters into slavery, Kelly informed the president that the great national crisis of 1863 was the abuse of a federal statute, the "malfunctioning of the preemption act of 1841."[24]

For many Californians—particularly both those squatting just outside the disputed city limits, such as George Fox Kelly, and those holding ambiguous titles to lots in the city of San Francisco—federal land policy was the most pressing political question the country faced. Unlike the battle over slavery along the Chesapeake, San Francisco's contest with federal authority would rage on for at least another decade. Californians appealed over one hundred of the decisions of the US Land Commission as far as the Supreme Court. Most of the cases took over a decade to be resolved, and some took far longer, even until the 1930s. Owners of some of the prime ranchos of El Partido de San Francisco, including first families such as the Bernals, the Haros, and the Briones, were not able to acquire clear titles until the 1880s.

Case No. 427 of the Northern District of California, on which hinged the right of the city to sell four leagues' worth of pueblo land, would not be resolved until 1866. The Pueblo Case was still on the court docket in 1860 under the title *The City of San Francisco v. the United States of America*. The city engineer, Milo Hoadley, denied that the federal government had any authority over the pueblo land, particularly the chunk of real estate called the Western Addition. Allied on the other side of the land case were those who claimed portions of the same territory according to the federal Preemption Act. If not exactly at war with the national government, the City of San Francisco brashly defied its authority in the 1860s, when the San Francisco Board of Supervisors carved the San Francisco Peninsula into lots and put them up for sale at the same time that its authority to do so was being disputed in the state and federal courts.[25]

The Pueblo Case lay dormant between 1857 and 1860 while the government in Washington was preoccupied with the sectional crisis. Since the federal government failed to challenge a decision of the California Supreme Court favorable to the city, the lawyers for the City of San Francisco presumed that they had won the Pueblo Case by default, and did not bother to pursue their claim further. That was not the end of the matter, however. Squatters on the outlying lands, both small farmers and speculators from back East, took one another to court to secure individual titles to the still disputed territory. In 1860, two disgruntled claimants to parcels on the margins of the city argued their case before the California Supreme Court. This litigation, *Hart v. Burnett*, became a critical test of municipal sovereignty.

The three judges hearing the case were well aware of "the immense interests involved," and therefore conducted yet another "laborious and careful examination" of the land practices of Spain, Mexico, and the United States. Justice Joseph Baldwin, writing for the majority, rehearsed the evidence presented by Dwinelle in *The City of San Francisco v. the United States*, from minute questions of geography to broad issues of Mexican and US law. The California Supreme Court upheld the right of the city, subject to affirmation by the state government, to control all the pueblo land. The court noted that a statute to this effect, the Van Ness Ordinance, had already been enacted by the City of San Francisco and confirmed by the state legislature. It "was a legal and proper exercise of this sovereign power," said the court.[26]

The decision in *Hart v. Burnett* was a triumph for local and states' rights. On this score, two of the three judges of the Supreme Court of California, Baldwin and Stephen J. Field, were adamant, stating that, "The pueblo lands of San Francisco were public and municipal, subject to the control of the state sovereignty, but not to that of the federal government." One sharply worded aside in the *Hart v. Burnett* decision suggests that the jurists were aware of a larger national and sectional context for their decision. The justices observed that to transfer state land rights to the national government would be "disastrous to the United States," and "very soon it would utterly corrupt our Federal administration, and destroy our Federal organization."[27] The decision was announced in April 1860, at a time when the doctrine of states' rights was fueling sectional animosity. To challenge an assertion of state sovereignty at that critical moment, even in far distant California, would have been perilous. By 1864, however, the tide of war had shifted in favor of

———

the Union, and proponents of states' rights were in retreat. Those who had coveted land claimed by the City of San Francisco renewed their challenge to the decision in *Hart v. Burnett* with an appeal to the federal judiciary. The next venue for adjudicating the gnarly matter of California land rights was the United States Circuit Court, where Stephen J. Field now presided. Arguing against the California city, attorney John Williams reinterpreted the political geography of New Spain and Mexico yet again. He contended that, according to both the Spanish constitution of 1812 and the laws of the Republic of Mexico, sovereignty rested in the Diputación of San Francisco, not with any single *ayuntamiento* located at a specific municipal site, such as the Presidio, Dolores, or Yerba Buena. Because there was no single center of municipal government from which a pueblo could extend out four leagues, the political boundaries of the Mexican territory were coterminous with the Partido de San Francisco. This interpretation of the complicated political geography of Alta California would grant control over a huge territory to the federal government.[28]

Williams's reading of the historical record was not without merit, but it did not persuade the justice presiding over the United States Circuit Court. Judge Field marshaled precedents set by the US Supreme Court to defend the interests of both the cities and the states in which they were located. Citing *The City of New Orleans v. the United States*, he ruled that when sovereignty passed from one nation to another (as it had between France and the United States in 1803), the state, and not the federal government, retained control over public lands. The argument relied on the interpretation of the Pueblo Case that was originally supplied by the lawyers for the city, Peachy and Dwinelle. In ruling in favor of the municipality of San Francisco, Field sounded impatient: "The decision not being subject to appeal, the controversy between the city and the Government is closed, and the claims of the city stand precisely as if the United States owned the land and by an Act of Congress had ceded it, subject to certain reservations to the city in trust for its inhabitants."[29]

One more legal challenge to San Francisco's land titles, *Townsend et al. v. Greeley*, heard by the US Supreme Court in 1866, reiterated the ruling that the ownership and control of the San Francisco Peninsula remained in state rather than federal hands. At the same time, the Court did not grant absolute autonomy to the municipality. Rather, it ruled that the city was "subject to the control of the state sovereignty," a position consistent with the ruling of Chief Justice John Marshall in his opinion in the Dartmouth Case of 1819.

———

The ruling in *Townsend v. Greeley* granted California ultimate authority over the San Francisco Peninsula. The deciding opinion, again written by Justice Field, carefully calibrated the division of authority among the municipality, the state, and the federal government. The Pueblo Case was put to rest in late December 1866, after almost twenty years of confused or suspended sovereignty over increasingly valuable real estate.[30]

One man, Stephen J. Field, was at the right place at the right time to exercise decisive authority over the public land around San Francisco Bay. Originally from Connecticut, Field had arrived in California before the Gold Rush and had soon become *alcalde* of the northern Sierra Nevada town of Marysville. He quickly moved on to become a justice of the peace in Sacramento and then a judge in the California Supreme Court, acquiring titles to California land wherever he went. The locals classified him a "great capitalist." Field rose up the California judicial hierarchy in time to rule on behalf of the City of San Francisco in its suit against the US government in 1860. In 1863, within days of upholding the city's position in *Hart v. Burnett*, Field ascended to the bench of the US Supreme Court. Lincoln had chosen him, a Union Democrat, in hopes of maintaining sectional and partisan balance on the nation's highest court. In 1864, and again in 1866, Field ruled in favor of the city when the question of the custody of pueblo land came before the federal judiciary. Presiding over another land case some years later, and once again ruling in favor of San Francisco and against the federal government, he received a note of appreciation from the *Alta*: "Judge Field has shown himself a true friend of San Francisco," said the newspaper, "and it is a matter of congratulations that he should have been here to try the case." Stephen Field rose up the scales of sovereignty with consummate agility, pursuing his own interests as well as those of San Francisco.[31]

Neither San Franciscans nor Baltimoreans were insulated from the sectional strife of the Civil War era. Their quarrels over sovereignty did not, however, align along the North/South border. The most wrenching social divisions within the cities were not about slavery. Know-Nothings and Vigilante Committee supporters, for example, divided the city along the lines of ethnicity, religion, and property, including the differences between squatters and those who held titles to city land. These cities were not preoccupied with opposing the federal government on the constitutional principle of states' rights. Sometimes, especially in the case of Baltimore, cities acted to defend their sovereignty against the state government rather than against the federal union. Baltimore chafed under the authorities in Annapolis, a conflict that climaxed on the eve of the Civil War, when the Maryland General Assembly unseated the Know-Nothing delegates from Baltimore and took over such vital municipal matters as the police, liquor licensing, and election monitoring.[32] The thorn in the side of the municipality of San Francisco was federal interference in land titles. It agitated the city government for decades, but it did not forestall the continuous taking of Mexican territory in order to shape it into an American city. Moreover, wily California lawyers like Stephen J. Field managed to use all the scales of sovereignty, local, state, and federal, to their own advantage.

RESHAPING THE CITY: BALTIMORE

Throughout the 1860s, the governments of both bay cities maneuvered within the constraints of divided sovereignty in order to create and maintain commodious spaces for their constituents. By 1870 the city astride the Chesapeake had become home to more than 250,000 people, while San

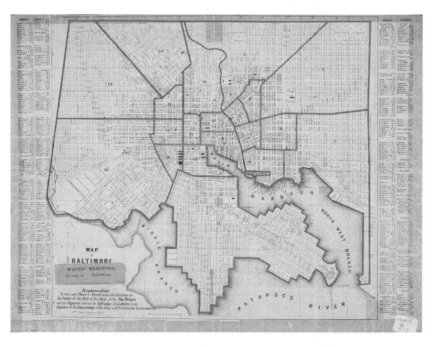

Map of Baltimore, *1859, Baltimore City Sheet Maps Collection.*
Courtesy of the Sheridan Libraries, Johns Hopkins University.

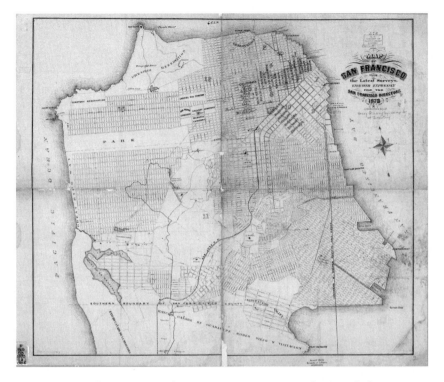

Map of San Francisco from Latest Surveys Engraved Expressly for
the San Francisco Director, Bancroft's Official Guide, *1873. Courtesy of the
David Rumsey Historical Map Collection, Stanford University.*

Francisco's population reached nearly 150,000. Both cities also burst the
seams of their old grids and stretched their urban boundaries outward to
accommodate tens of thousands of new residents. Baltimore spoke of its
"suburban" precincts, while realtors marked out "subdivisions" along the city
limits of San Francisco. Each city could also boast of grafting a new urban
landmark onto the street grid in the 1860s—a great park. Those who walked
the streets of either city, or took a horse-drawn railway to the city limits,
would feel at home in a modern urban space. The leaders and the citizens
of both Baltimore and San Francisco also modernized their political institutions, further refining and adjusting the relationship between capitalism
and local government.

In the border city of Baltimore, the prospects for innovative city planning
were bleak in the 1860s. Nonetheless, city boosters rushed to improve the

urban landscape even in the face of impending Civil War. They schemed to take and even *make* land. In the spring of 1859, the city council entertained the bizarre idea of converting the waters of the Basin into real estate. John Latrobe endorsed this plan to drain and fill the harbor in order to convert it into a valuable tract of lots at the crowded city center. The project as presented before the city council was both audacious and simple: it would level Federal Hill and fill up the Basin in one act of efficient and lucrative earth-moving. Latrobe called in "enlightened and scientific observers" to testify to both the feasibility and the healthy consequences of converting a "useless" geological formation into hundreds of salable properties. The cost of reshaping the central topographical feature of the city of Baltimore would be substantial—$765,346, by Latrobe's exacting estimate—but he deemed it well worth the expense. "Comparatively valueless" in its current condition, the spot chosen for the project, reshaped into real estate, would recover triple its cost in tax revenue. Latrobe further argued that collecting taxes on this virginal, manmade land would not produce the "litigation and contest that the assessment of the damages" on existing property entailed. Latrobe dared to do both nature and municipal capitalism one better: he would convert water into land and generate taxes without assessing property owners. Latrobe presented his plan to the city council in the spirit of the Monumental City, as another municipal project "typical of all great improvements."[33]

Fortunately, the impending sectional conflict put a damper on this profligate urban renewal project, but even on the eve of the Civil War, Baltimoreans kept up a campaign of urban improvement. The unflappable Latrobe went on to champion another, more tenable proposal for reshaping the city and enhancing Baltimore's reputation as a showcase for public architecture and urban landscaping. Billed as yet another attempt to replace the outdated Poppleton Plan, this proposal was sponsored by the direct descendants of Baltimore's founding fathers, including Latrobe, James Carroll, and Fielding Lucas Jr. (scion of the first family of surveyors and mapmakers). The audacity and novelty of the proposal is apparent in its title, "The Boundary Plan." The first daring innovation proposed by these distinguished, long-term residents of Baltimore was to devise a full-fledged urban "plan," an artful reshaping of a wide swath of urban space to be executed by the municipality. Second, the precocious planners dared to draw a border around the sprawl of settlement out from the old city. Their plan would draw the disarray of lots, squares, and housing tracts together and tie them up in a pastoral green border. Third, the Boundary Plan would be a thoroughly public project. It would require "a large outlay from the common purse," rather than fractional payments from the immediately interested parties, the abutting owners. Although the commission assumed that the project would yield the usual profit in real estate values and tax revenue, it could not pretend to be able to raise the upfront cost, estimated at $300,000, from special assessments.[34]

The design of the Boundary Plan broke with previous ways of taking the land and making space; it proposed to abruptly interrupt the amoeba-like expansion of settlement and encircle the city with a ribbon of parkland. The size of the proposed boundary avenue was unprecedented, 250 feet wide, with a promenade in the middle lined with trees and strewn with benches. Wherever it intersected with the major thoroughfares that jutted out from the city center, the boundary would be punctuated with a park. The architects of the Boundary Plan were agnostic about linear streets, orthogonal city blocks, and public squares. They dismissed the thoroughfare that led to the fashionable neighborhood of Jackson Square as an example of outmoded urban design, finding Broadway "objectionable on account of its glare and dust while at the same time its open character recommends it." The boundary avenue would be separated by a median and planted with sufficient greenery to relieve the eye of the "glare of the pavement." The avant-garde city planners had become somewhat resistant to the tyranny of the grid: "That same direction and grade should not be allowed to impair the picturesque as connecting with the avenue—while, at the same time, curved lines, which, on reflection, were found to be inconsistent with the value of adjacent lots for building purposes, were not permitted." This eclectic urban plan, with its curving border avenue and modified grid, was as innovative and stylish as Frederick Law Olmsted and Calvert Vaux's greensward plan for Central Park in New York. Moreover, the greenery was not to be confined within a single district, but threaded around the cityscape. Typical of the Chesapeake city, the Baltimore experiment in picturesque landscape planning showcased not a park, but a kind of street, and a curving one. In one critical way, however, the Boundary Plan was naïve and shortsighted. It conspired to draw a blunt line around the margins of urban settlement, presuming that the expanse of capitalist real estate could be confined within a neat, finite border.[35]

By the time the final report of the Boundary Park committee was submitted to the city council and circulated in the daily papers, the estimated cost had escalated to $500,000. The costly civic project was soon abandoned, lost in the mounting sectional conflict. The space of urban modernization slowed, and the public spaces around the harbor fell into civic neglect.

A member of the second branch of the city council was moved to alarm and nostalgia in 1859, when the first branch threatened to close the city spring on Calvert Street. Once the carefully manicured ornament to the top of the central north/south artery of the city, the Calvert Spring was prized as both "a pleasing object to all passers by" and "a place of resort for children and others, who cannot get into the country" in the summer months. The councilman forwarded a petition from his constituents with a plea to preserve this remnant of a bygone spatial order: "This city spring is the only open place retained by the City near its centre, and at one time helped to give a name to Baltimore as the city of Fountains, as well as Monuments, and the undersigned think it would be a small and false economy and an unworthy act in the Government of a great City (which has so few and insignificant public squares), to close their small place in order to save the annual expense necessary to keep it in order."[36]

Seemingly oblivious to the impending national crisis, the indefatigable Mayor Thomas Swann, in league with the city press, continued the campaign to develop the "unimproved" land at the city's margins. Ruminating on the subject, the editor of the *Sun* worried that the city had "lost sight of her true interest" by permitting anarchic growth and failing to balance "individual and aggregated interests." The editor believed the mania for carving the city into lots had gotten out of hand:

> The general idea is that landholders can dispose of their ground more profitably for building lots, and as a consequence they go to work and lease hundreds and hundreds of parcels of ground, twelve or fifteen feet by fifty or a hundred, at the low sum of one dollar per foot. Of these, small tenements are hurried up soon to dilapidate. We could point to scores of such streets as have been opened and built upon in this miserable manner. The eastern part of Baltimore abounds with them. They meet the view in the most indescribable irregularity, intersecting each other at all degrees of angles.[37]

The city council and the mayor echoed the *Sun*'s critique of Baltimore's chaotic development, but could find no way to contravene it. The mayor discouraged the municipal investment in yet another square, to be named for Lafayette. He calculated the cost in the old-fashioned way: the project would ask the city, rather than abutting owners, to bear the financial burden of paving, grading, and repairing the streets around the square. City boosters proposed the development of an alternative public space at a spot of commanding natural and historical prominence, the high point of Federal Hill, overlooking the Patapsco as it flowed out to the Chesapeake. Called a park and not a square, the proposed remodeling of Federal Hill was envisioned as an open recreational space for the workers and immigrants occupying the cramped houses and narrow alleys of South Baltimore. Although the development of Federal Hill Park would be postponed by the calamitous national events of the 1860s, it augured a new way of organizing urban space, something akin to the public playgrounds of the Progressive Era.[38]

In the months immediately preceding the outbreak of the war, Baltimore did manage to undertake two major renovations of the urban landscape: the first a municipal streetcar line, and the second a grand public park. The streetcar came to Baltimore through a familiar process of popular debate and municipal ingenuity. While conservatives, such as reform leader George Brown, opposed building a passenger railway out to the city limits, fearing it would "change the habits" of the people in disconcerting ways, middle-class citizens pressed for modern modes of public transportation. Over one thousand citizens petitioned the city council to provide streetcar service on Sundays. They argued that rapid urban transportation was essential to their spiritual welfare; without it, they could not bridge the distance between their suburban homes and their houses of worship, which were still clustered near the city center. The desire for urban locomotion could not be squelched. Between 1858 and 1861, as the nation was coming unraveled below the Mason-Dixon Line, the leaders and citizens of Baltimore went to work stitching the outlying neighborhoods together with the city center. By midcentury, private companies were providing regular omnibus service out to Franklin Square and across town to Jackson Square, the fashionable neighborhood on the east side. Then, in the late 1850s, the horse cars were placed on iron tracks, making the commute both quicker and more comfortable. Promoters of west-side development lobbied for a railway line out the "suburban avenue" to Reisterstown.[39]

Linking the urban core to the expanding suburbs would require political will and public action, both additional capital and new methods of municipal finance. The parsimonious civic leaders of the capitalist city were resistant to raising taxes for another costly public improvement. They resorted instead to the financial tool now labeled a franchise: licensing a private company to provide public services such as transportation. This expedient amalgam of public welfare and private profit did not meet with immediate approval.

—

As George Brown put it, the franchise for the street railway effectively rented out the city's most fundamental public property, the street bed. Inflicting further insult on the citizens of Baltimore, the first railway franchise was issued to a company based in Philadelphia. Mayor Swann took particular umbrage at this cavalier disregard for local sovereignty. In a seven-page diatribe against the plan, Swann argued that at the very least, the people of Baltimore were entitled to the same stake in the street railway that they once held in the B&O: "Any citizen" of Baltimore should have the right "to participate in the organization of the company" by purchasing stock. He deemed the grant of a franchise to Philadelphia an insufferable insult to the Monumental City, a municipality that had been "preeminent for more than half a century in the schemes of internal improvement." An astute member of the city council saw the franchise as a usurpation of a fundamental local prerogative, a transfer of the "extraordinary power . . . to take possession of the principal streets" to "nonresident capitalists."[40]

The opposition to the franchise was sufficient to derail the original contract for a street railway, which the city council declared null and void. Mayor Swann, facing another election, went back to the drawing board and came up with an ingenious compromise. Ever the enterprising businessman, Swann, the former president of the B&O, now saw a chance to make a deal between the public and private sectors. "It occurred to me," said the mayor, "that an opportunity was offered." The idea actually originated with a correspondent to the *Evening Bulletin* who called himself "Public Good." The mayor crafted the proposal into a contract that was more favorable to the city. It would impose a special city tax on the railroad company. Although the company would pass the tax on to the passengers in the form of a one-cent increase in the fare, the citizens of Baltimore were promised a kickback. The municipal revenue generated by the railroad tax would be used to provide for the "comfort, health and recreation of the inhabitants, and place Baltimore in advance of any other city," all "without a direct tax upon the treasury." On June 13, 1860, in accordance with Swann's plan, the city council passed an ordinance that taxed the street railway and allocated one-fifth of the five-cent fare to a "Park Fund."[41]

Initially, the revenue from the fare tax was earmarked for the creation and maintenance of green spaces throughout the city. It might have been allocated to funding the proposed Boundary Boulevard, improving Patterson Park, planting trees on the squares, or even upgrading the Calvert Street Spring or other central spaces. In the fertile imagination of Thomas Swann, however, the plan quickly mushroomed into the vision of a "grand park" spanning hundreds of acres. Support for the plan soon emerged in many quarters of the city. Different districts, east, west, north, and south, volunteered their neighborhoods as the site for this urban amenity. The citizens of South Baltimore renewed their appeal for a park on Federal Hill. Laboring men saw it as a construction site and source of jobs. The elite stewards of civic improvements, including John H. B. Latrobe and Columbus O'Donnell, who were appointed as park commissioners, saw it as an enhancement of the city's reputation. Swann's editorial allies at the *American* concurred with the opposition paper, the *Sun*, in endorsing the project. The *Sun* opined that the days of small squares were over and proceeded to expand the ideal scale of city planning to "a veritable park of five hundred—why not say a thousand—acres, and all the variety of wood, shrubbery, lake, flowers, etc., etc."[42]

The daily papers were not building parks in the air; they rushed to recommend specific pieces of urban turf as the location of the project. The *Sun* proffered, "For instance—a line extending from the Northern Avenue, along

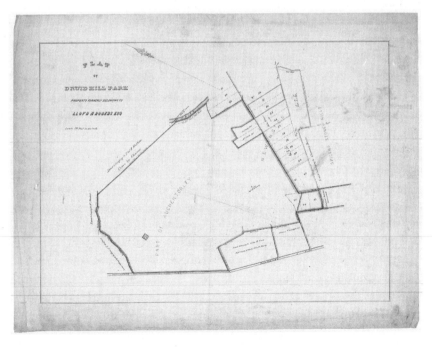

"Plat of Druid Hill Park," 1860. Courtesy of the Milton S. Eisenhower Library, Sheridan Libraries, Johns Hopkins University.

the York road, to the three mile stone, at Shaw's Hill; thence easterly, along by Teakle's place and Nizer's including Sterling's, on the Hillen road; thence southerly to the Harford road, and along that road to the Northern Avenue again, this avenue being the Southern boundary of the park." Whatever the favored site, all the proposals for a grand park imagined a public space of similar dimensions: it would be big, it would be placed in a remote part of the city, and it would be bounded not by city streets, but by country roads. The ideal park would also serve a novel, specialized function, that of wholesome outdoor recreation.[43]

Affixing the idea of a grand park onto the actual physical space of the city ignited a debate between different neighborhoods. As soon as the press proposed that the park be located on the northeastern side of the city, a correspondent to the *Sun* objected, saying that "Baltimore city is destined more particularly to extend and increase toward the west and northwest." When the park commission chose the west-side site, Druid Hill, the *Sun* summoned its rhetorical power to oppose the plan. The editor likened the park commissioners to Baron Haussmann, whose massive renovations of Paris under Napoleon III had been conducted "utterly without representation." The commissioners were giving the people "no voice in the matter," and had sited the park in the "aristocratic section of the city." The "infamous Park Tax" further inflamed the class conflict: the fare hike would cost the workingmen and women of the city, while the park would serve the wealthy residents of distant suburbs. The opposition to the park also had ethnic inflections. The *Sun* upbraided Mayor Swann for failing to invite the Irish to the opening ceremonies for the park, and branded the whole plan as the work of the Know-Nothings. In the opinion of the editor, Druid Hill Park exemplified the "ostentatious fraud, corruption and extravagance which have disgraced authority in Baltimore for some years." Finally, the *Sun* issued a threat to the partisans of the northwest park site. Although the people were as yet "utterly without redress" against the actions of the park commission, the issue would be in the voters' hands on election day, which was just weeks away.[44]

On October 31, 1860, the electorate followed the *Sun*'s advice, ousted Thomas Swann, and placed the reformer George Brown in the Mayor's Office. But the outgoing mayor and the park promoters would not stand by as their plans for urban development were stopped in their tracks. Just in the nick of time, the City of Baltimore took the first steps to convert large portions of those marginal spaces into the latest fashion in public space, not streets, not squares, but a grand park. As Lincoln was voted into office, and states to the south plotted secession, outgoing mayor Thomas Swann led a civic procession along the pathway of the new street railway to celebrate the groundbreaking for Druid Hill Park. As of November 1860, the plans to modernize the city had not yet been aborted.

Five months later, the Union Army marched into the city and threw the new mayor, George Brown, into jail on suspicion of being a Confederate sympathizer. While Brown languished in prison, the city continued to pay his salary, and the president of the first branch of the city council assumed the office of mayor. But the foundation for Druid Hill Park had been laid and would become the beachhead for a major reorganization of urban space and city life. The street railway would carry those citizens who could afford the fare out to the park and into districts of relative affluence and specialized residential use. The search for a park site was conducted, as the press put it, "mostly in the suburbs," and it would be sited on private land, purchased by the taxpayers and lying outside the city limits just beyond North Avenue. This spatial expansion had political and economic consequences. To the *Sun*, it was "the inexcusable folly of the Druid Hill purchases," something to benefit the county at the expense of city-dwellers. This line upon the land, the ominous divide between suburb and city, would be etched deeply into the everyday lives and politics of Americans. It would, as George Brown put it, "change the habits" of the people.[45]

Once war broke out in April 1861, many urban improvements, as small as Calvert Spring and as ambitious as Druid Hill Park, were put on hold. Some were literally blocked by the Civil War. The long-awaited park on Federal Hill became the encampment of Union troops. Public squares and buildings were converted into military hospitals. When Mayor Brown took up office late in 1860, he eviscerated Swann's agenda: he jettisoned the city hall project, nixed the harbor improvements, opposed appropriations for the grand park, and presided over a precipitous retrenchment in public expenditures. The growth in municipal expenditures between 1860 and 1865 was less than half of that which occurred between 1855 and 1860. Municipal services were recalibrated, but not curtailed. Proposals for civic improvements went through the two branches of the city council and on for the mayor's signature in the same deliberative process: balancing cost and benefits, considering the opinions of different classes and constituencies, weighing the interests of the various wards, and parrying the influence of different urban entrepreneurs. The long delayed building of a city hall was a case in point. The city council first voted to erect a house of government worthy of the Monumental City soon after it obtained its first charter. The project was periodically abandoned, revived, shelved, and proposed once again. Only after the Civil War, in 1868, was it finally approved. It was funded with a $1 million bond, and would rise proudly on the skyline in the 1870s.[46]

Although wartime austerity would reinforce the long-term trends of taxpayer frugality and municipal retrenchment, Baltimore muddled through the years of national carnage. The city would grow in the time-honored fashion, along the same methodical procession of streets, row houses, special assessments, and piecemeal additions to the Poppleton Plan. While the abutting owners still complained about the expense, the street commissioners made aggressive efforts to collect the cost of assessments from property owners. One frustrated council member despaired of ever bringing order and efficiency to the system of special assessments and recommended that the city assume the entire expense. Yet the municipal leaders could not summon the will to fundamentally reform the now antiquated and unwieldy compendium of street ordinances. The city's vital arteries became clogged with traffic as the population ventured out to "the precincts" and "the suburbs." Those who could afford it traveled the expanding urban spaces by new methods of transportation—chiefly horse-drawn omnibuses that were set on iron tracks and operated on a regular schedule.

Parks and suburbs would deliver fresh air, capacious public space, and the bounteous, intoxicating foliage of a Baltimore spring to some citizens, but not to everyone. Workingmen and women, including African Americans and the freed slaves streaming into the city after emancipation, were quartered in the small alley houses at the old city center or the new industrial districts to the south and the east. They had limited access to the grand park. The end of the Civil War did not portend a grant of equal urban space for all men and women. Another public notice appeared in the press amid the debate about Druid Hill Park. Dated May 31, 1860, it outlawed "all meetings or assemblages of colored persons in the city, except for religious worship, without permit from the mayor, and the presence of at least one white person." The vote was 14 to 5. In Baltimore, the end of the Civil War would be the beginning of an era of increasingly glaring and entrenched racial segregation.[47]

RESHAPING THE CITY: SAN FRANCISCO

At the outset of the Civil War, San Francisco was already beginning to resemble East Coast cities such as Baltimore. The municipal engineers had marked out a honeycomb of streets jutting off from the shoreline of Yerba Buena Cove, creating a municipal map that was more precise than Poppleton's plan for Baltimore. Remote from the battlefields, and with its sovereignty over public land secure, the city by San Francisco Bay proceeded to remodel and expand its capitalist urban space. After experiencing the Mexican-American War, the Gold Rush, and repeated plunges in the real estate market, the Civil War was just another seismic wave in the city's tempestuous history. Boosters shrugged it off as the distraction of the sectionalism gripping the East and continued carving up the San Francisco Peninsula at a frantic pace.

Heedless of any constitutional constraints, or even the authority of the Supreme Court of the United States, the municipality took charge of the pueblo lands and plotted out more lots in the Western Addition and beyond. The condition of the preemption grant originally awarded in 1850 to Merritt Welton exemplifies the jolting pace of the real estate market. The tract was still a warren of disputed titles twenty years later, after the death of the original grantee. Titles had been repeatedly forfeited, by "default," "foreclosure," "lien," "sheriff's sales," "quitclaims," and "complaint to recover possession," and that financial transaction that would bind owners to bankers for years to come, the "mortgage." A deed dated October 1865, for example, was riddled with references to mortgages. It reserved to the title-holder the right "to borrow money upon the whole or any part of the said real estate for the Improvement of the same etc. And for the purpose to execute any Mortgage or Mortgages with the usual terms, etc., provided that he shall include in the respective Mortgages in each instance his own interest in the land so mortgaged." The whirligig of mortgages and other financial vehicles made the land around San Francisco Bay the hostage of a tempestuous market for real estate.[48]

Despite all the pens, ink, and energy expended in buying, selling, exchanging, and mortgaging land, the Western Addition had not been shaped into a coherent plan, and certainly not into anything resembling the parallel lines of a street grid. Land sales in the Western Addition had not turned out to be a bountiful source of municipal revenue. City surveyor Milo Hoadley estimated that despite ten thousand expressions of interest in the Van Ness properties, only thirty people had succeeded in quieting their claims and thereby generating tax revenue for the city. The estimates of delinquent taxes at the time ran as high as $400,000. The Western Addition was far from the tax-rich residential district of an assessor's imagination. Most lots remained unsold, and those five public squares promised in the Van Ness Ordinance

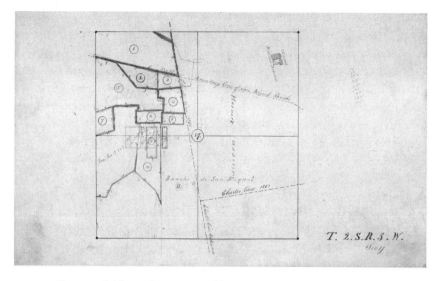

Abstract of titles to the Western Addition, MSS2002/51 CV2. Courtesy of the Bancroft Library, University of California, Berkeley.

of 1856 were disheveled open fields. In February 1863, officials reported that "some difficulty has already arisen from parties taking possession of public squares, and enclosing of such public lots may prevent much trouble and expense thereafter." The maps that appended the abstract of titles of the Welton tract looked nothing like the city survey of 1856 that marked off the Western Addition as an orderly expanse of rectangular blocks and lots. In fact, it looked more like a Mexican *diseño*, a hodgepodge of obliquely angled properties scattered around a crude representation of the old Mission church. As a material space, rather than a matrix for real estate speculation, much of the land on the southern tier of the city and county of San Francisco remained untamed desert.[49]

But the appetite for gobbling up land on the San Francisco Peninsula was not yet sated. Squatters and speculators alike looked greedily for more investments. A tract of land near Mission Creek opened up for business under the federal statute that permitted the sale of marginal wetlands and swamp. San Francisco developers quickly bought up the soggy soil, bridged it, filled it in, and expanded the landmass into San Francisco Bay. Not satisfied, the land grabbers next set their sights farther south. One 160-acre section out near the border of the Buri Buri Ranch and the San Mateo county line was hastily surveyed into fifty-square-vara lots, enclosed with a flimsy brush fence, and labeled the Beideman tract. With the swagger of a "big squatter," Mr. Beideman (also known for his fisticuffs in the city legislature) cordoned off his land first with brush and then with thirty thousand to forty thousand square feet of lumber, the makings of "a good substantial boarded fence." Finally, Beideman planted his land with turnips and stocked it with cows and hogs, all to prove he was a bone fide homesteader and qualified for a preemption grant. When Beideman's claim was challenged before the California Supreme Court, one of the justices called it typical of the "long and bitter controversies, which, for years have divided the bar and the bench." In the boundless imagination of Beideman and other land grabbers, the former ranchland of the Californios was yet another urban frontier. They called it simply "the Outside Lands." During and after the Civil War, the Outside Lands became the template on which to conduct yet further experiments in reshaping the land around San Francisco Bay.[50]

The annual municipal report for 1861 found city officers still struggling to shape the recalcitrant landscape around the San Francisco Bay into a proper, East Coast–style city. Under budgetary restraints similar to those of cities back East, San Francisco officials resorted to some cruder methods of financing infrastructure. For example, the Board of Supervisors put prisoners to work on public works, but allowed one humane concession: "No person sentenced to labor in the public works shall be compelled to wear any chain or Manacle."[51] At the same time, street construction had become a more routinized and bureaucratized process, even in the wilder West. The salaries of city and county employees, including the new police department, mounted to almost $140,000. Under the surveillance of municipal government, property owners cared for their streets and neighborhood more through fees and fines than through volunteering and collaborating. The revised street ordinance addressed citizens in the manner of a strict and punitive parent:

> All property holders or tenants of property upon any street already graded, planked or paved, which require or may require local repairs in grading, planking, paving, sidewalk, sewers or other wise, neglecting or refusing to make such repairs when so required by a notice from the superintendent of streets and highways, shall be deemed guilty of a misdemeanor, and on conviction shall be punished by fine not less than five dollars nor more than one hundred dollars, or by imprisonment in the county jail not less than two days nor more than fifty days, at the discretion of police judge

for each and every week he or they may so neglect or refuse counting from the date of the notice.

This was a far cry from the voluntary community efforts that had characterized Baltimore in the early nineteenth century when abutting owners came together to open and maintain their streets.[52]

Laying out, grading, and repairing the streets, including miscellaneous expenses, such as paying off "coupons due in New York" amounting to $20,000, consumed a major portion of San Francisco's municipal capital. While a large portion of the cost of street maintenance was still charged to abutting owners, that tax revenue was often difficult to recover. Contractors hired to excavate, fill, and plank Mission Street had to sue the city to recover $82,000 of unpaid bills. The job of the city engineer, Milo Hoadley, entailed more than opening and maintaining the streets and sidewalks. His job included cutting down inconvenient obstructions of commerce, such as Rincon Hill, south of Market Street, and depositing them in the bay, thereby creating level waterfront lots. He described his technique of making land as a two-step process of "excavating" and "embarkation": "Excavation," he said, "is where we are cutting down a hill and taking it away. Embarkation is where we are filling it in, to fill up, to make a filling." Hoadley used his bureaucratic authority to run roughshod over the land around the bay. He reported that his crew had rearranged close to fifty thousand yards of San Francisco land.[53]

San Francisco's city boosters searched for economic opportunities far beyond the local streetscape. They claimed a hinterland that extended "to the distant parts of the earth," and pledged to make San Francisco an international commercial hub "centralizing the commerce of the Pacific," a region they said extended to "Japan, China, Australia, Central and South America, as well as most of those countries bordering upon the Atlantic." In the imperial imagination of San Francisco's entrepreneurs, Yerba Buena Cove became a dock for shipbuilding, a depot for oceangoing vessels, and a distribution center for a full market basket of agricultural products: grain, flour, cotton, tobacco, wool, and hemp. However, it would take a major investment of municipal capital to convert the frontier market town into an international entrepôt.[54]

In 1858, John Van Ness rallied his fellow citizens to undertake a major improvement of the port. "Nature having given us a safe and commodious harbor," he boasted, "it is for the hand of art to make the port commensurate with the requirements of a great commercial Metropolis." As gold had rushed

---

William Hahn, Market Scene Sansome Street,
San Francisco, 1873. Wikimedia Commons.

in and out of San Francisco in the 1850s, all manner of dirt, debris, abandoned ships, and cargo had piled up in the harbor. The initiative to clear the clogged waterfront and prevent further obstruction came from a consortium of merchants inspired by what Van Ness called "the constant tendency of commerce to unite." The merchants proposed, and the Board of Supervisors endorsed, a plan to fortify the shipping channels with a giant bulkhead.[55]

Not everyone in San Francisco bought into this imperial project. One citizen saw the bulkhead proposal as an "unholy crusade against the use of our land." Others objected to the mode of financing this improvement, the grant of a franchise to a private company for a period of fifty years. To Democrats, among others, the franchise amounted to "the erection of a monster monopoly . . . a dishonest robbery of the city of San Francisco." In a letter home in May 1860, Robert Wallace, a young clerk trying to make a living in the mercurial Gold Rush economy, presented the controversy as public theft: "Taking from the city forever the right to her City front on the Bay and asking for the privilege of building a Bulkhead with foreign Capital." Other critics spread the rumor that the members of the Board of Supervisors who sponsored the bill were "heavy stockholders in this franchise," which was to be awarded to "foreigners" flush with "foreign capital." The chief local sponsor of the bulkhead project was actually the People's Party, or the Tax Payers' Union, whom the opposition Democrats branded the "subverters of our laws, and the avowed revolutionists of our government." In the favored political vilification of the 1860s, they were "Black Republicans."[56]

Caught in the political crossfire of 1860, the bulkhead project went down to defeat. In this instance of sectional politics, state authority thwarted the will of the mayor and the Board of Supervisors of the City and County of San Francisco; the governor vetoed the bulkhead ordinance and became a local hero. Robert Wallace deemed this a victory of states' rights over the municipal authorities. It had inspired "one of the greatest receptions to our city," as he put it, complete with the salute of hundreds of guns, the illumination of the streets, and "the military, and citizens[,] all turning out in Procession."[57]

The principles of political economy and vested private interests were both at stake in the bulkhead controversy, as documented in a flurry of speeches and pamphlets in the spring of 1860. The leading opponents of the project owned property near or on the waterfront. Addressing a "Mass Meeting" in March 1860, one speaker asked, "What right has this company, under these circumstances, to fence in this land to exclude the owners of these wharves from the enjoyment of their prosperity?" The rebuttal of proponents of the

---

bulkhead appealed not to land values but to the capitalist marketplace. They issued a pamphlet advising the public that "the stocks of those wharves, which are complained of for doing a good business, can be had on the streets every day in the week. They may be purchased sometimes at public but always at a private sale for those who wish to buy." The supporters of the bulkhead project proclaimed their boldfaced allegiance to the private sector: the pamphlet, titled "The Bulkhead Question Completely Reviewed," concluded that "THIS WORK MUST BE DONE BY PRIVATE CAPITAL." Harbor improvement, which had been the object of civic pride and public beneficence in early Baltimore, had become, in the city of San Francisco, "just one of those improvements to be left to private capital and enterprise." "The state," as the argument for the bulkhead continued, "should never come in as a distinct corporation and on its own account engage in operations of this kind." For government to interfere in the operation of private capital was simply "odious." Its proper function was the "conservation of public interest and public freedom." The only legitimate governmental functions that the proponents of the bulkhead identified were jails, penitentiaries, and provisions for "the sick, the insane, and the idiotic." The political economy of the City of San Francisco had been divided along a now familiar ideological border between private enterprise and municipal responsibility.[58]

The line that the self-proclaimed capitalists of San Francisco drew between private business and the public domain was actually serpentine, elastic, and penetrable. Funded by a franchise, the bulkhead project would have converted a public need into private profits, all with the approval and assistance of the municipal government. Although the concerted opposition of citizens, including local landowners with a vested interest in the waterfront, halted the bulkhead project, no one came up with an alternative plan to clean up San Francisco Harbor or to fund many of the other needed civic improvements. Unlike Baltimore and other American cities, San Francisco did not hasten to create a municipal waterworks, for example. For decades to come, the job of meeting this fundamental need of the men, women, and children of San Francisco was entrusted to the Spring Valley Water Company and its irascible owner, William Ralston, who made, and lost, his fortune importing water into the arid city. The 1860s was not a hospitable time to undertake expensive projects of internal improvement or public service, in either San Francisco or Baltimore. Given the exigencies of the Civil War and the mandate of fiscal conservatism, the best either municipality could do was to delegate the public weal to private companies in the form of lucrative franchises.[59]

Unlike Baltimore, however, San Francisco could still claim another source of revenue, the public land that remained around the bay, now called "the Outside Lands." The People's Party (or Tax Payers' Union) continued to calculate the revenue that could be generated by selling the land that the city lawyers had cannily claimed as a former Mexican pueblo. One of their publications estimated that the value of the pueblo lands was such that, "if sold," it "could pay the whole city debt of less than $3 million and build school houses, jails and other public structures." Standing in the way of this financial boon, according to the Tax Payers' Union, were the "specula- tors and 'land grabbers' who by fraud or force, or both combined, under some pretext or other, pounce upon public property, which they hold in their tenacious grips." A letter to the *Alta* in April 1861 laid claim to the Outside Lands with a familiar salvo: "The title is clear. They belong to the city. They are the last fragment of its patrimony. They are worth millions of dollars—worth more than the whole amount of our funded debt." The letter was signed "a taxpayer." His wishes were realized in a municipal statute on the model of the Van Ness Ordinance called "Shafter's Land Bill," later known as the "Clement Ordinance." The legislation offered titles to current occupants of the Outside Lands provided they paid the city five years' worth of taxes. Aware that the Pueblo Case was still before the federal courts, the city officials once again finessed the legal technicalities. "Not wishing to be disrespectful to the Supreme Court," the emissary of the San Francisco Board of Supervisors said, the decisions of the federal judiciary on the matter "had been multifarious." Along with the Clement Ordinance, the municipal leaders carried a supporting petition to Sacramento. It was signed by eight thousand citizens, with merchants outnumbering occupants of the disputed territory by four to one. A squatter on the Outside Lands shot back to the city officials: "You are selling my land to pay your debt."[60]

With state approval of the Clement Ordinance in 1866, the conversion of land into lots could continue its course farther down the San Francisco Pen- insula. The ordinance granted clear titles to those who had settled a given plot and paid their back taxes along with an additional 10 percent of the estimated value of the land. With the claims quieted, the municipal authori- ties began to shape the lots in the Outside Lands into an urban residential district. Section 2 of the Clement Ordinance mandated that the city "make a map showing streets and public highways, blocks formed by the intersection of that street and public highways, and the lots on which said blocks shall be subdivided." Furthermore, "upon such map shall be designated the portions

———

of land set apart for public uses." One citizen called for starting out on a clean slate to plot the Outside Lands. He would abandon ancient Spanish and Mexican precedents—"the whole absurd system of town commons." This amateur urban planner was equally dismissive of the blueprint for the Western Addition—the city was "studding the surface of the city map with little problematical squares, doomed, if ever properly reserved, to neglect and solitude." This anonymous pamphleteer envisioned another kind of urban shape: a "broad avenue . . . for rides and drives" going out to the "very spot which Nature has prepared for our Park."[61]

The final plan for the Outside Lands was drafted in the civic vernacular of the late nineteenth century. Incorporated into a map dated 1868, the Outside Lands looked like a large patch within a patchwork of patchworks, one division among multiple "subdivisions," another grid stitched into the contiguous grids of downtown, the Mission District, and the Western Addition. Partitioned into 1,255 numbered lots, with a vacant rectangle at their center labeled "PARK" (see *Map of San Francisco from Latest Surveys Engraved Expressly for the San Francisco Director*), the Outside Lands made up the biggest patch of the urban landscape. The map of the newly acquired Outside Lands was at first an extravagant fantasy written on sand and sagebrush in an area occupied by coyotes, jackrabbits, and squatters. It was also a recipe for more municipal squabbling and a forecast for urban sprawl. The actual conversion of these lands into housing tracts awaited the transportation technology that could mount steep hills. Horse-drawn railways, not in service until 1867, stopped a mile short of the proposed park; the technology capable of mounting the hills of San Francisco—the cable car—was not introduced until 1875. But the municipal planners looked confidently ahead to "enabling men of modest means to procure a homestead far from the business centers."[62]

One component of the modern plan for the Outside Lands began to materialize soon after the Civil War: Golden Gate Park. The city engineer marked off the site of the West Coast's answer to New York's Central Park within a massive grid miles from the city center. San Francisco's grand park was a testament to the political ingenuity that reshaped the city in the latter half of the nineteenth century. It was the spatial production of pragmatic deal-making politicians, including San Francisco's mayor from 1867 to 1869, Frank McCoppin. Mayor McCoppin helped broker the deal between land developers, legislators, and squatters that cleared the titles to the Outside Lands. The fine print of the Clement Ordinance stipulated that the 10 percent tax upon the squatters would be set aside to fund a park. McCoppin began the park planning on a high note by enlisting the services of Frederick Law Olmsted, who happened to be in California in 1864 and 1865. Olmsted owed his appointment as the overseer of Central Park to his Republican credentials and had not yet claimed landscape architecture as his profession. He was in San Francisco working his way out of bankruptcy after a failed business enterprise in the mining district and eking out a living by obtaining occasional landscaping contracts. Olmsted's "Plan of Public Pleasure Ground for San Francisco" strove to meet the naturalistic and romantic standards that he and Calvert Vaux had designed for New York's Central Park, adapting them to the topographical and climatic challenges of the San Francisco Peninsula. His design essentially slashed a broad promenade across Van Ness Street down to the bay, scattering a parade ground, a garden, and a playground along the way. Olmsted tucked the pleasure garden awkwardly into the San Francisco street grid and despaired of ever transforming the barren hillsides and sand dunes into a verdant garden. Although Olmsted tried to integrate nature into San Francisco's defiant grid, the two remained at war with one another. The Board of Supervisors found the plan too costly, and Olmsted returned to the East.[63]

San Francisco's grand park would not finally take shape until the 1870s, when William Hammond Hall, an engineer hailing from Hagerstown, Maryland, managed to anchor the sands with vegetation and lay out walkways and playgrounds within a rectangular segment of the Outside Lands. Golden Gate Park was a consolation prize for the conversion of a vast parcel of public land into private lots as authorized by the Clement Ordinance. The city's crafty politicians, acting in league with fiscal conservatives and stingy taxpayers, rescued those one thousand acres of windblown sand from the grasp of scheming realtors and land-hungry squatters. Those who campaigned to create a great park in San Francisco seldom echoed Olmsted's rhapsody about the civilizing power of nature. They were more likely to speak in the vernacular of the capitalist city, calculating how Golden Gate Park could simultaneously increase tax revenues and shore up real estate values in the Outside Lands. The *Alta* aptly described the function of the park: "increasing assessable values of the property and adding to the wealth and comfort of the citizen."[64]

In the end, the landscaping of Golden Gate Park, not unlike that of New York's Central Park, was a product of urban *realpolitick*. Both parks, moreover, took the same spatial form, a giant green space set in a grid remote from the demographic center of the city and inaccessible to most of its residents. In the 1860s and 1870s, most of the visitors to the parks were relatively affluent citizens who had access to horses, carriages, or a pricey streetcar fare. For all its limits, compromises, and inequities, however, San Francisco, like Baltimore, had managed to set aside hundreds of acres of coveted land as public space. It did so, moreover, at the same time that the nation was embroiled in a civil war and then preoccupied with the reconstruction of the South.[65]

As the Civil War ravaged the battlefields across the South, the cities of Baltimore and San Francisco managed to create spaces for leisure, recreation, and public sociability. With their grand parks set in proto-suburban spaces, the two cities on opposite coasts were looking remarkably similar, and much like other modern American cities. That resemblance between the vernacular urban plans of the two cities might suggest that urban history had moved from east to west according to models of residential squares and "central" parks originating on the Atlantic side of the continent. A closer look around the shore of San Francisco Bay suggests that landscape history, like Frederick Law Olmsted himself, moved in both directions during the 1860s. In 1865, Olmsted was also employed on the east side of San Francisco Bay—he had been commissioned to lay out the campus of the University of California. His plan called for a spiral of greenery climbing and circling the hillside above the academic buildings, presaging the curvilinear streets that he and Vaux would design for the suburb of Riverside, Illinois, in 1869. That example of American urban planning was a harbinger of what the cultural and urban history scholar David Schuyler has called "the new urban landscape." Like other harbingers of the novel landscape—picturesque cemeteries, Regent Park in London, and Llewellyn Park in West Orange, New Jersey—Olmsted's plan for the Berkeley campus and for Riverside placed home sites along winding roadways outside the city, circumventing rather than remodeling the urban street grid. His plan for the Berkeley campus placed domestic residences in open fields, distanced both from one another and from the village grid down the hill. Olmsted's imagination remained slanted toward a rural and domestic sensibility; his suburban plans reinforced the dividing line between city and country.[66]

While Olmsted and company were laying out suburbs and parkland back East, including in Baltimore, San Francisco continued to project a pattern of rectangular lots ever outward from the city center. One piece of visual evidence, however, suggests that California land developers were beginning to break with the hegemony of the grid and take the idea of the curvilinear street a significant step further. In 1867, the San Francisco developers Louis

Alfred Prioche and L. L. Robinson advertised the sale of lots on a tract called the "Subdivision of a Part of the San Miguel Rancho." The ad was embellished with a map of the available home sites. The lots were not plotted as a grid of perpendicular streets, like those that had been imposed over the beach and hills of Yerba Buena—and on much of the rest of urban America—during the nineteenth century. Nor did the plan for the San Miguel subdivision mimic the suburban pattern Olmsted had adapted from the plan of Llewellyn Park, New Jersey: residential parcels of one to five acres scattered through parkland. Rather, the narrow house lots of the San Miguel subdivision were lined up cheek and jowl along streets that twisted up and around the hillside, following the contours of the land. The curving streets were connected not by regular ninety-degree intersections but by rustic pathways. The advertisement for the subdivision was an uncanny forecast of the suburban housing tracts of the 1950s.[67]

Prioche and Robinson anticipated that the completion of the transcontinental railroad would lead to rapid sales in the subdivision. In fact the company failed in the depressed economy that followed the Civil War.

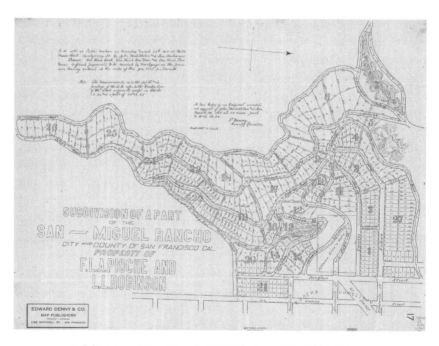

Subdivision of San Miguel, 1867. Courtesy of the Earth Science and Map Library, University of California, Berkeley.

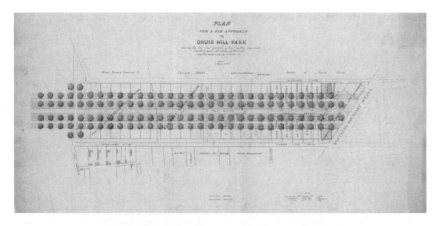

Plan for the street to Druid Hill Park, ca. 1860.
Courtesy of the Sheridan Libraries, Johns Hopkins University.

The hillside above the former mission would remain barren of housing until the 1870s, when the first homes began to cluster there. They were not "Suburban Villas" but tiny worker cottages, mostly built by their owners, possibly squatters. The original residential buildings that remain today on the tract of the San Miguel subdivision occupy winding streets with modesty and pride. Small, single-story dwellings, separated by the thinnest ribbon of open space, and sometimes ornamented with the Italianate cornices fashionable in the 1870s and 1880s, they stand witness to an egalitarian process of land-taking, at least relative to the cost of real estate in Llewellyn Park or Riverside, or contemporary San Francisco. The modest homes of Twin Peaks also testify to the exercise of local sovereignty. The street that crowns the neighborhood does not bear the name of President Lincoln, as first advertised, but of Peter Burnett of San Francisco, who convened the California Constitutional Convention from the old Mexican plaza, and who featured prominently in the litigation over the pueblo lands. The name of a local politician on a picturesque street of San Francisco is a fitting emblem of vernacular urban design. Producing space in San Francisco, including Golden Gate Park and the San Miguel subdivision, was not just a matter of adapting architectural plans from back East. It was the accomplishment of local people, working in tandem, in association with their municipal government and within the limits of their natural habitat.

The San Miguel subdivision was named after the ranch of José Jesús Noé. An overactive historical imagination can see in the map of the subdivision a

—

Taking land and making space continues at the
site of Rancho San Miguel. Author's photo.

reflection of the curving lines of a *diseño* and an echo of the paths that the Ohlone took along Mission Creek and out to the bay hundreds of years ago. (Some local residents maintain that what is now called Corbett Street was once an Indian trail.) The neighborhoods of Bernal Heights and the Twin Peaks, like the row houses that continue to line the streets of Baltimore, are tokens of the crisscrossing regional and cultural variety that survived the unification of the East and the West under one federal government during the 1860s. Whereas the subdivision of San Miguel anticipated the curvaceous roadways of modern suburbs, Baltimore towed the line of the grid, connecting the park to the city by way of a straight street lined with trees.

Baltimore's row houses and centering public squares have proven as durable as San Francisco's subdivisions, serving as blueprints for a "new urbanism." As the California way of shaping the city relieves the obsessive linearity of the grid, Baltimore's denser spaces tame the extravagance of sprawl. Although the cities of Baltimore and San Francisco are linked together under one nation, and resemble each other as political economies, each retains its unique spatial features. These two different urban landscapes are recollections of a long history, the heritage of Spain and of England, grafted onto the lands long tended by the Ohlone and the Powhatans. Each stands witness to the vernacular art of making a city and continues to set the daily rhythms of how people live, work, play, and struggle onward together.

———

EPILOGUE

T hose who sailed up the Chesapeake to the mouth of the Patapsco River or navigated the narrow entryway to San Francisco Bay in the 1860s would find modern cities gripping the shoreline. Men and women had occupied the bays for millennia and had made a succession of stunning alterations of their environment. They had also executed the kinds of massive changes that historians divide into great segments of time, such as the Paleolithic, Neolithic, feudal, and capitalist eras. The peoples who tended the land around the Chesapeake and San Francisco Bays were the architects of both these epochal historical spaces and an array of more intimate and material places, all the local sites of everyday life, personal affiliation, generational bonds, and historical memory. Those who lived and labored around the great bays created an abundance of distinctive places: shell mounds, cornfields, streets, squares, plazas, parks, neighborhoods, and homes.

It took countless hands and minds, working together over many generations, to fashion this plentitude of spaces and places. The first and most arduous spatial production was the work of the Paleo-Indians who made the

---

shores of the receding glaciers into a human habitat. Their remote progeny converted the littoral environment into complex economies: the Ohlone's expert hunting and gathering, and the agricultural villages of the Powhatans and the Piscataway. When seafarers entered the estuaries, after crossing the Atlantic or sailing up along the Pacific coast, they brought with them something more than guns and horses. Both the English and the Spanish came to the New World with plans to leave their imperial marks around the bays. The Spanish Empire brought elaborate designs for presidios, missions, pueblos, and multiple categories of public land. The English came with the tools of surveyors designed to carve the land into parcels of private property. They adapted the town charters and market regulations of England to the exigencies of organizing an economy along the western shore of the Atlantic. The settlers of the Chesapeake port and the *pobladores* of San Francisco Bay refashioned those European precedents into the incorporated town of Baltimore and a semblance of a pueblo near Yerba Buena Cove.

Those who founded Baltimore Town and the pueblo of Yerba Buena contributed to the distinctive aura and character of the bay cities. The "land hunters" who plotted patents at an inlet of the Patapsco River sited an international port along a wide, curving waterway, and converted the Basin into the harbor that still anchors B'more's civic identity. The early inhabitants graced the landscape with local whimsy as well as civic pride. They marked off the spaces and places of Baltimore in a fine hand, platting small lots along narrow streets that marched up toward the fall line and thus molding an urban geography that was neither as monotonous as a classic grid nor as curvaceous as either a medieval town or a modern suburb. The Californios occupied the land around San Francisco Bay in a more casual and open manner. They scattered to their ranchlands and reassembled around a series of ramshackle plazas, giving shape to a free-form rendition of Spanish urban plans and the directives from Mexico City.

The vernacular place-making of Baltimore and San Francisco created something more than a built environment: it nurtured a resilient sense of place. The distinctive street grid of Baltimore was etched deep into the local consciousness. Lined with row houses and marble stoops, it served as a place of everyday sociability and a fervid loyalty to neighborhood, a quotidian reminder that the citizens of the city by the bay were all in the same municipal boat. Seeing the statue of George Washington bobbing into view as one drives down the Jones Falls Expressway, or looking up at the Battle Monument on the way into the courthouse for jury duty, Baltimoreans are

---

reminded of their distinguished history.[1] The streets of San Francisco also inspire epiphanies of local allegiance. When an obstinate city engineer plotted a street grid up the steep hillsides, he left generations to make the laborious ascent and then exhale with civic pride while taking in the breathtaking view below.[2] The mestizo legacy of San Francisco would never be erased. Spanish-speaking immigrants reclaimed their place in California over the course of the twentieth century and are expected to become the largest single ethnicity in the state. The result can be seen in the "Mission District," the harbor for immigrants from Europe in the late nineteenth century and still a resilient and diverse ethnic neighborhood. Its streets, still bearing the names of Noe, Guerrero, and Vallejo, have been revivified by immigrants from Central America. Moreover, the municipality of San Francisco continues to assert its sovereignty, refusing, for example, to conform to the deportation policies of the federal government.[3]

The mundane actions of settlers, citizens, civic leaders, and democratically elected officials multiplied over many generations so as to create these two unique urban spaces. Baltimore and San Francisco were but two points in a network of cities around which two North American republics would be built. As Tamar Herzog demonstrated in tracing the fluid borders between Spain and Portugal in the Old World, and the complex process of taking possession of the land in the New, the actions of local settlers and municipal bodies could be at least as influential as diplomats and treaties. Similarly, tracking history through ordinary places, such as the cities built upon the shores of the San Francisco and Chesapeake Bays two hundred years ago, led to a close encounter with major events in national and world history. Baltimore and San Francisco framed a continent, embracing a Latin American as well as an Anglophone past, and therefore tell a two-pronged history of the hemisphere and the world. The Spanish Empire had a head start across the Atlantic and around the world. Its silver mines in South and Central America provided the capital that first linked the Eastern and Western Hemispheres in one continuous commercial market. As late as 1848, Mexico had nominal possession of most of the trans-Mississippi West, cutting the eastern United States off from the Pacific and its vast mineral wealth.[4]

The history of North America cannot be bluntly segregated into two alien nations. As one historian put it, the United States and the Republic of Mexico were the work of "peoples emerging from long interactions" who had "shared legacies and integrated histories."[5] Both republics came into being amid the ideological and historical changes that gripped the Old World in

---

the eighteenth century. At about the same time that Britain's colonies on the North Atlantic were declaring independence, the *visitador generál* of New Spain sent a waft of Bourbon reforms into Latin America and up the Pacific highway to California, advancing liberalism on the western coast of the hemisphere. The federal constitution drafted in Philadelphia in 1789 served as a model for that of Mexico in 1824. The collision of these two histories during the Mexican-American War of 1846–1848 created a whiplash that would fracture both republics. The amputation of its northern territory commenced decades of instability in the Mexican Republic, replete with popular insurrections, provincial rivalries, a French invasion, and a brutal civil war to install a centralized nation-state.

Events in the Republic of Mexico had a parallel impact in the United States. The Mexican Republic differed from the United States in one critical feature: it outlawed slavery in 1829. As recounted in Chapter 8, the prohibition of slavery in the territory ceded from Mexico in 1848 delivered something like a Trojan horse to the slave states of the American South. When the Constitutional Convention of the State of California outlawed slavery in 1850, it disrupted the balance between the slave and free states and sped the nation toward civil war. This unraveling of the national fabric can be traced not just to events in the territory ceded from Mexico but also to that quintessentially Californian urban space, the Plaza of San Francisco, where the Forty-Niners preempted the US Congress by calling the state convention that undermined the national compromise with slavery. To watch history unfold along the two estuaries is to stray from the straight and narrow path of national history, either American or Mexican, and to acknowledge a history that encompasses both.

This bifocal vantage point takes in the multiplicity of people and places that shaped two nations and challenges the presumption of a singular and decisive site of state authority. It recognizes that political power is dispersed along shifting borders, distributed between and within federated states, and practiced vigorously at the level of the municipality as well as the sub-national state. Viewed from such out-of-the-way places as the Plaza of San Francisco or Baltimore's Monument Square, history swerves off from another teleological channel, the ever-advancing juggernaut of capitalism. History looks more complicated and drastically foreshortened when examined from the perspective of the bays of San Francisco and the Chesapeake. Our species lived on the shores of the great estuaries for a score of millennia without taking the land or marking it off as private property. As late as three hundred years ago, the monarchs of Europe, the proprietors of Maryland, and the *pobladores* of Alta California were still imposing substantial limits on the taking of land in North America. Even as international commerce in agricultural commodities flourished at the ports along the estuaries, the municipality of Baltimore restricted free trade, regulated prices, and initiated major public improvements, while the Mexican pueblo reserved land for common pasture and multiple public uses. It was not until the third decade of the nineteenth century that capital in its quintessential form—the credit, debt, stocks, bonds, mortgages, and municipal deficits dispersed by banks and corporations—overwhelmed the public economy and made private enterprise the leading edge of economic growth.

Early in the nineteenth century, before private capital became hegemonic, the merchants who docked on the two estuaries built cities in collaboration with municipal governments. The pace of political and economic change accelerated in the port towns of the Mid-Atlantic. The founders of Baltimore adapted the English traditions of corporate charters and market regulations to build a municipality that became strong enough to fight off the British Empire in 1776, and again in 1814. On the Pacific side at the turn of the eighteenth century, Mexico reissued Spanish guidelines for urban development in North America and thereby multiplied the municipalities of Alta California, among them a pueblo and an *ayuntamiento* on the shores of San Francisco Bay. The town and cities, the pueblos and *diputacións*, became centers of political innovation. Constructing urban spaces on relatively open land required immense political effort and ingenuity. Accordingly, the town of Baltimore and the pueblo of San Francisco played outsized roles in crafting the proudest ideological construction of the New World, representative democracy. When Baltimore expelled the British in the War of 1812, and when, a decade later, the *pobladores* of San Francisco deposed both the Franciscan missionaries and the Spanish Crown, the cities pushed political change onward, beyond republican constraints and toward a more broadly representative democracy, on the two sides of the continent.

The Chesapeake city, in particular, was a strategic launching site for democracy in America. Born without a colonial history, and the first city incorporated in the immediate aftermath of the War of Independence, Baltimore quickly instituted republican institutions. It secured a city charter that featured annual elections, robust participation in the municipal legislature, and close, ward-level bonds between the citizens and their representatives. The heterogeneous population of the Chesapeake city practiced self-government

———

with boisterous protests and ardent support for the Jeffersonian and Jacksonian parties. Baltimoreans found the space in which to exercise democracy just down the street, where they mobilized neighbors to repair the pavement, and at the offices of the mayor and the city council, where they presented their grievances, sent a voluminous stream of petitions, and proposed all manner of civic projects. They regularly gathered in Monument Square for protest meetings and party rallies.

These urban political spaces also helped to advance capitalism across the continent. The coordinated actions that made Baltimore the fastest-growing city in the new nation were conducted in the offices of the city council, the mayor, and the street commissioners. Initially dominated by the merchant elite and a few professionals, but soon joined by a significant number of artisans, tradesmen, and small-time manufacturers, the municipal government summoned the capital for projects of internal improvement that were deemed essential for the city to prosper, everything from dredging the harbor to bankrolling the Baltimore and Ohio Railroad. Providing for economic prosperity as well as the general good was part of the genetic inheritance of Baltimore. Not even the impending Civil War distracted the electorate and city officials from investing in public welfare and economic growth. By popular vote, they taxed themselves to build a public water system, begrudgingly paid off the debts incurred by the railroad and canal companies, and made ingenious investments in urban transportation and parkland.

The symbiotic but strained relationship between democracy and capitalism was forged under unique historical conditions. The citizens of Baltimore could see and share in the benefits of public investment. Special assessments improved the streets; voluntary subscriptions graced the skylines with monuments; taxes kept the harbor in top-notch shape and bustling with commerce. Thanks to things like ground rent and modest row houses, a relatively large portion of the population had a material and spatial stake in the urban commonweal. The advances of this modern economy were propelled not just by the production of commodities like cotton or steel but also by the marketing of land in the form of small lots and modest row houses. In antebellum Baltimore, democracy was grounded in private property, the ownership of all those modest homes lined up on a tight web of streets. Small-scale local capitalism undergirded democracy, and democracy fostered local economic growth.

The interdependence of property and democracy was a fragile marriage of convenience and subject to at least two major strains. First, property owners could be jealous about their investments and insistent that they

---

362

benefit directly and personally from paying taxes. When investments in the city, whether special assessments or direct taxation, did not deliver palpable benefits, individual taxpayers could become stingy, and politicians began to preach retrenchment. Given the regular disruptions of the business cycle, calls for tax cuts became endemic to the modern capitalist city. Second, especially over the longer term, the close entanglement between democracy and capitalism could be a recipe for growing inequality. The economic divisions and social distances between citizens became wider as the scale of capital increased, as market regulation gave way to laissez-faire economics, and as the public and the private sectors grew further apart. Accidents of birth, the caprice of personal luck, the subordination of wage labor, and the fissures of racial, ethnic, and gender inequity all built economic conflict into the modern capitalist city. On occasion, conflict veered off into violence, including the expressly capitalist example of Baltimore's Bank Riot of 1835. But, buoyed up by its civic traditions, the Monumental City kept this internecine conflict within manageable boundaries even as the Civil War raged just outside the city limits.

The settlers of San Francisco did not organize their polity as cohesively as the citizens of Baltimore did theirs. Dispersed to their ranches or divided between the two separate pueblos, Yerba Buena and Dolores, the Californios did not develop the sustained habits of collaboration and the political skills that came with sharing city streets and the city council chambers. Consequently, San Francisco was ill prepared to meet the dual invasions from the East in the 1840s, first the Mexican-American War and then the Gold Rush. A tidal wave of unregulated capitalism hit the shores of San Francisco Bay and pressed the *pobladores* to make the transition to modernity in a fraction of the time it took the people of Baltimore. The happenstance of time conspired with the irregularities of space to deposit an especially virulent form of real estate capitalism in San Francisco. The Californios watched from the sidelines while makeshift governments of Forty-Niners, vigilantes, and Tax Payers' Unions conducted a fire sale of public land. Real estate, the most robust sector of the urban economy, enrolled countless small investors and homeowners in the ranks of bickering capitalists. The contrast between the political economies of Baltimore and San Francisco is emblematic of the erratic course of history through time and place. San Francisco was a congenial habitat for advancing capitalism, but less hospitable to the responsible practice of municipal sovereignty.

Land-taking reached an apotheosis in the "instant city" of San Francisco.

It was not a simple case of private enterprise, however; rather, it was the work of mayors, and the elected members of successive municipal legislatures—the *ayuntamientos* and Legislative Assembly, the Town Council, the San Francisco Common Council, and finally the Board of Supervisors of the City and County of San Francisco. In the short term, the machinations of San Francisco's public realtors had an unexpected democratizing effect. After ousting the Mexicans and selling off the public domain for municipal revenue, the politicians of San Francisco threw up their hands and enacted ordinances that conveyed thousands of lots to "squatters." The result of the reluctant municipal giveaway won the approval of Henry George, a newcomer to San Francisco who was soon to become a renowned land reformer. Speaking of San Francisco in 1869, George said, "There is probably a larger proportion owning homesteads and homestead lots than in any other city of the United States. The product of the rise of real estate will thus be more evenly distributed, and the social and political advantages of this diffused proprietorship cannot be overestimated." When Henry George cited the "homesteads and homestead lots" of San Francisco as the foundation of economic equality, he might have been recalling the municipal largesse that granted plots to squatters in the Western Addition and the Outside Lands, or the worker cottages that were beginning to rise up the hillsides where the Noés and the Bernals once ranched.[6]

George was right to acknowledge that "diffuse proprietorship cannot be overestimated." Nor should it be taken for granted. Even as Henry George wrote his first essay on land reform in 1869, he was losing hope that moderate measures, such as a more generous Homestead Act, would preserve democracy and equality in America. Writing from San Francisco after the Civil War, George also regretted that the pueblo lands had not been distributed "free or almost free to actual settlers . . . instead of being allowed to pass into the hands of a few, to make more millionaires." Absent some intervening political action, he foresaw the land rights of Californians in jeopardy: "All over the state the surveyors, speculators and railroads were busy grabbing up the public domain by the hundreds of thousands of acres." A decade later, George would publish *Poverty and Progress*, the best-selling nonfiction book of the nineteenth century, and a direct challenge to the American faith in unfettered private property. George proposed that governments impose a tax on land substantial enough to make speculation unprofitable and thereby break up large holdings and redistribute this most fundamental natural resource more equitably. Although political economists of George's generation, and the populists and progressives that followed him, raised a direct challenge to laissez-faire land policies, their proposals to rely on tax policy to modify the unequal distribution of landed property did not portend a reversal in the course of real estate capitalism. During and after the Civil War, more power accrued to corporations whose reach spanned the continent. The bounty of lots that the municipality of San Francisco awarded to the squatters paled beside the millions of acres the federal government granted to the railroad corporations.[7]

The cities survived the Civil War and continued upon the path of "improvement," seldom questioning the imperative of capitalist growth. Land speculation continued around the great bays, much of it focused on the territory beyond the bounds of city sovereignty—those places called the "Outside Lands" in San Francisco. Settlement outside the city limits tended to be amorphous, in a hodgepodge of small municipalities and unincorporated suburban clusters that were detached from the urban core. The more affluent population of Baltimore moved far from Monument Square, auguring a time when suburbs would displace cities as the leading sector of demographic growth. The boundary of settlement on the San Francisco Peninsula kept creeping southward until it reached the border of another pueblo, San Jose.

At the end of the twentieth century, a new kind of space and a postmodern economy took shape at the southern terminus of San Francisco Bay. It acquired a placeless name with no apparent political nucleus or boundary: the Silicon Valley. The technology companies and venture capitalists agglomerating along the freeways of the South Bay augured another spatial revolution, one that seemed to transcend local and material places and blanket the world in a fog of digital images and electronic communication. The new economy has boomeranged up the peninsula to the City of San Francisco, where the high cost of housing mocks Henry George's memory of egalitarian homesteads. We may be on the precipice of another epochal change in the social and political construction of space. If so, we might be at risk of losing the political energy, relative economic equality, and urban pleasure that once thrived in the streets, squares, plazas, neighborhoods, and vigorous municipal institutions of cities like Baltimore and San Francisco.[8]

UNITED CITIES AND DIVIDED PEOPLES

The sovereignty of the cities was challenged in the 1860s. Wartime soldered together the union of states, expanded the reach of the federal government, and solidified national sovereignty. Emboldened by the Union victory, the Radical Republicans in Congress took decisive action to remove the most egregious exception to the promise that "all men are created equal" by amending the Constitution to abolish slavery and confer the full rights of citizenship to people of all races, colors, and creeds. The Thirteenth, Fourteenth, and Fifteenth Amendments repaired the most glaring contradictions of democracy in America. While racial minorities continued the battle to secure their civil rights, only a few belittled champions of women's rights objected to the fact that approximately half the population, whatever their race, creed, or previous condition of servitude, were still denied full citizenship. The Fourteenth Amendment granted the privileges and immunities of US citizenship to "male inhabitants," and the Fifteenth granted the right to vote exclusively to men. That major roadblock in the path of freedom accounts for the minor, usually offstage, roles that women have played in this account of city-building. A contingent of women who were recognized in the records of the mayor and city council in 1859, for example, addressed the mayor and council in the language not of civil rights, but of political subordination and domestic responsibility: "We the undersigned Ladies of Old Town, think that we should have the privilege of expressing our opinion in regard to the hour of holding the Bell Air market, as it devolves upon us, in a great measure to attend the said market for the purpose of purchasing marketing for our families." Those few women who harbored more entrepreneurial ambitions sometimes wandered off the path of "true womanhood" by accumulating their capital as the proprietors of Baltimore's bawdy houses or the madams of Gold Rush San Francisco.[9]

For all their essential labors—gathering subsistence, tending cornfields, sustaining families, and caring for the poor in their communities—women rarely controlled property, and never cast votes or held municipal office. They were denied the most basic political tools necessary for taking land and shaping cities. They were only beginning, with much effort, to leave a public impression on the urban landscape. At the same time, wives and mothers maintained the bedrock of real estate capitalism by tending the single-family residences that lined the streets of Baltimore and rose up the hills of San Francisco. Although gender historians, including this one, have uncovered masses of evidence that women commanded authority in churches, in voluntary associations, and in the domestic sphere, it would take several generations, and Herculean effort, for them to win a place, much less parity, in the sovereign spaces of North American government.[10]

In some ways, the marks of gender difference and racial inequality stood out even more starkly upon the urban landscape in the decades after the Civil War, when they were cemented by blunter lines of residential segregation. African Americans of either sex and along both sides of the continent would struggle for another century and more to convert the promises of radical reconstruction into actual equality. In the West, racial inequality took on new dimensions. Once the borders of the United States were extended from the Atlantic to the Pacific, race in America became more multifaceted than the dualism of black and white. The Mexicans who settled Alta California late in the eighteenth century were mestizos who readily formed marital alliances with the Europeans who ventured into San Francisco Bay after 1820. As a result, an extraordinary mix and mingling of ethnicities gathered in the village of Dolores and the Port of Yerba Buena, where all but the indigenous peoples were accounted citizens of Alta California. The ferocious real estate capitalism of the Civil War era would, however, soon displace the mestizo settlers of Dolores, Yerba Buena, and the ranches from their land, and reduce those of Mexican descent to a subordinated minority.

Meanwhile, another wave of immigration streamed into San Francisco Bay from the Pacific. Thousands of Chinese joined the rush to "gold mountain" in the 1850s. The First Transcontinental Railroad, completed in 1869, brought thousands more immigrants from China to the United States, where they performed the dangerous work of laying rails and digging tunnels through the mountains of the West. Soon thereafter, white working men of San Francisco, many of them immigrants, would take the lead in pressuring the Congress of the United States to bar the Chinese from citizenship.

More than a century later, the democracy of the streets, squares, and plazas is sometimes hard to locate within that sprawling landscape of private property and in the growing gulf between the rich and the poor. It is especially distressing to see the monuments of Baltimore become the backdrop to a decaying industrial city, where racial inequality first degenerated into Jim Crow and then metastasized into the police violence that provoked the desperate and chilling assertion that "Black Lives Matter." Today, the broken promise of equality is written on the streets of San Francisco by the encampments of homeless men, women, and children lined up along the streets and huddled under the concrete shelters of the freeways.

The people of San Francisco and Baltimore could never have predicted such developments as the Civil War came to an end. During the presidential campaign of 1864, Monument Square was festooned with a huge banner reading "Lincoln and Johnson—a free Union—a Free Constitution and Free Labor." Those citizens who had maintained loyalty to the North, and were therefore entitled to vote, carried the city for Lincoln. The "Recent Union Victories" warranted a citywide celebration on April 7, 1865. According to the *Baltimore Sun*, "The national flag was displayed at all prominent points as well as from innumerable private residences during the day, giving the principal thoroughfares, as well as many of the more retired[,] a gay and lively aspect." At 8:00 p.m., a "merry peel" of church bells, along with salutes fired from Fort McHenry and the Washington Monument, signaled the illumination of stores, homes, and streets across the city. Candles, Chinese lanterns, and fireworks flickered over the skyline. The brightest light radiated from the stately new depot that had been built by the Baltimore and Ohio Railroad. The windows and cupola of Camden Station were set ablaze by the blinding power of locomotive headlights.[11]

The power of the railroad to light the streets of Baltimore reflected the ties that bound the city and the nation together at the close of the Civil War. By 1865, Maryland and Baltimore were securely realigned with the Union and bound to northern capital. They had been drawn into the wide orbit of a national industrial economy that was now leaning decisively toward the West. The exigencies of war and the policies of the Lincoln administration had dramatically shortened the distance between Baltimore and San Francisco: the iron grip of the First Transcontinental Railroad would link East to West in one powerful national economy; the Morrill Acts funded the land-grant universities that would spread higher learning across the nation; and the Homestead Act promised a portion of the public domain to those who settled the West. Hence, the applause that greeted the reunification of the nation in Baltimore reverberated across the continent, echoing as far as San Francisco.

The afterglow of the Union victory and the impact of Republican policies also forecast another kind of national unity, that "rebirth of freedom" that Lincoln prayed would bring former slaves and persons of color under the protection of the US Constitution. Baltimore's free colored men and women had not waited until war's end (or until the Maryland Constitutional Convention of 1864 had emancipated the slaves who remained in the city and state at that time) to claim their rights as citizens. Well before the Civil War commenced, they exerted their political influence at national conventions of free men and women and met to claim their civil rights at scores of local churches and public places, such as one they named Liberty

———

Hall near downtown Baltimore. When war broke out, ten thousand black men from Maryland marched off into the Union Army. In the 1860s, the African Americans of Baltimore created their own public forum not far from the city center and named it after their own municipal hero, calling it the Douglass Institute. From this urban public base, Baltimoreans of color took their cause into the streets. Widows of Union soldiers claimed seats on the new street railways, becoming the vanguard of desegregation in advance of the Civil Rights Act of 1866 and the Fourteenth Amendment. Baltimore's African Americans stepped into the municipal public sphere in the moment of celebration, and soon thereafter, of national mourning. They joined the civic procession that lined up behind Lincoln's funeral cortege, albeit at the back of the line of march.[12]

The Union victory in the Civil War carried promises of freedom into the streets and across a continent. Off in San Francisco, African Americans made January 1 their own holiday in celebration of the Emancipation Proclamation. In 1866, the orator of the day exclaimed: "Our country is truly free. . . . [W]e can join in the ever onward march of progress." And march they did. Taking off from the African Methodist Episcopal Church at Powell and Market Streets, the African American citizens of San Francisco proceeded "to Broadway, to Dupont St., down Clay, through Sansome to Market, cross to Second, to Folsom, to Fourth, down Mission to Third, cross Market, up Montgomery to Washington and Stockton to the Church." The Pacific Brass Band provided musical accompaniment while the marching men held aloft a banner; it had an image of Lincoln on one side and the text of the Emancipation Proclamation on the other. From this auspicious moment onward, the march of racial progress would proceed forward at a jolting and painfully slow pace toward a still elusive goal of full equality.[13]

And yet the immediate aftermath of the Civil War was a time for celebrating the prospects for liberty and equality in the cities of the West and the East. It is therefore fitting to close with a celebration of equal rights in urban space. The occasion was the passage of the Fifteenth Amendment in Baltimore on May 19, 1870. The procession set out from beneath the Washington Monument in Mount Vernon, passing along the marble mansions of Baltimore's most affluent and honored citizens. Their front porches served as viewing stands for the parade. A souvenir lithograph colored the complexions of the audience in both black and white. The fashionable ladies posing on the front lawns included daughters of Africa. A dark-skinned boy was pictured scaling the ionic column of a mansion in order to wave the Stars

---

and Stripes. Portraits of antislavery heroes, John Brown as well as Frederick Douglass, framed the scene. At the center of the celebration was a contingent of African American Civil War veterans taking to the streets of Baltimore in full regalia before an audience estimated at ten thousand. Their destination was Monument Square. The featured speaker of the day was Frederick Douglass himself; his podium was the base of the Battle Monument. The young slave who had tasted the first elixir of freedom on the pavements of Fells Point had trodden a long and difficult road toward the still distant goal of freedom and equality for all. That journey continues to find momentum in city streets and summons power from public places like Monument Square in Baltimore.

The Result of the Fifteenth Amendment, *published by Metcalf & Clark.*
Hambleton Print Collection. Courtesy of the Maryland Historical Society.

Unknown photographer, Baltimore's African Americans Celebrate the
Fifteenth Amendment Establishing the Right of Suffrage, *1870. Courtesy*
of the Maryland Historical Society.

ACKNOWLEDGMENTS

The covers of this book enclose something more than the results of a research project. They capture the preoccupations of a long career as a teacher and a historian. As a consequence, *Taking the Land to Make the City* is the work of teams of faculty and students who came together within two academic institutions, the University of California at Berkeley and the Johns Hopkins University. It is also a record of a time when I turned my attention to the study of urban history, and to the material landscape of American cities, in particular. My first acknowledgment, therefore, must go to these two universities and to the two places where they are located, San Francisco, California, and Baltimore, Maryland. Shuffling back and forth between these two homes for nearly twenty years has been my intellectual sustenance, my source of political engagement, and my personal pleasure.

I first embarked on the path toward this publication when I journeyed across the Berkeley campus to the School of Environmental Design, where the architectural historians Paul Groth and Dell Upton taught me how to discover the past in the contemporary landscape. Teaching seminars with

——

Paul and Dell, and the wonderful graduate students they brought to Berkeley, was an interdisciplinary feast. So educated, I began to teach the history of San Francisco with the support of the Richard and Rhoda Goldman Fund and with the sponsorship of the History Department and the Program in American Studies. The inventive American Studies curriculum at Berkeley was crafted under the guidance of its wizard director Kathleen Moran, who is also a mainstay of the reading group that suffered through several messy drafts of these chapters. I owe many thanks to these friends, including Paul Groth, Richard Hutson, Margaretta Lovell, Don McQuade, Louise Mozingo, and Chris Rosen; I gamely strove to absorb their multidisciplinary advice, and their kindly criticism has made this a better book.

Over a decade ago, the trail of my intellectual debts turned east to Baltimore and Johns Hopkins. This book benefited immeasurably from the famed seminars of the Hopkins History Department, and especially the opportunity to co-teach with my colleagues Toby Dietz, Judith Walkowitz, and Nathan Connolly. I am indebted to Toby, Judy, and Nathan not just for their critical acumen as historians, but also for their examples as graduate teachers in the fields of gender, race, and urban history. The exemplary practice of graduate education at Hopkins spun off lively seminars that were given affectionate nicknames by the students, such as "the geminar" and "the charm school of Baltimore History." To the members of the latter group I owe many hours of practical research assistance as well as troves of insights, ideas, and evidence that found a place in the chapters on Baltimore. My deep gratitude goes to the "charmers": Robert Gamble, Paige Glotzer, Katie Hemphill, David Schley, and Mo Speller. Rob deserves a special merit badge for heroically saving me from drowning in the details of producing the final manuscript. On the Berkeley side, Sophie Fitzmaurice and Erika Lee provided critical research assistance; I am also grateful for the forbearance Sophie showed toward my clerical foibles.

Taking the Land to Make the City was also fashioned from the collections of the Bancroft Library, Berkeley, and the Baltimore City Archives, the California Historical Society, the Maryland Historical Society, the Maryland State Archives, the Berkeley Earth Science Map Library, the San Francisco Public Library, and the Sheridan Libraries of Johns Hopkins—including the Eisenhower, Special Collections, the Peabody, and the Garrett. Therefore this book rests on the shoulders of many archivists and librarians. Among the countless able staff members of these institutions, I am especially indebted to James Gillispie for guiding me through the maps from the JScholarship digital repository at the Sheridan Library, Johns Hopkins; to Ed Papenfuse, Maryland State Archivist and savior of Baltimore's municipal records; to Rob Schoeberheim, the caretaker of the treasures of the Baltimore City Archives; to Theresa Salazar, the ever helpful and deeply knowledgeable curator of Western Americana at the Bancroft; and to José Adrián Barragán-Álvarez, curator of Latin Americana at the Bancroft Library. The David Rumsey Historical Map Collection at Stanford deserves profuse thanks for making its collection available to the public.

When, with all of this help, I finally managed to create a manuscript, a number of colleagues took the time to read through the draft and offered expert criticism and suggestions for revision. They included Karen Caplan, Mathew Crenson, Marta Gutman, David Henkin, David Igler, Alan Lessoff, and an anonymous reviewer for the University of Texas Press. Along with my appreciation I absolve everyone from responsibility for the errors and limitations that remain, which are solely mine.

Bringing this project to fruition as a printed volume was made both possible and pleasurable by the University of Texas Press. Special thanks go to Sarah McGavick, who cheerfully and expertly transformed my bundle of images into a gallery of illustrations, and to Katherine Streckfus for heroic copyediting. Robert Devens is the dream editor, acutely smart about writing history, savvy about how to produce a book, and stalwart in support of the author.

Lastly, on the family front, thanks go to Anne Busacca-Ryan for adding her knowledge of the law to the pleasures of her company, especially in excursions up and down the western side of the continent from Nicaragua to Mexico City to Los Angeles and along both shores of San Francisco Bay. This book is dedicated to Robert Roper, in gratitude for the inspiration of his prose, the reinvigoration of our outdoor adventures, and the routine joys that sustained me over the years it took to make this book.

NOTES

INTRODUCTION

1. Benjamin Wingate, Correspondence with His Family, 1850–1854, BANC Film 2083, May 1, 1853, Online Archive of California, University of California, Berkeley, July 15, 1852, July 1, 1851.
2. Ibid., March 15, 1854.
3. Ibid., July 1, 1851.
4. Henri Lefebvre, *The Social Production of Space*, trans. Donald Nicholson-Smith (Malden, MA: Blackwell, 1992); David Harvey, "Between Space and Time: Reflections on the Geographical Imagination, *Annals of the Association of American Geographers* 80, no. 3 (September 1990): 418–434; Edward S. Casey, "How to Get from Space to Place in a Fairly Short Stretch of Time," in *Senses of Place*, eds. Steven Feld and Keith H. Basso (Santa Fe, NM: School of American Research Press, 1996); Simon Gunn, "The Spatial Turn: Changing Histories of Space and Place," in *Identities in Space: Contested Terrains in the Western City Since 1850*, eds. Simon Gunn and Robert J. Morris (Burlington, VT: Ashgate, 2001), 1–14; Carol Shammas, "The Space Problem in Early United States Cities," *William and Mary Quarterly* 57, no. 3 (July 2000): 505–542; Richard White, "What Is Spatial History?" Spatial History Project, Stanford University, February 1, 2010, web.stanford.edu/group/spatialhistory/cgi-bin/site/pub.php?id=29 (last accessed June 6, 2017); Tamar Herzog, *Frontiers of Possession: Spain and Portugal in Europe and the Americas* (Cambridge, MA: Harvard University Press, 2015).
5. John Brinckerhoff Jackson, *Discovering the Vernacular Landscape* (New Haven, CT: Yale University Press, 1984), xii. See also Dell Upton, *Another City: Urban Life and Urban Spaces in the New American Republic* (New Haven, CT: Yale University Press, 2008); Dell Upton, *What Can and Can't Be Said: Race, Uplift, and Monument Building in the Contemporary South* (New Haven, CT: Yale University Press, 2015); Paul Groth, *Living Downtown: The History of*

Residential Hotels in the United States (Berkeley: University of California Press, 1999); Paul Groth and Todd W. Bressi, *Understanding Ordinary Landscapes* (New Haven, CT: Yale University Press, 1997); Marta Gutman, *A City for Children: Women, Architecture, and the Charitable Landscape of Oakland, 1850–1950* (Chicago: University of Chicago Press, 2014); Anne Vernez Moudon, *Built for Change: Neighborhood Architecture in San Francisco* (Cambridge, MA: MIT Press, 1986); Hilary Ballon, *Paris of Henry IV: Architecture and Urbanism* (Cambridge, MA: MIT Press, 1994); Hilary Ballon and Kenneth T. Jackson, eds., *Robert Moses and the Modern City: The Transformation of New York* (New York: W. W. Norton, 2008); Jane Jacobs, *The Death and Life of Great American Cities* (New York: Vintage, 1992 [1961]).

6. Hendrick Hartog, *Public Property and Private Power: The Corporation of the City of New York in American Law, 1730–1870* (Ithaca, NY: Cornell University Press, 1983); Elizabeth Blackmar, *Manhattan for Rent, 1785–1850* (Ithaca, NY: Cornell University Press, 1989); Russell Shorto, *The Island at the Center of the World* (New York: Vintage, 2005); Ted Steinberg, *Gotham Unbound: The Ecological History of Greater New York* (New York: Simon and Schuster, 2014); Catherine McNeur, *Taming Manhattan: Environmental Battles in the Antebellum City* (Cambridge, MA: Harvard University Press, 2014); William Cronon, *Nature's Metropolis: Chicago and the Great West* (New York: Norton, 1991); Robin L. Einhorn, *Property Rules: Political Economy in Chicago, 1833–1872* (Chicago: University of Chicago Press, 1991); Carl Smith, *Urban Disorder and the Shape of Belief: The Great Chicago Fire, the Haymarket Bomb, and the Model Town of Pullman* (Chicago: University of Chicago Press, 1995); Carl Smith, *The Plan of Chicago: Daniel Burnham and the Remaking of the American City* (Chicago: University of Chicago Press, 2006); Carl Smith, *City Water, City Life: Water and the Infrastructure of Ideas in Urbanizing Philadelphia, Boston, and Chicago* (Chicago: University of Chicago Press, 2013); Robin F. Bachin, *Building the South Side: Urban Space and Civic Culture in Chicago, 1890–1919* (Chicago: University of Chicago Press, 2004); Davarian L. Baldwin, *Chicago's New Negroes: Modernity, the Great Migration, and Black Urban Life* (Chapel Hill: University of North Carolina Press, 2007); Shannon Lee Dawdy, *Building the Devil's Empire: French Colonial New Orleans* (Chicago: University of Chicago Press, 2008); Ari Kelman, *A River and Its City: The Nature of Landscape in New Orleans* (Berkeley: University of California Press, 2003); Eberhard L. Faber, *Building the Land of Dreams: New Orleans and the Transformation of Early America* (Princeton, NJ: Princeton University Press, 2015); Catherine Cangany, *Frontier Seaport: Detroit's Transformation into an Atlantic Entrepôt* (Chicago: University of Chicago Press, 2014); Jesús F. Teja, *San Antonio de Béxar: A Community on New Mexico's Northern Border*, (Albuquerque: University of New Mexico Press, 1995); Alan Lessoff, *Where Texas Meets the Seas: Corpus Christi and Its History* (Austin: University of Texas Press, 2015).

7. Sherry H. Olson, *Baltimore: The Building of an American City*, rev. ed.

(Baltimore: Johns Hopkins University Press, 1997); Matthew A. Crenson, *Baltimore: A Political History* (Baltimore: Johns Hopkins University Press, 2017); Garrett Power, *Chesapeake Bay in Legal Perspective* (Washington, DC: US Department of the Interior, 1970); Richard A. Walker, *The Conquest of Bread: 150 Years of Agribusiness in California* (New York: The New Press, 2004); Philip J. Dreyfus, *Our Better Nature: Environment and the Making of San Francisco* (Norman: University of Oklahoma Press, 2008); Robert Cherny and William Issel, *San Francisco: Presidio, Port, and Pacific Metropolis* (San Francisco: Boyd and Fraser, 1981); Roger W. Lotchin, *San Francisco, 1846–1856: From Hamlet to City* (Urbana: University of Illinois Press, 1997); Leonard L. Richards, *The California Gold Rush and the Coming of the Civil War* (New York: Vintage, 2007); Michael Rawson, *Eden on the Charles: The Making of Boston* (Cambridge, MA: Harvard University Press, 2010); David Hamer, *New Towns in the New World: Images and Perceptions of the Nineteenth Century Urban Frontier* (New York: Columbia University Press, 1990).

8. Neil Brenner and Roger Keil, eds., *The Global Cities Reader* (New York: Routledge, 2006).

9. Richardson Dilworth, ed., *The City in American Political Development* (New York: Routledge, 2009); Katherine M. Johnson, "'The Glorified Municipality': State Formation and the Urban Process in North America," *Political Geography* 27 (2008): 400–417; Gerald E. Frug, *City Making: Building Communities Without Building Walls* (Princeton, NJ: Princeton University Press, 1999); Helen Nader, "The Spain That Encountered Mexico," in *The Oxford History of Mexico*, eds. William H. Beezley and Michael C. Meyer (New York: Oxford University Press, 2010), 11–72.

10. Sven Becket and Seth Rockman, eds., *Slavery's Capitalism: A New History of American Economic Development* (Philadelphia: University of Pennsylvania Press, 2016).

11. Neil Brenner, *New State Spaces: Urban Governance and the Rescaling of Statehood* (New York: Oxford University Press, 2004); Jesús Escobar, *The Plaza Mayor and the Shaping of Baroque Madrid* (New York: Cambridge University Press, 2003); Jordana Dym, *From Sovereign Villages to National States: City, State, and Federation in Central America, 1759–1839* (Albuquerque: University of New Mexico Press, 2006); Tamar Herzog, *Defining Nations: Immigrants and Citizens in Early Modern Spain and Spanish America* (New Haven, CT: Yale University Press, 2003); Cynthia Radding, *Landscapes of Power and Identity: Comparative Histories in the Sonoran Desert and the Forests of Amazonia from Colony to Republic* (Durham, NC: Duke University Press, 2006); Michael Peter Smith, *City, State, and Market: The Political Economy of Urban Society* (Oxford: Basil Blackwell, 1988); Liam O'Dowd, "Contested States, Frontiers and Cities," in *A Companion to Border Studies*, eds. Thomas M. Wilson and Hastings Donnan (Malden, MA: Wiley-Blackwell, 2012), 158–176; Jaime E. Rodríguez O., *"We Are Now the True Spaniards": Sovereignty, Revolution, Independence, and the*

———

Emergence of the Federal Republic of Mexico, 1808–1824 (Stanford, CA: Stanford University Press, 2012); John Tutino, *The Mexican Heartland: How Communities Shaped Capitalism, a Nation, and World History, 1500–2000* (Princeton, NJ: Princeton University Press, 2017).

12. Fawwaz Traboulsi, "Public Spheres and Urban Space: A Critical Comparative Approach," *New Political Science* 27, no. 4 (December 2005): 529–541.

13. Martin Ridge, ed., *History, Frontier, and Section: Three Essays by Frederick Jackson Turner* (Albuquerque: University of New Mexico Press, 1993), 59–60; Alex Wagner Lough, "Henry George, Frederick Jackson Turner, and the 'Closing' of the American Frontier," *California History* 89, no. 2 (2012): 4–54; John Mack Faragher, ed., *Rereading Frederick Jackson Turner: 'The Significance of the Frontier in American History' and Other Essays* (New Haven, CT: Yale University Press, 1994); Stephen J. Hornsby, *British Atlantic, American Frontier: Spaces of Power in Early Modern British America* (Lebanon, NH: University Press of New England, 2005).

14. David Harvey, "Flexible Accumulation Through Urbanization: Reflections on 'Post Modernism' in the American City," *Perspecta* 26 (1990): 251–272.

PART I: TAKING THE LAND

1. J. B. Harley, *Maps and the Columbian Encounter: An Interpretive Guide* (Milwaukee: University of Wisconsin–Milwaukee Press, 1990); John Rennie Short, *Representing the Republic: Mapping the United States, 1600 to 1900* (London: Reaktion Books, 2001).

CHAPTER I: BEFORE THE LAND WAS TAKEN

1. Greg Castro, "The People Gather," *News from Native California* 25, no. 1 (2011): 40–43; Les W. Field, "Unacknowledged Tribes, Dangerous Knowledge: The Muwekma Ohlone and How Indian Identities Are 'Known,'" *Wicazo Sa Review* (Fall 2003): 79–91.

2. Randall Milliken, "The Costanoan-Yohuts Language Boundary in the Contact Period," in *The Ohlone Past and Present: Native Americans of the San Francisco Bay Region*, ed. Lowell J. Bean (Menlo Park, CA: Ballena Press, 1994), 181; Russell K. Skowronek, "Sifting the Evidence: Perceptions of Life at the Ohlone (Costanoan) Missions of Alta California," *Ethnohistory* 45, no. 4 (1998): 675–708; Edward M. Luby, Clayton D. Drescher, and Kent G. Lightfoot, "Shell Mound and Mounded Landscapes in the San Francisco Bay Area: An Integrated Approach," *Journal of Island and Coastal Archaeology* 1 (2006): 191–214.

3. James D. Rice, *Nature & History in the Potomac Country* (Baltimore: Johns Hopkins University Press, 2009); Malcolm Margolin, *The Ohlone Way: Indian Life in the San Francisco–Monterey Bay Area* (Berkeley, CA: Heyday Books, 1978).

4. Deborah R. Harden, *California Geology* (Upper Saddle River, NJ: Prentice Hall, 1998), 7, 18.
5. Kent G. Lightfoot, "Cultural Construction of Coastal Landscapes: A Middle Holocene Perspective from San Francisco Bay," in *The Archaeology of the California Coast During the Middle Holocene*, eds. Jon M. Erlandson and Michael A. Glassow (Los Angeles: Cotsen Institute of Archaeology, University of California, 1997), 129–141; James W. Bartolome, "Ecological History of the California Mediterranean-Type Landscape," in *Landscape Ecology: Study of Mediterranean Grazed Ecosystems, Man and the Biosphere*, ed. W. J. Clawson (Proceedings of Man and the Biosphere Symposium, 16th Annual Grasslands Conference, Nice, France, 1989), 1–15; Brian F. Atwater, Charles W. Hedel, and Edward J. Helley, "Late Quaternary Depositional History, Holocene Sea-Level Changes, and Vertical Crustal Movement, Southern San Francisco Bay, California" (US Geological Survey, Professional Paper 1014, 1977); W. Jacquelyne Kious and Robert I. Tilling, *The Dynamic Earth: The Story of Plate Tectonics* (US Geological Survey, 1996), fn. 12.
6. Helen C. Rountree, Wayne E. Clark, and Kent Mountford, eds., *John Smith's Chesapeake Voyages, 1607–1609* (Charlottesville: University of Virginia Press, 2007).
7. Martin F. Schmidt Jr., *Maryland's Geology* (Centreville, MD: Tidewater Publishers, 1993), 111, 140.
8. Henry M. Miller, "Living Along the 'Great Shellfish Bay': The Relationship Between Prehistoric Peoples and the Chesapeake," in *Discovering the Chesapeake: The History of an Ecosystem*, eds. Philip D. Curtin, Grace S. Brush, and George W. Fisher (Baltimore: Johns Hopkins University Press, 2001), 109–126; Bartolome, "Ecological History of the California Mediterranean-Type Landscape"; Terry L. Jones and Kathryn A. Klar, eds., *California Prehistory: Colonization, Culture and Complexity* (Lanham, MD: AltaMira Press, 2007).
9. Kent G. Lightfoot and Otis Parrish, *California Indians and Their Environment: An Introduction* (Berkeley: University of California Press, 2009); Frank W. Porter, *Maryland Indians, Yesterday and Today* (Baltimore: Maryland Historical Society, 1983).
10. Miller, "Living Along the 'Great Shellfish Bay'"; Porter, *Maryland Indians*; Lightfoot and Parrish, *California Indians and Their Environment*, 10; Jones and Klar, *California Prehistory*, 35–47.
11. Jeanne E. Arnold, Michael R. Walsh, and Sandra E. Hollimon, "The Archaeology of California," *Journal of Archaeological Research* 12, no. 1 (2004): 1–73; Martin Gallivan, "The Archaeology of Native Societies in the Chesapeake: New Investigations and Interpretations," *Journal of Archaeological Research* 19, no. 3 (2011): 281–325; John N. Wilford, "From Spearheads, New Ideas About First North Americans," *New York Times*, July 13, 2012; Jon M. Erlandson, Torben C. Rick, Terry L. Jones, and Judith G. Porcasi, "One If by Land, Two If by Sea: Who Were the First Californians?," in Jones and Klar, *California Prehistory*.

———

12. Herbert S. Klein and Daniel C. Schiffner, "The Current Debate About the Origins of the Paleoindians of America," *Journal of Social History* 37, no. 2 (Winter 2003): 483-492; Todd J. Braje and Jon M. Erlandson, "Looking Forward, Looking Back: Humans, Anthropogenic Change, and the Anthropocene," *Anthropocene* 4 (January 2014): 116-121.

13. Rountree et al., *John Smith's Chesapeake Voyages*, 2; Porter, *Maryland Indians*; Richard J. Dent Jr., *Chesapeake Prehistory: Old Traditions, New Directions* (New York: Plenum Press, 1995); Arnold et al., "Archaeology of California."

14. Dent, *Chesapeake Prehistory*; Lightfoot and Parrish, *California Indians*; Bartolome, "Ecological History of the California Mediterranean-Type Landscape"; Porter, *Maryland Indians*.

15. Miller, "Living Along the 'Great Shellfish Bay.'"

16. Lightfoot and Parrish, *California Indians*.

17. Luby et al., "Shell Mounds and Mounded Landscapes," 191-241; Edward M. Luby and Mark F. Gruber, "The Dead Must Be Fed: Symbolic Meanings of the Shellmounds of the San Francisco Bay Area," *Cambridge Archaeological Journal* 9, no. 1 (April 1999): 95-108.

18. Arnold et al., "Archaeology of California."

19. M. Kat Anderson, *Tending the Wild: Native American Knowledge and the Management of California's Natural Resources* (Berkeley: University of California Press, 2005), 5; Kent G. Lightfoot and Edward M. Luby, "Temporal Trends in the Use and Abandonment of Shell Mounds in the East Bay," in *Catalysts to Complexity: Late Holocene Cultural Complexity on the California Coast*, eds. Jon M. Erlandson and Terry L. Jones (Los Angeles: Cotsen Institute of Archaeology, University of California, 2002), 262-281.

20. Arnold et al., "Archaeology of California"; L. Mark Raab and Terry L. Jones, eds., *Prehistoric California: Archaeology and the Myth of Paradise* (Salt Lake City: University of Utah Press, 2004); Jack M. Broughton, *Resource Depression and Intensification During the Late Holocene, San Francisco Bay* (Berkeley: University of California Press, 1999); Brian Fagan, *Before California: An Archaeologist Looks at Our Earlier Inhabitants* (Lanham, MD: Rowman and Littlefield, 2003).

21. Milliken, "Costanoan-Yohuts Language Boundary"; Randall Milliken, *A Time of Little Choice: The Disintegration of Tribal Culture in the San Francisco Bay Area, 1769-1810* (Menlo Park, CA: Ballena Press, 1995); Andrew Galvan, Lecture on Ohlone (University of California, Berkeley, July 26, 2001); *San Francisco Chronicle*, January 1, 2001; Lightfoot and Parrish, *California Indians and Their Environment*, 1-151; Raab and Jones, *Prehistoric California*.

22. Lowell Bean and Thomas King, eds., *ANTAP: California Indians, Political and Economic Organization* (Ramona, CA: Ballena Press, 1974); Margolin, *The Ohlone Way*.

23. Lynn H. Gamble, *The Chumash World at European Contact: Power, Trade, and Feasting Among Complex Hunter-Gatherers* (Berkeley: University of California Press, 2008).

———

24. Anderson, *Tending the Wild*, chaps. 1, 4, and 6.

25. Ibid., 34–40.

26. Robert L. Bettinger, *Orderly Anarchy: Sociopolitical Evolution in Aboriginal California* (Berkeley: University of California Press, 2015).

27. Rountree et al., *John Smith's Chesapeake Voyages*, 38.

28. Ibid., 41–51.

29. Gallivan, "Archaeology of Native Societies," 281–325.

30. Porter, *Maryland Indians*; Dent, *Chesapeake Prehistory*; Helen C. Rountree and E. Randolph Turner, *Before and After Jamestown: Virginia's Powhatans and Their Predecessors* (Gainesville: University Press of Florida, 2002); Martin D. Gallivan, "Powhatan's Werowocomoco: Constructing Place, Polity, and Personhood in the Chesapeake, C.E. 1200–C.E. 1609," *American Anthropologist* 109, no. 1 (March 2007): 85–100.

31. J. Frederick Fausz, "Present at the 'Creation': The Chesapeake World That Greeted the Maryland Colonists," *Maryland Historical Magazine* 79, no. 1 (Spring 1984): 7–20.

32. Jose Barreiro, "'The Earth Is Us': A Case of Sacred Right," *Southern Exposure* 3 no. 2 (1986): 21–23; L. E. Wildesen, "Notes of an Archaeologist: Ohlone Indian Prehistory," *Indian Historian* 2 (1969): 25–28; Field, "Unacknowledged Tribes"; Gabrielle Tayac, "'So Intermingled with This Earth': A Piscataway Oral History," *Northeast Indian Quarterly* 5, no. 4 (Winter 1988): 4–17.

CHAPTER 2: THE BRITISH AND THE AMERICANS TAKE THE CHESAPEAKE

1. Quoted in W. Stitt Robinson, "Conflicting Views on Landholding: Lord Baltimore and the Experiences of Colonial Maryland with Native Americans," *Maryland Historical Magazine* 83, no. 2 (1988): 85–97.

2. Michael Leroy Oberg, *Dominion and Civility: English Imperialism, Native America, and the First American Frontiers, 1585–1685* (Ithaca, NY: Cornell University Press, 1999).

3. Ken MacMillan, "Centers and Peripheries in English Maps of America, 1590–1685," in *Early American Cartographies*, ed. Martin Brückner (Chapel Hill: University of North Carolina Press, 2011), 67–92.

4. Gavin Hollis, "The Wrong Side of the Map? The Cartographic Encounters of John Lederer," in Brückner, *Early American Cartographies*, 145–168; James D. Rice, *Nature & History in the Potomac Country* (Baltimore: Johns Hopkins University Press, 2009); Margaret Beck Pritchard and Henry G. Taliaferro, *Degrees of Latitude: Mapping Colonial America* (Williamsburg, VA: Colonial Williamsburg Foundation, 2002), 122.

5. Calvert quoted in Frank W. Porter, *Maryland Indians, Yesterday and Today* (Baltimore: Maryland Historical Society, 1983); Smith quoted in Lyon Gardiner Tyler, ed., *Narratives of Early Virginia, 1606–1625* (New York: Charles Scribner's Sons, 1907), 42–63; James H. Merrell, "Cultural Continuity Among the

Piscataway Indians of Colonial Maryland," *William and Mary Quarterly* 36, no. 4 (October 1979): 548–570.

6. Rice, *Nature & History*, chaps. 4 and 5, esp. 108–109; Merrell, "Cultural Continuity"; Porter, *Maryland Indians*.

7. Porter, *Maryland Indians*, 181; Helen C. Rountree and E. Randolph Turner, *Before and After Jamestown: Virginia's Powhatans and Their Predecessors* (Gainesville: University Press of Florida, 2002), chap. 5.

8. Quoted in Stephen R. Potter, *Commoners, Tribute, and Chiefs: The Development of Algonquin Culture in the Potomac Valley* (Charlottesville: University of Virginia Press, 1994), 195.

9. John Kilty, *The Land-Holder's Assistant and Land-Office Guide; Being an Exposition of Original Titles, as Derived from the Proprietary Government, and More Recently from the State, of Maryland* (Baltimore: G. Dobbin and Murphy, 1808), 21, 35, 108–132.

10. Kilty, *Land-Holder's Assistant*, 354.

11. Rice, *Nature & History*, 139–141; Merrell, "Cultural Continuity," 563; Robert Paulett, *An Empire of Small Places: Mapping the Southeastern Anglo-Indian Trade, 1732-1795* (Athens: University of Georgia Press, 2012).

12. Quoted in Robinson, "Conflicting Views on Landholding"; John Smith, *A True Relation of Virginia* (Boston: Wiggin and Lunt, 1866), 57.

13. Quotes from Kilty, *Land-Holder's Assistant*, 351–355.

14. Robinson, "Conflicting Views on Landholding"; Oberg, *Dominion and Civility*; Merrell, "Cultural Continuity."

15. Quotes from Kilty, *Land-Holder's Assistant*, 358; Michael Witgen, *An Infinity of Nations: How the Native New World Shaped Early North America* (Philadelphia: University of Pennsylvania Press, 2012); Stuart Banner, *How the Indians Lost Their Land: Law and Power on the Frontier* (Cambridge, MA: Belknap Press of Harvard University Press, 2005).

16. Andro Linklater, *Owning the Earth: The Transforming History of Land Ownership* (New York: Bloomsbury, 2013), 33; Edward T. Price, *Dividing the Land: Early American Beginnings of Our Private Property Mosaic* (Chicago: University of Chicago Press, 1995).

17. Quoted in Andro Linklater, *Measuring America: How the United States Was Shaped by the Greatest Land Sale in History* (New York: Plume, 2003), 28, 78.

18. Quoted in Jess Edwards, "A Compass to Steer By: John Locke, Carolina, and the Politics of Restoration Geography," in Brückner, *Early American Cartographies*, 93–115; Linklater, *Owning the Earth*, 79–86.

19. Alison Bell, "White Ethnogenesis and Gradual Capitalism: Perspectives from Colonial Archaeological Sites in the Chesapeake," *American Anthropologist* 107, no. 3 (September 2005): 446–460.

20. Quoted in Robinson, "Conflicting Views on Landholding."

21. Kilty, *Land-Holder's Assistant*, 125.

22. Ronald Hoffman, *Princes of Ireland, Planters of Maryland: A Carroll Saga,*

1500-1782 (Chapel Hill: University of North Carolina Press, 2000); Kilty, *Land-Holder's Assistant*, 128–130.

23. Willie Graham, Carter L. Hudgins, Carl R. Lounsbury, Fraser D. Neiman, and James P. Whittenburg, "Adaptation and Innovation: Archaeological and Architectural Perspectives on the Seventeenth-Century Chesapeake," *William and Mary Quarterly* 64, no. 3 (July 2007): 451–522; D. W. Meinig, *The Shaping of America: A Geographical Perspective on 500 Years of History*, vol. 1, *Atlantic America, 1492-1800* (New Haven, CT: Yale University Press, 1986), 150–153; David W. Schneider, "Effects of European Settlement and Land Use on Regional Patterns of Similarity Among Chesapeake Forests," *Bulletin of the Torrey Botanical Club* 123, no. 3 (July–September 1996): 223–239.

24. John T. Scharf, *The Chronicles of Baltimore; Being a Complete History of "Baltimore Town" and Baltimore City from the Earliest Period to the Present Time* (Baltimore: Turnball Brothers, 1874), 122; "A True Relation by Captain John Smith, 1608," in Tyler, *Narratives of Early Virginia*, 33; Christian J. Koot, "The Merchant, the Map, and Empire: Augustine Herrman's Chesapeake and Interimperial Trade, 1644–73," *William and Mary Quarterly* 67, no. 4 (October 2010): 603–644.

25. Scharf, *Chronicles of Baltimore*; Garrett Power, "Parceling Out Land in the Vicinity of Baltimore, 1632–1796," pt. 1, *Maryland Historical Magazine* 87, No. 4 (Winter 1992): 453–466.

26. William Ridgeway, *Community Leadership in Maryland, 1790-1840: A Comparative Analysis of Power in Society* (Chapel Hill: University of North Carolina Press, 1979).

27. Entries of September 18, 1747, p. 21, and April 10, 1795, p. 95, *First Records of Baltimore Town and Jones' Town, 1729-1797* (Baltimore, 1905).

28. Entry of September 18, 1747, *First Records*, 21; Scharf, *Chronicles of Baltimore*; Power, "Parceling Out Land."

29. *First Records*, xvii.

30. Garrett Power, "Parcelling Out Land in the Vicinity of Baltimore: 1632–1798," *Maryland Historical Magazine* 87, no. 4 (1993): 453–465 (Part I), and 88, no. 2 (1993): 151–167 (Part II).

31. Entries of January 1729 to March 16, 1746, *First Records*, 3–19; Robert J. Brugger, *Maryland: A Middle Temperament, 1634-1980* (Baltimore: Johns Hopkins University Press, 1988), 102–106.

32. Cartographic Records, BRG-12, Baltimore City Archives (BCA hereafter).

33. Entry of July 14, 1729, *First Records*.

34. "Act of 1745 by Virtue of Which Baltimore and Jones Towns Were Consolidated Under Name of Baltimore Town," *First Records*, xvii–xxiii.

35. Entries of 1733 to 1750, *First Records*, 13–32; Power, "Parceling Out Land."

36. Entries of July 10, 1733, to July 24, 1747, *First Records*, 9–19.

37. Entries for September 10, 1750, *First Records*.

38. Sherry H. Olson, *Baltimore: The Building of an American City*, rev. ed.

(Baltimore: Johns Hopkins University Press, 1997), 7; Garrett Power, "Parceling Out Land," 160–163; Exact Platt of Baltimore Town; Thomas W. Griffith, *Sketches of the Early History of Maryland* (Baltimore: Frederick G. Schaeffer, 1821), 31–32.

39. "Act of 1745," *First Records*, xi, xx, xxiii.
40. Ibid.
41. *First Records*, 46; Gerald E. Frug, *City Making: Building Communities Without Building Walls* (Princeton, NJ: Princeton University Press, 1999); Charles Belfoure and Mary Ellen Hayward, *The Baltimore Rowhouse* (New York: Princeton Architectural Press, 2001); Sherry H. Olson, *Baltimore: The Building of an American City* (Baltimore: Johns Hopkins University Press, 1980), chap. 2; Garrett Power, "Entail in Two Cities: A Comparative Study of Long Term Leases in Birmingham, England, and Baltimore, Maryland, 1700–1900," *Faculty Scholarship*, no. 262 (1992), digitalcommons.law.umaryland.edu/fac_pubs/262 (last accessed July 8, 2017).
42. Entry of July 2, 1791, *First Records*, 72.
43. *First Records*, xii; Dennis Rankin Clark, "Baltimore, 1729–1829: The Genesis of a Community" (PhD diss., Catholic University of America, 1976).
44. Philip A. Crowl, *Maryland During and After the Revolution: A Political and Economic Study* (Baltimore: Johns Hopkins University Press, 1943); Brugger, *Maryland*, chap. 3.
45. Scharf, *Chronicles of Baltimore*, 130–133.
46. Leroy Graham, *Baltimore: The Nineteenth-Century Black Capital* (Lanham, MD: University Press of America, 1982), 20–25; Christopher Phillips, *Freedom's Port: The African American Community of Baltimore, 1790–1860* (Urbana: University of Illinois Press, 1997); T. Stephen Whitman, *Challenging Slavery in the Chesapeake: Black and White Resistance to Human Bondage, 1775–1865* (Baltimore: Maryland Historical Society, 2006).
47. Quoted in Phillips, *Freedom's Port*, 52.
48. Quoted in Christopher J. Young, "Mary K. Goddard: A Classical Republican in a Revolutionary Age," *Maryland Historical Magazine* 96, no. 1 (Spring 2001): 4–27.
49. Scharf, *Chronicles of Baltimore*; Crowl, *Maryland During and After the Revolution*; Charles G. Steffen, *The Mechanics of Baltimore: Workers and Politics in the Age of Revolution, 1763–1812* (Urbana: University of Illinois Press, 1984).
50. Steffen, *Mechanics of Baltimore*, 73.
51. "A Supplementary and Additional Act to the Act Entitled, An Act for Erecting a Town on the North Side of Patapsco, in Baltimore County" (1745), *Proceedings and Acts of the General Assembly*, in *Archives of Maryland*, eds. William Hand Browne et al. (Baltimore and Annapolis, 1883–), 44:214.
52. Entry of July 11, 1768, *First Records*, 38.
53. Entry of July 12, 1793, *First Records*, 85.
54. Entry of November 16, 1793, *First Records*, 87.

55. Olson, *Baltimore*, 1997, 6–7.
56. Christian Fritz, *American Sovereigns: The People and America's Constitutional Tradition Before the Civil War* (New York: Cambridge University Press, 2008); Dana D. Nelson, *Commons Democracy: Reading the Politics of Participation in the Early United States* (New York: Fordham University Press, 2015).
57. Herbert Baxter Addams, "Maryland's Influence upon the Land Cessions to the United States: With Minor Papers on George Washington's Interest in Western Lands, the Potomac Company, and a National University," Johns Hopkins University, Studies in Historical and Political Science, vol. 111 (1885); John R. Van Atta, *Securing the West: Politics, Public Lands, and the Fate of the Old Republic, 1785–1850* (Baltimore: Johns Hopkins University Press, 2014); Linklater, *Owning the Earth*, 216.

CHAPTER 3: THE LAND OF SAN FRANCISCO BAY

1. Stephen J. Hornsby, *British Atlantic, American Frontier: Spaces of Power in Early Modern British America* (Lebanon, NH: University Press of New England, 2004); D. W. Meinig, *The Shaping of America: A Geographical Perspective on 500 Years of History*, vol. 1, *Atlantic America, 1492–1800* (New Haven, CT: Yale University Press, 1986).
2. Barbara E. Mundy, *The Death of Aztec Tenochtitlan: The Life of Mexico City* (Austin: University of Texas Press, 2015); Helen Nader, "The Spain That Encountered Mexico," in *The Oxford History of Mexico*, eds. William Beesley and Michael C. Meyer (New York: Oxford University Press, 2010), 11.
3. Alan Taylor, *American Revolutions: A Continental History, 1750–1804* (New York: W. W. Norton, 2016), 15, 21; John Tutino, ed., *Mexico and Mexicans in the Making of the United States* (Austin: University of Texas Press, 2012); John Tutino, *Making a New World: Founding Capitalism in the Bajío and Spanish North* (Durham, NC: Duke University Press, 2011).
4. José De Gálvez, "1768: The Decision to Move Farther North," in *Lands of Promise and Despair: Chronicles of Early California, 1535–1846*, eds. Rose Marie Beebe and Robert M. Senkewicz (Berkeley, CA: Heyday Books, 2001), 111.
5. Ibid.; Julia G. Costello and David Hornbeck, "Alta California: An Overview," in *Columbian Consequences*, vol. 1, *Archaeological and Historical Perspectives on the Spanish Borderlands West*, ed. David Hurst Thomas (Washington, DC: Smithsonian Institution Press, 1989).
6. Arrell Morgan Gibson and John S. Whitehead, *Yankees in Paradise: The Pacific Basin Frontier* (Albuquerque, NM: University of New Mexico Press, 1993); James P. Delgado, *Gold Rush Port: The Maritime Archaeology of San Francisco's Waterfront* (Berkeley: University of California Press, 2009); Nancy Olmsted, *Vanished Waters: A History of San Francisco's Mission Bay* (San Francisco: Mission Creek Conservancy, 1986).
7. John P. Langellier and Daniel B. Rosen, *El Presidio de San Francisco: A History*

Under Spain and Mexico, 1776–1846 (Norman, OK: Arthur H. Clark Company, 1996).

8. Quoted in Langellier and Rosen, *El Presidio de San Francisco*, 2; Junípero Serra, "1770: A Beachhead at Monterey," in Beebe and Senkewicz, *Lands of Promise and Despair*, 139–141.

9. Francisco Palóu, "1776: The Beginnings of San Francisco," in Beebe and Senkewicz, *Lands of Promise and Despair*, 205; Frank M. Stanger and Alan K. Brown, *Who Discovered the Golden Gate? The Explorers' Own Accounts* (Redwood City, CA: San Mateo County Historical Society, 1969); Zoeth Skinner Eldredge, *The Beginnings of San Francisco from the Expedition of Anza, 1774 to the City Charter of April 15, 1850* (San Francisco: Zoeth S. Eldredge, 1912).

10. *Fray Juan Crespi: Missionary Explorer of the Pacific Coast*, ed. and trans. Herbert Eugene Bolton (Berkeley: University of California Press, 1927), 28–32, 37, 47, 143, 220–229, 237, 291.

11. Ibid.

12. Ibid.

13. Ibid.

14. Alan Brown, ed. and trans., *With Anza to California, 1775–1776: The Journal of Pedro Font, O.F.M.* (Norman, OK: Arthur H. Clark Company, 2011), chap. 1; Vincente de Santa María, "1775: Encounter in San Francisco Bay," in Beebe and Senkewicz, *Lands of Promise and Despair*.

15. *Fray Juan Crespi*, 234; Santa María, "1775: Encounter," 178–185, 193–204; Vladimir Guerrero, *The Anza Trail and the Settling of California* (Santa Clara, CA: Santa Clara University Press, 2006), 195, 199; Brown, *With Anza to California*, chap. 1, 305.

16. Santa María, "1775: Encounter," 180.

17. Quoted in Langellier and Rosen, *El Presidio de San Francisco*, 28.

18. Quoted in Guerrero, *Anza Trail*, 199; Palóu, "1776: The Beginnings."

19. Palóu, "1776: The Beginnings."

20. Ibid.

21. Ibid., 206–208.

22. Barbara L. Voss, *The Archaeology of Ethnogenesis: Race and Sexuality in Colonial San Francisco* (Berkeley: University of California Press, 2008).

23. Ibid., 178; Bernard Moses, *The Establishment of Municipal Government in San Francisco* (Baltimore: John Murphy and Company, 1889), 7; Julia G. Costello and David Hornbeck, "Alta California: An Overview"; Leon G. Campbell, "The Spanish Presidio in Alta California During the Mission Period, 1769–1784," *Journal of the West* 16, no. 14 (1977): 65–77.

24. Quoted in Langellier and Rosen, *El Presidio de San Francisco*, 599; Voss, *Archaeology of Ethnogenesis*, 180; Kent G. Lightfoot, *Indians, Missionaries and Merchants: The Legacy of Colonial Encounters on the California Frontier* (Berkeley: University of California Press, 2006), chap. 7.

25. Quoted in Langellier and Rosen, *El Presidio de San Francisco*, 108.

26. David J. Garr, *Hispanic Urban Planning in North America* (New York: Garland Publishing, 1991), 7–19; James A. Sandos, *Converting California: Indians and Franciscans in the Missions* (New Haven, CT: Yale University Press, 2004); Harold Kirker, *California's Architectural Frontier: Style and Tradition in the Nineteenth Century* (Layton, UT: Gibbs Smith, 1986); John Reps, *Cities of the American West: A History of Frontier Urban Planning* (Princeton, NJ: Princeton University Press, 1979); Fray Martin de Landaeta, *Noticias Acerca del Puerto de San Francisco* (Mexico City: Antigua Librería Robredo, 1949), 47, 61.

27. Quoted in Louis Choris, *San Francisco One Hundred Years Ago*, trans. Porter Garnett (San Francisco: A. M. Robertson, 1913), 7.

28. Steven W. Hackel, "The Staff of Leadership: Indian Authority in the Missions of Alta California," *William and Mary Quarterly* 54, no. 2 (1997): 347–376; Daniel Garr, "Planning, Politics and Plunder: The Missions and Indian Pueblos of Hispanic California," *Historical Society of Southern California Quarterly* 54, no. 5 (1979): 291–312; Carey McWilliams, *North from Mexico* (Philadelphia: J. B. Lippincott, 1948).

29. Dora P. Crouch, Daniel J. Garr, and Axel I. Mundigo, *Spanish City Planning in North America* (Cambridge, MA: MIT Press, 1982); Mark A. Burkholder, "An Empire Beyond Compare," in *Oxford History of Mexico*, 111—142, 123; Don Jose Figueroa, *Manifesto to the Mexican Republic* (Oakland, CA: BioBooks, 1952).

30. Philip Dreyfus, *Our Better Nature: Environment and the Making of San Francisco* (Norman: University of Oklahoma Press, 2008), 27; Felipe de Neve, John Everett Johnson, and Oscar Lewis, *Regulations for Governing the Province of the Californias, Approved by His Majesty by Royal Order, Dated October 24, 1781* (San Francisco: Grabhorn Press, 1929), 44.

31. Albert L. Hurtado, *Indian Survival on the California Frontier* (New Haven, CT: Yale University Press, 1988); David Igler, *The Great Ocean: Pacific Worlds from Captain Cook to the Gold Rush* (New York: Oxford University Press, 2013), chap. 2; Dreyfus, *Our Better Nature*.

32. Lightfoot, *Indians, Missionaries and Merchants*, chaps. 2, 3, and 7; Pedro Font, "1776: The San Francisco Bay Region," in Beebe and Senkewicz, *Lands of Promise and Despair*, 198; Pedro Fages, *A Historical, Political, and Natural Description of California*, trans. Herbert Ingram Priestley (Berkeley: University of California Press, 1937).

33. Gregorio Mora-Torres, ed. and trans., *Californio Voices: The Oral Memoirs of José María Amador and Lorenzo Asisara* (Denton: University of North Texas Press, 2005), 95, 113, 123.

34. Ibid.; José María Fernández, "1797: Treatment of the Indians at Mission San Francisco," in Beebe and Senkewicz, *Lands of Promise and Despair*, 262; José Argüello, "1797: Military Interrogation of San Francisco Indians," in Beebe and Senkewicz, *Lands of Promise and Despair*, 267–268.

35. Fernández, "1797: Treatment," 262; Argüello, "1797: Military Interrogation," 267–268.

---

36. Argüello, "1797: Military Interrogation," 267.

37. Robert H. Jackson, "The Changing Economic Structure of the Alta California Missions: A Reinterpretation," *Pacific Historical Review* 61, no. 3 (1992): 387–415.

38. Louis Choris, *San Francisco One Hundred Years Ago*, trans. Porter Garnett (San Francisco: A. M. Robertson, 1913).

39. Antonio de la Concepción Horra and Fermín Francisco de Lasuén, "1798–1801: The Mission System Evaluated and Defended," in Beebe and Senkewicz, *Lands of Promise and Despair*, 272, 273–274.

40. Ibid.

41. United States Land Commission, "US District Court of California, Northern District, California Land Cases," A300, Bancroft Library, University of California, Berkeley (hereafter Land Case ND), Land Case 427ND; Stephen W. Silliman, *Lost Laborers in Colonial California: Native Americans and the Archaeology of Rancho Petaluma* (Tucson: University of Arizona Press, 2004), chap. 7.

42. Sandos, *Converting California*, 13–17.

43. Julia G. Costello and David Hornbeck, "Alta California: An Overview," in Thomas, *Columbian Consequences*; M. Kat Anderson, Michael G. Barbour, and Valerie Whitworth, "A World of Balance and Plenty: Land, Plants, Animals, and Humans in a Pre-European California," *California History* 76, no. 2/3 (1997): 12–47; William Preston, "Serpent in the Garden: Environmental Change in Colonial California," in *Contested Eden: California Before the Gold Rush*, eds. Ramón A. Gutiérrez and Richard J. Orsi (Berkeley: University of California Press, 1998), 260–298.

44. Quoted in Daniel Garr, "Planning, Politics and Plunder: The Missions and Indian Pueblos of Hispanic California," *Historical Society of Southern California Quarterly* 54, no. 5 (1979): 301–302.

45. Fond, "1776: The Beginnings," 204; Maria Raquél Casas, *Married to a Daughter of the Land: Spanish-Mexican Women and Interethnic Marriage in California, 1820–1880* (Reno: University of Nevada Press, 2007), 30; Garr, *Hispanic Urban Planning*; Jay Kinsbruner, *The Colonial Spanish-American City: Urban Life in the Age of Atlantic Capitalism* (Austin: University of Texas Press, 2005); Iris H. W. Engstrand, "The Legal Heritage of Spanish California," *Southern California Quarterly* 75, no. 3/4 (1993): 205–236.

46. Neve et al., *Regulations*, 14; Elizabeth Milroy, "Repairing the Myth and the Reality of Philadelphia's Public Squares, 1800–1850," *Change over Time* 1, no. 1 (2009): 52–78; Jesús Escobar, *The Plaza Mayor and the Shaping of Baroque Madrid* (New York: Cambridge University Press, 2003).

47. Neve et al, *Regulations*, 14.

48. Engstrand, "Legal Heritage," 230.

49. Robert C. West, *Sonora: Its Geographical Personality* (Austin: University of Texas Press, 1993); Stuart F. Voss, *On the Periphery of Nineteenth-Century*

Mexico: Sonora and Sinaloa, 1810-1877 (Tucson: University of Arizona Press, 1982).

50. Voss, *Archaeology of Ethnogenesis*; Mora-Torres, *Californio Voices*, introduction.

51. William M. Mason, *The Census of 1790: A Demographic History of Colonial California* (Menlo Park, CA: Ballena Press, 1998). See also Voss, *Archaeology of Ethnogenesis*, chap. 3; Eldredge, *Beginnings of San Francisco*, 102.

52. Eldredge, *Beginnings of San Francisco*, 102; Voss, *Archaeology of Ethnogenesis*; Brown, *With Anza to California*, 138-139.

53. Voss, *Archaeology of Ethnogensis*; Lightfoot, *Indians, Missionaries and Merchants*, chap. 7.

54. Land Case 424ND: José Yves Limantour, November 12, 1775.

55. Ibid.; María Raquél Casas, *Married to a Daughter of the Land: Spanish-Mexican American Women and Interethnic Marriage in California, 1820-1880* (Reno: University of Nevada Press, 2007).

56. J. N. Bowman, "Juana Briones de Miranda," *Historical Society of Southern California Quarterly* 39, no. 3 (1957): 227-241.

57. Land Case 353ND: José R. Valencia; Land Case 389ND: Candelario Valencia, p. 5, Petition of Candelario Valencia, February 11, 1852.

58. Land Case 8ND: J. K. Rose.

59. Ibid.

60. Ibid.

61. Tutino, *Making a New World*, 477; Helen Nader, "The Spain That Encountered Mexico" in *Oxford History of Mexico*; Karen D. Caplan, *Indigenous Citizens: Local Liberalism in Early National Oaxaca and Yucatán* (Stanford, CA: Stanford University Press, 2010).

62. The line referred to is from Robert Frost's the "The Gift Outright," which Frost read so poignantly at the inauguration of President John F. Kennedy.

63. François-Xavier Guerra, "El Soberano Y Su Reino: Reflexiones sobre la génesis del ciudadano en América Latina," *Ciudadanía politica y formación naciones* (1999): 33-61; Tamar Herzog, *Defining Nations, Immigrants and Citizens in Early Modern Spain and Spanish America* (New Haven, CT: Yale University Press, 2003); Nader, "The Spain That Encountered Mexico," 18-21.

64. Antonio Annino and Marcela Ternavasio, eds., *El laboratorio constitucional iberoamericano: 1807/1808-1830* (Madrid: Iberoamericana-Estudios AHILA, 2012); Tutino, *Making a New World*, 485, 466-486.

PART II: MAKING THE MUNICIPALITY

1. John Melish, *A Geographical Description of the United States, with the Contiguous British and Spanish Possessions, Intended as an Accompaniment to Melish's Map of These Countries* (Philadelphia: John Melish, 1816), 4.

2. Ibid., 54-56.

CHAPTER 4: ERECTING BALTIMORE INTO A CITY

1. "An Act to Erect Baltimore Town, in Baltimore County, into a City and to Incorporate the Inhabitants Thereof," *Acts of the General Assembly of Maryland,* November 1796, Chapter LXVIII, 281–282.

2. Chapter 68 (1796), *Laws of Maryland* (Annapolis: Frederick Green, 1797), 256. For municipal corporations, see Jerome Hodos, "Against Exceptionalism: Intercurrence and Intergovernmental Relations in Britain and the United States," in *The City in American Urban Development,* ed. Richardson Dilworth (New York: Routledge, 2009), 44–63; Jason Kaufman, "Town and Country in the Redefinition of State-Federal Power: Canada and the United States, 1630–2005, in Dilworth, *City in American Urban Development,* 64–74; Simon Middleton, *From Privilege to Right: Work and Politics in Colonial New York City* (Philadelphia: University of Pennsylvania Press, 2006); Andrew M. Schocket, *Founding Corporate Power in Early National Philadelphia* (Dekalb: University of Northern Illinois Press, 2007); Alan DiGaetano, "The Birth of Modern Urban Governance: A Comparison of Political Modernization in Boston, Massachusetts, and Bristol, England, 1800–1870," *Journal of Urban History* 35, no. 2 (January 2009): 259–287.

3. Ernest S. Griffith, *History of American City Government: The Colonial Period* (New York: Oxford University Press, 1938); Russell Shorto, *Island at the Center of the World: The Epic Story of Dutch Manhattan and the Forgotten Colony That Shaped America* (New York: Doubleday, 2004).

4. Chapter 68 (1796), *Laws of Maryland,* 258–264; *American and Commercial Advertiser,* February 4, 1808.

5. Ordinance No. 12 (1797), No. 15 (1797), No. 14 (1797), in *Ordinances of the Corporation of the City of Baltimore, 1797–1802* (Baltimore: John Cox, 1875), 44–47, 58–64, 54–58.

6. *Ordinances* (1800), 174.

7. Leonard P. Curry, *The Corporate City: The American City as a Political Entity, 1800–1850* (Westport, CT: Greenwood Press, 1997), 36; Ordinances of 1804, in *Ordinances of the Corporation of the City of Baltimore from 1803 to 1812, Inclusive* (Baltimore: John Cox, 1876), 42.

8. Gary Lawson Browne, *Baltimore in the Nation: 1789–1861* (Chapel Hill: University of North Carolina Press, 1980).

9. Curry, *Corporate City,* 36–37; Robert Gamble, "Civic Economies: Commerce, Regulation, and Public Space in the Antebellum City" (PhD diss., Johns Hopkins University, 2014).

10. City Council Records, 1799:219, 219a, RG16-1, BCA; *Ordinances* (1797), 161; *Proceedings of the First Branch of the City Council,* February 13, 1804, March 5, 1806, February 15, 1821, and January 16, 1826. The records of the *City Council Proceedings* are available in manuscript form on microfilm at the Maryland State Archives and transcribed into printed annual volumes, available at the

Legislative Law Library at Baltimore City Hall. Specific citations are identified here by date and page in the printed volumes.

11. *City Council Proceedings*, February 14 and 25, 1803, February 8, 1809, March 17 and February 29, 1820; Mayor's Message, February 15, 1821, February 12, 1824, RG9-2, BCA.

12. *Ordinances* (March 7, 1801), 289–291; City Council Records, 1802:294, RG16-1, BCA; *City Council Proceedings*, February 4, 1803.

13. Curry, *Corporate City*, 16.

14. Ibid., v, ix.

15. *Ordinances* (1807–1808), 238–243; William G. LeFurgy, "Baltimore's Wards, 1797–1978: A Guide," *Maryland Historical Magazine* 75, no. 2 (June 1980): 145–153; Charles G. Steffen, *The Mechanics of Baltimore: Workers and Politics in the Age of Revolution, 1763–1812* (Urbana: University of Illinois Press, 1984), 125–126, 209–227; Curry, *Corporate City*; Marianna L. R. Dantas, *Black Townsmen: Urban Slavery and Freedom in the Eighteenth-Century Americas* (New York: Palgrave MacMillan, 2008).

16. Whitman H. Ridgway, *Community Leadership in Maryland, 1790–1840* (Chapel Hill: University of North Carolina Press, 1979).

17. Howard B. Rock, Paul A. Gilje, and Robert Asher, eds., *American Artisans: Crafting Social Identity, 1750–1850* (Baltimore: Johns Hopkins University Press, 1995).

18. Brooke Hunter, "Wheat, War, and the American Economy During the Age of Revolution," *William and Mary Quarterly* 62, no. 3 (July 2005): 505–526; Richard Chew, "'Far Short of Our Expectations': Baltimore and the Atlantic World Trade in the Confederation Period," *Maryland Historical Magazine* 98, no. 4 (Winter 2003): 408–439; Richard Chew, "Certain Victims of an International Contagion: The Panic of 1797 and the Hard Times of the Late 1790s in Baltimore," *Journal of the Early Republic* 25, no. 4 (Winter 2005): 563–613; *American and Commercial Advertiser*, February 4, 1808.

19. Jeffrey L. Pasley, *"The Tyranny of Printers": Newspaper Politics in the Early American Republic* (Charlottesville: University of Virginia Press, 2001).

20. *American and Commercial Daily Advertiser*, October 6, 1808; Michael Leib, *A Portrait of the Evils of Democracy, Submitted to the Consideration of the People of Maryland* (Baltimore, 1816); *The Three Patriots, or, The Cause and the Cure of Present Evils Addressed to the Voters of Maryland* (Baltimore: Arthur B. Edes, Printer, 1811).

21. *Federal Gazette*, July 1, 1809; *Baltimore Daily Intelligencer*, February 24, 1794.

22. William Leigh Pierce, *The Year: A Poem, in Three Cantos* (New-York: David Longworth, 1813); *American and Commercial Advertiser*, June 18, 1812.

23. Paul A. Gilje "The Baltimore Riots of 1812 and the Breakdown of the Anglo-American Mob Tradition," *Journal of Social History* 13, no. 4 (Summer 1980): 547–564; Charles Royster, *Light-Horse Harry Lee and the Legacy of the American Revolution* (New York: Knopf, 1981); Paul A. Gilje, "'Le Menu Peuple'

in America: Identifying the Mob in the Baltimore Riots of 1812," *Maryland Historical Magazine* 81, no. 1 (Spring 1986): 50–66.

24. Henry Lee, *A Correct Account of the Conduct of the Baltimore Mob* (Winchester, VA: John Heiskell, 1814), 4, 12, 17.

25. Ibid., 7, 9, 6, 8, 13.

26. Ibid., 11; "Report of the Committee of Grievances," pamphlet, Peabody Library, Sheridan Libraries of Johns Hopkins University, 208–209.

27. Edward Johnson to the City Council, August 3, 1812, City Council Records, 1812:555, BCA; *Address of the Committee Appointed to Inquire into the Causes and Extent of the Late Commotion in the City of Baltimore* (Baltimore: Printed for Baltimore City Council, 1812), 3.

28. *Report of the Committee of Grievances.* 29–43.

29. Ibid., 260, 327; *Causes and Extent of the Late Commotion*, 18–22.

30. *Report of the Committee of Grievances*, 208–209.

31. James Clifford, "The Battles That Saved America: Northpoint and Baltimore, September 1814," *On Point: Journal of Army History* 10, no. 2 (September 2004): 9–15; Charles G. Muller, *The Darkest Day: The Washington-Baltimore Campaign During the War of 1812* (Philadelphia: University of Pennsylvania Press, 2003).

32. Muller, *Darkest Day*; Mayor's Message, February 14, 1814, 379, 380, BRG 16-1, BCA.

33. Mayor's Message, February 14, 1814, City Council Records, 1814:379, 380, BRG 16-1, BCA.

34. *Proceedings Relative to the Erection of a Monument to the Memory of Those Who Fell at the Battle of North Point; Including the Prayer of Bishop Kent, and the Address of the Rev. Doctor Inglis* (Baltimore: Neal, Wills, and Cole, 1815), 24. For a fuller account of Baltimore's antebellum monuments, see Mary P. Ryan, "Democracy Rising: The Monuments of Baltimore, 1809–1842," *Journal of Urban History* 36, no. 2 (March 2010): 127–150.

35. *Federal Gazette*, July 15, 1815. Comegys is quoted in "1915 Washington Monuments Centennial Records," Washington Monument Papers, 1810–1843, Maryland Historical Society, MS 876.

36. The Baltimore Monumental Subscription Book, BMS3, BCA.

37. *Baltimore Patriot*, August 28, 1815, March 21, 1815, July 29, 1815; Baltimore Monumental Subscription Book, BCA; Resolution of March 18, 1819, *Ordinances of the Corporation of the City of Baltimore, 1813-1822* (Baltimore: John Cox, 1876), 250; Ordinance No. 52, *Ordinances* (1821), 345–346; Ordinance No. 13 (1825), *Ordinances of the Corporation of the City of Baltimore, 1823-1827* (Baltimore: John Cox, 1876), 116–117.

38. Robert Mills Notebook, Washington Monument Record Books, November 1813, Maryland Historical Society, MS 876.

39. Caroline V. Davison, "Maximilian Godefroy," *Maryland Magazine of History* 29, no. 3 (September 1934): 175–211; Robert L. Alexander, "The Public Memorial

and Godefroy's Battle Monument," *Journal of the Society of Architectural Historians* 17, no. 1 (March 1958): 19–24.

40. *City Council Proceedings*, March 24, 1818, 63; January 15, 1827, 412; January 5, 1834, 9.

41. *City Council Proceedings*, March 24, 1818, 63.

42. Ordinance No. 47, *Ordinances* (1797), 112–114; *City Council Proceedings*, May 26 to June 8, 1812, 174–177; Jehu Bouldin, "Survey of the limits of Baltimore City," 1817, Cartographic Records, BRG 12-4-31, BCA.

43. *City Council Proceedings*, May 26 to June 8, 1812, 174–177; March 28, 1840, 408.

44. Ordinance No. 17, *Ordinances* (1803), 27; Richard J. Cox, "Trouble on the Chain Gang: City Surveying, Maps, and the Absence of Urban Planning in Baltimore, 1730–1823; With a Checklist of Maps of the Period," *Maryland Historical Magazine* 81, no. 1 (Spring 1986): 8–49.

45. *First Records of Baltimore Town and Jones' Town, 1729–1797* (Baltimore, 1905), April 10, 1795, October 12, 1795.

46. Chapter 52 (1794), *Laws of Maryland* (Annapolis: Frederick Green, 1795); Chapter 17 (1782), *Hanson's Laws of Maryland* (Annapolis: Frederick Green, 1787); Ordinance No. 14, *Ordinances* (1797), 55.

47. *First Records*, February 10 and 17, 1794, April 23, 1795, 88–89, 95.

48. Ordinance No. 16, *Ordinances* (1799), 205–206; Samuel Green, "Survey of the Basin of Baltimore," 1807, Cartographic Records, BRG 12-4-2, BCA.

49. Francois Bedarida and Anthony Sutcliffe, "The Street in the Structure and Life of the City: Reflections on Nineteenth Century London and Paris," *Journal of Urban History* 6, no. 4 (August 1980): 379–396; Michael Bruce Kahan, "Pedestrian Matters: The Contested Meanings and Uses of Philadelphia's Streets, 1850s-1920s" (PhD diss., University of Pennsylvania, 2002).

50. *Ordinances* (1797), 66–67; *Ordinances* (1803), 27; Patrick Joyce, *The Rule of Freedom: Liberalism and the Modern City* (London: Verso, 2003).

51. Jehu Bouldin, "Survey to Alter and Extend Granby and Exeter Streets," 1806, Cartographic Records, RG12-2-42; Samuel Green, "Survey of the Basin of Baltimore," 1807, Cartographic Records, RG12-4-2; J. Lewis Wampler, "Survey of Jones Falls from the Baltimore Street Bridge to Bridge Street Bridge," September 12, 1811, Cartographic Records, RG12-3-37, BCA.

52. *City Council Proceedings*, February 27, 1804, 60.

53. Dantas, *Black Townsmen*, 147.

54. Petitions for the improvement of Harford Run, City Council Records, 1817:254–257; Petition outlining improvements to Jones Falls, City Council Records, 1818:437; Ordinance No. 41, *Ordinances* (1807), 214–219; Ordinance No. 17, *Ordinances* (1817), 120–122; Ordinance No. 29, *Ordinances* (1818), 190–191.

55. *City Council Proceedings*, March 29, 1803, 143; February 4, 1840, 278; Jill Jonnes, *Urban Forests: A Natural History of Trees and People in the American Cityscape* (New York: Viking, 2016).

56. *Ordinances* (June 17, 1816), 95–99; David. P. Erlick, "The Peales and Gas

Lights in Baltimore," *Maryland Historical Magazine* 80, no. 1 (Spring 1885): 9–18; Peter C. Baldwin, *In the Watches of the Night: Life in the Nocturnal City, 1820–1930* (Chicago: University of Chicago Press, 2012).

57. Ordinance No. 28, *Ordinances* (1816), 95–99; Ordinance No. 13, *Ordinances* (1799), 200–202; *City Council Proceedings*, March 17, 1803, 126; February 8, 1809, 144.

58. *City Council Proceedings*, February 14, 1814, 321–323; John H. B. Latrobe, *Picture of Baltimore: Containing a Description of All Objects of Interest in the City, and Embellished with Views of the Principal Public Buildings* (Baltimore: Fielding Lucas Jr., 1832); Ordinance No. 30, *Ordinances* (1810), 293.

59. Mary Ellen Hayward and Charles Belfoure, *The Baltimore Rowhouse* (New York: Princeton Architectural Press, 2001), 7–46; Mary Ellen Hayward, *Baltimore's Alley Houses: Homes for Working People Since the 1780s* (Baltimore: Johns Hopkins University Press, 2008); Garrett Power, "Baltimore After the War of 1812: Where Robert Mills Met His Waterloo and When James A. Buchanan Broke the Bank" (working paper, Digital Commons, University of Maryland, Francis King Carey School of Law, June 14, 2012).

60. M. P. Leone, The *Archaeology of Liberty in an American Capital: Excavations in Annapolis* (Berkeley: University of California Press, 2005).

61. Petition to Mayor, March 28, 1817, Mayor's Correspondence, RG9-2, BCA; Criminal Docket, 1831–1839, Baltimore City Justice of the Peace, C211-2, Maryland State Archives.

62. Criminal Docket, September 13, May 2, and August 21, 1821, Baltimore City Justice of the Peace, C211-1, Maryland State Archives.

63. William Leigh Pierce, *The Year: Poem in Three Cantos* (New York: David Longworth, 1813).

64. Mary E. Ellicott Book of Newspaper Clippings, E. B. Smith–E. E. Tyson Collection, 1795–1912 (MS 3057), Box 2, Folder 4, Maryland Historical Society.

65. The Female Humane Impartial Society and Aged Women's Home, *Act of Incorporation and By Laws of the Society and Rule for the Government of the Aged Women Home* (Baltimore: James Young, 1855).

66. Seth Rockman, *Scraping By: Wage Labor, Slavery and Survival in Early Baltimore* (Baltimore: Johns Hopkins University Press, 2009).

67. Curry, *Corporate City*.

68. Letters to Mayor, May 1 and May 7, 1816, April 24, 1830, Mayor's Correspondence, RG9-2, BCA; Robert J. Gamble, "The City That Eats: Food and Power in Early Baltimore's Public Markets," in *Baltimore Revisited: Social History for the 21st-Century City*, eds. Nicole King and Kate Drabinski (New Brunswick, NJ: Rutgers University Press, forthcoming).

69. Frederick Douglass, *My Bondage and My Freedom* (New York, 1855), 147; Browne, *Baltimore in the Nation*.

CHAPTER 5: SHAPING THE SPACES OF CALIFORNIA

1. William Hartnell Papers, September 1826, VMS Z8, California Historical Society; Robert G. Cowan, *Ranchos of Alta California: A List of Spanish Concessions, 1775–1822, and Mexican Grants, 1822–1846* (Fresno, CA: Academic Library Guild, 1956), 348, 406, 71, 249; "US District Court of California, Northern District, California Land Cases," A300, Bancroft Library, University of California, Berkeley, (hereafter Land Cases ND), Land Case 166ND: Heirs of Francisco de Haro.

2. Land Case 54ND: Rancho Pulgas.

3. Hilda Iparraguirre and Ma. Isabel Campos Goenaga, eds., *Hacia una nación moderna: La modernidad y la construcción de la nación en México* (Mexico City: Escuela Nacional de Antropología e Historia, 2011).

4. Francois-Xavier Guerra, "El soberna y su reino: Reflexiones sobre la génesis del ciudadano en América Latina," in *Ciudadanía politica y formacíon de las naciones: Perspectivas históricas de América Latina*, ed. Hilda Sábato (Mexico City: Colegio de México, 1999), 33–61; Jaime E. Rodríguez O., *"We Are Now the True Spaniards": Sovereignty, Revolution, Independence, and the Emergence of the Federal Republic of Mexico, 1808–1824* (Stanford, CA: Stanford University Press, 2012), 4–5, 336.

5. Don Jose Figueroa, *The Manifesto to the Mexican Republic* (Oakland, CA: BioBooks, 1952), 83.

6. Antonio Maria Osio, *The History of Alta California: A Memoir of Mexican California*, ed. Rose Marie Beebe and Robert M. Senkewicz (Madison: University of Wisconsin Press, 1996); Timothy J. Henderson, *The Mexican Wars for Independence: A History* (New York: Hill and Wang, 2009); Woodrow James Hansen, *The Search for Authority in California* (Oakland, CA: BioBooks, 1960).

7. J. N. Bowman, "Index of the Spanish-Mexican Private Land Grant Records and Cases of California," typescript, 1958, Bancroft Library, University of California, Berkeley, 208–210; C. Alan Hutchinson, *Frontier Settlement in Mexican California: The Híjar-Padrés Colony and Its Origins, 1769–1835* (New Haven, CT: Yale University Press, 1969), 161–174.

8. Tsim Duncan Schneider, "Placing Refuge: Shell Mounds and the Archaeology of Colonial Encounters in the San Francisco Bay Area, California" (PhD diss., University of California, Berkeley, 2010), 173–174; Hutchinson, *Frontier Settlement in Mexican California*, 161–174.

9. Land Case 425ND: San Francisco de Asís Mission, p. 461, Exhibit VIII, Act of Departmental Assembly (of Alienation), October 28, 1845; Roberta S. Greenwood, "The California Ranchero: Fact and Fancy," in *Columbian Consequences*, vol. 1, *Archaeological and Historical Perspectives on the Spanish Borderlands West*, ed. David Hurst Thomas (Washington, DC: Smithsonian Institution Press, 1989); "Documents Relating to Early San Francisco Government, 1835–1857," C-A 370, Box 1, Bancroft Library, University of California, Berkeley.

---

10. Halleck, Peachy and Billings Papers, C-B 421, Dolwe 298 Sesione Publica, 1840, Bancroft Library, University of California, Berkeley.

11. Land Case 424c, 2481; Hansen, *Search for Authority*, 15-68; Francis F. Guest, "Municipal Government in Spanish California," *California Historical Society Quarterly* 46, no. 4 (1967): 307-335; David J. Garr, *Hispanic Urban Planning in North America* (New York: Garland Publishing, 1991), 24-28; Iris H. W. Engstrand, "The Legal Heritage of Spanish California," *Southern California Quarterly* 75, no. 3/4 (1993): 205-236.

12. David Hornbeck, "Land Tenure and Rancho Expansion in Alta California, 1784-1846," *Journal of Historical Geography* 4, no. 4 (1978): 371-390.

13. J. N. Bowman, "Index of the Spanish-Mexican Private Land Grant Records and Cases of California 1956," typescript, Bancroft Library, University of California, Berkeley; John Ryan Fischer, *Cattle Colonialism: An Environmental History of the Conquest of California and Hawai'i* (Chapel Hill: University of North Carolina Press, 2015), chaps. 2, 5.

14. W. W. Robinson, *Land in California: The Story of Mission Lands, Ranchos, Squatters, Mining Claims, Railroad Grants, Land Scrip, Homesteads* (Berkeley: University of California Press, 1979), chap. 5; Fischer, *Cattle Colonialism*, chap. 5.

15. Bowman, "Index of the Spanish-Mexican Private Land Grant Records."

16. Land Case 401ND: Depositions, September 29-October 23, 1855.

17. Ibid., 1-14.

18. Land Case 5ND: Rancho Rincón de las Salinas y Potrero Viejo, pp. 1-25, 39, 44, 161-165, Petition of the Heirs of José Cornelio Bernal and Depositions, February 9, 1852-September 27, 1854.

19. Ibid.

20. Land Case 389ND: Candelario Valencia, p. 9, Petition of Candelario Valencia, February 11, 1852; p. 18, Translation of Expediente, May 23, 1851.

21. Land Case 353ND: José R. Valencia, p. 12, Deposition of Candelario Valencia, September 13, 1854; p. 15, Annex to the Deposition of Juan Alvarado, June 30, 1835.

22. Land Case 353ND: p. 13, Deposition of Candelario Valencia, September 13, 1854; p. 10, Deposition of Manuel Castro, May 9, 1854.

23. Land Case 387ND: Rancho Las Camaritas, pp. 22-23, Petition of José Jesús Noé to the Prefect of the First District, October 3, 1839; Mae Silver, *The Last Mexican Alcalde of Yerba Buena, Jose de Jesus Noe* (San Francisco: M. Silver, 1991).

24. Land Case 387ND: p. 19, Ruling, January 1, 1840; p. 22, Petition of José Jesús Noé to the Prefect of the First District, October 3, 1839.

25. Ibid., p. 12, Deposition of José de la Cruz Sanchez, March 31, 1854.

26. Land Case 6ND: Josefa de Haro; Mae Silver, *Rancho San Miguel: A San Francisco Neighborhood History* (San Francisco: Ord Street Press, 2001).

27. Ibid.; Land Case 166ND; Land Case 380ND.

28. Land Case 166ND: pp. 8-11, Translation of Petition and Grants, March 2, 1853;

Decree, March 2, 1853; pp. 66–69, Depositions in Heirs of Francisco de Haro case, August 14, 1862; pp. 72–82, Testimony in Heirs of Francisco de Haro case, July 24, 1862; Land Case 173ND: Heirs of Francisco de Haro, pp. 58–73, Deposition of Tiburcio Vasquez, August 27, 1862; pp. 8–11, Transcript of the Proceedings, August 29, 1854; pp. 66–69, Deposition of José Fernandez, August 28, 1862; pp. 72–82, Deposition of Francisco Sanchez, August 28, 1862.

29. Land Case 166ND: pp. 66–80, Depositions of José Fernandez and Francisco Sanchez, August 14, 1862; Land Case 173ND: p. 145, Deposition of Francisco Sanchez, August 27, 1862; p. 63, Deposition of Tiburcio Vasquez, July 31, 1862.

30. Land Case 166ND: August 15–16, 1843.

31. Land Case 166ND: p. 7, Expediente, March 2, 1853; p. 27, Final Decree, August 24, 1857; pp. 4–11, Deposition of Francisco Sanchez, August 31, 1853; pp. 76–78, Deposition of Francisco Sanchez, August 14, 1862; Land Case 173ND: pp. 123–124, 136, 146, Deposition of Francisco Sanchez, August 1, 1862; Stefanos Polyzoides and Chris Wilson, eds., *The Plazas of New Mexico* (San Antonio: Trinity University Press, 2011), chap. 2.

32. Francis J. Weber, comp. and ed., *Mission Dolores: A Documentary History of San Francisco Mission* (Hong Kong: Libra Press, 1979).

33. Charles Brown, "Statement of Recollections of Early Events in California," Bancroft Dictation, Bancroft Library, University of California, Berkeley, 1878.

34. Richard N. Schellens Papers, California Historical Society, clipping from the *Honolulu Pacific Advertiser*, 1870.

35. Jeanne Farr McDonnell, *Juana Briones of Nineteenth-Century California* (Tucson: University of Arizona Press, 2008); J. N. Bowman, "Juana Briones de Miranda," *Historical Society of Southern California Quarterly* 39, no. 3 (1957): 227–244; Land Case 424aND: José Yves Limantour, pp. 32–61, Deposition of William A. Richardson, September 6, 1853; Land Case 427aND: City of San Francisco.

36. Land Case 424aND: pp. 32–37, Deposition of William A. Richardson, September 6, 1853.

37. Figueroa, *Manifesto to the Mexican Republic*, 98.

38. David Igler, *The Great Ocean: Pacific Worlds from Captain Cook to the Gold Rush* (New York: Oxford University Press, 2013), 185, chap. 1, conclusion.

39. Harlan Hague and David Langum, *Thomas O. Larkin: A Life of Patriotism and Profit in Old California* (Norman: Oklahoma University Press, 1978), 40–42.

40. Papers of Jacob Leese, Collection MS OV 10, California Historical Society; William Heath Davis, Account Book, 1843–1845, California Historical Society.

41. William Leidesdorff Papers, Folder 5, MS Vault 86, California Historical Society, 1847.

42. Richard Henry Dana, *Two Years Before the Mast: A Personal Narrative* (New York: Harper and Brothers, 1840), chap. 26; Edward Kemble, "Yerba Buena—1846, A Backward Look," *Sacramento Union*, August 26, September 16, and October 14, 1871.

———

43. "Documents Relating to Early San Francisco Government, 1835–1857," C-A 370, Box 1, Bancroft Library, University of California, Berkeley; Land Case 424aND: pp. 661–664; John Henry Brown, *Reminiscences and Incidents of "The Early Days" of San Francisco* (San Francisco: Mission Journal Publishing Company, 1886), 20–22; Frank Soulé and John H. Gihon, *The Annals of San Francisco*, reprint ed. (Whitefish, MT: Kessinger Publishing, 1966), 82.

44. Brown, *Reminiscences and Incidents*, 19–23; John Henry Brown, *Yerba Buena, 1846: A Description of the Town with an Account of Its Early Inhabitants* (San Francisco: Grabhorn Press, 1939), 7; Land Case 166ND; Fischer, *Cattle Colonialism*.

45. McDonnell, *Juana Briones of Nineteenth-Century California*, 27–28, 68, 105, chap. 8.

46. Ibid., 116; Jacob N. Bowman, *The Peraltas and Their Houses* (Oakland, CA: Alameda County Historical Society, 2001).

47. Quoted in C. Alan Hutchinson, *Frontier Settlement in Mexican California* (New Haven, CT: Yale University Press, 1969), 199–200; Hansen, *Search for Authority*, chap. 1.

48. "Documents Relating to Early San Francisco Government, 1835–1857," Bancroft C-A, Box 2, August 8, 1844, October 8, 1844, Box 1, August 4, 1837, December 5, 1845, August 8, 1844, Bancroft Library, University of California, Berkeley.

49. Land Case 424cND: José Yves Limantour, p. 2480, December 13, 1835; *The Works of Hubert Howe Bancroft, History of California*, ed. Wallace Hebberd, vol. 20 (Santa Barbara, CA: Wallace Hebberd, 1966), 665–668.

50. Land Case 424c: José Yves Limantour, p. 2481.

51. "Documents Relating to Early San Francisco Government, 1835–1857," Box 1, folders 18, 141, 151, 161, 162, Bancroft Library, University of California, Berkeley.

52. Ibid., "CA of California," Box 2, folders 136, 138.

53. Land Case 424cND: p. 2506, Office of the Prefect of the First District, April 23, 1841; Iris H. W. Engstrand, "The Legal Heritage of Spanish California," *Southern California Quarterly* 75, no. 3–4 (1993): 205–236; "Documents Relating to Early California," Box 2, folder 28, Bancroft Library, University of California, Berkeley; Hutchinson, *Frontier Settlement in Mexican California*, 211–212.

54. "Documents Relating to Early California," Box 1, December 31, 1837, Bancroft Library, University of California, Berkeley.

55. "Documents Relating to Early California," Box 1, folder 2, September 23, 1835, Box 2, April 23, 1841, Bancroft Library, University of California, Berkeley; *The Works of Hubert Howe Bancroft*, 20:665–668, 20:703–706.

56. Land Case 424aND: pp. 652–664, Depositions of Robert Ridley and William Richardson, September 6, 1853.

57. Land Case 424cND: 2481, 2506; Land Case 425ND: Bishop Joseph S. Alemany, pp. 37–50, Testimony of Jose Castro, April 23, 1841; Land Case 427aND: pp. 85–89, Deposition of John Vioget, April 13, 1854.

58. Quoted in Hutchinson, *Frontier Settlement in Mexican California*, 341.

59. For the concept of the multilocal, see Matt K. Matsuda, *Pacific Worlds: A History of Sea, Peoples, and Cultures* (New York: Cambridge University Press, 2012).

60. Land Case 424aND: pp. 15-19, Deposition of Manuel Jimeno, February 15, 1853.

61. Hansen, *Search for Authority*, 68.

62. Soulé and Gihon, *Annals of San Francisco*, 187.

63. "Documents Relating to Early California," Box 1, folder 162, Bancroft Library, University of California, Berkeley.

64. Ibid., Box 1, folder 162; Benjamin Madley, "Understanding Genocide in California Under United States Rule, 1846-1873," *Western Historical Quarterly* 47 (Winter 2016): 449-462.

CHAPTER 6: MAKING BALTIMORE A MODERN CITY, 1828-1954

1. George McCreary, *The Ancient and Honorable Mechanical Company of Baltimore* (Baltimore, 1901), 82.

2. *City Council Proceedings*, March 15, 1835, February 1, 1844, February 6, 1851, and November 14, 1854.

3. Robert E. Shalhope, *The Baltimore Bank Riot: Political Upheaval in Antebellum Maryland* (Urbana: University of Illinois Press, 2009).

4. Mayor's Message, November 14, 1854.

5. J. H. Hollander, *The Financial History of Baltimore* (Baltimore: Johns Hopkins University Press, 1889), 172-194; Robin Einhorn, *American Taxation, American Slavery* (Chicago: University of Chicago Press, 2006); Leonard P. Curry, *The Corporate City: The American City as a Political Entity, 1800-1850* (Westport, CT: Greenwood Press, 1997), 43, 54.

6. *City Council Proceedings*, February 8, 1808; March 24, 1818, 64; January 10, 1839, 20; Hollander, *Financial History*.

7. *Ordinances of the Corporation of the City of Baltimore, 1823-1827* (John Cox, City Printer: Baltimore, 1876), July 23, 1824, to February 16, 1825; *City Council Proceedings*, January 2, 1826, 266.

8. Quoted in James D. Dilts, *The Great Road: The Building of the Baltimore and Ohio, the Nation's First Railroad, 1828-1853* (Stanford, CA: Stanford University Press, 1993), 7-11.

9. *City Council Proceedings*, P. W. Thomas to the City Council, February 1831; Mayor's Message, January 2, 1832.

10. John Pendleton Kennedy, *Letters of a Man of the Times to the Citizens of Baltimore* (Baltimore: Sands and Neilson, 1836).

11. Buckler Family Papers, MS 2786, folder 1832-1838, Maryland Historical Society; *Niles Weekly Register*, August 15, 1835; John T. Scharf, *The Chronicles of Baltimore; Being a Complete History of "Baltimore Town" and Baltimore City from the Earliest Period to the Present Time* (Baltimore: Turnball Brothers, 1874), 475-79; David Grimsted, *American Mobbing, 1828-1861: Toward Civil War* (New York: Oxford University Press, 1998), 7-12; Frank Otto Gatell, "Secretary

Taney and the Baltimore Pets: A Study in Banking and Politics," *Business History Review* 39, no. 2 (1965): 205–227.

12. Robert E. Shalhope, *The Baltimore Bank Riot: Political Upheaval in Antebellum Maryland* (Urbana: University of Illinois Press, 2009), 66, chap. 2.

13. Quote from *Niles Weekly Register*, August 15, 1835; Scharf, *Chronicles of Baltimore*, 475–480.

14. Samuel Smith, *The Address of the City of Baltimore to the Citizens of Maryland Made in Pursuance of Resolutions Passed in Town-Meeting, on the 6th Inst.* (Baltimore[?], 1836).

15. John Pendleton Kennedy, *Proceedings of the Convention on Internal Improvement of Maryland Held in Baltimore, May 2, 1836* (Baltimore: John Tay, 1836), 13; Kennedy, *Letters of a Man of the Times*; *City Council Proceedings*, February 13, 1837, 139.

16. *Baltimore Sun*, October 26, 1841.

17. Stuart Bruchey, *Enterprise: The Dynamic Economy of a Free People* (Cambridge, MA: Harvard University Press, 1990), chap. 7; Morton Horwitz, *The Transformation of American Law, 1780–1860* (Cambridge, MA: Harvard University Press, 1977).

18. Dilts, *Great Road*; *City Council Proceedings*, March 5, 1839, 275.

19. Hollander, *Financial History*, 100; Mayor's Correspondence, 1832:1026, BRG9-2, BCA.

20. Mayor's Message, January 2, 1832, and January 5, 1834; Hollander, *Financial History*.

21. City Council Records, 1840:337, RG16-1, BCA.

22. *City Council Proceedings*, December 16, 1842; January 22, 1843; April 6, 1843, 368–370; February 8, 1853, 217.

23. *City Council Proceedings*, January 7, 1830.

24. Gary Lawson Browne, *Baltimore in the Nation: 1789–1861* (Chapel Hill: University of North Carolina Press, 1980), 179.

25. Jason Kaufman, "Town and Country in the Redefinition of State-Federal Power: Canada and the United States, 1630–2005," in *The City in American Political Development*, ed. Richardson Dilworth (New York: Routledge, 2009), 64–74; Jason Kaufman, "Corporate Law and the Sovereignty of States," *American Sociological Review* 73 (June 2008): 402–415; Katherine M Johnson, "'The Glorified Municipality': State Formation and the Urban Process in North America," *Political Geography* 27 (2008): 400–417; Hendrik Hartog, *Public Property and Private Power: The Corporation of the City of New York in American Law, 1730–1870* (Chapel Hill: University of North Carolina Press, 1983), 4, 237.

26. David Schley, "Building the Capitalist City: The B&O Railroad and Urban Space in Baltimore, 1827–1877" (PhD diss., Johns Hopkins University, 2013).

27. Quoted in Sherry H. Olson, "Baltimore Imitates the Spider," *Annals of the Association of American Geographers* 69, no. 4 (December 1979): 560.

28. Ibid.

29. City Council Records, March 14, 1826, March 1828, pp. 457, 459–460, RG 16, BCA.

30. *City Council Proceedings*, February 24, 1840, 338; January 1828; March 17, 1836; February 24, 1840; May 14, 1837 (Second Branch), 253.

31. *City Council Proceedings*, February 21, 1828.

32. Mayor's Message, January 2, 1832, and June 10, 1834, p. 9.

33. City Council Records, 1832:572, 1849:526, RG16-1, BCA; *City Council Proceedings*, February 17, 1834; March 12, 1835, 215–217.

34. *City Council Proceedings*, April 22, 1857, 676–679.

35. *Charter and By-Laws of the Canton Corporation* (Baltimore: John Murphy, 1848); *City Council Proceedings*, February 25, 1836.

36. Charter and By-Laws of the Canton Corporation, 1818, pamphlet printed by John Murphy, 1948; City Council Records, February 25, 1836.

37. Olson, "The Spider"; Mary Ellen Hayward, *Baltimore's Alley Houses: Homes for Working People Since the 1780s* (Baltimore: Johns Hopkins University Press, 2008); Mary Ellen Hayward and Charles Belfoure, *The Baltimore Row House* (New York: Princeton Architectural Press, 1999); Martha J. Vill, "Building Enterprise in Late Nineteenth-Century Baltimore," *Journal of Historical Geography* 12, no. 2 (1986): 162–181.

38. Edward K. Muller and Paul A. Groves, "The Emergence of Industrial Districts in Mid-Nineteenth Century Baltimore," *Geographical Review* 69, no. 2 (April 1979): 159–178. Hayward, *Baltimore's Alley Houses*; Michael Franch, "Congregation and Community in Baltimore, 1840–1860" (PhD diss., University of Maryland, 1984).

39. City Council Records, March 18, 1845, p. 364; April 25, 1854, p. 574; February 16, 1846, p. 758.

40. Mary P. Ryan, "Democracy Rising: The Monuments of Baltimore, 1809–1842," *Journal of Urban History* 36 (2010): 127–150.

41. *Ordinances of the Corporation of the City of Baltimore* (Baltimore: John Cox, 1876), March 30, 1832, 87; *Baltimore Sun*, February 27, 1846, December 1, 1858; Muller and Groves, "Industrial Districts"; Mary Ellen Hayward, "Urban Vernacular Architecture in Nineteenth-Century Baltimore," *Winterthur Portfolio* 16, no. 1 (1980): 33–63; Hayward and Belfoure, *Baltimore Row House*.

42. *Baltimore Sun*, June 11, 1839, June 8, 1855, December 13, 1850.

43. *City Council Proceedings*, January 1, 1857.

44. *Baltimore Sun*, June 11, 1839.

45. *City Council Proceedings*, January 7, 1830; April 8, 1834, 296.

46. *Baltimore Sun*, June 1, 1839; Deed Book, January 1839, Maryland State Archives.

47. *Baltimore Sun*, June 12, 1839; Ordinance No. 47, *Ordinances* (April 23, 1839).

48. *Baltimore Sun*, April 11, 1844, January 15, 1854.

49. *City Council Proceedings*, 1855, 22.

50. *Baltimore Sun*, May 5, 1856, April 24, 1856, December 1, 1858.

51. *City Council Proceedings*, February 3, 1841, 34; February 6, 1843, 85; June 1, 1843, 259–272; February 2, 1841.

52. *Baltimore Sun*, September 9, 1846, November 18, 1858, May 10, 1859.

53. *Baltimore Sun*, February 7, 1852; *City Council Proceedings*, July 4, 1857.

54. City Council Papers, April 3, 1844, p. 463; April 26, 1850, pp. 318–319, RG16, series 2, Baltimore City Archives.

55. *City Council Proceedings*, February 5, 1844, January 21, 1850, March 20, 1850; *Baltimore Sun*, September 9, 1850.

56. *Gloucester Telegraph*, June 5, 1850.

57. *Baltimore Sun*, May, 5 1844, June 6, 1844.

58. Alexis de Tocqueville, *Journey to America*, trans. George Lawrence, ed. J. P Mayer (New Haven, CT: Yale University Press, 1960), 74–75; *City Council Proceedings*, June 15, 1853.

59. Tocqueville, *Journey to America*, 75.

60. *Baltimore Sun*, February 12 to February 19, 1853.

61. *Baltimore Sun*, March 31, 1848, September 11, 1831.

62. *Baltimore Sun*, October 1, 1844, September 7, 1850.

63. *City Council Proceedings*, June 15, 1853; Nelson Manfred Black, *Water for the Cities: A History of the Urban Water Supply Problem in the United States* (Syracuse, NY: Syracuse University Press, 1956), 63.

64. Black, *Water for the Cities*, 239; *City Council Proceedings*, February 8, 1853, February 7, 1853.

65. Browne, *Baltimore in the Nation*; William J. Novak, *The People's Welfare: Law and Regulation in Nineteenth-Century America* (Chapel Hill: University of North Carolina Press, 1996), 9; Sam Bass Warner Jr., *The Private City: Philadelphia in Three Periods of Its Growth* (Philadelphia: University of Pennsylvania Press, 1968).

66. *City Council Proceedings*, December 6 and 20, 1853, 53–92; Browne, *Baltimore in the Nation*, 202.

67. *City Council Proceedings*, May 26, 1853, 622.

68. *City Council Proceedings*, April 1, 1858, 269–277; May 5, 1858, 37; April 24, 1851, 475.

69. [John P. Kennedy], "Baltimore Long Ago," 17, 6, Pamphlet Collection, John Work Garrett Library, Johns Hopkins University.

70. *Gloucester Telegraph*, June 5, 1850.

CHAPTER 7: THE CAPITALIST "PUEBLO"

1. Roger W. Lotchin, *San Francisco, 1846–1856: From Hamlet to City* (Urbana: University of Illinois Press, 1997), 128–131; *Baltimore Sun*, March 25, 1850; William Hull Papers, diary, July 27, 1849, and undated speech, MS2135, Maryland Historical Society.

2. William D. M. Howard Papers, Vault MA 30, California Historical Society, Box 3, folder 5.

3. Ibid.; "Articles of Association and Agreement of the San Francisco Land

Association," 9, Bancroft Library, University of California, Berkeley; Thomas Hayes Miscellany, 1854–1896, MS 3182, California Historical Society.

4. A. M. Sakolski, *The Great American Land Bubble: The Amazing Story of Land-Grabbing, Speculations, and Booms from Colonial Days to the Present Time* (Eastford, CT: Martino Fine Books, 2011).

5. *Minutes of the Proceedings of the Legislative Assembly of the District of San Francisco, March 12, 1849, to June 4, 1849, and a Record of the Proceedings of the Ayuntamiento or Town Council of San Francisco, from August 6, 1849, until May 3, 1850* (San Francisco: Towne and Bacon, 1860), April 9, 1849.

6. *Manual of the Corporation of the City of San Francisco, Containing a Map of the City; The Declaration of Independence; the Constitution of the United States; the Constitution of the State of California; The Charters of the City; The Revised Ordinances; The General Repealing Ordinances; The Ordinances Still in Force, and Certain Laws Relating Particularly to the City of San Francisco* (San Francisco: G. K. Fitch and Company, 1852); Samuel W. Brown, "Journal of Sea Voyage to San Francisco in April of 1849," MS 236, California Historical Society.

7. Diary of Charles Theodore Hart Palmer, August 24, 1851, 222–226, Charles Theodor Hart Palmer Papers, BANC MSS C-B 560, Bancroft Library, University of California, Berkeley.

8. Memorial to the Legislature of the State of California, *San Francisco Miscellany*, 1–6, BANC MSS C-B 691, Bancroft Library, University of California, Berkeley.

9. Ibid.

10. *Proceedings of the Town Council of San Francisco, Alta California, 1849–50*, facsimile, Bancroft Library, University of California, Berkeley.

11. "An Act of Incorporation and Ordinances of the City of San Francisco, 1850," in *Manual of the Corporation*, 18–21.

12. "Charters of San Francisco" and "Act of Incorporation, Mayor's Message, 1853," in *Manual of the Corporation*, 17–24.

13. "Documents Relating to Early San Francisco Government, 1835–1857," Box 1, April 23, 1841, Bancroft Library, University of California, Berkeley; Halleck, Billings and Peachy Papers, Box 3, folders 298–304, copy of the document of the California Prefecture, April 23, 1841, BANC MSS C-B 421, Bancroft Library, University of California, Berkeley; David Weber, *The Mexican Frontier, 1821–1846: The American Southwest Under Mexico* (Albuquerque: University of New Mexico Press, 1982), 282; David Hornbeck "Land Tenure and Rancho Expansion in Alta California, 1784–1846," *Journal of Historical Geography* 4 (1978): 371–390; Alfred Wheeler, *Land Titles in San Francisco and the Laws Affecting the Same with a Synopsis of All Grants and Sales of Land Within the Limits Claimed by the City* (San Francisco: Alta California Printing Office, 1852), Schedule F.

14. *Minutes of the Proceedings of the Legislative Assembly of the District of San Francisco*; O'Farrell Papers, April 2, 1848, San Francisco History Center, San Francisco Public Library.

15. "Horace Hawes," photostat, California Historical Society; Horace Hawes, *Brief*

of an Argument Made by Horace Hawes on Behalf of the United States Before the US Board of Land Commissioners, for California (San Francisco: Times and Transcript Steam Press, 1854), California Historical Society; United States Land Commission, "US District Court of California, Northern District, California Land Cases," A300, Bancroft Library, University of California, Berkeley (hereafter Land Case ND), Land Case 305ND.

16. "Records of the Legislative Assembly" (1849), in *San Francisco, History, Incidents*, 283-241, xF869.s3.2 S15, Bancroft Library, University of California, Berkeley.

17. *Minutes of the Proceedings of the Legislative Assembly*, Appendix 4, 221-240.

18. Wheeler, *Land Titles in San Francisco*, Appendix I; Frank Soulé and John H. Gihon, *Annals of San Francisco*, reprint ed. (Whitefish, MT: Kessinger Publishing, 1966), 229-231.

19. "Peter H. Burnett Governor Overrules Hawes," photostat, California Historical Society.

20. Entries from March 12, 1849, to June 4, 1849, *Minutes of the Proceedings of the Legislative Assembly of the District of San Francisco* (San Francisco: Office of the Evening Press, 1850).

21. Wheeler, *Land Titles in San Francisco*. Wheeler's report was reprinted by two newspapers, the *Alta* in 1852 and the *Evening Picayune* in 1851.

22. Joseph Folsom Collection, Bill of City Taxes, 1851, MS758, California Historical Society.

23. Nancy Olmsted, *Vanished Waters: A History of San Francisco's Mission Bay* (San Francisco: Mission Bay Creek Conservancy, 1986), 22.

24. Adolphus C. Whitcomb Papers, MS 2309, California Historical Society; Jacob Leese to Thomas Larkin, January 19, 1849, Papers of Jacob Leese, Collection MS OV 10, Vault B-062, California Historical Society.

25. San Francisco Charter, Mayor's Message, in *Manual of the Corporation*, 12.

26. *Organization Act and Regulations of the US Land Commissioners for California* (San Francisco, 1852), Bancroft Negatives, Box 567:20, Bancroft Library, University of California, Berkeley.

27. Land Case 6ND: Josefa de Haro, p. 175, Decree, January 12, 1876; Halleck Peachy and Billings Papers, Bancroft Library, University of California, Berkeley, Box 1, folder 260; Land Case 5ND: José Jesús Bernal, pp. 209-212, Deposition of Helen Lowell, July 23, 1855.

28. Land Case 5ND: pp. 161-163, Deposition of Pedro Chaboya, September 27, 1854; Land Case 387ND: Rancho Las Camaritas.

29. Land Case 5ND: p. 178, Deposition of Jacob Leese, May 19, 1855; Land Case 387ND: p. 9, Deposition of José de la Cruz Sanchez, March 14, 1854.

30. Land Case 5ND: p. 214, Testimony of Helen Lowell, July 23, 1855.

31. Halleck, Billings and Peachy Papers, Box 3, folders 250-275 and 284-294, and Box 1, Bancroft Library, University of California, Berkeley.

32. Paul Gates, "Land Act of 1851," *California Historical Quarterly* (December 1971): 395-430; Opinion of Commissioner Wilson, "Organization Act and Regulations

of the US Land Commissioners for California," 58–59, in case of Widow Jose Bernal.

33. Land Case 424aND.

34. Land Case 424aND: José Yves Limantour, pp. 138–150, Deposition of Thomas Larkin, October 25, 1854.

35. *Manual of the Corporation*, "Charters of San Francisco," Article I, p. 1; John Dwinelle, *The Colonial History of San Francisco* (San Francisco: Towne and Bacon, 1863), 2.

36. Halleck, Peaching and Billings Papers, Box 3, folder 304, Bancroft Library, University of California, Berkeley; Land Case 427aND: City of San Francisco, p. 34, Testimony of William Richardson, August 20, 1853.

37. Dwinelle, *Colonial History*, 2.

38. Ibid., 1–21, 35, 56–61; Hawes, "Brief of an Argument" Addenda.

39. Dwinelle, *Colonial History*, Addenda XI, 21.

40. Land Case 427aND: pp. 32–49, Testimony of William Richardson, August 20, 1854; Pueblo Lands 59, 60.

41. Land Case 427aND.

42. Dwinelle, *Colonial History*, 144; *Proceedings of the Town Council of San Francisco, Alta California, 1849–50*, February 13, 1850, 72.

43. Dwinelle, *Colonial History*, Preface.

44. Land Case 427aND: pp. 50–55, Deposition of Julius K. Rose, August 30, 1853; Halleck, Peachy and Billings Papers, Bancroft Library, University of California, Berkeley, Box 3, folder 304–305; Palmer Diary, March 19, 1850.

45. Land Case 424aND, pp. 39–45, p. 322, Deposition of Henry S. Fitch, December 5, 1855.

46. Whitcomb Manuscript; "The Abstract of Titles to Part of the Western Addition," vol. 3, 170, BANC MSS 2002/51c; Land Case 387ND.

47. Land Case 166ND: Heirs of Francisco de Haro, p. 58, Deposition of J. J. Gardiner, August 13, 1862.

48. Land Case 6ND: pp. 22, 24–25, Protest of John B. Polley Against the Confirmation of This Claim, April 23, 1852; W. W. Robinson, *Land in California* (Berkeley: University of California Press, 1948), chap. 9, p. 113; *Daily California*, December 19, 1862.

49. "Prospectus of the California Land Distribution and Home Association," Bancroft Negatives, Box 567:20, Bancroft Library, University of California, Berkeley; Mae Silver, *Rancho San Miguel San Francisco* (San Francisco: Mouse Type, Inc., and Stanyan Printing, 1992).

50. *Alta*, July 5, 1851.

51. "California Taxpayer's Union," pamphlet, Bancroft Library, University of California, Berkeley; *Alta*, January 19, 1856.

52. "An Act Concerning the City of San Francisco and to Ratify and Confirm Ordinances of the Common Council, Approved March 11, 1858," pF869.S3.76.C2, Bancroft Library, University of California, Berkeley.

53. Ibid.; "An Act to Repeal the Several Charters of the City of San Francisco: To Establish the Boundaries of the City and County of San Francisco, and to Consolidate the Government Thereof," BANC MSS C-B 526 v.2:4.

54. *Proceedings of the Town Council of San Francisco, Upper California* (San Francisco: Alta California Press, 1850), 52nd Meeting, February 5, 1850; 46th meeting, January 16, 1850, xF869.S3.2.S169, Bancroft Library, University of California, Berkeley; *San Francisco in the 1850s: 33 Photographic Views by G. R. Fardon* (New York: Dover Publications, 1977).

55. Palmer Diary, February 3, 1850.

56. Land Case 424ND: Richardson Testimony; see map in chap. 5.

57. Soulé and Gihon, *Annals of San Francisco*, 161–162; Eric Sandweiss, "Claiming the Urban Landscape: The Improbable Rise of an Inevitable City," in *Eadweard Muybridge and the Photographic Panorama of San Francisco, 1850–1880*, eds. David Harris and Eric Sandweiss (Montreal: Centre Canadien d'Architecture, 1993), 15–33.

58. "An Act Concerning the City of San Francisco," Second Section, 51.

59. *Alta*, February 2, 1851, March 25, 1851, April 29 1952.

60. *Alta*, August 18, 1850, March 25, 1851, July 31, 1851, April 29, 1852, August 1, 1854.

61. *Alta*, February 3, 1851, January 17, 1860.

62. "Ordinances and Joint Resolutions of the City of San Francisco: Together with a List of the Officers of the City and County and Rules and Orders of the Common Council" (San Francisco: Monson and Valentine, 1854), xF869.S3S31, Bancroft Library, University of California, Berkeley.

63. Charles Gibson to Billings, October 3, 1855, Halleck Peachy and Billings Papers, Box 1, Bancroft Library, University of California, Berkeley; "Articles of Association of the San Francisco Land Association," 2–3.

64. John Coffin Jones to Thomas Larkin, in *The Larkin Papers: Personal, Business and Official Correspondence of Thomas Oliver Larkin*, ed. George P. Hammond (Berkeley: University of California Press, 1951); W. K. Weston to H. L. Weston, May 31, 1852, William Weston Papers, California Historical Society; letter fragment, June 23, 1857, "Thomas Hayes Miscellany, 1854–1896," California Historical Society; Peter R. Decker, *Fortunes and Failures: White-Collar Mobility in Nineteenth-Century San Francisco* (Cambridge, MA: Harvard University Press, 1978), 34.

65. J. N. Bowman, "Juana Briones de Miranda," *Historical Society of Southern California Quarterly* (1957): 227–244; letter fragment, 1857, Thomas Hayes Miscellany.

66. Charles Brewster Letters, January 29, 1851, MS 213, California Historical Society; Stark B. Smith to Sallie, September 11, 1853, BANC MS 98/c, Bancroft Library, University of California, Berkeley.

67. DeWitt Family Papers, February 27, 1850, BANC MSS 73/163, Bancroft Library, University of California, Berkeley.

68. George Hollingsworth Letters, July 18, 1852, May 28, 1854, December 2, 1854,

MS 1016, California Historical Society; Joseph F. Emery to John R. Emery, February 28, 1855, Emery Papers, San Francisco History Center, San Francisco Public Library.

69. Palmer Diary, "Letter to the Journal of Commerce," 220–228; Robert B. Wallace, May 21, 1854, March 14, 1860, Robert B. Wallace Letters, MS Vault 63, California Historical Society.

70. Papers of Jasper O'Farrell, Letter to "Friend" MacCorkle, 10/6/?, MS Vault 101, California Historical Society.

71. John Coffin Jones to Thomas Larkin, *Larkin Papers*, vol. 9, 88; Peter DeWitt to Alfred Dewitt, October 10, 1850, DeWitt Family Papers, BANC MSS 73/163c, Bancroft Library, University of California, Berkeley.

CHAPTER 8: BALTIMORE, SAN FRANCISCO, AND THE CIVIL WAR

1. *Baltimore Sun*, May 11, 1860, November 2, 1860; Frank Towers, *The Urban South and the Coming of the Civil War* (Charlottesville: University Press of Virginia, 2004), 109, 116.

2. *Baltimore Sun*, June 19, 1860.

3. *Baltimore Sun*, June 21, 1860, June, 23, 1860; David Goldfield, *America Aflame: How the Civil War Created a Nation* (New York: Bloomsbury, 2011), 67–68.

4. Leonard L. Richards, *The California Gold Rush and the Coming of the Civil War* (New York: Vintage, 2007), 228–229.

5. Calvin Schermerhorn, "The Coastwise Slave Trade and a Mercantile Community of Interest," in *Slavery's Capitalism: A New History of American Economic Development*, eds. Sven Beckert and Seth Rockman (Philadelphia: University of Pennsylvania Press, 2016), 209–224; John R. Killick, "The Cotton Operations of Alexander Brown and Sons in the Deep South, 1820–1860," *Journal of Southern History* 13, no. 2 (May 1977): 169–194.

6. Bernard C. Steiner, *The Life of Reverdy Johnson* (Baltimore: Norman Remington Company, 1914), 95, passim.

7. Arthur Quinn, *The Rivals: William Gwin, David Broderick and the Birth of California* (New York: Crown, 1994), 255; Woodrow James Hansen, *The Search for Authority in California* (Oakland: BioBooks, 1960), 168.

8. John Tutino, *Making the New World: Founding Capitalism in the Bajío and Spanish North* (Durham, NC: Duke University Press, 2011); Hilda Iparraguirre and Ma. Isabel Campos Goenaga, eds., *Hacia una nación moderna: La modernidad y la construcción de la nación en México* (Mexico City: Escuela Nacional de Antropología e Historia, 2011).

9. Rachel St. John, *Line in the Sand: A History of the Western US–Mexico Border* (Princeton, NJ: Princeton University Press, 2011); Robert E. May, *Slavery, Race, and the Conquest of the Tropics* (New York: Cambridge University Press, 2013); Amy Greenberg, *A Wicked War: Polk, Clay, Lincoln and the 1846 Invasion of Mexico* (New York: Knopf, 2012); Rachel St. John, "The Unpredictable

America of William Gwin: Expansion, Secession, and the Unstable Borders of Nineteenth-Century North America," *Journal of the Civil War Era*, 6, no. 1 (2016): 56–84.

10. Goldfield, *America Aflame*; Eric Foner, "The Wilmot Proviso Revisited," *Journal of American History* 56, no. 2 (September 1969): 262–279.

11. Robert W. Johnson, ed., *The Lincoln-Douglas Debates of 1858* (New York: Oxford University Press, 1965), 15–16, 39, 212, 254; Michael A. Morrison, *Slavery in the American West: The Eclipse of Manifest Destiny and the Coming of the Civil War* (Chapel Hill: University of North Carolina Press, 1997), 40; Eric Foner, *Free Soil, Free Labor, Free Men: The Ideology of the Republican Party Before the Civil War* (New York: Oxford University Press, 1970).

12. Goldfield, *America Aflame*, 167–168, 178; Jonathan H. Earle, *Jacksonian Antislavery and the Politics of Free Soil, 1824–1854* (Chapel Hill: University of North Carolina Press, 2004).

13. Steiner, *Reverdy Johnson*, 26; Peter H. Burnett, *Recollections and Opinions of an Old Pioneer* (New York: Da Capo Press, 1969 [1880]), 196; Hansen, *Search for Authority*, chap. 22; Judge H. S. Brown, Bancroft Dictation, BANC MSS C-D, Bancroft Library, University of California, Berkeley, 19–22.

14. Hansen, *Search for Authority*, chap. 39, 168; Jeremy Adelman, *Sovereignty and Revolution in the Iberian Atlantic* (Princeton, NJ: Princeton University Press, 2006), 188.

15. Andrew Slap and Frank Towers, eds., *Confederate Cities: The Urban South During the Civil War Era* (Chicago: University of Chicago Press, 2015).

16. *City Council Proceedings*, January 18, 1858, 6–7; Jean H. Baker, *Ambivalent Americans: The Know-Nothing Party in Maryland* (Baltimore: Johns Hopkins University Press, 1977); Philip J. Ethington, *The Public City: The Political Construction of Urban Life in San Francisco, 1850–1900* (New York: Cambridge University Press, 1994); Mary P. Ryan, *Civic Wars: Democracy and Public Life in the American City in the Nineteenth Century* (Berkeley: University of California Press, 1997), 139–151.

17. *Baltimore Sun*, September 5, 1859; Tracey Mathew Melton, *Hanging Henry Gambril: The Violent Career of Baltimore's Plug Uglies, 1854–1860* (Baltimore: Maryland Historical Society, 2005); Michael Holt, *The Rise and Fall of the American Whig Party* (New York: Oxford University Press, 1999).

18. George William Brown, *Baltimore and the Nineteenth of April 1861: A Study of the War* (Baltimore: Isaac Friedenwald, 1867).

19. *City Council Proceedings*, January 16, 1860, 4.

20. Jonathan W. White, ed., "Forty-Two Eyewitness Accounts of the Pratt Street Riot and Its Aftermath," *Maryland Historical Magazine* 106, no. 1 (2011): 70–90; Charles W. Mitchell, "'The Whirlwind Now Gathering': Baltimore's Pratt Street Riot and the End of Maryland Secession," *Maryland Historical Magazine* 97 (2002): 203–232; Harry A. Ezratty, *Baltimore in the Civil War: The Pratt Street Riot and the Occupied City* (Charleston, SC: Arcadia Press, 2010).

21. Ezratty, *Occupied City*.
22. Ibid., 44; Brown, *Nineteenth of April*, 15; Robert Schoeberlein, "A Fair to Remember: Maryland Women in Aid of the Union," *Maryland Historical Magazine* 90, no. 4 (Winter 1995): 466–488.
23. See, for example, Land Case ND166: July 13, 1858.
24. George Fox Kelly, *Land Frauds of California, Startling Exposures: Government Officials Implicated, Appeals for Justice—The Present Crisis* (Santa Rosa[?], 1864), Bancroft Library, University of California, Berkeley.
25. *Land Titles in San Francisco; Addresses by Honorable William J. Shaw and Honorable Nathaniel Bennett Giving Facts the Laws and the Character Effects of Legal Decisions Thereon, in Regard to the Land Titles of San Francisco* (San Francisco: S. T. Valentine and Company, 1862), Bancroft Negatives Box, 793:8, Bancroft Library, University of California, Berkeley.
26. *Hart v. Burnett*, 15 Cal. 530, 553–554 (1860); *Testimony Showing the Time of Possession, etc., of the Beideman Tract and the Decision of the Supreme Court of California Thereon* (San Francisco: Towne and Bacon, 1861).
27. *Hart v. Burnett*, 562.
28. United States Circuit Court, *The City of San Francisco v. the United States*, reprinted in Land Case 427ND: pp. 732, 793–821.
29. Ibid.
30. *Townsend et al. v. Greeley*, 72 US 326 (1866).
31. Paul Klens, *Justice Stephen Field: Shaping Liberty from the Gold Rush to the Golden Age* (Lawrence: University Press of Kansas, 1997). For Field, the gradations of sovereignty were stepping stones in a long political career. Field lived long enough to vote on two momentous Supreme Court decisions not related to the local land tussle: he upheld both corporate personhood in *Santa Clara v. the Southern Pacific* (1886) and racial segregation in *Plessy v. Ferguson* (1896).
32. Sherry H. Olson, *Baltimore: The Building of an American City*, rev. ed. (Baltimore: Johns Hopkins University Press, 1997), 142.
33. *City Council Proceedings*, June 15, 1859, 782.
34. *City Council Proceedings*, April 1, 1858, 269–270; May 5, 1858, 37; April 24, 1851, 475.
35. Ibid.
36. *City Council Proceedings*, 1859, 164.
37. *Baltimore Sun*, January 22, 1852.
38. *Baltimore Sun*, December 1, 1858.
39. *City Council Proceedings*, April 1861, 233–241; Joseph L. Arnold, "Suburban Growth and Municipal Annexation in Baltimore, 1745–1918," *Maryland Historical Magazine* 73, no. 2 (June 1978): 109–128.
40. *City Council Proceedings*, March 2, 1859, 332–341; March 22, 1859, 432–439.
41. Quoted in David Schley, "Landscape and Politics: The Creation of Baltimore's Druid Hill Park, 1860," *Maryland Historical Magazine* 103, no. 3 (2008): 294; David Schuyler, *The New Urban Landscape: The Redefinition of City Form in*

Nineteenth-Century America (Baltimore: Johns Hopkins University Press, 1986), 108–113.

42. *Baltimore Sun*, June 19, 1860.

43. *Baltimore Sun*, June 8, June 13, and June 16, 1860.

44. *Baltimore Sun*, July 11, July 18, July 15, July 26, October 4, and October 6, 1860.

45. Paige Glotzer, *Building Suburban Power: The Business of Exclusionary Housing Markets* (New York: Columbia University Press, 2019).

46. *City Council Proceedings*, January 20, 1858, 32; J. H. Hollander, *The Financial History of Baltimore* (Baltimore: Johns Hopkins University Press, 1889), 381; Arnold, "Suburban Growth."

47. *Baltimore Sun*, May 31, 1860; Schley, "Landscape and Politics"; Eden Unger Bowditch and Anne Draddy, *Druid Hill Park: The Heart of Historic Baltimore* (Charleston, SC: History Press, 2008).

48. "The Abstract of Titles to the Western Addition," October 28, 1865, Bancroft Library, University of California, Berkeley.

49. *Report of the Executive Committee of the Tax Payers' Protective Union, Approved and Adopted at the General Meeting of Members Held on the 14th of August, 1861* (San Francisco: Commercial Book and Job Steam Press, 1861).

50. *Testimony Showing the Time of Possession, etc., of the Beideman Tract*, 53–55.

51. *Codified Ordinances of the City and County of San Francisco Comprised in General Order No. 4113* (San Francisco: Towne and Bacon, 1861), 6.

52. "Codified Ordinances," "Auditor's Report," and "Act to Re-Incorporate" (1851), in *Manual of the Corporation of the City of San Francisco, Containing a Map of the City; The Declaration of Independence; the Constitution of the United States; the Constitution of the State of California; The Charters of the City; The Revised Ordinances; The General Repealing Ordinances; The Ordinances Still in Force, and Certain Laws Relating Particularly to the City of San Francisco* (San Francisco: G. K. Fitch and Company, 1852), 7–9.

53. "State of California District Court of the Fourth Judicial District, The City of San Francisco, April 24, 1854," 13–14, Pamphlet Collection, Bancroft Library, University of California, Berkeley; "Codified Ordinances" and "Report of the Board of Engineers upon the City Grades," June 30, 1860, in *Manual of the Corporation*; State of California District Court, Fourth Judicial District, *Felis Argenti v. the City of San Francisco*, April 24, 1859, pamphlet, California Historical Society.

54. *The Antidote for the Poison of Speeches and Documents Against the Parson Bulkhead, Published by the Citizens Anti-Bulkhead Committee of San Francisco* (San Francisco: Towne and Bacon, 1860), 21.

55. J. H. Purkitt, "Letter on the Water Front Improvement," in *The Bulkhead Question Completely Reviewed: The Law and the Testimony, and Speeches* (Sacramento: Daily Standard Office, 1860).

56. Wallace Papers, MSS 26620.U5W3, no. 8, Bancroft Library, University of California, Berkeley; *Antidote to the Poison*.

57. Robert B. Wallace to Bill [?], May 5, 1860.

58. "Letter on the Water Front Improvement," in *San Francisco History, Incidents,* 13–23, Bancroft Library, University of California, Berkeley.

59. Gray Brechin, *Imperial San Francisco: Urban Power, Earthly Ruin* (Berkeley: University of California Press, 2006), pt. 1.

60. *Alta*, April 30, 1861, March 16, 1862, January 14, 1863; *The Question of the Title to the Outside Lands, Settler (in proper) vs. the City of San Francisco, Argument for the Plaintiff* (San Francisco: Book and Job Printer, 1866), 3, Bancroft Negative, Box 792-9, Bancroft Library, University of California, Berkeley.

61. *Alta*, April 30, 1861, March 16, 1862, January 14, 1863; *Question of the Title to the Outside Lands*, 5, 13.

62. *The Clement Ordinance for Settling the Title to the Outside Lands of the City and County of San Francisco Approved October 12, 1866* (San Francisco: Towne and Bacon, 1866); Chas. Stanyan, A. J. Shrader, R. Beverly Cole, Chas. Clayton, and Monroe Ashbury, "Map of the Outside Lands of the City and County of San Francisco Showing Reservations Selected for Public Purposes Under the Provision of Order 800" (1868), Bancroft Library, University of California, Berkeley. See also Terence Young, *Building San Francisco's Parks: 1850-1930* (Baltimore: Johns Hopkins University Press, 2004); see *Map of San Francisco from Latest Surveys Engraved Expressly for the San Francisco Director*.

63. Victoria Post Ranney, ed., *The Papers of Frederick Law Olmsted*, vol. 5, *1863-1865: The California Frontier* (Baltimore: Johns Hopkins University Press), 519–546.

64. *Clement Ordinance*; *Evening Bulletin*, August 4, 1865; *Papers of Frederick Law Olmsted*, 5:519–546.

65. Roy Rosenzweig and Elizabeth Blackmar, *The Park and the People: A History of Central Park* (Ithaca, NY: Cornell University Press, 1992).

66. Schuyler, *New Urban Landscape*; John Archer, "Country and City in the American Romantic Suburb," *Journal of the Society of Architectural Historians* 42, no. 2 (May 1982): 139–156.

67. Michael R. Corbett, "Corbett Heights, San Francisco (Western Part of Eureka Valley) Historic Context Statement," courtesy of the author.

EPILOGUE

1. Linda G. Rich, Joan Clark Netherwood, and Elinor B. Cahn, *Neighborhood: A State of Mind* (Baltimore: Johns Hopkins University Press, 1981).

2. Gary Kamiya, *Cool Gray City of Love: 49 Views of San Francisco* (New York: Bloomsbury Press, 2013).

3. Ocean Howell, *Making the Mission: Planning and Ethnicity in San Francisco* (Chicago: University of Chicago Press, 2015).

4. See Tamar Herzog, *Frontiers of Possession: Spain and Portugal in Europe and the Americas* (Cambridge, MA: Harvard University Press, 2015).

---

5. John Tutino, *Mexico and Mexicans in the Making of the United States* (Austin: University of Texas Press, 2012), 69, 75.

6. Kenneth C. Wenzer, ed., *Henry George: Collected Journalistic Writing*, vol. 1, *The Early Years, 1860-79* (Armonk, NY: M. E. Sharpe, 2003); Edward T. O. O'Donnell, *Henry George and the Crisis of Inequality: Progress and Poverty in the Gilded Age* (New York: Columbia University Press, 2015).

7. Richard White, *Railroaded: The Transcontinentals and the Making of Modern America* (New York: W. W. Norton, 2011).

8. Louise Mozingo, *Pastoral Capitalism: A History of Suburban Corporate Landscapes* (Cambridge, MA: MIT Press, 2011); Andrew Blauvelt, ed., *Worlds Away: New Suburban Landscapes* (Minneapolis: Walker Art Center, 2008).

9. City Council Papers, May 15, 1849, 629, BRG 16, Baltimore City Archives; Katie Hemphill, "Bawdy City: Commercial Sex, Capitalism, and Regulation in 19th Century Baltimore" (PhD diss., Johns Hopkins University), 201; Faye E. Dudden, *Fighting Chance: The Struggle for Woman Suffrage and Black Suffrage in Reconstruction America* (New York: Oxford University Press, 2001).

10. See Marta Gutman, *A City for Children: Women, Architecture, and the Charitable Landscape of Oakland, 1850-1950* (Chicago: University of Chicago Press, 2015); Mary P. Ryan, *Mysteries of Sex: Tracing Women and Men Through American History* (Chapel Hill: University of North Carolina Press, 2006), chap. 4; Mary P. Ryan, *Women in Public: Between Banner and Ballots, 1825-1880* (Baltimore: Johns Hopkins University Press, 1990).

11. *Baltimore Sun*, April 7, 1865.

12. Leroy Graham, *Baltimore: The Nineteenth Century Black Capital* (Lanham, MD: University Press of America, 1982), 132-137; Charles Lewis Wagandt, *The Mighty Revolution: Negro Emancipation in Maryland, 1862-1864* (Baltimore: Johns Hopkins University Press, 1964); Kenneth J. Zanca, "Baltimore Catholics and the Funeral of Abraham Lincoln," *Maryland Historical Magazine* 98, no. 1 (2003): 91.

13. *The Elevator*, January [?] 1865; Frank H. Goodyear, "Beneath the Shadow of Her Flag: The Elevator and the Struggle for Enfranchisement, 1865-1870," *California History*, Spring 1999, 27-39.

INDEX

corporations, 11, 130, 196
Cortes de Cádiz, 10, 176
Costanoans, 24, 25, 91
cotton trade: and capitalist development,
    11, 13, 315–316, 362; and Civil War's
    impact on Baltimore, 323; and impact
    of Civil War in Baltimore, 326; and port
    facilities at Yerba Buena, 346
Council of Maryland, 53–54
courthouses, 66, 82
Covenant Chain of the Iroquois, 55
coyote, 116
Coyote (spirit), 23
Coyote Hills, 22, 33, 44
credit, 75
Crespí, Juan, *92*, 93–95
Crèvecoeur, Jean, 117
cronoco, 41
Cronon, William, 6
cultural assimilation, 104–105
curfews, 259

Daily Alta California, 292, 297–299, 331,
    350, 352
Dana, Richard Henry, 197
*Danse des habitantes de Californie a la
    mission de San Francisco* (Choris), *105*,
    insert
Darnall, Henry, 60–61
Dartmouth Case, 330–331
David's Fancy, 63
Davis, Jefferson, 318
Davis, Juan, 203
Davis, William Heath "Guillermo," 174,
    196–198, 295
Davis and Company, 197
Declaration of Independence, 14, 77, 79–80
deer, 93–94
Democracy in America (Tocqueville), 9, 251
Democratic Party: and civic engagement
    in Baltimore, 313–314; and civic life of
    Baltimore, 250–252; and Civil War–era
    politics, 318–319; and Civil War–era
    sovereignty claims, 331; and Civil War's
    impact on Baltimore, 322–324; and

political factionalism in San Francisco,
    304; and racial politics of Baltimore,
    316; and urban planning/development
    in San Francisco, 348; and vigilantism
    in San Francisco, 266
Democratic Republicans, 141, 148
democratization, 12–13, 159, 256
Democrats, 250–252
demographic changes, 78, 105–106,
    197–198, 249, 352–353, 365
Dennison, Andrew, 192, 198
DeWitt's Coffee House, 81
"Dios y Libertad" (God and Freedom), 175
Diputación de la Jurisdicción del Partido
    de San Francisco: and Civil War–era
    sovereignty claims, 330; and early
    settlement of San Francisco, 201, 204;
    and land-taking under Republic of
    Mexico, 176–178, 180; and Mexican
    settlement near Mission Dolores,
    187–188, 193; and privatization of San
    Francisco property, 269; and the Pueblo
    Land Case, 287; and urban develop-
    ment in San Francisco, 209
diseases and epidemics, 8, 105–106
diseños: described, 181; Plaza San
    Francisco, *insert*; and *pobladores*
    land-taking, 210; and pueblos,
    287–288; Rancho San Leandro, *180*,
    insert; Rancho San Miguel, *189*, *356*;
    as support for land claims, 185; and
    Vioget's maps, 207; and the Western
    Addition, 344
Disturnell, John, *213*
diversity, 62–63, 138, 166
DNA, 29–30
docks and wharves, 9, 66, 82, 132, 134, 136,
    221
Dolores creek, 102
Dolores Mission. *See* Misión San Francisco
    de Asís
Douglas, Stephen, 313–314, 316–319
Douglass, Frederick, 171, 370
Douglass Institute, 369
Drake, Francis, 18, 90